GIRDLESTONE'S
SYNONYMS
OF THE
OLD
TESTAMENT

GIRDLESTONE'S
SYNONYMS
OF THE
OLD
TESTAMENT

R. B. Girdlestone

HENDRICKSON PUBLISHERS

Girdlestone's Synonyms of the Old Testament
Hendrickson Publishers, Inc.
P.O. Box 3473
Peabody, Massachusetts 01961-3473

Printed in the United States of America
ISBN 1-56563-558-2

Hendrickson Publishers' edition reprinted by arrangement with Baker Book House Company.

First Printing — March 2000

Contents

Publisher's Preface

In the author's preface to the second edition, he said that, while revising the text, "I have kept before me, first, the needs of busy people who have not time to learn Hebrew, and secondly, the requirements of beginners in Hebrew."[1]

The third edition seeks to advance the author's purpose, particularly for laymen and students in the late twentieth century. Those who do not read Hebrew and Greek will find most useful the numbers following each word in these scripts, numbers that correspond with those in *Strong's Exhaustive Concordance*. By referring to the latter work, one can discover how a Hebrew or Greek word is pronounced, how it is translated in the Authorized (or King James) Version, and in what biblical passages it appears. The number after a certain Hebrew or Greek word will also allow one to refer immediately to any of the lexicons that have also been coded to Strong's concordance.[2]

English readers will appreciate as well the definitions that accompany Latin words and abbreviations, the translations of all foreign-language quotations, the list of abbreviations, and the glossary. All of these features are unique to this edition.

In addition to resetting the entire text in a more readable and pleasing typeface, some typographical changes have been introduced. These involve minor changes in spelling, capitalization, punctuation, and wording, all designed to modernize (and in a few

---

1. *Synonyms of the Old Testament*, 2d ed. (London: J. Nisbet & Co., 1897), p. vii.

2. For the O.T. there are the Hebrew lexicons of Gesenius (Baker Book House, 1979) and of Brown, Driver, and Briggs (Associated Publishers and Authors, 1981); for the N.T., the Greek lexicon of Thayer (Baker Book House, 1977).

cases to Americanize) the text. Vowel points have been added to the Hebrew words, making recognition and pronunciation much simpler for beginning students of the language.

This edition is released with the hope that the life of a classic, already more than a century old,[3] will be extended many more decades.

---

3. The first edition was published in London by Longmans and Green in 1871.

Author's Preface

In selecting subjects, it was hard to know where to stop. But the leading topics of religious thought have been the same in all ages of the church, and the writer's aim has been to investigate the usage of the terms in which these subjects were originally brought before the human mind by the great Author of our being. While admitting the importance of studying the writings of the early Fathers, and the works of English and foreign divines of various schools, the writer holds that the pious, diligent, and accurate study of the sacred text is the appointed means of obtaining a wise and practical understanding of the truth, both as it regards the character and work of God and the duty and hopes of man.

To be unbiased is impossible, but the writer has never wittingly evaded any text or any consideration that seemed to militate against a previously formed impression. He has endeavored to work as a student, not as a controversialist; and the various chapters have been worked out independently, not as parts of a system, although as a matter of fact they have thrown much light on each other. Some readers will object that too many controverted points are introduced, while others will complain that the writer's views on doctrinal subjects are not sufficiently pronounced. Believing that sound theology ought to be based on accurate biblical criticism, the writer could not discuss sacred words without touching upon their doctrinal import. On the other hand, having put together the materials that could best aid in the formation of a judgment on the chief doctrines of the Bible, it seemed both unwise and unnecessary, even if there had been time and space for the undertaking, to work out the details of a theological system.

A secondary aim has not been overlooked in preparing the following pages, namely, to illustrate the importance of the study of Hebrew. The difficulties at the outset are considerable, but when they are once overcome, every hour spent on the Hebrew Bible amply repays the student.

Having to do solely with the meaning and usage of words, I have avoided all reference to modern critical theories of the Old Testament.

The English translations of texts do not always follow the Authorized Version, nor has elegance been aimed at in translation, the object being the greatest possible clearness. Sometimes an alternative rendering or a paraphrase has been incorporated into the text, in order to bring out the sense more clearly.

The chief books that have been used in the course of the preparation of the work are the Bible in various languages, Wilson's *English-Hebrew Concordance* (Macmillan), a most valuable work; Fürst's *Hebrew Concordance;* the *Englishman's Hebrew Concordance* (Longman); and the Greek concordances of Kircher, Trommius, and Bruder. Buxtorf's rabbinical dictionary has also been referred to, in order to ascertain the (comparatively) modern usage of Hebrew terms. But rabbinical studies, while deeply interesting, do not contribute so much to the understanding of the Scriptures as might be supposed.

I must add an expression of thanks to my friend Prof. Sayce, who has kindly added references to the corresponding Assyrian words throughout.

In conclusion, the author earnestly desires that readers of this book may gain—as *he* has gained in writing it—a deepened conviction of the truth, the unity, and the authority of the Scriptures, and that it may influence members of various parties and denominations to enter on a critical and systematic study of the sacred records in their original languages. They will thus be drawn nearer to one another, and will be stimulated to live "in unity of spirit, in the bond of peace, and in righteousness of life," awaiting the Master's return to reward all who have labored in His spirit and on His side: "and then shall every man have praise of God."

Abbreviations

A.V.   Authorized Version (1611). The version known popularly as the King James Version.

A.S.V. American Standard Version (1901). The American edition of the R.V.

LXX   Septuagint (see glossary)

L–S   Liddell and Scott, *A Greek-English Lexicon*, 9th ed. (1940)

N.T.   New Testament

O.T.   Old Testament

R.V.   Revised Version (1885). A revision of the A.V.

Glossary

Chaldee Targums—translations or interpretations of all or portions of the Hebrew Bible. The Targums (a word meaning "translations") arose out of the synagogal practice of accompanying the reading of the Hebrew text with an Aramaic (or Chaldee) translation.

Luther—the German translation of the Bible made by Martin Luther (1483–1546). The N.T. appeared in 1522; the entire Bible, twelve years later.

Majority (or Received) text—the Greek N.T. text widely accepted as definitive before the critical editions of the Greek N.T. published in the nineteenth century. The majority of Greek manuscripts (though not the older ones discovered in modern times) support this text. It was first called the Received Text in the edition published by Elzevir in 1633.

Masoretic text—the definitive (received) text of the O.T., determined by Jewish scholars (known as Masoretes) between the sixth and tenth centuries

Received Text. *See* Majority text *and* Masoretic text

Septuagint—the first Greek translation of the O.T., made by Jews of Alexandria in the second century B.C. The translators, according to tradition, numbered seventy; hence the translation's name and abbreviation.

Sinaiticus—a fourth-century manuscript of portions of the O.T. and all of the N.T., discovered in the nineteenth century in a monastery on Mt. Sinai

Syriac—dialect of Eastern Aramaic which was spoken by many early Christians and into which the Bible was translated either late in the fourth century or early in the fifth

Talmud—a massive compilation of Jewish teaching, consisting of the Mishnah (a collection of oral traditions and rabbinical exegesis, mostly legal in content) and the Gemara (Aramaic commentary on the Hebrew Mishnah). The word *talmud* means "study, learning."

Vulgate—the Latin translation of the Bible made by Jerome late in the fourth century. It has been widely used in the Western church since then, having been declared by the Council of Trent (1546) to be the Roman Catholic Church's official Bible.

Wycliffe—the English translation of the Bible made by John Wycliffe (ca. 1329–1384) and his associates. The first edition of this translation was completed before Wycliffe's death, the second by about 1395.

1

On the Translation and Interpretation of Biblical Terms

§1. *Need of Accuracy in the Translation and Interpretation of Scripture*

The controversies that exist in the Christian Church are a source of trouble and perplexity to every thoughtful mind. It might naturally be supposed that those who profess to follow one and the same Master, to venerate one and the same Book as the final court of appeal in matters pertaining to religion, would agree on all questions of faith and ecclesiastical order; but this is far from being the case. Roman Catholic theologians have sometimes asserted that Protestantism is the real source of religious dissensions, inasmuch as it exposes the Scripture to the private judgment of the individual; and they tell us that there would be no differences of opinion among Christians if all were to abide by the teaching of the Papal Church. There are many reasons, however, that may fairly lead us to doubt the propriety of such a solution. In the first place, controversy did not spring up with the Reformation. There were nearly a hundred shades of opinion, more or less erroneous, which had to be contended against in the earliest ages of the Church; and there were as hot discussions on theological questions in the Middle Ages as there are now. Second, there are far greater divergences of thought in religious matters among adherents of the Papacy than the world generally suspects.[1] Third, it is to be observed, that though

---

1. Jeremy Taylor, in his *Liberty of Prophesying*, gives an almost interminable list of the differences of opinion that have existed in the Church of Rome.

the modern Church of Rome has laid down in the decrees of the
Council of Trent a scheme or basis of doctrine according to which
all Scripture is to be interpreted, yet she has never ventured to
publish an infallible commentary that should explain all the hard
passages of Scripture. Thus even under Roman rule the door of
controversy is practically left open. There were expositors of the
Scripture in the Church long before Christians were divided into
Roman Catholics, Greek Church, and Protestants. Which of them
shall we follow? Shall it be Origen or Chrysostom, Jerome or Augustine? The answer that the Church of Rome, in common with all
other Churches, has to give is that no interpretations of Scripture by
an individual, however learned, are to be regarded as infallible; all
that can be done by the authorized leaders of the Church is to
indicate a certain line of faith, ecclesiastical order, and practice,
according to which the Bible ought to be interpreted, and by which
all commentators ought to be guided and tested.

In accordance with this view, one of the most learned of Roman
Catholic divines, Cardinal Cajetan, says, that if a new sense be
discovered for a text, though it is opposed to the interpretation of a
whole torrent of sacred doctors, it may be accepted, provided it be
in accordance with the rest of Scripture, and with the teaching of
the Church.[2] To Scripture alone, he adds, do we reserve this author-

2. Cajetan, *Praef. in Pent.* The original passage is as follows: "Si quando occurrerit
novus sensus Textui consonus, nec a Sacra Scriptura nec ab Ecclesiae doctrina dissonus,
quamvis a torrente Doctorum sacrorum alienus, aequos se praebeant censores. Meminer-
int jus suum unicuique. Solis Scripturae Sacrae autoribus reservata est haec autoritas, ut
ideo credamus sic esse, quia ipsi ita scripserunt: alios autem, inquit Augustinus, ita lego,
ut quantalibet sanctitate doctrinaque praepolleant, non ideo credam sic esse, quia ipsi
ita scripserunt. Nullus itaque detestatur novum Scripturae sensum, ex hoc quod dissonat
a priscis Doctoribus; sed scrutetur perspicacius Textum ac contextum Scripturae; et si
quadrare invenerit, laudet Deum, qui non alligavit expositionem Scripturarum Sacrarum
priscorum Doctorum sensibus, sed Scripturae integrae sub Catholicae Ecclesiae censura."
Translation of Latin: "If at any time a new, fit understanding to a text should appear,
differing neither from sacred Scripture nor the teaching of the Church (although differing
from a torrent of sacred teachers), let judges prove themselves impartial. Let them
remember that they are independent with respect to everyone. This authority to correct
a horde of sacred theologians has been reserved by teachers to sacred Scripture alone;
not only should we believe this to be so, but also that they themselves thus wrote:
indeed, Augustine wrote (so I read), that they powerfully surpassed in sanctity and
doctrine others ever so great; for that reason should I not likewise believe this to be,
because they themselves have written so. Consequently, no one should despise a new
understanding of Scripture because it differs from the ancient teachers; but let the text as
well as the context be examined minutely; and if it be found to agree, one should praise
God, Who did not bind exposition of sacred Scripture by the understanding of the

ity, that we believe a thing *to be so* because it is *written so*. The conclusion is that the more thoroughly we study the Bible in a right spirit and on just principles of interpretation, so much the more closely shall we draw near to one another in faith and life.

The Bible is to be regarded in two aspects. It has its use for the unlearned, and its use for the teacher. The O.T. tells the story of God's dealings with man in language that is plain to the most unlettered. The N.T. likewise unfolds the truth concerning the Lord Jesus in terms that come home to every heart. The little child and the untaught man will find many hard words, many puzzling arguments, many allusions to Eastern customs and to points of contemporary history of which they know nothing; but they will also find certain solid facts that they can grasp, and they will meet with living words that will arrest their attention and cause them to regard God in a new light. The simple student may thus become a theologian in the true old sense of the word, though ignorant of what modern writers sometimes call theology: he may attain that loving and reverential disposition toward his Maker and Redeemer that is described as "the beginning of wisdom" (Prov. 1:7), though knowing nothing of the early Church Fathers or of the German school of thought.

It has been held in all ages of the Church that the humble and devout reading of the Scriptures is one of the most profitable sources of growth in godliness; and nothing but the exigencies of controversy can have led the authorities of the Church of Rome to discourage the study of the Bible by the laity.[3]

---

ancient teachers, but all Scriptures are under the Catholic Church." Cardinal Pallavicini (*Hist. Conc. Trid.* vi. 18) discusses the view thus boldly enunciated by his brother Cardinal—a view by no means generally approved of—and says that it is not contrary to the decrees of the Council of Trent, as they simply declare heretical any doctrine or exposition that is opposed to the universal teaching of Fathers, Popes, and Councils.

3. No translation of the Bible can be circulated with the sanction of the Papacy unless it be made from the Latin Vulgate, and be accompanied with notes taken from the "Catholic doctors"; and even then no layman is (theoretically) permitted to read it unless he have a license from his priest. The practical consequence of these steps has been that the Bible is almost an unknown book among the Roman Catholic laity. *Editor's Note:* Since the papal encyclical of Pius XII published in 1943, entitled *Divino Afflante Spiritu,* Roman Catholic Biblical scholars have been officially instructed to produce new translations based on the original languages. Also, since the Second Vatican Council, the laity have been officially encouraged to engage in regular devotional reading of the Bible in ecclesiastically authorized versions. See the Preface to *The New American Bible* (Paterson, N.J.: St. Anthony Guild Press, 1970).

Jerome, the prince of translators, and a "churchman" of the highest order, speaks soundly on this point. So does Augustine; and so do Chrysostom, Ambrose, Basil, and the leading Fathers of the early Church. They knew that "as the body is made lean by hunger and want of food, so is the soul that neglects to fortify itself by the Word of God rendered weak and incapable of every good work."[4]

It may, however, be said that the reading of the Bible should at any rate be confined to those who are previously instructed in Christianity. But there is nothing in its pages that calls for such restriction. Practically, also, it is found that the Scriptures in the mother tongue have penetrated further than the living voice of the missionary, and in hundreds—nay, probably thousands—of instances they have been the means of leading men to the knowledge of God. "Missionaries and others," says Sir Bartle Frere in his essay on Missions, "are frequently startled by discovering persons, and even communities, who have hardly ever seen, and perhaps never heard, an ordained missionary, and who have nevertheless made considerable progress in Christian knowledge, obtained through the medium of an almost haphazard circulation of tracts and portions of Scripture." The Reports of the British and Foreign Bible Society and the records of the various Missionary Societies abundantly testify to this point.

But the Bible is also the textbook for the theological teacher, and the final court of appeal on all religious questions. Even the Church of Rome, though putting her ecclesiastical traditions on a level with the Scripture, generally seeks to obtain the sanction of God's Word for her teaching, and never professedly holds any doctrine that, according to her interpretation, is positively opposed to the Bible. To this Book, then, all churches and denominations turn for support; and whatever our view of inspiration may be, we practically take its words as the basis of our teaching and as the standard of our orthodoxy.

4. Augustine. Compare the words of Ambrose, "Omnes aedificat scriptura divina." Translation of Latin: "Divine Scripture builds up all men." The acrimony with which the circulation of the Scriptures has been opposed by the Popes and their subordinates since the days of the Reformation presents a painful contrast with the earnest exhortations of men such as Jerome and Augustine.

§2. *Text and Linguistic Peculiarities of the Hebrew O.T.*

It would be quite beside the present purpose to discuss theories of inspiration, to attempt a solution of the various questions that relate to the Canon, or to weigh the authority of different texts, MSS., and readings. Suffice it to say that, with regard to the O.T., the text as now received, with the punctuation and accentuation[5] that represent the traditional way of reading it in early times, may be taken as substantially the same as that which existed when our Lord gave the weight of His authority to "the Scriptures." Several hundred Hebrew MSS. have been brought to light in modern times, and by their aid the Received text might be considerably amended;[6] but the changes thus introduced, though very numerous, and often of the deepest interest, would not affect the body of the book. The same is true in the case of the N.T., in which we have substantially (whether in the Received or the Revised Text) the writings that were regarded as authoritative in the early Church.

5. By *punctuation* is here signified, not the marking of pauses in the sense, but the determination of the vowel sounds. Supposing that in some old English inscription we met with the abbreviated word BRD, we might have to determine whether it stood for BREAD, BIRD, BARD, BEARD or BOARD. This we could usually do by means of the context; but there might be doubtful cases, and if such existed we should be glad to know how the word had been understood by others in past times. Thus tradition would come in to aid our reasoning powers, though, after all, tradition itself might sometimes be at fault. This just illustrates the case of the Hebrew points. They were added to MSS. somewhere about the fifth century after Christ, in order to perpetuate the traditional mode in which the Hebrew words of the Bible used to be pronounced. Generally speaking, they are undoubtedly right; but they are not infallible, and sometimes they are capable of correction by means of MSS. and early versions. The case of the word *bed* for *staff*, in Gen. 47:31, is the most familiar sample of the existence of two traditional modes of giving vowel sounds for a word whose consonants are the same.

The *accents* mark the tones, the emphasis, and the pauses in Hebrew, and thus they too at times affect the sense and even the division of the verses.

6. Kennicott's two Dissertations, his Introduction to the Hebrew Bible (which he edited), and the posthumous volume of his criticisms, illustrate what may be done in this direction. He may have been led to speak too strongly against what he conceives to be the willful corruption of the text by the Masoretic Jews, but he has conferred a benefit by his labors upon both Jew and Christian, which, alas, neither the one nor the other has yet learned to appreciate. Döderlein and Meisner's Critical Hebrew Bible contains the most convenient collection of readings from Kennicott's and De Rossi's MSS. Reference may here be made to *Deuterographs* (published by the Oxford Press), where the parallel texts of Kings and Chronicles and other books are so printed that the textual variations may be seen at a glance.

The more closely we study the Hebrew Bible, the more we shall be struck with the uniform precision with which doctrinal terms are used throughout its pages. However we may choose to account for this fact, its practical bearing is manifest. If the Hebrew Scriptures use theological terms with marked exactitude, translations made from them are plainly missing something of Divine truth unless they do the same.[7]

There are some 1860 Hebrew roots in the O.T., many of which represent theological, moral, and ceremonial ideas, and our first business must be to find out their exact meaning. The opinion formerly held by some scholars, that all Hebrew words are equivocal, is now generally regarded as an exaggeration; and, although there are differences of opinion as to the meaning of some words, the dictionaries of such men as Gesenius and Fürst, being the embodiment of Jewish tradition confirmed and checked by investigations into cognate languages, give us a fair general idea of the meaning of the roots. This, however, is not enough. The Bible being regarded as a statute book among Christians, the exact shade of meaning to be given to each Hebrew word ought, if possible, to be ascertained; and this can only be effected by an induction of instances leading to a definite conception of the sacred usage in each case.[8] When this has been discovered, the student is naturally led to inquire how far the sense thus arrived at has been, or can be, represented in other languages.

In making a translation of the Bible, it is impossible at first to find adequate words for some of the ideas that it contains; and there must always be a risk of considerable misunderstanding for a time. It is only gradually that the Biblical usage of a word becomes engrafted into a national language; and it has been noticed that the

---

7. The rule that each word of the original shall always have the same rendering is not to be pressed too far, but in argumentative and doctrinal passages it is very important. It would be easy to name a hundred passages, even in our Revised Version, that have seriously suffered through the neglect of this principle.

8. The founder of Inductive Science has not neglected to remind us that its principles are applicable to the study of the Bible. He urges an inquiry into "the true limits and use of reason in spiritual things," which would "open men's eyes to see that many controversies do merely pertain to that which is either not revealed or positive, and that many others do grow upon weak and obscure inferences or derivations"; he calls men to investigate the Scriptures themselves instead of resting in Scholastic Divinity, because "the more you recede from the Scriptures by inferences and consequences, the more weak and dilute are your positions"; and he extols "positive divinity, collected upon particular texts of Scriptures." Bacon's *Advancement of Learning*, last chapter.

more fixed a language is at the time the translation is made into it, the greater is the difficulty of diverting words from their general use to the sacred purposes of the Bible.[9] The Hebrew language, though poor in some respects, for example, in tenses, is rich in others; and probably no better language could have been selected for the purpose of preparing the way for Christ. Its variations of stem give shades of meaning that cannot be found in the Indo-European languages. Its definite article, the way in which genders are marked in the verb as well as in the noun, its mode of marking emphasis and comparison, the gravity and solemnity of its structure, the massive dignity of its style, the picturesqueness of its idiom—these make it peculiarly fitting for the expression of sacred truth. Indeed, it is often a lesson in moral philosophy to take a Hebrew dictionary and trace the gradual growth of meaning in certain words as their signification advances from things that are seen and temporal to those which are not seen and eternal. Persons who have made this point a study can well sympathize with the saying of Luther, that he would not part with his knowledge of Hebrew for untold gold.[10]

But how is it possible that a translation (unless it be in a cognate language such as Arabic) should bring out all the shades of thought that are to be found in the Hebrew Bible? Thus the play on words,[11] which is so frequent in the original, as in the naming of Jacob's sons or in the blessing pronounced upon them by their father, can rarely be reproduced in another language. Such distinctions as exist between the *rest* that means cessation and that which signifies quietness, or between the *fear* that signifies terror and that which

9. See Rhenius on the principles of translating the Bible.

10. "Hac quantulacunque cognitione infinitis millibus aureorum carere nolim" (*Prol. in Ps.* 45). Translation of Latin: "I would not want to be without this knowledge (however small) for countless thousands of gold coins." Mr. Craik, in his little work on the Hebrew language (Bagster), gives a few apt illustrations of the original meanings of its words. "It has been well observed," he says, "that the original notions inherent in the Hebrew words serve to picture forth with remarkable distinctness the mental qualities which they designate. Thus, for instance, the usual term for 'meek' is derived from a root which signifies to afflict. The usual term for 'wicked' comes from a root that expresses the notion of restlessness. A 'sinner' is one who misses the mark. To 'delight' in anything is literally to bend down towards it. The 'law' is that which indicates the mind of God. 'Righteousness' is that which is perfectly straight. 'Truth' is that which is firm. 'Vanity' that which is empty. 'Anger' is derived from a root meaning to breathe, quick breathing being a sign of irritated feeling. To 'trust' is to take shelter under, or to lean upon, or to cast oneself on. To 'judge' is radically [as to its root meaning] to smooth or make equal."

11. A large number of instances of *paronomasia* will be found at the end of Canon Wilson's *Hebrew Concordance* (Macmillan).

marks respect, are often left unnoticed by translators. Again, who would have supposed that three Hebrew words are rendered *window* in the account of the Deluge, three rendered *sack* in the story of Joseph's brethren in Egypt, three rendered *leaven* in the account of the Passover, three rendered *ship* in the first chapter of Jonah, and five rendered *lion* in two consecutive verses of Job (4:10, 11)? There are many other curiosities in Hebrew that cannot be reproduced, such as the strange fact that the same word is sometimes used not only in different senses, but even with flatly contradictory meanings. For example, one word signifies both *to bless* and *to curse;* the same is the case with words signifying *to redeem* and *to pollute; to join* and *to separate; to afflict* and *to honor; to know* and *to be strange; to lend* and *to borrow; to sin* and *to purge; to desire* and *to abhor; to hurt* and *to heal.*[12] Again, how much significance lies in the circumstance that a common word for buying and selling also means corn, that a name for money also means a lamb, that the general word for cattle is adopted to signify possession, and that the common name for a merchant was Canaanite?

As an illustration of the richness and variety of the Hebrew language, it may be mentioned that seven different words are rendered *black* in the A.V.; there are eight words for an *axe*, for an *archer*, for a *hook;* nine are rendered *wine;* twelve words stand for *beauty*, and the same number for *body;* thirteen for *light*, for *bough*, and for *hand;* fourteen are rendered *dark;* sixteen are rendered *anger* and *chief;* eighteen are rendered *fear;* twenty are rendered *bind* and *cry.* The words *afraid* or *affrighted* stand for twenty-one Hebrew words; *branch* for twenty-two; *deliver* for twenty-five; *cover* for twenty-six; *gather* for thirty-five; *cut* for forty-two; *come* for forty-seven; *destroy* for fifty-five; *break* for sixty; *cast* for sixty-one; *bring* for sixty-six; *go* for sixty-eight; and *take* for seventy-four.

§3. *The LXX a Connecting Link between the Hebrew O.T. and the Greek N.T.*

We now pass from the Hebrew original to the ancient Greek version, commonly called the Septuagint (LXX); and we may take as our starting-point the remark of a late scholar,[13] that the Christian

---

12. The stem, however, is not always the same in these cases.

13. Professor Duncan. Cappellus expressed the same sentiment in almost the same words.

revelation must be regarded as *Hebrew thought in Greek clothing.* No human language is capable of setting forth adequately the truth about the Divine Being; but it is a great help that the Scripture is written in *two* languages, one of a Semitic type and the other Aryan, the latter being not mere ordinary Greek, such as might be found in Plato or Demosthenes, but Greek of a peculiar kind, the leading words of which conveyed to the *Jewish* mind ideas that the Hebrew O.T. had originated.

Very different estimates have been formed respecting the value of the LXX by various writers. In the early days of Christianity both Jews and Christians were inclined to regard it as a work of inspiration; and most of the early versions of the O.T. were made from it. But when the Jews found that it was so freely quoted and so much used by Christians, they took refuge in the assertion that it was not a faithful translation; and on this account the Greek versions of Theodotion, Aquila, and Symmachus were made. It was too late, however, to disparage a version that had been prepared before the days of controversy between Jew and Christian had begun; and the charges made against it were really the means of confirming its value, for Jerome was led to make his version from the Hebrew, partly at least that Christians might see that both Hebrew and Greek practically taught the same truth.

Modern critics have sometimes run to extremes in dealing with the LXX. Isaac Voss held that it was inspired; Cappellus, Munster, and Buxtorf attached but little value to it; Morinus respected it highly, but was inclined to correct it by the Latin Vulgate. Perhaps the fairest estimate of its value is to be found in the work of Hody on early versions, and in the criticisms of Kennicott.

This early Greek translation is, indeed, of the greatest value to the Biblical student, partly because it contains certain readings of importance that are not to be found in the existing Hebrew Bibles; partly also, because its renderings, though often free and para-phrastic, and sometimes even illiterate and unintelligible, frequently represent the traditional sense attached to the sacred text among the Alexandrian Jews. But, after all, the main value of the LXX lies in this, that it represents in a great measure the Greek religious language of many of the Jews of our Lord's time, and by its pages the Greek of the N.T. may be illustrated at every turn. Those who have access to Grinfield's Hellenistic Greek Testament, or any similar book, are aware that there is hardly a verse in the N.T. the phraseology of which may not be illustrated, and to some extent explained, by reference to the LXX. This fact, which is allowed by all students, has, nevertheless, hardly received that full attention from translators that it deserves. The idea that the LXX is often an indifferent authority from a literary and critical point of view, has caused them to neglect its study;[14] whereas it ought to be regarded as a sort of dictionary in which every N.T. word and phrase ought to be sought out, in order that its usage in Judeo-Greek might be ascertained. Philo is good, Josephus is good, but the LXX is best of all: both because of its subject matter, and because of the influence that it has exercised over Christian theology.

It has often been remarked how much the English language now owes to the Authorized Version of the Bible. Many English words and phrases used in tracts and sermons, and other religious writings, can be understood only by reference to the Bible. The words themselves may sometimes be found in the works of authors who lived before our version was prepared, and also in the writings of many whose acquaintance with religious topics is very limited; but it is to the Bible that we turn for an explanation of such words as *edify, justify, atonement, faith,* and *grace.* These and many other words have been taken out of their ordinary secular usage, and have been adopted for Christian purposes. Little by little the new sense has eclipsed and obscured the old, so that in some cases the latter has vanished altogether. As generations succeed one another, if religious instruction and conversation continues, and if our Bible is not materially altered, Biblical language may become still more naturalized among us.

What is true in the case of the English language has also been perceived in many other languages—wherever, in fact, the Bible is much studied. It often happens that missionaries gather their knowledge of a new language, not from native literature, for perhaps there is none, but from a translation of the Scriptures. This forms the basis of their vocabulary, and the standard of their idiom. Mr. Medhurst, in one of his works on the Far East, notices that this was the case in Malacca, where "the style of preaching and writing became in consequence very stiff and unidiomatic, and so a new

---

14. Certainly, if the Hebrew original were lost and our translation were made from the LXX, each word being rendered according to classical usage, while the substance of the O.T. would remain the same, we should have a very different (and a very mistaken) idea of many of its details.

and barbarous dialect sprang up among the professors of Christianity, which was in many instances barely intelligible to the Mahometan population who speak the regular Malayan tongue."

To take one other illustration of the mode in which a religious language is formed, the reader may be reminded of the vocabulary at the end of Dean Nowell's Catechism. It contains a list of Latin words and modes of expression peculiar to Christians, and differing from the ordinary classical usage.[15] We find among them the words for angel, apostle, flesh, believe, create, crucify, demon, devil, elect, gospel, Gentile, idol, justify, sanctify, mediator, minister, mortify, repentance, resurrection, sacrament, scripture, temptation, tradition, and Trinity.

Applying these remarks to the influence of the LXX on Judeo-Greek, we may cite the opinion of Father Simon, who points out[16] that the versions made by the Jews have been servile renderings, and that style has never been considered in them. "The words employed in these versions are not used in the ordinary style; rather the Jews, in their desire to give a verbal rendering to the words of the Hebrew text, have formed a certain strange language, which one might call the language of the synagogue. The Greek of the Septuagint version, and even that of the N.T., is of this nature. . . . It is this that has led certain learned critics to call it Hellenistic, so as to distinguish it from ordinary Greek."

The late Dr. Campbell, of Aberdeen, ought to be named as having forcibly expounded the same view in his "Preliminary Dissertations."

The LXX may thus be regarded as a linguistic bridge spanning the gulf that separated Moses from Christ. Thus, to take a single short book, in the Epistle of James we meet with certain Greek words rendered *dispersion, temptation, trial, doubting, firstfruits, respect*

---

15. "Vocabula nostratia, et loquendi formae Christianorum propriae, in quibus a communi more verborum Latinorum discessum est." Translation of Latin: "The vocabulary of our country and peculiar patterns of speaking of Christians has been set apart in those ways in which it differs from the common use of Latin words."

16. *Critique V. T.* 2:3. Similar remarks are made by this acute writer in the very interesting preface to his French translation of the N.T. This work, including the Preface, was translated into English by William Webster, Curate of St. Dunstan's-in-the-West; and printed by Charles Rivington, in St. Paul's Churchyard, in 1730. Simon's rendering of the Greek would be generally regarded as too free, though not so paraphrastic as the version made by De Sacy. While aiming at "expressing the pure word of God with all possible exactness," he was the very opposite of a *servile* translator. His remarks on the Greek particles and prepositions, viewed in relation to the Hebrew, are very instructive.

of persons, Lord of Sabaoth, in the last days, stablish your hearts, justify, double minded, longsuffering, of tender mercy, faith, spirit, wisdom, the judge. A Jew trained in the use of the LXX would naturally give to these words a peculiar richness and fullness of meaning from their usage in the Law and the Prophets when they appear as the rendering of certain Hebrew words and phrases.

The same would be the case with such expressions as "son of perdition," "children of wrath," "if they shall enter into my rest," "by the hand of a mediator," "go in peace," "living waters."[17]

It may be objected, however, that the use of the LXX was confined to a small portion of the Jews, that most of them spoke Aramaic, or (as it is called in the N.T.) Hebrew, and that therefore we must not press the resemblances between the Greek Testament and the LXX too far. The popular belief certainly is that our Lord and His disciples spoke in Aramaic,[18] an idea that is usually based on the fact that three or four words of this dialect are found amidst the Greek of the N.T. When Diodati propounded his view that our Lord was in the habit of speaking in Greek, it met with general contempt. De Rossi, no mean critic, controverted this novel view (as it was considered) in a treatise of some learning, though of short compass.[19] Dr. Roberts, in his "Discussions on the Gospels," has taken up the subject again, and has upheld the views of Diodati with much skill; but his arguments do not altogether carry conviction. It is strange that there should be any uncertainty about a point of such deep interest. There is probably more to be said on each side than has yet been said. The fact is, that a large number of the Jews in our Lord's time were bilingual: they spoke both Aramaic and Judeo-Greek. We know that Paul's speech in Acts 22 was delivered in Hebrew, while that given in Acts 24 must have been delivered in Greek. While, therefore, some of the discourses contained in the Greek Gospels must be

17. Mr. Webster rightly states, in his *Grammar of New Testament Greek,* that the influence of Hebrew on the Greek Testament is lexical rather than grammatical, but he somewhat underrates the bearing of the Hebrew stems, tenses, particles, and prepositions on N.T. Greek. Dr. Delitzsch, in the learned introduction to his translation of the Epistle to the Romans into Hebrew (Leipzig, 1870), has some interesting remarks on this subject.

18 A compound of Aramaic and perhaps Arabic dialects, of which there were two or three forms, e.g., the Galilean, which was ruder than that spoken in Jerusalem. See Walton's *Prolegomena* on this subject; also De Rossi's work, referred to below; and compare Neubauer in *Studia Biblica.*

19. Dissertazioni della lingua propria di Cristo [*Dissertations concerning the Actual Language of Christ*], Milan, 1842.

considered as translations, others may possibly give us the *ipsissima verba* [the exact words] of Him who spake as never yet man spake. One thing is certain, that if the Greek Gospels do not give our Lord's original discourses, it is in vain to look to any other source for them. If *they* are not originals, we have no originals. The Syriac version of the N.T. bears evident traces of having been made from the Greek; so does the early Latin; so do all the other early versions; nor is there any other practical conclusion to be arrived at than this, that the Greek Gospels are to be taken as accurate accounts of the words and deeds of the Savior, written in a tongue that was intelligible to most Jews, to all Greeks, to many Romans, and to the great bulk of people whom the Gospel could reach in the course of the first century.

The LXX had certainly received a quasi-authorization by age and custom in our Lord's time. Father Simon considers that it may have obtained its name from the fact that it was sanctioned by the Sanhedrin, which consisted of seventy members. He remarks that the Synagogue was used not only for a place of religious service, but as a school. And whereas the Talmud prohibited the reading of the law in any language but Hebrew during divine service, the LXX and also the Chaldee Targums were the main basis of teaching during school hours. Thus the Hebrew sacred books constituted the canon, while the LXX, so far as its rendering of those sacred books is concerned, became what we may call the Authorized Version in daily use in the school, and to a certain extent in the family; and the style of the N.T. would naturally be accommodated to it.[20]

20. NOTE ON MATTHEW'S GOSPEL—A possible solution of a long-standing difficulty may be here presented for the consideration of the learned. The old tradition is that Matthew wrote his Gospel in Hebrew, and there is no reason to doubt it; but the opinion of some modern scholars who have subjected the matter to the severest criticism is that it was written in Greek. But, even if their view is correct, some copies may have been specially prepared *in Hebrew characters* for those Jews who spoke Greek but did not read it. In the present day we find Greek, Spanish, German, Polish, Persian, and the Arabic works (especially Bibles) written and printed in Hebrew characters. Occasionally in the time of Origen, the Hebrew Scriptures were written in Greek letters. Why, then, should not the Greek Scriptures have been written in Hebrew characters for the benefit of a portion of the Jewish people who would otherwise have been debarred from access to them? Transliteration is very common now. Arabic Scriptures are printed in Syriac characters, Turkish in Armenian, Turkish in Greek, Kurdish in Armenian, Indian languages in Arabic, Malay and even Chinese in Roman. The version that the Karaite Jews especially esteem is a Greek Pentateuch, printed at Constantinople in Hebrew characters. According to the opinion of most scholars, the whole Hebrew Scriptures have been transliterated from Samaritan characters, while the Samaritans still retain a text of the Pentateuch in their own characters. There would, therefore, be nothing novel or extraordinary in the plan that is here conjectured to have been adopted by Matthew or some of his followers,

The whole Bible may be regarded as written "for the Jew first";[21] and its words and idioms ought to be rendered according to Hebrew usage. The shades of meaning represented in the Hebrew stems ought to be borne in mind by the translator, the *Piel* or intensive being peculiarly a technical or ceremonial stem. Where critics or theologians differ as to the sense conveyed by the original, the translator must content himself by adhering to the most literal or the most natural rendering of the text. The great danger is the tendency to paraphrase. This may be illustrated by Martin Luther's translation of δικαιοσύνη θεοῦ (simply, "the righteousness of God") as "the righteousness which is valid before God."[22] The phrase certainly needs exposition, as many similar condensed expressions do, but the translator must leave this task to the expositor.

§4. *Our Lord's Method of Interpreting the O.T.*

There are about 600 quotations from the O.T. in the N.T. The great proportion of these are in accordance both with the Hebrew original and with the LXX, and where they vary it is frequently owing to textual corruption. They present us, when taken together, with a systematic key to the interpretation of the O.T. But it is curious to observe the great variety of deductions that have been made from examining the mode of citation. Father Simon, in his "Critique" on the O.T. (lib. i. chap. 17), tells us that our Lord followed the method of interpreting the Scriptures that was adopted by the Pharisees, while He condemned their abuse of those traditions that had no solid foundation. "St. Paul," he continues,

> whilst he was one of the sect of the Pharisees, had interpreted Scripture in the light of tradition; and the Church apparently from the beginning preferred this mode of elucidating the Bible to that adopted by modern grammarians who stick to the words. Thus neither our Lord nor His apostles appear to have taken pains to cite passages of Scripture word for word; they have had more regard for

---

namely, to make copies of the Gospel in Hebrew characters. Any person not versed in the study of Hebrew would naturally suppose, on seeing such a copy, that it was written in the Hebrew language. It is true that scholars such as Origen and Jerome would not be so imposed on; but there is no proof that either of these learned men had ever held the book in their hands.

21. It may be objected that some portions at least of the N.T. were intended for Gentile readers; this *may* have been the case, but they were written by Jews, and consequently more or less in the Judeo-Greek diction.

22. *Die Gerechtigkeit, die vor Gott gilt.*

the sense than for the letter of the text. . . . Their citations were made after the method of the Pharisees, who took no exact account of the words of the text when they cited it, being persuaded that religion depended more on the preconceived opinions (*préjugés*) obtained by tradition than on the simple words of Scripture which were capable of diverse explanations.

This bold statement, which if true would be very convenient for the Church to which Father Simon belonged, requires considerable modification. There were two schools among the Jews of our Lord's day who tampered with the letter of Scripture. There were the Pharisees, who so overlaid Scripture with legal niceties of man's invention, that the Word of God was practically made void by their traditions. And there were the Cabbalists, who applied a mystical interpretation to the very letters of which the words of Scripture were composed, and thus lost the plain sense that lay on the surface. In opposition to these two schools, our Lord generally adopted the plan of interpreting the Scripture by its context, and with a due regard both to the claims of grammar and the harmony of the Divine plan of revelation. In this respect, as in others, He left us an example that we should follow in His steps.

§5. *Illustrations of the Use of the LXX in Translating the N.T.*

A few instances may be given, in conclusion, to illustrate the bearing that the language and idiom of the LXX has on the meaning of the N.T.

(a) In II Thess. 3:5, we read, "And the Lord direct your hearts into the love of God, and into the patient waiting for Christ." The latter words are more literally rendered in the margin and in the R.V.: "the patience of Christ." This expression would not convey much sense to the reader unless he took it to signify "the patience that Christ exhibited when he suffered," or "the patience that Christ bestows on His people." Were our translators right in departing from the literal rendering and in giving a clear and definite meaning to the Apostle's words, one that is in strict conformity with the context? Yes, they have doubtless hit the sense. And their view of the passage is confirmed by the Greek rendering of Ps. 39:7, which literally runs thus: "And now what is my patience? is it not the Lord?" This answers to the rendering of the A.V. and R.V.: "And now, Lord, what wait I for? my hope is in thee." It may well be supposed that if this passage from the LXX was not in the Apostle's mind as he wrote, yet the phraseology of it, which was so familiar to him, gave form to his thought.

(b) In a Greek Testament that is in the hand of every student, it is said in a note on II Thess. 1:11 (on the words "fulfil all the good pleasure of his goodness") that "ἀγαθωσύνη (19) will not refer with any propriety to God, of whom the word is *never* used."[23] Accordingly, it is altered in the R.V. But the usage of the LXX should be considered before the question be thus summarily decided. Accordingly, on turning to that book, we find that the word ἀγαθωσύνη (19) is used of God in at least three passages.

(c) Readers of the English Bible must have experienced some surprise at meeting twice over with the singular expression, "thy holy child Jesus" in Acts 4:27 and 30 (see also Acts 3:13, 26). The Greek word παῖς (3816) may certainly be rendered *child*, though the diminutive παιδίον (3813) is more usually adopted in the N.T. for this purpose. But why should the Christians make such special mention of "the holy child?" The usage of the N.T. may first be consulted. The word occurs at most twenty-five times. In seven or eight of these passages it is rendered *servant*, while in others it is rendered *child*. It is first applied to our Lord in Matt. 12:18, where the prophecy of Isaiah (42:1) is referred to. Our translators here wisely allowed themselves to be guided by the Hebrew word, of which παῖς (3816) is the rendering, and to translate "Behold my servant, whom I have chosen." In accordance with this passage the Virgin Mary sings of God, "He hath holpen his servant [παῖς, 3816] Israel" (Luke 1:54), and Zacharias praises God for raising up a horn of salvation (i.e., a mighty Savior) in the house or family of His servant (παῖς, 3816) David. It is natural to suppose that the Christians referred to in Acts 4:27, 30, did not mean to speak of Christ as God's child, but His servant. This view is borne out by the fact that they had in the very same prayer in which the words occur used the same expression with reference to David's saying, "Lord, thou art God . . . who by the mouth of thy servant [παῖς, 3816] David hast said, why did the heathen rage? . . ." For these reasons it would be well to translate παῖς (3816) *servant* in the four passages in the Acts in which it is used of our Lord.

An examination of other passages in which David is called God's

---

23. See Alford in loco.

servant will greatly tend to confirm the rendering given above. See Jer. 33:15–22; Ezek. 34:23, 24; 37:24, 25.

These samples, perhaps, are sufficient to illustrate the way in which the LXX forms a connecting link between the O.T. and the N.T. Many more will be brought to light in the course of the following pages, in which the leading Hebrew terms relating to the nature of God and man, the work of redemption, the ministrations under the law of Moses, together with other important topics, are discussed. If all difficult passages in the N.T. were dealt with in accordance with the principles thus illustrated, it does not seem too much to say that many obscurities would be removed, and the perplexities in which the plain English reader often finds himself involved would be considerably reduced.

Before closing this chapter a word must be added concerning the language in which the earliest pages of the Bible were written. It is, to say the least, possible that the records of the events that happened before Abraham's time are themselves pre-Abrahamic. If so, they may have been written in a language or dialect very different from Biblical Hebrew. The same hypothesis would hold good in a measure with reference to the records of the period between Abraham and Moses. All that we can do, however, is to take the Book of Genesis as it stands, and to discuss its words as if they were the original, or at any rate as if they fairly represented it, just as we take the Greek of the Gospels as an adequate representation of the language in which our Lord usually spoke.

2

The Names of God

A translator of the Bible into the languages of heathendom finds his work beset with difficulties at every step. He has to feel about for bare words, and this not merely in matters such as weights, measures, animals, and trees, but in others of far greater importance. He constantly has to pause and consider whether he had better use a native word that but indifferently represents the original, or whether it is preferable to transfer or transliterate a word from the Hebrew, Greek, or some other language. In the one case he is in danger of creating a misunderstanding in the mind of his readers; in the other he is certain to convey no sense at all until by oral teaching, or otherwise, the newly grafted word has become familiar. He wants to speak of angels, and must choose between messengers and genii; he wants to write of the kingdom of heaven, and finds that such a thing as a kingdom is unknown; he has to speak concerning the soul and the spirit to those who are apparently without a conception of anything beyond the body, as was the case with the Bechuana tribes.[1] Thus a version of the Scripture must needs be full of anomalies and obscurities at first, and though the substantial facts contained therein may be plainly set down, a clear understanding of its details will be arrived at only after much study on the part of native readers.

The difficulty of the translator usually begins with the name of God. To us English people this is so much a thing of the past that we cannot understand it; but, as a matter of fact, it has caused

---

1. See Moffat's *South African Sketches*. Things are very different among Bechuanas now.

perplexity, if not dissension, in the case of many new translations. In China the missionaries of the various Christian bodies are not to this day agreed as to the right word to be adopted, and consequently they will not all consent to use the same editions of the Bible. Some approve of the name *Tien-Chu,* a title which signifies "the Lord of heaven," which has been adopted for three centuries by the Roman Catholics; some adopt *Shang-ti,* the Confucian name for "the Supreme Ruler"; others are in favor of *Shin,* which is generally supposed to mean "spirit." The controversy between the upholders of these various opinions has been very warm and earnest, and has called forth several deeply interesting essays. The arguments have usually gathered around one question: ought we to choose a *generic* name for God, i.e., a name that represents to the heathen mind a *class* of beings, or ought we to choose what may be called a *proper* name, even though that name may present a most unworthy notion of the Deity?

§1. *The Name* 'ĔLÔHÎYM

The general Hebrew name for God is 'Ĕlôhîym (אֱלֹהִים, 430). Sometimes it is used with a definite article, sometimes without. Altogether it occurs 2555 times. In 2310 of these instances it is used as the name of the living and true God, but in 245 passages it appears to be adopted in lower senses.

Although plural in form,[2] the name is generally used with a singular verb when it refers to the true God.[3]

This name properly represented One only Being, who revealed Himself to man as Creator, Ruler, and Lord. It was His own peculiar title, and ought to have been confined to Him. Accordingly we read, "In the beginning God ['Ĕlôhîym, 430, in the plural] created [in the singular] the heavens and the earth" (Gen. 1:1).

The first hint at the possibility that the title 'Ĕlôhîym (430) might be shared by others besides the Creator is to be found in the ser-

---

2. This is indicated by the termination *-im,* as in such words as Cherub-im and Seraph-im. Dr. Sayce tells me that in the Tel el Amarna tablets Pharaoh is addressed as *gods.*

3. The exceptions are in Gen. 20:13; 35:7; II Sam. 7:23 (but in I Chron. 17:12). The Samaritan Pentateuch has altered those in Genesis to the singular. Sometimes the adjective that agrees with 'Ĕlôhîym is plural, as in Josh. 24:19; sometimes singular, as in II Kings 19:4.

pent's suggestion, "Ye shall be as 'Ĕlôhîym [430], knowing good and evil" (Gen. 3:5). The translators of the A.V. render the word *gods*, but our first parents only knew of one 'Ĕlôhîym (430); they heard His voice from time to time, and perhaps they saw His form; they addressed Him in the singular number; and the idea of any other being to be called 'Ĕlôhîym (430) but this One could not have entered their imaginations until the Tempter said to them, "Ye shall be as God, knowing good and evil" (see R.V.).

In after ages the worship of the Creator as 'Ĕlôhîym (430) began to be corrupted. The Name, indeed, was retained, but the nature of Him who bore it was well-nigh forgotten. When men were divided into different nations, and spoke various dialects and languages, they must have carried with them those notions of 'Ĕlôhîym (430) that they had inherited from their fathers, but the worship that was due to Him alone was in the lapse of ages transferred to the souls of the departed, to the sun, moon, and stars, and even to idols made by men's hands.

It has been supposed that some sanction is given to the theory that the name 'Ĕlôhîym (430) is generic by the fact that idols are called by this name in Scripture. Some instances of this usage may therefore be cited for examination.

In Gen. 35:1, 2, 4, we read as follows:

> And 'Ĕlôhîym [430] said unto Jacob, Arise, go up to Beth-el and dwell there, and build there an altar, unto the 'Ĕl [410] that appeared to thee when thou fleddest from before thy brother Esau. Then Jacob said to his house and to all that were with him, Put away the strange 'Ĕlôhîym [430] that are among you . . . and they gave unto Jacob all the strange 'Ĕlôhîym [430] that were in their hands, and their earrings which were in their ears, and Jacob hid them under the oak which was by Shechem.

The 'Ĕlôhîym (430) in this case seem to have been images, perhaps charms worn on the person, similar to those which the ancient Egyptians used to wear, and which have been exhumed or manufactured by the hundreds in modern days. The word **Nâkar** (נָכַר, 5234), here rendered *strange*, is used in Scripture in two opposite senses, for *to know*, and *not to know*; it here probably means *foreign* or *alien*, in which sense it is frequently applied to idolatrous worship in Scripture.

In Gen. 31:19, we read that Rachel had stolen her father's images (Teráphîym, 8655[4]), but Laban calls them his 'Ĕlôhîym (430—v. 30), and Jacob, adopting the word, says, "with whomsoever thou findest thine 'Ĕlôhîym (430), let him not live" (v. 32). Laban, then, worshiped Teráphîym (8655) as 'Ĕlôhîym (430), though he ought to have known better, for he knew the name of Jehovah (3068—Gen. 30:27; 31:49), and he was not ignorant of the real 'Ĕlôhîym (430), whom his own father had worshiped (Gen. 31:29, 50, 53).

We also read of "the 'Ĕlôhîym [430] of Egypt" (Exod. 12:12, A.V. gods; the margin has princes, but see Num. 33:4); of molten 'Ĕlôhîym (430—Lev. 19:4); of the 'Ĕlôhîym (430) of the heathen (Exod. 23:24); also of Chemosh, Dagon, Milcom, and other idols that were designated as 'Ĕlôhîym (430). When the Israelites made the molten calf out of their golden earrings (Exod. 32:3, 4), they said of it, "These be thy 'Ĕlôhîym [430], O Israel," by which they practically meant "this is thy God," for they regarded the image as a representation of Jehovah (3068, v. 5).[5]

Jethro, the father-in-law of Moses, draws a distinction between the true and the false 'Ĕlôhîym (430), when he says, "Now know I that Jehovah [3068] is greater than all the 'Ĕlôhîym [430]: for in the matter wherein they dealt proudly he was above them" (Exod. 18:11); yet this very confession is so worded as to imply not only that the priest of Midian had hitherto been in the dark on the subject, but also that he still had a lingering belief in the existence of inferior 'Ĕlôhîym (430). The same ignorance and superstition was to be found among the children of Israel; and the primary lesson that the Lord sought to teach them during their journeyings in the wilderness was that they were to restore the name 'Ĕlôhîym (430) to its original and sole owner. "Thou shalt have no other 'Ĕlôhîym [430] before me"[6] (Exod. 20:3). "Make no mention of the name of other

---

4. For further remarks on the nature of the Teraphim, see chap. 27, 7.

5. David Mill, in one of his Dissertationes Selectae, discusses the symbolical meaning of the golden calf, and comes to the conclusion that it represented, not Apis, but Typhon (i.e., Set), to whom the Egyptians attributed all evil. The people of Israel knew full well that their God had looked with no favoring eye upon Egypt, and it is therefore not improbable that in choosing a symbol to represent Him they would select that which the Egyptians regarded as their evil genius.

6. Literally, "in addition to my face." Some Hebrew students regard this expression not merely as a Hebrew idiom, but as setting forth that the Face or Manifestation of God is God. They have hence argued for the Deity of Christ; but the argument in the form in which it is sometimes advanced is rather perilous, because it is inapplicable to other

'Ĕlôhîym [430], neither let it be heard out of thy mouth" (Exod. 23:13). "Jehovah [3068] he is 'Ĕlôhîym [430] in heaven above, and upon the earth beneath: there is none else" (Deut. 4:39). So in the Song of Moses (Deut. 32:37, 39) we read concerning the heathen, "Where are their 'Ĕlôhîym [430], the rock on which they leaned? . . . I, even I, am he, and there is no 'Ĕlôhîym [430] with me." Once more, the utter anomaly of using the word 'Ĕlôhîym (430) for others than the true God is clearly indicated in the prayer of Hezekiah (II Kings 19:17, 18): "Of a truth, Jehovah [3068], the kings of Assyria have destroyed the nations and their lands and have cast their 'Ĕlôhîym [430] into the fire: for they were no 'Ĕlôhîym [430], but the work of men's hands, wood and stone: therefore they have destroyed them."

§2. *The Name* 'ĔLÔHÎYM *and the Trinity*

It is clear that the fact that the word 'Ĕlôhîym (430) is plural in form does not at all sanction polytheism; but we have now to consider whether it may fairly be taken as a testimony to the plurality of Persons in the Godhead. It is certainly marvelously consistent with this doctrine, and must remove a great stumbling block out of the path of those who feel difficulties with regard to the acknowledgment of the Trinity in Unity. Great names are to be cited for taking a step further, and for adducing, as a proof of the Trinity, the words, "'Ĕlôhîym [430] said, Let *us* make man in *our* image, after *our* likeness" (Gen. 1:26). Father Simon notes that Peter Lombard (c. A.D. 1150) was the first to lay stress on this point, though probably the argument was not really new in his time. Many critics, however, of unimpeachable orthodoxy, think it wiser to rest where such divines as Cajetan in the Church of Rome and Calvin among Protestants were content to stand, and to take the plural form as a *plural of majesty,* and as indicating the greatness, the infinity, and the incomprehensibleness of the Deity. Perhaps the idea unfolded in the plural form 'Ĕlôhîym (430) may be expressed more accurately by the word *Godhead* or *Deity* than by the word *God;* and there is certainly nothing unreasonable in the supposition that the name of

---

passages, e.g., Exod. 33:20: "Thou canst not see my face, for there shall no man see me and live." It is nevertheless true that we do behold "the glory of God in the face [or person] of Jesus Christ" (II Cor. 4:6).

the Deity was given to man in this form, so as to prepare him for the truth that in the unity of the Godhead there are three Persons.

As long as the passage quoted above stands on the first page of the Bible, the believer in the Trinity has a right to turn to it as a proof that *plurality* in the Godhead is a very different thing from *polytheism*, and as an indication that the frequent assertions of the Divine Unity are not inconsistent with the belief that the Father is God, the Son is God, and the Holy Ghost is God. It is well known that the Hebrews often expressed a word in the plural, so as to give it a special or technical meaning, as in the case of the words *blood, water, wisdom, salvation, righteousness, life;* and this is in favor of what has just been advanced. The use of the plural in the language of majesty and authority tends to the same conclusion. In these cases it is implied that the word in the singular number is not large enough to set forth all that is intended; and so in the case of the Divine Name the plural form expresses the truth that the finite word conveys an inadequate idea of the Being Whom it represents.

Other names of God will be found to be in the plural also; and it is worthy of notice that in the well-known passage in Ecclesiastes (12:1) the Hebrew runs thus: "Remember now thy Creators in the days of thy youth."

§3. *Secondary Uses of the Name* 'ĔLÔHÎYM

Another use of the word 'Ĕlôhîym (430) has now to be noticed. We read in Exod. 4:16, that God said to Moses, with reference to his brother Aaron, "thou shalt be to him in the place of 'Ĕlôhîym [430]." From these words it would appear that Moses was to be regarded by Aaron as standing in immediate relation to God,—not, however, as on a level with Him, for God did not say, "thou shalt be *as* [כְּ] 'Ĕlôhîym [430]," but *"for* [לְ] 'Ĕlôhîym [430]."[7] Moses was instructed to convey the Divine message to Aaron, who, in his turn, was to announce it to Pharaoh. Similarly in Exod. 7:1 the Lord says to His

---

7. The R.V. is in error here. In Exod. 6:7, we have the same expression (לַאלֹהִים) rendered in the A.V., "I will be to you *a God."* It might be best, therefore, to consider the emphatic verb *to be* in the above passage as signifying (in conjunction with the preposition) *to represent*—"Thou shalt represent 'Ĕlôhîym [430] to him." In Zech. 12:8 there is a more remarkable expression. It is said that "the House of David shall be as God, as the Angel of the Lord before them." Here we have not representation but equality; and the passage has its fulfillment in Christ.

servant, "Behold I have appointed thee 'Ĕlôhîym [430] to Pharaoh, and Aaron shall be thy prophet." It is evident that the name of God was here given to His human representative, as such. In Exod. 4:16, the LXX says, "and thou shalt be to him [i.e., to Aaron] *in things pertaining to God"* (τὰ πρὸς τὸν θεόν—3588, 4314, 3588, 2316).

The use of the word in these passages may be illustrated by a reference to our Lord's teaching. When accused by the Jews of making Himself God, He answered, "Is it not written in your law, I said, Ye are gods? If he called them gods, unto whom the word of God came, and the scripture cannot be broken; say ye of him, whom the Father hath sanctified, and sent into the world, Thou blasphemest; because I said, I am the Son of God?" (John 10:34–36). The passage that our Lord here refers to is in Psalm 82:1, and begins thus: "'Ĕlôhîym [430] taketh his stand [נצב, 5324] in the gathering of 'Êl [410]; in the midst of 'Ĕlôhîym [430] he doeth judgment." The Psalmist proceeds to rebuke this gathering of 'Ĕlôhîym (430), who were evidently judges, and who were responsible for judging in accordance with the word of the LORD: "How long will ye administer perverted justice, and favor wicked men? Deal justly with the poor and fatherless: acquit the afflicted and needy. Deliver the poor and needy: rescue them from the hand of wicked men" (vv. 2–4). Yet the rebuke was unheeded. Alas! "They know not, neither do they perceive; they go on walking in darkness: all the foundations of the land [i.e., its judges] are moved from their course" (v. 5). Then comes the retribution following on their neglect of these august privileges and duties. "It is I myself[8] that said ye are 'Ĕlôhîym [430], and all of you children of the Highest. Yet after all ye shall die as Adam, and as one of the princes shall ye fall" (vv. 6, 7). The Psalmist concludes with the prophetic aspiration, "Arise, thou 'Ĕlôhîym [430], administer just judgment in the land: for it is thou that hast all the nations for thine inheritance" (v. 8). Our Lord, by referring to this Psalm, evidently meant His hearers to understand that if earthly judges were called *gods* in Scripture because they were to regulate their decisions by the Word of God, it could be no blasphemy in Him whom the Father had sent into the world to call Himself God's Son. If *they* represented God, how much more did *He.*

---

8. It is only in some such way as this that one can express the force of the emphatic Hebrew personal pronoun. Our translators have not often adopted this plan, but in other versions (e.g., the French of Ostervald) the distinction between the expressed and the unexpressed pronoun has been marked in this way. The R.V. fails here.

In accordance with the words of the Psalm just referred to, we read in Exod. 22:8, 9, "If the thief be not found, then the master of the house shall be brought unto *the judges* [ha-'Ělôhîym, 430], to decide whether he hath put his hand unto his neighbour's goods.... the cause of both parties shall come before the judges [ha-'Ělôhîym, 430]; and whom the judges ['Ělôhîym, 430] condemn, he shall pay double to his neighbour." In verse 28, where our translators have somewhat unfortunately put "thou shalt not revile the gods," we read 'Ělôhîym (430) again; and consistently with the previous passages we should render it, "thou shalt not revile *judges,* nor speak evil of a leader among thy people." See R.V., margin. This passage was referred to with a latent shade of irony by the Apostle Paul when he was called to account for speaking sharply to Ananias, who professed to judge him according to the law while causing him to be smitten contrary to the law (Acts 23:5).

The judges are also called 'Ělôhîym (430) in Exod. 21:6, where the account is given of the master boring his servant's ear in the presence of the magistrates. It is possible that the witch of Endor, when she said, "I see 'Ělôhîym [430] ascending from the earth," used the word in this sense: "I see *judges* ascending from the earth." Both the noun and the participle are in the plural number in this passage.[9] The R.V. has noted this point.

In all these passages the word 'Ělôhîym (430) indicates not beings who are to be worshiped, but a body of responsible magistrates who are called by this name because they represent the only true 'Ělôhîym (430), who is God of gods and Lord of lords. Accordingly we read that "the men between whom there is a controversy shall stand before Jehovah [3068], before the priests and the judges" (Deut. 19:17).

§4. *The Application of the Name* 'ĚLÔHÎYM *to Angels*

There is yet another use of the word 'Ělôhîym (430) that must not be passed over. The Samaritan Pentateuch and also the LXX have adopted the word *angels* to represent it in several places, and the English translators, partly guided by the teaching of the N.T., have occasionally followed their example.

---

9. See Chapter 26, §3, for a further reference to the scene here noticed.

Some critics have been inclined to render the words in Gen. 3:5, "Ye shall be as angels"; but there is no ground for such an interpretation. In Job 38:7, "the sons of God" who shouted for joy are designated *angels* by the LXX, but this is by way of commentary rather than translation. Compare Ps. 138:1.

In Heb. 1:6, we read, "when he bringeth the firstbegotten into the world, he saith, And let all the angels of God worship him." The writer here cites words that are to be found in some copies of the LXX in the Song of Moses (Deut. 32:43), but there is no Hebrew equivalent for them in our existing text. The words that follow carry the reader on from the day of Moses to a time yet to come when God "will avenge the blood of his servants and will render vengeance to his adversaries, and will be merciful to his land, and to his people." This will be at the time of the restitution of all things that has been spoken of by all the holy prophets from old time (Acts 3:21). While the writer of the Epistle to the Hebrews probably had the Song of Moses in his mind when he quoted the words of the LXX, there may be a secondary reference to Psalm 97:7, where we read, "worship him, all ye gods ['Ĕlôhîym, 430]," but where the LXX has rendered, "worship him, all ye his angels."

In Ps. 8:4–6 the A.V. runs thus, "What is man, that thou art mindful of him? and the son of man, that thou visitest him? For thou hast made him a little lower than the angels, and hast crowned him with glory and honour. Thou madest him to have dominion over the works of thy hands." Here the Hebrew has 'Ĕlôhîym (430), and were it not for the sanction given to the LXX interpretation in Heb. 2:7, our translators would probably have given a literal rendering, as the R.V. has done.

Gesenius, Hengstenberg, and other critics understood the Psalmist to mean that the Son of Man should be but little below the glory of God. So Calvin *"parum abesse eum jussisti a divino et coelesti statu"* (translation of Latin: "you have decreed him to be not very far from a Divine and heavenly position"). We might, perhaps, paraphrase the words, "thou hast *bereft*[10] him for a little while of the Divine glory." Compare Phil. 2:7. In giving this interpretation of the words, though we do not adopt the exact rendering of the LXX, we arrive at a substantial agreement with its teaching. The fact announced in the Hebrew text with regard to man generally is fulfilled

10. The word is so rendered in Eccles. 4:8.

with regard to Christ in such a mode as the LXX describes, and as
the writer of the Epistle to the Hebrews sanctions.

§5. *Difficulties in Translating*
the Name 'ĔLÔHÎYM

We have seen that the name 'Ĕlôhîym (430) is properly a title
belonging to one Being, who is the Creator of heaven and earth and
the Sustainer of all existence. The question now returns, how is the
word to be dealt with in translation: Three possible courses present
themselves. The Hebrew word might be transliterated, as is sometimes done with the name Jᴇʜᴏᴠᴀʜ; or the name of some native
object of worship might be substituted for it; or the original meaning
of the word might be reproduced by a translation.

To deal with the last proposal first, there could be no valid objection to such a course, if no better plan presented itself. It is agreed
by almost all scholars that the name 'Ĕlôhîym (430) signifies the
Putter forth of power. He is the Being to whom all power belongs.
The lowest of heathen tribes are compelled to acknowledge that
there is a Power in existence greater than their own, and the missionary constantly has to take this acknowledgment as a basis on
which he may plant a more complete theology.

The proposal that the Hebrew name for the Divine Being should
be transliterated, and used alone or in combination with those of
native deities, has been received with greater favor by some missionaries. They have looked on it as a means of avoiding the danger
in which every translator is manifestly involved, of giving a seeming
sanction to false religion by the adoption of a name that conveys
false ideas. But, after all, while seeking to escape one evil, the trans-
literator runs into another; for he would be laying himself open to
the charge that he was setting forth strange gods.

The other plan is to single out that name which is, on the whole,
the best representative of a personal and powerful Being, leaving it
for the general teaching of Scripture and for the oral instruction of
the missionary to lift up men's minds to higher ideas of this Being
than they had done before.

If all the names of God were to be rejected that had ever been
used for idolatrous purposes, it is hard to know what would be left.
'Ĕlôhîym (430) itself was so used; the same is the case with the
Arabic form *Allah,* with the Greek *Theos* (Θεός, *2316*), the Ethiopic

Amlak (cf. *Moloch*), the Egyptian *Nout*, the Hungarian *Isten*, the Albanian *Pernti*, the Tartar *Tengri*, and many others, which are sanctioned in time-honored versions. Nay, what would happen to the Georgian *Ghut*, the Persian *Khuda*, the German *Gott*, and the English *God*? Fortunately our idea of God comes not from the etymology of the word, nor from its use in the days of our heathendom, but from the truths that we have been taught about Him from our childhood. This is exactly the point to be borne in mind. The truth about God is gathered not so much from the Name as from what is taught concerning Him who bears it. The knowledge of the nature and character of God is gradually acquired through the study of the Scriptures.

The American Bishop Boone, in his contribution to the Chinese discussions, says that we should render the name of God by the highest generic word that represents an object of worship. If this theory were to be carried out, then the first verse of the Bible would practically run thus: "In the beginning an object of worship created the heavens and the earth." This, however, would be an inversion of the right order of thought. God is to be worshiped because He is Creator. His works constitute, in great measure, His claim to worship. The same writer also quotes Lactantius and Origen in favor of a generic name for God. These learned men wrote centuries after the matter had been practically settled, so far as regards the Greek language, by the usage of the LXX, and when it would have been too late, even if it had been good for any reason, to substitute *Zeus* (Ζεύς, 2203) for *Theos* (Θεός, 2316). Dr. Malan, indeed, has shown, in his work on the Names of God,[11] that *Zeus* and *Theos* were originally, in all probability, the same word. But we have a greater witness than Dr. Malan, even that of the Apostle to the Gentiles, who, after quoting two heathen hymns written in honor of *Zeus*, argues from them in favor of the spiritual nature of *Theos*, who made the world.

The passage in the Acts (chap. 17) referred to here deserves special notice. When Paul reached Athens he found that it was wholly given to idolatry (κατείδωλον, 2712), an expression that falls in all too well with the Roman satirist's remark that it was easier to find a god than a man in that city. Accordingly, the Apostle held constant discussions (διαλέγομαι, 1256), not only with the Jews and proselytes whom he found in the synagogue,[12] but also with anybody

---

11. *Who Is God in China?*—a powerful argument in favor of *Shang-ti*.
12. The A.V. (v. 17) runs thus: "Therefore disputed he in the synagogue with the Jews,

whom he could meet with in the Agora. Here certain of the Epicureans, who were Atheists, and of the Stoics, who were Pantheists, fell in with him from day to day;[13] and while some spoke of him with utter scorn—his Gospel being "foolishness" to them—others came to the conclusion that he was setting forth certain *demons* (A.V. "gods") that were foreign to their city. By "demons" these philosophers meant very much the same as the Muslims mean by their *genii;* their ideas about them would be very vague. Sometimes they seem to have been regarded as the souls of the departed, sometimes as guardian angels, sometimes as evil influences, sometimes as what we call *demi-gods.*[14]

Here, Paul found himself confronted with idolatry and demon-worship, the two substitutes for the worship of the living God that are to be found among almost all the nations of the earth. Even the *fetish* of the African rainmaker is connected with a mysterious unseen power, which is supposed to work on a man's life and possessions. The acknowledgment of such hidden influence harmonizes all too readily with Pantheism, and is not inconsistent even with Atheism. A man may be a Positivist and yet a Spiritualist. He may, in profession at least, deny that there is a personal *causa causarum* [cause of causes], and yet may give way to a superstitious respect for certain shadowy powers, which are to him realities, and which exercise an appreciable influence on his thoughts and ways. This arises from the necessity of his nature. His consciousness announces to him the reality of unseen and immaterial entities, though he does not care to proclaim the fact to the world. If he is highly civilized and scientific, he may dismiss these phantoms as creations of the imagination. But if he is a member of a barbarous and uncultivated tribe from which the true idea of God has apparently died out, he will become the prey of the rainmaker, the conjurer, or the witch, by whose arts his superstition will be systematically developed. The *fetish* or object that he regards with awe,

---

and with the devout persons"; but there ought to be no comma after the word *Jews.* The σεβόμενοι (4576), or devout proselytes, went to the synagogue, where Paul doubtless discoursed in Greek. The R.V. is correct.

13. The imperfect tense is used throughout.

14. No distinction can be drawn between δαίμων (1142) and δαιμόνιον (1140); both were applied to the deity, to fortune, to the souls of the departed, and to genii or demi-gods, beings part mortal part divine (μεταξὺ θεοῦ τε καὶ θνητοῦ) [intermediate, (partaking) both of divine and of mortal] as Plato calls them (*Symp.* p. 202 d.).

whether it be merely a bit of rag or a bundle of feathers, becomes to him an embodiment of the dark and terrible side of his spiritual feelings. As long as the sun shines and the rain descends and the fruits of the earth abound—as long as a man has health, and strength, and prosperity—he cares little about fetish or demon, and still less about God. But when trouble comes he will follow the example of Jonah's mariners, who "cried every man unto his god," and will seek by magic or superstitious arts to avert the misfortunes that have befallen him and to propitiate the evil spirit whom he has unwittingly offended. This sad story of human superstition is well known to every missionary who has labored among rude tribes of idolaters; and it may help us to understand the state of things which Christianity has had to displace ever since its earliest promulgation.

But to return to Paul's speech at Athens. "He seemeth," said the sage (v. 18), "to be a setter forth of strange [i.e., foreign] demons."[15] Accordingly, impelled by curiosity, they gather round the Apostle, and lead him out of the bustling Agora up the steps hewn out of the rock by which we still mount to the Areopagus. There to his male and female audience, half-cynical, half-interested, the Apostle of the Gentiles delivered a model missionary address, and conferred a luster on Athens that neither the oratory of Demosthenes, the states-manship of Pericles, the philosophy of Plato, nor the art of Phidias can surpass. "Athenians!" he seems to say, "ye appear to me to be far too much given to demon-fearing already; it is a mistake therefore to suppose that I have come to set forth more demons for your acceptance. My mission is a very different one; for while coming through your city, and inspecting the objects that you regard with reverence, I met with an altar on which was written, 'To GOD THE UNKNOWN.' Besides the demons whom you fear, then, there is evi-dently a being called GOD, whom you regard with reverence, even though you are ignorant about His true nature. *This* is the Being whom I am setting forth to you."[16]

Having thus awakened the attention of his hearers, he concen-trated their mind on the word GOD. "The God who made the *cosmos* and all that is in it, He, being Possessor and Ruler of heaven and

---

15. The very charge made against Socrates (Xen. *Mem.* 1:1:2; Plato, *Ap.* 24*b*).

16. καταγγέλλω (*2605—declare, set forth, make known*); compare the ξένων δαιμονίων καταγγελεὺς (*3581, 1140, 2604*—lit., *of foreign demons* [or *deities*] *a proclaimer*).

earth, cannot have His Presence confined within the minute space that human hands are able to compass round with walls (and here no doubt the speaker pointed to the buildings that lay at his feet), neither can He be ministered to (θεραπεύω, 2323) by hands of mortal men, as if He had any necessities that they could relieve—seeing that it is He that is the Giver of life in all its aspects to all men. The nations that dwell on the face of the whole earth have sprung from one source, and have been distributed through many ages, and among various countries, by His will and agency. And it is for them to seek God,[17] if haply they may feel Him[18] and find Him. And, after all, He is not far off from any single person among us, for it is through union with Him that we have life, movement, and even bare existence; as some of your own poets[19] have said, 'For we are His offspring.' Seeing, then, that there is such a relationship existing between God and man, we ought to know better than to suppose that the Deity (τὸ θεῖον—3588, 2304) can be really like a cleverly carved piece of stone or metal. If these things do not represent the real life of man, how can they possibly represent Him from whom that life flows?"

Paul's argument rested not on the name of God, but on the Divine operations and attributes. He knew full well that the word *Theos* did not convey the whole truth about the Divine Being to the mind of his hearers, and that *Zeus* was still further from being a fair representative of 'Ĕlôhîym (430); but he confirmed what he had to say about the *Theos* who made the heaven and the earth by reference to two hymns dedicated to *Zeus*, who was also described as maker of all things. He thus worked round to the original idea of 'Ĕlôhîym (430), and laid the foundations of sound Gospel teaching on one of the noblest products of natural theology.

§6. *Other Names for God*

Although the plural 'Ĕlôhîym (430) is ordinarily used for God, the singular form 'Ĕlôwahh (433) is found in fifty-seven passages, most

17. Not "the Lord," as A.V.

18. The point is somewhat obscured in the A.V. and R.V., which read, "feel *after* him." The verb ψηλαφάω (5584) means to *handle* (I John 1:1); hence, to feel an object in the dark. The nations were intended to have an *impression* of God's existence, though they were in darkness as to His real nature.

19. The hymns to Zeus that he quotes were written by Cleanthes the Stoic, of Assos (300 B.C.), and by Aratus of Soli, near Tarsus (270 B.C.).

of which are in the Book of Job. Only six times is 'Ĕlôwahh (433) applied to any but the true God.

The Aramaic form 'Ĕlâhh (426) is found thirty-seven times in Ezra, once in Jeremiah, and forty-six times in Daniel. Of the eighty-four passages where it occurs, seventy-two refer to the True God. The Assyrian form is *Ilu.*

The more simple and elementary form 'Êl (410), which is frequently adopted either alone or in dependence on another substantive, to express power or might, is used of the true God in 204 passages, and of others in eighteen passages. It is found especially in Job, Psalms, and Isaiah.

The names Êl (410), 'Ĕlâhh (426), 'Ĕlôwahh (433), and 'Ĕlôhîym (430) seem to express the same idea, even if they are not all connected etymologically—though it may prove that they are. All occur, together with Jehovah (3068), in Deut. 32:15–19.

The plural of 'Êl (410) is 'Êlîym (410), which is supposed to be used of false gods in Exod. 15:11; Ps. 29:1; 89:6; and Dan. 11:36; in each of which passages, however, the word may be rendered *mighty ones.* 'Êlîym (410) is never used of the true God.

'Êl (410) is sometimes used in compound names, as 'Êl-Shadday (410, 7706), rendered in the A.V. "Almighty God," Bêyth-'Êl (1008), "the house of God"; and in other cases it is used apparently to add force and sublimity to an idea, as when we read of "mountains of 'Êl [410]," i.e., "mighty mountains."

The titles of the Messiah contained in Isa. 9:6 have been subjected to a good deal of criticism from Jewish and Gentile pens, partly, no doubt, because the name 'Êl (410) occurs in the expression that our translators have rendered "the mighty God." In this passage we read, "His name shall be called Wonderful, Counsellor." These words may, perhaps, be taken in their connection with one another as a parallel to Isa. 28:29, where the same words in rather different forms are rendered "wonderful in counsel" and applied to the LORD of hosts.[20] Again, "His name shall be called . . . the Mighty God." In the LXX, Luther's, and other versions, we find this title broken up into

---

20. The word for *wonderful* is literally *a wonder* (see Isa. 29:14). The verb related to it is constantly used of God's *wonderful* works. Sometimes it signifies that which is *hidden,* or *difficult,* as in Gen. 18:14, "is anything too *hard* for the LORD?" In Judg. 13:18 we read, "Why askest thou my name, seeing it is *secret?*" Perhaps *wonderful* would be a better rendering here; the cognate verb occurs in the next verse, where we read that the angel did *wondrously.*

two, and translated "Mighty, Hero," or "Mighty, Powerful"; but the order of the Hebrew words is in favor of A.V., which is consistent with Isa. 10:21 and Jer. 32:18 where the expression reappears. The remaining title, the Everlasting Father, has been rendered in some recensions of the LXX and in the Vulgate "the Father of the Coming Age," and in other versions "the Father of Eternity"; the last, which is the best rendering when read in the light of the N.T., would signify that the Messiah was to be the Father, Spring, or Source of Everlasting Life to all the world. Lastly, as He was to be the Father of Eternity, so was He to be called the Prince of Peace, one whose dominion should establish a holy peace (in all the fullness of meaning of that word) throughout the world.

§7. *The Almighty*

The name **Shadday** (שַׁדַּי, 7706) is always rendered *Almighty.*

The LXX renders it by the word θεός (2316), κύριος (2962), and παντοκράτωρ (3841), *God, Lord,* and *Almighty.* In five passages we find ἱκανός (2425), which we might translate *All-sufficient.* Jerome adopted the word *Omnipotens,* Almighty, and other versions have followed in his track.

The title **Shadday** (7706) really indicates the fullness and riches of God's grace, and would remind the Hebrew reader that from God comes every good and perfect gift—that He is never weary of pouring forth His mercies on His people, and that He is more ready to give than they are to receive. The word is connected with a root that signifies a *breast,* and hence the idea is similar to that contained in our word *exuberance.* Perhaps the expressive word *bountiful* would convey the sense most exactly.[21] This rendering will be illustrated and confirmed by a reference to some of the passages in which **Shadday** (7706) occurs, as they will be found specially to designate God as a bountiful Giver. The first passage in which the word is found is Gen. 17:1, where we read that "Jehovah appeared to Abram, and said, I am 'Êl Shadday [410, 7706]; walk before me, and be thou perfect. And I will make my covenant between me and thee, and will multiply thee exceedingly . . . and thou shalt be a father of a multitude of nations. Neither shall thy name any more be called

---

21. Compare the rendering *allgenugsame* (German—*all-sufficient*) in the Berlenburger Bible.

Abram, but thy name shall be Abraham; for a father of a multitude of nations have I made thee. And I will make thee exceeding fruitful, and I will make nations of thee, and kings shall come out of thee."

The title is next found in Gen. 28:3, where Isaac says to Jacob, "'Êl Shadday [410, 7706] bless thee, and make thee fruitful, and multiply thee, that thou mayest be an assemblage of peoples."

The third passage is Gen. 35:11, where God says to Jacob, "I am 'Êl Shadday [410, 7706]: be fruitful and multiply; a nation and an assemblage of nations shall be of thee, and kings shall come out of thy loins" (cf. Gen. 48:3).

The fourth passage is Gen. 43:14, where Jacob, in the intensity of his anxiety on behalf of his youngest son whom he is about to send into Egypt, throws himself upon the tender compassion of the All-Bountiful God, and says, "'Êl Shadday [410, 7706] give you tender mercy before the man, that he may send away your other brother and Benjamin."

There is only one other place in Genesis in which this name is found, namely, Gen. 49:25, where Jacob is blessing his son Joseph, and says, "From the 'Êl (410) of thy father, there shall be help to thee; and with Shadday (7706), there shall be blessings to thee, blessings of heaven above, blessings of the deep that lieth under, blessings of the *breasts* [here the word Shad (שַׁד, 7699) is used in its original sense], and blessings of the womb."

These passages appear to establish the fact that while the name 'Êl (410) sets forth the might[22] of God, the title Shadday (7706) points to the inexhaustible stores of His bounty.

Passing by the reference to this name in Exod. 6:3, which will be discussed in a later section, it may be noticed that Shadday (7706) is only once again used in combination with 'Êl (410), namely, in Ezek. 10:5; without 'Êl (410) it is used twice by Balaam (Num. 24:4, 16), twice by Naomi (Ruth 1:20, 21), twice in the Psalms (68:14; 91:1), and three times by the prophets (Isa. 13:6; Ezek. 1:24; Joel 1:15). These are the only places in which it is to be found in the Bible except in the Book of Job, in which we meet with it thirty-one times.

---

22. When we read of the Mighty One of Israel, or the Mighty God of Jacob or Israel, the word for Mighty is usually Abbîyr (אָבִּיר, 47), a word marking strength and excellence. Sometimes Gâdôwl (גָּדוֹל, 1419), *great,* is used, e.g., in Deut. 7:21; and in one or two cases the Hebrew name for a Rock is used to set forth the firmness of the Divine power: see, for example, Isa. 30:29. The 50th Psalm begins with the three names 'Êl (410), 'Êlôhîym (430), Jehovah (3068—A.V. The Mighty God, even the LORD).

§8. *The Lord*

The word usually rendered *Lord,* or *my Lord,* is 'Ădônây (אֲדֹנָי, 136). This is a special form of 'Ădôwn (113), a word that signifies *master;* and that exactly answers to the Greek Κύριος (2962). 'Ădôwn (113) is sometimes rendered *sir* in the A.V., as in Gen. 43:20; *owner,* as in I Kings 16:24; but generally *master,* as in Gen. 24:9. The plural form 'Ădônîym (113) and its plural construct form 'Ădônêy (113) are used in the same sense; but when the word is applied to God, the form 'Ădônây (136) is adopted. The termination of the word, as in the case of **Shadday** (7706), may mark an ancient plural form, but this is uncertain. In the A.V., as in other versions, 'Ădônây (136) is frequently rendered *my Lord.* The title indicates the truth that God is the owner of each member of the human family, and that He consequently claims the unrestricted obedience of all. It is first used of God in Gen. 15:2, 8, and again in 18:3. It is rare in the Pentateuch and historical books, but frequent in the Psalms, Isaiah, Jeremiah, Ezekiel, Daniel, and Amos.

The words that we read in the 110th Psalm and the first verse, if literally translated, would run thus: "Jehovah (3068) said unto my Master,[23] sit thou on my right hand until I make thine enemies thy footstool." And our Savior's comment might be rendered, "If David then call him Master, how is he his son?" (Matt. 22:45).

The expression "the Lord GOD," which first occurs in Gen. 15:2, and is frequently found in the O.T., especially in the prophetical books, is literally "my Lord Jehovah."

When we meet with the title "Lord of lords," as in Deut. 10:17, the words are literally "Master of masters," i.e., Divine Master of all those who possess or obtain authority.

In the Psalms and elsewhere there is found that significant title that the Apostle Thomas gave to the Lord Jesus when he had optical and sensible demonstration that He was risen from the dead. Thus in Ps. 35:23, the sacred writer uses the double title 'Ĕlôhay (430) and 'Ădônây (136), "my God and my Lord"; and in Ps. 38:15 we find 'Adônây 'Ĕlôhay (136, 430), "my Lord, my God."

The claim on man's service that is set forth in the title 'Ădônây (136) is well illustrated by Mal. 1:6, where Jehovah says, "A son

---

23. According to the present Masoretic punctuation the word is in the singular— 'Ădônîy (113), not 'Ădônây (136).

honoureth his father, and a servant his master [or masters]; if, then, I be a father, where is mine honour? and if I be a master ['Ădônîym, 113[24]], where is my reverential fear?"

§9. *The Most High*

The Hebrew title rendered *Most High* is 'Elyôwn (עֶלְיוֹן, 5945), for which the LXX usually has the reading ὁ ὕψιστος (*3588, 5310*), the Highest. The word 'Elyôwn (5945), however, is not confined to this sacred use. It is found in Gen. 40:17; I Kings 9:8; II Kings 18:17; II Chron. 7:21; 23:20; 32:30; Neh. 3:25; Jer. 20:2; and 36:10.

This title is first applied to God in the account of Melchizedek (Gen. 14:18–22); it is used by Balaam, who "knew the knowledge of the Most High" (Num. 24:16); and Moses adopts it when he speaks of the Most High dividing the earth among the nations (Deut. 32:8; cf. Acts 17:26). It occurs also several times in the Psalms: Ps. 18:13 says, "The Highest gave his voice"; Ps. 78:35 declares, "They remembered that God was their rock, and the High God their redeemer." In Ps. 89:27, this title is applied to the Messiah: "I will make him my firstborn, higher than the kings of the earth."

When we read of the Most High God in Micah 6:6, the Hebrew Mârôwm (מָרוֹם, 4791), *exalted,* is used. Compare Ps. 99:2; 113:4; 138:6; and Isa. 57:15. In these texts a simpler form of Mârôwm (4791), Râm (רָם—from רוּם, 7311), is rendered *high,* and applied to God.

§10. *Jehovah*

All the titles by which the living and true God was made known to Israel have been brought under consideration with the exception of one, Yᵉhôvâh, or the familiar Jehovah (יְהֹוָה, 3068), which occurs about 5500 times in the O.T. This name has been preserved by our translators in a few passages, but the word LORD, spelled in small capitals, has usually been substituted for it. The LXX set a precedent for this course by almost invariably adopting the word Κύριος, (*2962*), *Lord,* as a rendering, the only exception being Prov. 29:26, where δεσπότης, (*1203*), *Ruler* or *Master,* is found.

The shorter form, Yâhh or Jah (3050), occurs in Exod. 15:6 and 17:16, in each of which passages our translators have rendered it

---

24. Some MSS. here read 'Ădônây (136).

LORD; it is also found a few times in Isaiah, and in thirty-five passages in the Psalms, the earliest instances being Ps. 77:11 and 89:8. We are familiar with it in the expression *Hallelujah*, i.e., *Praise* Jah, also as a suffix or prefix in compound names such as Elijah and Jehoshua.

It is a strange fact, with respect to the word Jehovah (3068), that critics should differ as to its pronunciation, its origin, and its meaning. The first difficulty has arisen from the mystery with which the Jews have always surrounded this sacred and (as they hold) incommunicable name; but we may rest content with the traditional pronunciation of the word until there is stronger reason than appears at present for the substitution of Jahveh, or of some other form. The Assyrians represent it in Israelitish names by the form *Yahu* and *Yahava* (Sayce). The doubt about the signification of the name is owing probably rather to the finiteness of the human understanding than to any uncertainty as to the revelation of Jehovah (3068) contained in Scripture.[25]

Whatever may be the opinion about 'Ĕlôhîym (430), it is generally agreed that Jehovah (3068) is not a generic or class name, but a personal or proper name. Maimonides says that all the names of God that occur in Scripture are derived from his works except one, and that is Jehovah; and this is called "the plain name," because it teaches plainly and unequivocally of the substance of God. A Scottish divine has said,

> In the name Jehovah the Personality of the Supreme is distinctly expressed. It is everywhere a proper name, denoting the Person of God, and Him only; whence Elohim partakes more of the character of a common noun, denoting usually, indeed, but not necessarily or uniformly, the Supreme. The Hebrew may say *the* Elohim [430], the true God, in opposition to all false Gods; but he never says *the* Jehovah [3068], for Jehovah is the name of the true God only. He says again and again *my God*, but never *my* Jehovah [3068], for when he says "my God" he means Jehovah. He speaks of *the God of Israel*, but never of *the* Jehovah [3068] *of Israel*, for there is no other Jehovah. He speaks of *the living God*, but never of *the living* Jehovah [3068], for he cannot conceive of Jehovah as other than living.[26]

25. In some foreign translations of the Bible the name Jehovah is rendered *The Eternal*. Perhaps there is no word that, on the whole, conveys the meaning of the name so well; but, after all, the truth that it represents is too many-sided to be rendered by any one word.

26. See Fairbairn's *Dictionary of the Bible*, article on *Jehovah*.

The meaning, and, in all probability, the etymology[27] of this name, is to be looked for in Exod. 3:14, 15, where, in answer to the question of Moses as to the name of the 'Ĕlôhîym (430) who was addressing him, the LORD said to Moses, "I AM THAT I AM."[28] "Thus shalt thou say unto the children of Israel, I AM hath sent me unto you. . . . Jehovah [3068], the 'Ĕlôhîym [430] of your fathers, the 'Ĕlôhîym of Abraham, and of Isaac, and of Jacob, hath sent me unto you: this is my Name for ever, and this is my Memorial[29] unto all generations." Again, in Exod. 6:2, 3, we read, "I am Jehovah [3068], and I appeared unto Abraham, and unto Isaac, and unto Jacob, by the name of 'Êl Shadday [410, 7706], and, as regards my name Jehovah [3068], I was not fully known by them; yet, verily, I have established [or rather, taking the tense as a prophetic future, I will establish] my covenant with them, to give them the land of Canaan." These two passages taken together elucidate the following points: (1) that though the name Jehovah (3068) was in frequent use as the title of the 'Ĕlôhîym (430) of the Patriarchs, yet its full significance was not revealed to them; (2) that it was to be viewed in connection with the fulfillment of God's covenant and promise that now, after the lapse of some four hundred years, the true import of the name was to be unfolded by the manifestation of a personal living Being, working in behalf of Israel, so as to fulfill the promises made to the Fathers. Thus the sublime idea of an unchanging, ever-living God, remaining faithful to His word through many generations, began to dawn on the mind of Israel. And that which was hoped for, and

27. There has been much difference of opinion as to the formation of the word; but it may be noted that the *v* introduced into the name may be illustrated by the *v* in the name of *Eve*.

28. The words above rendered "I AM THAT I AM" are almost unapproachable, after all. Owing to the vagueness of the Hebrew tense (which is the same in both parts of the sentence) we might render them in various ways, but none are better than our own, denoting as they do a personal, continuous, absolute, self-determining Existence. It ought to be observed that the Hebrew word rendered I AM occurs in several important prophetic passages, in which it has generally been rendered *"I will be."* Thus, right here in Exod. 3:12 we read, "Certainly *I will be* with thee"; so also in Gen. 26:3, *"I will be* with thee and will bless thee"; and in Gen. 31:3, *"I will be* with thee." In these and similar passages we might render the words *"I AM* with thee." They mark an eternal, unchanging Presence. Compare the identical words used by the Lord (Jesus Christ?) in Acts 18:10, *"I AM* with thee, and no man shall set on thee to hurt thee"; also John 8:58, "Before Abraham came into being I AM"; and in Matt. 28:20, "And lo, I AM with you all the days until the consummation of the age."

29. Compare Hos. 12:5, "Jehovah [3068] is his memorial," i.e., the name by which His attributes were always to be brought to mind.

sealed up in the name during the Patriarchal age, began to work itself out into a substantial reality. God's personal existence, the continuity of His dealings with man, the unchangeableness of His promises, and the whole revelation of His redeeming mercy gather round the name Jehovah (3068). "Thus saith Jehovah [3068]," not "thus saith 'Ĕlôhîym [430]," is the general introduction to the prophetic messages. It is as Jehovah (3068) that God became the Savior of Israel, and as Jehovah (3068) He saves the world; and this is the truth embodied in the name of *Jesus* (2424), which is literally *Jehovah-Savior.*

It is supposed by some critics that the contributors to the early books of the Bible were of different schools of thought, some believing in 'Ĕlôhîym (430), some in Jehovah (3068), and some in both. This is no place for discussing such a supposition. Undoubtedly some writers preferred to use one name and some another. This is demonstrated by a comparison of parallel texts in Kings and Chronicles.[30] Taking the books as they stand, the important point to notice is that the various names of God are used by the sacred writers advisedly, so as to bring out the various aspects of His character and dealings. Thus, the first chapter of Genesis sets forth Creation as an act of power; hence 'Ĕlôhîym (430) is always used. The second chapter, which properly begins at the fourth verse, brings 'Ĕlôhîym (430) into communion with man; hence He is called Jehovah 'Ĕlôhîym (3068, 430).[31] In the third chapter it may be observed that the Serpent avoids the use of the name Jehovah (3068). In the fourth chapter the offerings of Cain and Abel are made to Jehovah (3068), and this is the case with the whole sacrificial system both under the Patriarchal and the Levitical dispensation. In many cases the offerings to Jehovah (3068) are accompanied by a calling on His name (see Gen. 12:8; 13:4); and probably from the earliest days the Name of Jehovah (3068) was taken as the embodiment of that hope for the human race that found its expression in sacrifice and in prayer (see Gen. 4:26).

30. See *Deuterographs.*

31. Editor's note: Sometimes Jehovah (יְהֹוָה, 3068) is spelled Yᵉhôvîh (יְהֹוִה, 3069), in which case it is translated GOD in the A.V., as in the expression "GOD the Lord" (Ps. 68:20) or "Lord GOD" (Ps. 71:5). In both instances it is joined with 'Ădônây (אֲדֹנָי, 136), translated "Lord" in the A.V. In the book of Ezekiel the Divine names are characteristically joined in this way, Adonay Jehovih (136, 3069). The A.V. consistently renders this "Lord GOD," whereas the N.I.V. renders it "(the) Sovereign Lord."

Although man had fallen, Jehovah (3068) had not forsaken him. His Spirit still strove with man (Gen. 6:3); but the judicial aspect of His nature had to be exercised in punishment, as we see from the history of the Deluge, the confusion of tongues, and the destruction of Sodom and Gomorrah. In Gen. 9:26, Jehovah (3068) is called the God of Shem; and in 14:22 He is identified by Abram with 'Êl 'Elyôwn (410, 5945), "the Most High God," who is "the Possessor of heaven and earth."

In Gen. 15:1, we are introduced to the expression that afterwards became so familiar, "the Word of Jehovah [3068]"; and throughout that remarkable chapter the name 'Ĕlôhîym (430) does not occur, because it is the name Jehovah (3068) that God adopts when making His communications and covenants with man. In Gen. 16 "the angel of Jehovah [3068]" is spoken of for the first time, and appears to be identical with Jehovah (3068) himself; He is also described by Abraham as "the Judge of all the earth" (Gen. 18:25).

The Patriarchs are frequently represented as worshiping and holding spiritual communication with Jehovah (3068). He seems to have revealed Himself in a human form to these privileged children of Adam, whether through visions or otherwise (see Gen. 18:1, 2; 28:13–17; 32:24–30).

In Exod. 24:10, 11, we are told of the seventy elders of Israel that "they saw[32] the God of Israel. . . . and did eat and drink." What a marvelous sight, and what a mysterious feast is here recorded! But this God of Israel must have been Jehovah (3068), whom Jacob or Israel worshiped, and who was now revealing Himself in order to fulfill the promises made to the fathers.

Jehovah (3068) is represented as in constant communication with Moses. And when he threatened that he would not go up to the land of Canaan with the people because of their idolatry, the lawgiver took the sacred tent that already existed (for there must have been worship from the beginning) and pitched it without the camp; and "the cloudy pillar descended, and stood at the door of the tabernacle, and Jehovah [3068] talked with Moses. . . . And Jehovah [3068] spake unto Moses face to face, as a man speaketh unto his friend" (Exod. 33:9–11). Then it was that Moses besought this august

32. The LXX had not the courage to translate this literally, but rendered it, "They saw *the place where* the God of Israel *stood.*"

Being to show him His glory, and His merciful answer was given and the revelation made:

> Jehovah [3068], the merciful and gracious 'Êl [410], longsuffering, and abounding in lovingkindness and truth. Keeping lovingkindness for thousands, pardoning iniquity and transgression and sin, and that will by no means hold men guiltless; visiting the iniquity of the fathers upon the children, and upon the children's children, unto the third and fourth generation (Exod. 34:6, 7).

Here, then, we have the full meaning of the name Jehovah (3068). We find that it sums up both the merciful and the judicial aspects of the Divine character. While the title 'Ělôhîym (430) sets forth God's creative and sustaining power, Shadday (7706) His bounty, and 'Elyôwn (5945) His sublimity, the name Jehovah (3068) sets forth His essential and unswerving principles of mercy and judgment. It presents Him as a Father, a Friend, and a Moral Governor.

§11. *The Lord of Hosts*

The title Jehovah Tsebâ'ôwth (3068, 6635) is often found represented in the expression "the LORD of Hosts" and "the LORD of Sabaoth," the former being a translation of the latter.[33] This title first appears in I Sam. 1:3. The LXX sometimes retains Σαβαώθ (4519; cf. Rom. 9:29; James 5:4), and sometimes renders it ὁ Κύριος τῶν δυνάμεων (3588, 2962, 3588, 1411—*the Lord of forces* or *armies*), and sometimes παντοκράτωρ (3841), *Almighty*. Occasionally the name 'Ělôhîym (430) is combined with or substituted for Jehovah (3068) in this connection, as in Ps. 80:4, 7, 14, 19; Amos 5:27.

In Exod. 12:41, the Israelites are called "the Hosts of the LORD," and hence it has been supposed that the title above mentioned signifies the Captain or Defender of the hosts of Israel. Others regard the expression as referring to God's governments of the "host of heaven," i.e., the stars; while others connect it with the fact that God is attended by hosts of angels who are ever ready to do His pleasure.

---

33. The French translation (Ostervald) has *l'Eternel des armées* (*the Eternal of Armies*); hence, no doubt, is derived the questionable title "the God of battles." Luther has *Herr Zebaoth* (*Lord of Hosts*). Where we read of "the God of Forces" in Dan. 11:38, a different word is used, which literally means *strength*. Dr. Sayce compares the Assyrian title *Bil Kissati*, "lord of legions."

This title is often used in the minor prophets with special reference to God's majesty, sometimes also with reference to His care for Israel (II Sam. 7:26; Ps. 46:7; 48:8; Zech. 2:9). Probably the name would indicate to a Jew that God was a Being who had many material and spiritual agencies at His command, and that the universe of matter and the world of mind were not only created, but also ordered and marshalled[34] by Him who "telleth the number of the stars, and calleth them all by their names" (Ps. 147:4; cf. Isa. 40:26).

§12. *The Angel of the Lord*

The name Jehovah (3068), again, is always used in the familiar expression, "the angel of the LORD." This title, in the opinion of some scholars, specially belongs to the Messiah. The late Dr. McCaul, in his Notes on Kimchi's Commentary on Zechariah, briefly states the reasons that led him to this conclusion. First, as to the word Mal'âk (מַלְאָךְ, 4397), he reminds us that it simply signifies a *messenger;*[35] leaving the rank and nature of the person so designated out of the question. Thus in Gen. 32:1, 3, the word is applied first to God's angels, and, secondly, to Jacob's messengers. Then, as to the full expression Mal'âk Jehovah (4397, 3068), he opposes the opinion occasionally advanced that it should be rendered "the Angel Jehovah." Again, he opposes the translation adopted by modern Jews, "an angel of the Lord," though it is occasionally sanctioned by the A.V., as in Judg. 2:1. The absence of the article is no guide here, because the word angel is *in regimen* (Latin—*within the regulations of, governed by*), i.e., is limited or defined by the word that follows it. Though the second word under such circumstances generally has a definite article, yet this would be impossible in the present instance since יְהֹוָה (Jehovah, 3068) never receives one. Dr. McCaul thus reaches the conclusion that "the angel of the LORD" is the right rendering, and he affirms that one and the same person is always designated thereby, as the expression is never used in the plural number. He then proceeds to show that "the angel of God" occa-

---

34. The *collocation*, as distinct from the *creation*, of the heavenly bodies, is dwelt upon with great force by Dr. Chalmers in his Bridgewater Treatise.

35. More literally, an *agent* or *worker.* The word is found in another form in Gen. 2:2, of God's *works* (4399); there is, therefore, nothing unbecoming in applying the title to a Divine Being. Dr. Sayce points out that in some Assyrian inscriptions Nebo is called the *Sukkul,* or messenger of Bel Merodach.

sionally spoken of in the singular number is the same person as "the angel of the LORD." This he does by citing Judg. 6:20, 21, and also Judg. 13:3, 9. In Gen. 16:7-13, "the angel of the LORD" is identified with "the LORD" (i.e., Jehovah, 3068) and with 'Êl (410). The same is the case in Judg. 6:11-16, and in Josh. 6:2. A still more remarkable identification is found in Zech. 3:2, when the angel of Jehovah (3068) is not only spoken of as Jehovah Himself, but is also represented as saying, "Jehovah [3068] rebuke thee."

But the writer proceeds to discuss Gen. 31:13, where "the angel of Jehovah [3068]" says of Himself, "I am the God of Bethel, where thou anointedst the pillar, and vowedst the vow unto me." On referring to the vision at Bethel, we read that this Being said, "I am Jehovah [3068], the God of Abraham thy father, and the God of Isaac." Dr. McCaul justly adds, "Where the law of Moses sets before us a Being who says of Himself that He is the God of Bethel, and that He is the object of Jacob's worship, what else can we conclude but that He is Very God, especially as the great object of this law throughout is to enforce the unity of God?" A similar inference may be gathered from Exod. 3:4-6.

The arguments above prove that in *some*[36] cases there is a remarkable identification between Jehovah (3068) and the Agent who carried into effect the Divine purposes. When our Lord said, "My Father worketh hitherto, and I work," this great truth appears to have been in His mind. And it almost dawned on the minds of His hearers, for we read that "the Jews sought the more to kill him, because he said that God was his Father, making himself equal with God" (John 5:17, 18). The whole mission of Christ was regarded and set forth by Him as the doing of the Works of God. Thus He was truly what the O.T. indicates that He was to be: the Angel or Agent of Jehovah (3068), giving effect and embodiment to the will of His Father. Moreover, as the priest was the agent (A.V. messenger) of the Lord of Hosts under the Old Covenant (Mal. 2:7), so Christ became

---

36. The importance of making this qualification will be seen at once by pursuing the subject into the N.T. The "Angel of the Lord," in Matt. 2:13, cannot well be identified with "the young child" in the same verse. It may be noticed, however, that here (as in Matt. 2:19; 28:2; and elsewhere) the word *Angel* has no definite article in the original Greek text. In the O.T. we must look to the context to find out whether *an* angel is meant, or whether *the* Angel or Agent of the Divine Will is referred to. In Zech. 1:12, there is evidently a distinction of persons between the Angel of the LORD and the LORD of Hosts; the former intercedes with the latter on behalf of Israel. See also Jude 13.

the True Priest or Agent who should bring about a more spiritual system of worship and a closer union between God and man.

§13. *How Translators Deal with the Name Jehovah*

It has been urged with some force that the name Jehovah (3068) ought to have been adopted more generally in translations of the Bible, whereas it is confined to a very few.[37] Putting aside the difficulty as to the right spelling of the word, it may be observed that the LXX had set an example before our Lord's time that would not be easy to depart from now. If that version had retained the word, or had even used one Greek word for Jehovah (3068) and another for 'Ădônây (136), such usage would doubtless have been retained in the discourses and arguments of the N.T. Thus our Lord, in quoting the 110th Psalm, instead of saying, "The Lord said unto my Lord," might have said, "Jehovah [3068] said unto 'Ădônîy [113]." How such a course would have affected theological questions it is not easy to surmise; nor is it needful to attempt any conjectures on the subject, as the stubborn fact remains before us that 'Ădônây (136) and Jehovah (3068) are alike rendered *Lord* in the Septuagint, and that the LXX usage has led to the adoption of the same word in the N.T. It is certainly a misfortune, and cannot easily be rectified without making a gulf between the O.T. and the N.T. How can it be gotten over?

Suppose a Christian scholar were engaged in translating the Greek Testament into Hebrew, and would have to consider, each time the word Κύριος (2962) occurred, whether there was anything in the context to indicate its true Hebrew representative. This is the difficulty that would arise in translating the N.T. into all languages if the title Jehovah (3068) had been allowed to stand in the O.T. The Hebrew Scriptures would be a guide in many passages. Thus, wherever the expression "the angel of the Lord" occurs, we know that the word *Lord* represents Jehovah (3068). A similar conclusion as to the expression "the word of the Lord" would be arrived at if the precedent set by the O.T. were followed. So also in the case of

---

37. The Spanish translator De Reyna preserved Jehovah throughout the O.T., and his successor, Valera, though his version has since been altered, did the same. De Reyna defends the adoption of this course in his Preface at some length. Calvin also uses the word Jehovah in his Latin translation, and many modern translators have done the same.

the title "the Lord of Hosts." Wherever, on the contrary, the expression "my Lord" or "our Lord" occurs we should know that the word Jehovah (3068) would be inadmissible, and Ădônây (136) or Ădônîy (113) would have to be used. But many passages would remain for which no rules could be framed.

It is to be noticed, in connection with this subject, that there are several passages in the O.T. referring to Jehovah (3068) that are adopted in the N.T. as fulfilled in the Lord Jesus Christ. Thus in Joel 2:32 we read, "Whosoever shall call on the name of Jehovah [3068] shall be saved"; but these words are applied to Jesus Christ in Rom. 10:13. The Apostle John (12:41), after quoting a certain passage from Isaiah referring to Jehovah (3068), affirms that it was a vision of the glory of Christ (see Isa. 6:9, 10). In Isa. 40:3, the preparation of the way of Jehovah (3068) is spoken of, but John the Baptist adopts the passage as referring to the preparation of the way of the Messiah. In Mal. 3:1 there seems to be a very important identification of Jehovah (3068) with the Messiah, for we read, "Jehovah [3068], whom ye [profess to] seek, shall suddenly come to his temple, even the angel of the covenant[38] whom ye [profess to] delight in." In Rom. 9:33 and I Pet. 2:6–8, Christ is described as "a stone of stumbling and a rock of offence," titles that appear to be given to Jehovah (3068) in Isa. 8:13, 14. Again, in Isa. 45:23–25, Jehovah (3068) says, "Unto me every knee shall bow. . . . In Jehovah [3068] shall all the seed of Israel be justified." But in Phil. 2:9–11 we read that God "hath highly exalted [Christ Jesus], and hath given him a name which is above every name: that at the name of Jesus every knee should bow . . . and every tongue confess that Jesus Christ is LORD [surely Jehovah, 3068], to the glory of God the Father."

It would be deeply interesting to show how each of the names of God finds its embodiment in Him who is "the Word of the Father." Thus, as 'Ĕlôhîym (430), Christ exercised Divine power, and also communicated supernatural powers to others. As Shadday (7706) Christ was all-sufficient, possessed of unsearchable riches, and

---

38. There is some difficulty about this passage. It would seem that the Old Covenant is spoken of. Who, then, was its Angel? Possibly there is a reference to Exod. 23:20-23, "Behold, I send an Angel before thee to keep thee in the way, and to bring thee into the place which I have prepared. Regard him [not beware of him, A.V.], and obey his voice, provoke him not; for he will not pardon your transgressions: for My Name is in him." The coming of the Messiah was evidently to be the manifestation of One who had for a long time been in charge of the people of Israel. See Matt. 23:37.

always ready to pour forth His benefits on man. As 'Elyôwn (5945) Christ was exalted in moral and spiritual nature, and also, as to position, made higher than the heavens. Lastly, as Jehovah (3068), Christ is "the same yesterday, to-day, and for ever," ready to save to the uttermost, in close communion with His people, fulfilling all the Divine promises, and appointed to be "Judge of all the earth." "I am Alpha and Omega, the beginning and the end, saith the Lord, which is, and which was, and which is to come, the Almighty" (Rev. 1:8).

3

The Names of Man

If it is strange that man, gifted though he is with great intelligence, should need a special revelation of the nature and character of his Maker, still more surprising is it that he should have to learn from the pages of Scripture the story of his own origin and destiny. Human nature, as portrayed in the Bible, is full of incongruities that illustrate at once the greatness and the littleness of man, his nearness to God, and his fellowship with the dust. The very names of man used by the Hebrew writers indicate the anomalies of his condition, for the principal words that are used represent him in four apparently inconsistent aspects: as 'Âdâm (120), he is of the earth, earthy; as 'Îysh (376), he is endued with immaterial and personal existence; as 'Ĕnôwsh (582), he is weak or incurable; and as Geber (1397), he is mighty and noble.

§1. *The Name* 'Âdâm

The root word 'Âdâm (אָדָם, 120) signifies *to be red* or *ruddy,* and is the ordinary word used for that purpose. It designates Esau's red lentil pottage, and gives him his name, 'Ĕdôm (123; Gen. 25:30). It is used of the rams' skins dyed red in Exod. 25:5 and other places. It marks the color of the red heifer in Num. 19:2, and of the red horses in Zech. 1:8. It is the word used of the sardius stone or ruby in Exod. 28:17 and Ezek. 28:13; and of the ruddy tint of the flesh of human beings in Gen. 25:25; I Sam. 16:12; and Song of Sol. 5:10. In II Kings 3:22 it is applied to the water that was as red as blood, and in Isa. 63:2 to the red garments that He wore who came from Edom (123).

Nor should we omit to notice that the ordinary Hebrew word for blood, Dâm (1818), is possibly connected with the same root.[1]

Another form 'Âdâm (120) takes is 'Âdâmâh (127), *the earth* or *soil*, which may have received its name from its reddish tint. We here see why the first man was called 'Âdâm (121), and why the human race is generally called by the same name in the Hebrew Scriptures, *Homo ex humo* ("Man is from the ground"—Latin). Accordingly we read in Gen. 2:7 that "the LORD God formed *man* ['Âdâm, 120] of the dust of the *ground* ['Âdâmâh, 127]."[2]

The word 'Âdâm (120) is used in the O.T. for a *human being* in about 460 places. It is usually rendered in the LXX ἄνθρωπος (444), *a human being*, which occurs in 411 passages; ἀνήρ (435), *a man, a male*, is found only eighteen times, of which fifteen are in the Book of Proverbs; in Prov. 20:24, θνητός (2349), *mortal*, is used; in the Book of Job, βροτός (L-S 331A), *mortal*, is adopted four times; and in Jer. 32:20, we find γηγενής (L-S 347B), *earth-born*, which is the closest translation of any.

The word is generally used throughout the O.T. to signify *human nature* or the *human race* generally, as contrasted with God above, or with the brute creation below. Thus it is used with great fitness in Exod. 33:20, "There shall no man see me and live," and in Mal. 3:8, "Will a man rob God?" It is the word ordinarily used in the expression "children of men" (as in Gen. 11:5). It is also found in the title "son of man," which occurs fifty-seven times in Ezekiel and once in Daniel (8:17); compare also Ps. 8:4; Job 25:6; 35:8; et al. In all such passages special stress is laid on the fact that the person thus designated is a child of Adam by descent, one of the great family of man, with a body framed of earthy material. The Lord Jesus frequently used this title with respect to Himself in order to teach His disciples that though He "came down from heaven," and was "sent from God," yet He was in very deed and truth a man.[3]

1. See Gen. 9:6, where the two words are found together. Prof. Sayce points out a possible relationship in Assyrian between *Adamu*, man, and *Adman*, sanctuary.

2. It may also perhaps be inferred that primeval man was of a ruddy color. Lanci's translation of the word 'Âdâm (120) was *Il Rossicante* (Italian, meaning the *red-complexioned man*).

It is not always easy to determine when the word 'Âdâm (120) should be regarded as a proper name, and when as a generic title. In Job 31:33, we read of a man hiding his transgression *as* 'Âdâm (121), a remarkable reference to the story of the fall; but in Hos. 6:7, where the same form is found, our translators (A.V.) have put into the text, "they *like men* have transgressed the covenant," and have banished the name *Adam* to the margin. But see R.V. or A.S.V.

3. It is sometimes asked, How can a Person be at the same time God and the Son of

A few passages in which the word 'Âdâm (120) is used for *man* deserve special notice. In Dan. 10:16, 18, we read of "one like the similitude or appearance of a man"—*like* an 'Âdâm (120), and yet not an 'Âdâm (120), because not yet incarnate. In Ezek. 1:5, 8, 10, and 10:8, 14, we meet with a description of living creatures with "the likeness of a man," with "the hands of a man," and with "the face of a man"; and "upon the likeness of the throne was the likeness as of the appearance of a man above upon it"; and this, we are told, was "the appearance of the likeness of the glory of the Lord" (Ezek. 1:26, 28; see also 3:23 and 10:4). It may be inferred that the Being whom Ezekiel thus saw in his vision was represented in human form but clothed with Divine attributes—not yet "a son of 'Âdâm [120]," but "one *like* a son of 'Âdâm [120]."

These remarkable passages indicate that human nature is intended to occupy a very high position in the scale of Creation, and that human nature was originally so constituted as to be capable of becoming the dwellingplace of the Most High. They also prepared the mind for the truth set forth by the Apostle John, who thus wrote of the Lord Jesus: "The Word was made flesh, and dwelt [or *tabernacled*] among us, (and we beheld his glory, the glory as of the only begotten of the Father,) full of grace and truth" (John 1:14). What Ezekiel saw in vision John saw in reality; his eyes looked upon and his hands handled the Word of Life (I John 1:1).

Two other passages have often attracted the attention of students. In II Sam. 7 there is recorded, first, the promise of God to keep an unfailing covenant with the seed of David, whose throne should be established forever; and secondly, David's expression of thankfulness on account of this promise. In the opening of his song of praise (vv. 18, 19) he says, "Who am I, O Lord God? and what is my house, that thou hast brought me hitherto? And this was yet a small thing in thy sight, O Lord God; but thou hast spoken also of thy servant's house for a great while to come. And is this the manner of man, O Lord God?" The parallel passage (I Chron. 17:17) runs thus: "For thou hast also spoken of thy servant's house for a great while to come, and hast regarded me according to the estate of a man of high degree."

God? The answer partly lies in the parallel question, How can a Person be at the same time Man and the Son of Man? Christ was not the son of any individual man, but was a partaker of human nature; and this was what He signified by the title "Son of Man." Similarly, by the title "Son of God" He taught that He was a partaker of Deity.

The word translated *manner* in the one passage and *estate* in the other is Tôwrâh (8451), which is generally rendered *law*. The first passage might be rendered, "And this is the *law* [or *order*] of the man," and the second, "Thou hast regarded me according to the *law* [or *order*] of the man from on high."

Some versions have rendered these passages so as to bring out more distinctly a reference to the Messiah. Thus, in Luther's version of II Sam. 7:19, we read, "That is a way of a man, who is God the LORD";[4] while his rendering of I Chron. 17:17 is, "Thou hast looked upon me after the *order* [or *form*] of a man who is the LORD God on High."[5] The words are grammatically capable of this rendering; but it is more in accordance with the context, and also with the structure of the passage, to regard the name of the Lord God as in the vocative case, in accordance with the rendering given by our A.V. translators (see R.V. on II Sam. 7:19).

§2. *The Word* 'Îysh

The second name for man to be considered is 'Îysh (אִישׁ, 376). The original meaning of this word is doubtful. It is often supposed to be connected with 'Ĕnôwsh (582; see treatment below); and this theory receives a certain amount of confirmation from the fact that the plural of the latter word has almost always been used instead of the proper plural of 'Îysh (376). Others incline to the supposition that the word may bear some relationship to the verb—if it may be called a verb—Yêsh (יֵשׁ, 3426)—a root similar to the Latin *esse*, and to the English *is*. Others, again, connect it with the unused root 'Âshash, *to found* or *make firm*; or with the kindred unused root, 'Âshâh, *to prop* or *sustain*. These words may all spring from a common source.

The first passage in which 'Îysh (376) occurs is Gen. 2:23, where Adam said, "This is now bone from my bone, and flesh from my flesh; she shall be called woman ['Ishshâh, 802], because she was taken out of man ['Îysh, 376]."[6] Although great names may be cited to the contrary, there seems to be no valid reason for departing from the implied derivation of 'Ishshâh (802) from 'Îysh (376).[6] The word

---

4. Das ist eine Weise eines Menschen, der Gott der Herr ist.

5. Du hast angesehen mich als in der Gestalt eines Menschen, der in der Höhe Gott der Herr ist.

6. The Latin Vulgate keeps up the relationship between 'Îysh (376) and 'Ishshâh (802)

'Îysh (376), being first used by man of himself in contradistinction to a second being of his own kind and springing from him, must represent some personal feeling of a kind to which Adam had hitherto been a stranger. Instead of being isolated and without a fellow, having God far above him, and the beasts of the earth below him, Adam found that he had a companion of a nature congenial to his own, "a help," as Scripture says, "meet for [suited to] him"; there was an *I* and a *Thou*, a personal relationship between two *selves* or *existences*, an 'Îysh (376) and an 'Ishshâh (802), the one springing from the other and reflecting the other's nature—the same, yet distinct.

But whatever may be the origin of the word 'Îysh (376), its usage is very plain, and is illustrated by the fact that the LXX renders it by ἀνήρ (435) in about 1083 passages, and by ἄνθρωπος (444) only 450 times. 'Îysh (376) is rightly translated *a man* as contrasted with *a woman; a husband*[7] as contrasted with *a wife; a master* as contrasted with *a servant; a great and mighty man* as contrasted with *a poor and lowly one.*

'Îysh (376) is often used with qualifying nouns, as in Exod. 4:10, "a man of words." It sometimes implies greatness or eminence, and is thrown into contrast with 'Âdâm (120). Thus, in Ps. 49:2, the words "low and high" are literally "children of 'Âdâm [120] and children of 'Îysh [376]"; Ps. 62:9, "men of low degree [children of 'Âdâm, 120] are vanity, and men of high degree [children of 'Îysh, 376] are a lie"; so also in Isa. 2:9; 5:15; 31:8.

The word is often used in the sense of *each* or *every one*, e.g., Joel 2:7: "They shall march every one on his ways." It is used in the Hebrew idiom "a man to his brother," which signifies "one to another," as it is rendered in Exod. 25:20; Ezek. 1:11, etc., where reference is made to the wings of the living creature touching each other. The feminine form 'Ishshâh (802), is used in exactly the same way. Thus we read in Exod. 26:3, "The five curtains shall be coupled together, one to another"; literally, "a *woman* to her *sister.*" Probably

---

by rendering them *Vir* and *Virago*. In Latin *Vir* signifies *a man, a male person*. The fact that the word *Virility* is derived from *Vir* helps us understand the word's frequent use to emphasize a man's maturity, physical strength, character, or courage. *Virago* means *a man-like woman, a female warrior, a heroine.*

7. The word itself appears in Hos. 2:16, "Thou shalt call me 'Îyshîy" (376 plus first person singular possessive ending), that is, *My Husband.*

the much disputed passage, Lev. 18:18, which is so frequently discussed in relation to the marriage with a deceased wife's sister, ought to be rendered in accordance with this idiomatic form of expression.

The word is constantly used in such compound expressions as "man of Israel," "man of God," "man of understanding," and "man of sorrows."

Where we read in Exod. 15:3 that "the LORD is a man of war," the word 'Îysh (376) is used. The passage does not mean that He is a human being—*this* would have involved the use of the word 'Âdâm (120). Again, when the sacred writer tells us in Josh. 5:13 that "a man stood over against" Joshua, he does not use the word 'Âdâm (120), but 'Îysh (376), which both here and elsewhere can be rendered *Person* or *Being*. Compare also Dan. 9:21; 10:5; 12:6, 7; Zech. 1:8, etc., where the word is applied to beings (angelic or Divine), who presented themselves in vision to the eye of the prophet without being partakers of human nature.

There is a diminutive formed from the word 'Îysh (376), namely, 'Îyshôwn (אִישׁוֹן, 380), which signifies the *apple* or *pupil of the eye*, literally the "little man" that anyone may see reflected in another person's eye.[8] It occurs also in Deut. 32:10, and in Prov. 7:2.[9] In Lam. 2:18, the figure is slightly different, the expression being literally "the daughter of the eye"; and in Ps. 17:8, the two are combined, so that the literal rendering would be "keep me as the little man, the daughter of the eye." In Zech. 2:8, a different word is used for the pupil, representing the hole or gate of the eye rather than that which is reflected on it.

A verb has been derived from the word 'Îysh (376), and is used in the expression "shew yourselves men" (Isa. 46:8), answering well to the Greek ἀνδρίζεσθε (imperative plural of ἀνδρίζομαι, 407). Compare the English phrase "to be unmanned."

§3. *The Word* 'Ĕnôwsh

The third word for man is 'Ĕnôwsh (אֱנוֹשׁ, 582), which occurs very frequently in the O.T., and is generally considered to point to man's

---

8. This figure has found its way into other languages. See *Gesenius' Hebrew-Chaldee Lexicon to the Old Testament: a Dictionary Numerically Coded to Strong's Exhaustive Concordance* on this word.

9. In verse 9 of the same chapter it is rendered *black* (the idea being borrowed from the darkness of the pupil) and applied to night.

insignificance or *inferiority*.[10] This word, like 'Îysh (376), depends in some measure on its surroundings for its meaning, and often answers to our English word *person*, by which it has been rendered in the A.V. in Judg. 9:4 and Zeph. 3:4. Its plural form generally does duty for the plural of 'Îysh (376) as well. See, e.g., Gen. 18:2, 16, 22, where the "men" were angelic beings.

In poetry 'Ĕnôwsh (582) occurs as a parallel to 'Âdâm (120). Thus, "I will make a man ['Ĕnôwsh, 582] more precious than fine gold; even a man ['Âdâm, 120] than the golden wedge of Ophir" (Isa. 13:12). It is occasionally introduced as a parallel with Bên-'Âdâm (1121-120), the *son of man;* thus, "How much less man ['Ĕnôwsh, 582] that is a worm, and the son of man [Bên-'Âdâm, 1121-120] which is a worm" (Job 25:6); "What is man ['Ĕnôwsh, 582], that thou art mindful of him? and the son of man [Bên-'Âdâm, 1121-120], that thou visitest him?" (Ps. 8:4); "What is man ['Ĕnôwsh, 582], that thou takest knowledge of him? or the son of man [Bên-'Âdâm, 1121–120], that thou makest account of him?" (Ps. 144:3); "Thou turnest man ['Ĕnôwsh, 582] to destruction; and sayest, Return, ye children of men" (Bᵉnêy-'Âdâm, 1121 plural-120; Ps. 90:3). In these passages it will be noted that the *insignificance* of man is especially in the writer's mind. In Job 4:17, our translators have rendered it *mortal man:* "Shall mortal man ['Ĕnôwsh, 582] be more just than God? Shall a man [Geber, 1397][11] be more pure than his maker?" Here the word Geber (1397) must be used with a tinge of irony, as in Job 10:5: "Are thy days as the days of man ['Ĕnôwsh, 582]? are thy years as man's [Geber, 1397] days?"

There are other passages where the insignificance of man is specially brought out by the use of 'Ĕnôwsh (582), e.g., Job 7:17: "What is man, that thou shouldest magnify him? and that thou shouldest set thine heart upon him?" Witness also Job 9:2: "How should man be just before God?" See also Job 15:14; 25:4; Ps. 9:20; 103:15; Dan. 2:43.

'Ĕnôwsh (582) is sometimes used where man is brought into direct contrast with his Maker. Thus we read in Job 10:4, "Hast thou [O God] eyes of flesh? or seest thou as man seeth?" Job 33:12 says, "I will answer thee, that God is greater than man"; Isa. 7:13, "Is it a small thing for you to weary men, but will ye weary my God also?" See also Isa. 29:13 and 51:7, 12.

10. The Assyrian *niou* for *eniou* is taken by Dr. Sayce as answering to 'Ĕnôwsh (582).

11. See below, §4.

In Ezek. 24:17, the prophet is forbidden to mourn or to eat "the bread of men." Here the rabbinical commentators incline to take the word *men* as signifying *other* men, according to an ordinary Hebrew idiom, and they refer to the custom of the food of the mourner being supplied by a neighbor. Others read it "the bread of husbands," i.e., of widowed husbands, and the usage of the word in Ruth 1:11, and perhaps in Jer. 29:6 (in each of which passages 'Ĕnôwsh [582] occurs) gives some slight ground for this view. Others, again, consider the word here to signify *mortal men*.

The A.V. rendering of the word in I Sam. 2:33, "in the flower of their age," is hardly justified by other passages, and might well be replaced by a more literal translation without departing from English idiom; it has the sanction, however, of the Vulgate and of Luther (see R.V.).

When we come to inquire into the etymology and original meaning of the word, we find it connected with the Hebrew root 'Ânash (605). This word occurs (usually in the form 'Ânûwsh, passive participle of 605) in the following passages only: II Sam. 12:15, David's child was "very sick"; Job 34:6, "My wound is incurable"; Ps. 69:20, "I am full of heaviness"; Isa. 17:11, "desperate sorrow"; Jer. 15:18, "Why is my pain perpetual, and my wound incurable, which refuseth to be healed?"; Jer. 17:9, the heart is "desperately wicked"; Jer. 17:16, "Neither have I desired the woeful day" (LXX, "the day of man"); Jer. 30:12, "Thy bruise is incurable and thy wound is grievous"; Jer. 30:15, "Thy sorrow is incurable for the multitude of thine iniquity"; Micah 1:9, "Her wound is incurable."

These passages fix the meaning of the word. But it may be asked why a word that signifies *incurable* should be used to denote *man*. Perhaps the answer may be found in Gen. 4:26. Seth had been "appointed" in the place of Abel, but man remained unchanged and unredeemed; so Seth's son was called 'Ĕnôwsh (582). "Then began men to call upon the name of Jehovah." The race was "incurable," but the Lord was its hope. Thus, Seth's son may have been named 'Ĕnôwsh (582), that is to say "incurable," because he was utterly unable to redeem himself from the bondage of corruption. This view of the matter is taken by Cocceius, who says that, "as 'Âdâm [120] was the name given to all who sprang from the dust of earth, so 'Ĕnôwsh [582] became the title of all those who are heirs of corruption."

The Messiah was never designated by the name 'Ĕnôwsh (582),

because, though appointed to become a descendant of Adam, and destined to be made "in the likeness of sinful flesh," yet in Him there was to be no sin. But it is a remarkable thing that when the glorious coming of the Messiah to rule the nations is unfolded in Dan. 7:13, the Lord is described as "one like a son of 'Ĕnôwsh [582]." Compare the description in Rev. 5:6, "A Lamb as it had been slain," which indicates that the marks of His humiliation will accompany His glory.

§4. *The Word* Geber

The last name for man that has to be noticed is Geber (גֶּבֶר, 1397), which is used more than sixty times in the O.T., and represents man as *a mighty being*. This title is at first sight inconsistent with the name 'Ĕnôwsh (582); but no one can weigh well the facts that human nature daily presents to his observation without coming to the conclusion that man is a marvelous compound of strength and weakness, and that while he is rightly called 'Ĕnôwsh (582) by reason of the corruption of his nature, he may also lay claim to the title of Geber (1397) by virtue of the mighty energies that are capable of being exhibited in his life and character.

The Greek translators have rendered Geber (1397) by ἀνήρ (435) in the majority of places where it occurs, but in fourteen passages they have been content with the more general word ἄνθρωπος (444). In the English Bible it is usually rendered *man*, but in some places the original sense of the word has been adhered to, and it has been translated *mighty*.

The earliest passages where the word is found, with the exception of Gen. 6:4, are the following: Exod. 10:11, "Go now ye that are *men*"; and Exod. 12:37, "About six hundred thousand on foot that were *men*, beside women and children." Balaam uses this word when he designates himself "the *man* whose eyes are open" (Num. 24:3, 15). It is used of the male sex as opposed to the female in Deut. 22:5, and is rendered "man by man" where individuals are distinguished from tribes in Josh. 7:14 and I Chron. 23:3. It is twice applied to David with a significant reference to its real meaning, namely, in I Sam. 16:18, "A mighty valiant man" (lit. "a mighty man of strength"), and II Sam. 23:1, "The man who was raised up on high." See also I Chron. 12:8; 28:1; II Chron. 13:3; Ezra 4:21; 5:4, 10; 6:8.

The above-named passages plainly show the original meaning

and the general usage of Geber (1397), but in the poetical books, in which this word occurs with greater frequency, there is not always the same marked clearness of signification. In the Book of Job there appears to be a slight irony in its use: "Shall a man [mighty though he be in his own estimation] be more pure than his maker?" (4:17); "[mighty] man dieth and wasteth away" (14:10); "If a [mighty] man die, shall he live again?" (14:14); "Can a [mighty] man be profitable unto God?" (22:2); "that he may hide pride from [mighty] man" (33:17). See also Job 33:29; 38:3; 40:7.

The word is used in Ps. 34:8, "Blessed is the man that trusteth in him," where it points to the fact that however great a man may be, yet he is not to trust in his own strength but in the living God. The same explanation may be given of its use in Ps. 37:23, "The steps of a man [A.V. "of a good man"] are ordered [or established] by the LORD." Compare Ps. 40:4; 52:7; 94:12; and 128:4. In Ps. 88:4 we read, "I am as a [mighty] man that hath no strength"; the contrast here indicated between the name and the condition is very striking. The Psalmist says again (89:48), "What man is he that liveth and shall not see death?" The point of this question comes out far more clearly when the use of the word Geber (1397) is noticed, and the sentiment might be thus expressed, "Is there any living man so mighty as to be able to avoid death?"

Neither Isaiah nor Ezekiel uses the word Geber (1397) at all, but we meet with it eight times in the prophecy of Jeremiah, and four times in the Book of Lamentations. The following are the most interesting examples: Jer. 17:5, 7, "Cursed is the [mighty] man [Geber, 1397] that trusteth in man [Âdâm, 120, the earthy]. . . . Blessed is the [mighty] man that trusteth in the LORD." Jer. 23:9 says, "I am like a [mighty] man whom wine hath overcome." With what force is the power of strong drink here delineated! Geber (1397) is also found in Jer. 31:22, where the LORD says to the "Virgin of Israel" that He was about to create a new thing: "A woman shall compass a man."[12]

Several words are related to Geber (1397). There is the verb Gâbar (1396), which is found in twenty-three places, and is usually rendered *prevail*; in Ps. 103:11 and 117:2 it is used of the moral efficacy and prevailing power of God's mercy. Gᵉbîyr (1376) is used for "lord" in Isaac's blessing (Gen. 27:29, 37). Gᵉbîyrâh (1397) is sometimes used for a Queen; Gᵉbereth (1404) for a mistress (rendered *lady* in Isa.

12. Literally, "a female shall compass [or enclose] a Mighty One."

47:5, 7). G^ebûwrâh (1369) is rendered *force, mastery, might, power, strength.* Gibbôwr (1368) signifies *mighty,* and is frequently used both of God and man; it is found three times in the expression "the mighty God," namely, in Isa. 9:6; 10:21; and Jer. 32:18—passages that are deeply interesting in relation to the Deity of the Messiah.

The LXX has sometimes rendered Gibbôwr (1368) by γίγας (L-S 348B), *giant,* as in Gen. 6:4; 10:8, 9; I Chron. 1:10; Isa. 3:2; 13:3; Ezek. 32:21. The general Hebrew name for a *giant* is not Gibbôwr (1368), which refers to might rather than stature, but R^ephâ'îym (7497, plural), *Rephaites* or *sons of Raphah.* The word used in Gen. 6:4, and also in Num. 13:33, is N^ephilîym, which is derived from the Hiphil or causative form of Nâphal (5307), *to fall,* and hence signifies *tyrants,* or those who make use of their power to cast down others. In the former of these passages the Vulgate has *giants,* and Luther *tyrants;* in the latter the Vulgate has *monsters,* and Luther *giants (Riesen).*

The word M^ethîym (מְתִים, 4962, plural of מַת) is translated *men* in a few passages, chiefly in Job, Psalms, and Isaiah, also in Deut. 2:34. It perhaps means "mortal," but this is doubtful.

4

The Soul and the Spirit

When the writer of the Epistle to the Hebrews says that the word of God pierces "to the dividing asunder of soul and spirit" (Heb. 4:12), and when the Apostle Paul prays that the "spirit, soul, and body" of his converts may be preserved blameless (I Thess. 5:23), a psychological division of the immaterial part of human nature is drawn that is exactly similar to what we find running through the whole O.T. The Bible proceeds on the supposition that there are two spheres of existence that may be called *mind* and *matter*. It tells us that the key to the mystery of the universe is to be found—not in the material substance of which it is composed, nor in the agencies or influences that cause the phenomena of nature to follow one another in regular sequence, but—in a Mastermind, who plans all things by His wisdom and sustains them by His power. The Scriptures bring the immaterial world very close to every one of us; and while we are all only too conscious of our relation to things fleeting and physical, the Sacred Record reminds us on every page that we are the offspring of the absolute and unchanging Source of all existence. A man is sometimes tempted to say, "I will believe only what I see"; but the first puff of wind or the first shock of electricity tells him that he must enlarge his creed. If he still stops short by asserting his faith only in the forces that affect matter, he will find himself confronted by the fact that the matter that composes the human frame becomes by that very circumstance subject to forces and influences to which all other matter is a stranger. He finds a world within as well as a world without, and he is compelled to acknowledge that his physical frame is the tenement of a superphysical being that he calls *self*. Further, he finds that the self is on the one

70

hand a recipient of knowledge and feeling obtained through the instrumentality of the body, and on the other hand an agent originating or generating a force that has an effect on the outer world.

It is in respect to this inner life and its workings that man is the child of God. His structure is of soil—earthborn—allied with all physical existence, and subjected to the laws of light, heat, electricity, gravitation, and such like as much as if it were so many atoms of vegetable or mineral matter. But the immaterial existence that permeates that structure, investing it with consciousness, flooding it with sensibilities, illuminating it with understanding, enabling it to plan, to forecast, to will, to rule, to make laws, to sympathize, to love—this *ego*, this pulse of existence, this nucleus of feeling and thought and action, is a denizen of an immaterial sphere of being, though ordained by God its Father to live and grow and be developed within the tabernacle of flesh.

§1. *The Soul*

The Hebrew equivalent for the word *soul* in almost every passage in the O.T. is **Nephesh** (נֶפֶשׁ, 5315), which answers to ψυχή (*5590*) in the Greek. The cognate verb **Nâphash** (5314), *to refresh*, is found in Exod. 23:12; 31:17; and II Sam. 16:14.[1] The word **Nephesh** (5315) has various shades of meaning and of rendering, which must be gathered as far as possible under one or two heads. The soul is, properly speaking, the animating principle of the body, and is the common property of man and beast. Thus, in Lev. 24:18, we read, "He that killeth a beast shall make it good; beast for beast." This is literally, "He that smiteth the soul of a beast shall recompense it; soul for soul." It is also used with respect to the lower animals in Gen. 1:21, 24; 2:19; Lev. 11:46; et al., in which passages it has been rendered *creature*.

In some passages **Nephesh** (5315) has been rendered *anyone;* the word is thus used in an indefinite sense, the soul representing the person, as when we speak of a city containing so many thousand *souls*. Thus, we read in Lev. 2:1, "When any (lit. a *soul*) will offer a meat offering"; in Lev. 24:17, "He that killeth any man," lit. "that smiteth any soul of man"—the soul representing the life; in Num.

---

1. In Assyrian, *napistu*, which means *life*, is connected with *napâsu, to expand*, and hence *to breathe* (Sayce).

19:11, "He that toucheth the dead body of any man shall be unclean seven days," lit. "he that toucheth the dead [part] of any soul of a man shall be unclean seven days." See also Num. 19:13; 31:19; 35:11, 15, 30. In these passages a dead body is regarded as that which ought properly to be animated by the soul. But owing to the law whereby man has to return to the dust, the spectacle is seen of a soulless body that must be regarded as ceremonially unclean. Compare Lev. 21:11; Num. 5:2; 6:6, 11; 9:6, 7, 10.

In Ps. 17:9, "deadly enemies" are literally "enemies of my soul [or life]." In Job 11:20, "the giving up of the ghost" is "the puffing forth of the soul." So also in Jer. 15:9 the literal rendering is "she hath puffed forth the soul."

The soul is thus the source of animation to the body; in other words, it is the life, whether of man or beast. Accordingly, **Nephesh** (5315) is rendered *life* in Gen. 19:17, 19, where we read of Lot's life being saved; in Gen. 32:30, "I have seen God face to face, and my life is preserved"; in Gen. 44:30, "His life is bound up in the lad's life"; in Exod. 21:23, "Thou shalt give life for life"; in verse 30, "He shall give for the ransom of his life whatsoever is laid upon him."

In Deut. 24:7 we read, "If a man be found stealing any [lit. *a soul*] of his brethren," etc.; so also in Ezek. 27:13, "They traded the persons [lit. *the souls*] of men." By the use of the word **Nephesh** (5315) here the wickedness of treating men as goods and chattels to be bought and sold is practically reprobated. This doubtless is the crime referred to in Rev. 18:13. Perhaps the word *person* in the sense in which we speak of an offense against a man's person, or of a personal injury, is the best rendering in such passages. It is adopted in Gen. 14:21; Lev. 27:2 (where both men and beasts are referred to); Num. 5:6; 19:18; and Ezek. 16:5. A similar rendering is *self*, which is found in Lev. 11:43; I Kings 19:4; and Isa. 5:14.

In some passages the word *soul* is added to give emphasis, as in Gen. 27:31: "that thy soul may bless me." Compare Matt. 26:38.

In Hebrew, as in most other languages, the shedding of a man's blood was a phrase used to represent the taking of his life, for "the blood is the life." In this oft-repeated phrase (e.g., Lev. 17:11, 14) we see that the blood is (i.e., represents) "the soul"; and if the one flows out from the body, the other passes away, too. In Prov. 28:17, we read literally, "The man that doeth violence to the blood of a soul shall flee into the pit"; so in Ezek. 33:6, "If the sword come and take away a soul [A.V. *person*] from among them . . . his blood will I require at the watchman's hands"; so also in Jonah 1:14, "Let us not perish for this man's life, and lay not upon us innocent blood."

This mystical identification of the blood and the life is of great interest as bearing on the atoning work of Christ. We are told that He poured out His soul unto death, and that He shed His blood for the remission of sins. Evidently the shedding of the blood was the outward and visible sign of the severance of the soul from the body in death; and this severance is regarded as a voluntary sacrifice offered by the Divine Son, in accordance with His Father's will, as the means of putting away sin.

But the Nephesh (5315) or *soul* is something more than the bare animating principle of the body. If it is regarded in this light, a large view must be taken of that mysterious organism we call the body, and it must include the bodily appetites and desires. Nephesh (5315) is rendered *appetite* in Prov. 23:2, and Eccles. 6:7. Compare the words of Israel, "our soul loatheth this light food" (Num. 21:5). Other passages in which a similar idea is presented are Eccles. 6:9, et al. (desire); Isa. 56:11 (greedy); Exod. 15:9, et al. (lust); Ps. 105:22, et al. (pleasure); Deut. 21:14, et al. (will).

Nephesh (5315) is also rendered *mind* and *heart* in several places where these words are used in the sense of desire and inclination, e.g., Gen. 23:8; II Kings 9:15.

Thus the soul, according to the O.T., is the personal center of desire, inclination, and appetite, and its normal condition is to be operating in or through means of a physical organism, whether human or otherwise. Hence, when we read that man or Adam became a living soul (Gen. 2:7), we are to understand that the structure that had been molded from the dust became the habitation and, to a certain extent, the servant of an *ego* or conscious center of desire or appetite. When the soul departs (Gen. 35:18) the body becomes untenanted, and the *ego* that has grown with the growth of the body is dislodged from its habitation. It may, however, return again to its old home through the operation of God, as was the case with the widow's child (I Kings 17:21; cf. Ps. 16:10).

The fact that the desires to which the soul gives birth are often counter to the will of God fixes *sin* on the soul; accordingly, we read, "the soul that sinneth it shall die" (Ezek. 18:4). Hence the need of atonement for the soul (Lev. 17:11), and of its conversion or restoration to a life of conformity to God's law (Ps. 19:7; 34:22).

In the N.T. ψυχή (5590) often signifies *life*, as in Matt. 2:20, "Those who seek the life of the young child"; in Matt. 6:25, "Be not solicitous for your life" (i.e., life in the body). In Matt. 10:28, a distinction is drawn between the destruction of the body, which man can effect, and the perdition or ruin of the soul as well as the body in Gehenna, which only God can bring about. Sometimes there seems to be a play on the word, as when the Savior says, "he that loseth his life [in the ordinary sense of the word] shall find it [in a new and higher sense]" (Matt. 10:39; 16:25). When describing His mission, our Lord plainly said that He came to give His soul or life a ransom for many (Matt. 20:28). In Acts 2:27, the Apostle Peter quotes Ps. 16:10: "Thou wilt not leave my soul in Hades." This passage certainly *might* be taken to signify, "thou wilt not leave my dead body in the grave"; but it is far more in accordance with the usage of the two important words *soul* and *Hades* to understand that the animating principle, the *ego*, of our Savior was not to remain in the nether world.

§2. *The Spirit*

Very different is the idea that Scripture gives of the *spirit* from that which is to be understood by the word *soul*. With the exception of Job 26:4, and Prov. 20:27, where N^eshâmâh (נְשָׁמָה, 5397), *a breathing being*, is used, the word *spirit* always represents the Hebrew Rûwach (רוּחַ, 7307).[2] Compare the Assyrian *Rukhu*.

The word Rûwach (7307), like its Greek equivalents, $\pi\nu\epsilon\hat{\upsilon}\mu\alpha$ (4151) and $\H{\alpha}\nu\epsilon\mu o\varsigma$ (417), the Latin *spiritus*, and the English *ghost*, and similar words in other languages, originally signified *wind* or *breath*. It is the only word rendered *wind* in the O.T. It is rendered *whirlwind* in Ezek. 1:4, *tempest* in Ps. 11:6, *cool* (wind) in Gen. 3:8, *air* in Job 41:16, *blast* in Exod. 15:8 (as well as II Kings 19:7; Isa. 25:4; and 37:7). Thus, as *blood* represents the animal life, so does *wind* the spiritual element in life.

Rûwach (7307) is frequently rendered *breath*, as, e.g., in Gen. 6:17: "the *breath* of life." As long as this breath is sustained in a man, he lives (Job 27:3); when it goes forth, he returns to his earth (Ps. 146:4). The most remarkable passage in which the action of breath and wind is identified with the source of life is the vision of the dry

2. There are two verbs cognate with this word: one (רָוָה, 7304) signifies *to be refreshed* (I Sam. 16:23; Job 32:20; see also Jer. 22:14, where *large* signifies *airy* or *ventilated*); the other (רוּחַ, 7306) signifies *to smell*, hence *to be keen* or "of quick understanding" (Isa. 11:3).

bones in Ezek. 37. In this, as in some other passages, it is not easy to distinguish between the physical and the superphysical breath, both of which are gifts from God.

In Josh. 2:11, where we read that "there remained no more *courage* in any man," the word might be rendered *breath.* In Judg. 8:3, deep breathing is a sign of *anger,* and accordingly the word is so rendered. In I Sam. 1:15, it is a sign of earnest prayer, or perhaps of the agitation of the heart. In Gen. 26:35, it is a sign of grief; it is there rendered *mind* instead of *spirit,* unfortunately, as has also been the case in Prov. 29:11; Ezek. 11:5; 20:32; and Hab. 1:11.

It is clear that the wind is regarded in Scripture as a fitting emblem of the mighty penetrating power of the Invisible God. Moreover, the breath is supposed to symbolize not only the deep feelings that are generated within man, such as sorrow and anger, but also kindred feelings in the Divine nature. God is not set forth in Scripture as a *soul*[3]—i.e., the center of physical appetite and the animating principle of a body—but as a *spirit,* that is, an unseen living being capable of deep emotions. Moreover, it is revealed that God and God alone has the faculty of communicating His Spirit or life to His creatures, who are thus enabled to feel, think, speak, and act in accordance with the Divine will.

§3. *The Spirit of God*

References in the O.T. to the Spirit of God and to the Spirit of the Lord are more numerous than is sometimes imagined. In upwards of twenty-five places this Divine Spirit is spoken of as entering man for the purpose of giving him life, power, wisdom, or right feeling. God, moreover, is called "the God of the spirits of all flesh" in the O.T., as He is called the "Father of our spirits" in the N.T.; and it is everywhere taught or implied that the personal agency of God is in contact with the center of life in every child of man. How He acts we know not; in what mode He enlightens, inspires, comforts, and warns we cannot tell. We see and feel the results, but we are unable to comprehend the processes.

---

3. It is true that the Hebrew word Nephesh (5315) is used in certain idiomatic expressions with reference to the Divine Being, but not in such a way as to invalidate what is affirmed above.

§4. *Meanings of the Word Spirit in N.T.*

A full examination of the usage of the word $\pi\nu\epsilon\hat{\upsilon}\mu\alpha$ (spirit, *4151*) in the N.T. would be a work of great interest, but of no little difficulty. The passages in which it occurs may be generally classified as follows:

First, there are various references to the spirit of man, that part of human nature that is breathed into him by God.

Second, mention is often made of evil spirits, which are spoken of as personal beings capable of allying themselves with men and inflicting various evils on them.

Third, there are references to the work of the Holy Spirit of God in John the Baptist and others *before* the day of Pentecost.

Fourth, some passages are found that speak of the Spirit of God dwelling and working in our Savior during His earthly ministry.

Fifth, there are a number of passages that imply a special agency of the Holy Spirit, which has come into operation in consequence of the mediatorial work of the ascended Lord.

Last, there are texts that speak of the effects produced in man by the Spirit of God, and that combine under the same designation both the Worker and the effect produced.

The first and third of these classes naturally associate themselves with similar passages in the O.T. The second is deeply mysterious and interesting, but does not call here for special discussion. There remain three others on which a few remarks may be offered.

The Lord Jesus, *as man*, possessed spirit, soul, and body; and His spirit was in a special sense the dwellingplace of the Holy Spirit. He was filled with the Spirit, who was given to Him without measure.[4] He was guided in His movements by the Spirit; His wisdom and

---

4. It is almost dangerous, and yet it may be helpful to some minds, to take an illustration of this difficult subject from nature. As it is true that no man has seen God at any time, so it may be said that no one has seen electricity. But as a man may be charged with electricity without losing his personal identity, and may thus become not only an embodiment of that unseen agency but also capable of communicating it to others by contact, so the Son of Man contained the fullness of the Spirit. This indwelling agency had complete possession of His human nature, so that in Him the manhood was taken into the Godhead. By the touch of faith we draw the virtue or force of the Spirit from Him into ourselves; we thus become partakers with Him of the Spirit of God. The relationship between the three Persons of the Godhead is utterly beyond human conception. The Father is represented in Scripture as the Source of life, will, and affection; the Son is the obedient Agent of the Father's will working on the creature *ab extra* [from without]; the Spirit works on the creature *ab intra* [from within].

discernment, His power over evil demons, and perhaps we may say all His words and deeds, were wrought through the agency of the Spirit. See Matt. 1:18; 4:1; 12:18, 28; Luke 4:1, 14, 18; John 3:34.

A special point in the teaching of John the Baptist was that Jesus, the Lamb of God, should baptize with the Holy Ghost; and our Lord, in His conversations with Nicodemus, the Samaritan woman, and others, teaches that those who believed in Him would become partakers of a new life, which would be in a peculiar sense the work of the Holy Ghost. In the course of these conversations He put forth this truth in various forms. There was the heavenly birth, the living water, the bread of life, the resurrection life, the sap of the vine, each in turn taken as the central point in a discourse, leading up to the truth that (after His glorification) those who believe in Him should receive the Holy Ghost. Our Lord's last conversations with His disciples before His crucifixion were full of this subject; and when He rose from the dead He indicated by the symbolical act of breathing on His disciples the truth that through His mediatorial agency they were to receive the promised blessing of the Spirit. When the Day of Pentecost was fully come, this Divine gift was showered down. A life of praise, of sonship, of love, of boldness, and of missionary labor was inaugurated. The disciples were organized through this new influence into a Church, which breathed the spirit of Christ and did the work of Christ on earth. For a time the Christian life and preaching were accompanied by special miracles, as our Lord's own life had been. These were intended to give an authoritative seal to the mission of the original disciples, just as similar works had testified a few years earlier to the mission of the Son of God.

If it be asked in what way the work of the Holy Spirit of God differs now from what it was in earlier ages of the world's history, it may be sufficient for the present purpose to answer that, though the Agent is the same, the Truth whereby He operates on the feelings and affections of man is much more developed now than in old days. Formerly, the way of redemption from sin and corruption was only dimly shadowed forth. Now, the substance has been wrought out: Christ has been lifted up, and all men are being drawn to Him. And those who believe in Him enter thereby into a special relationship with Him so that they live in Him and He in them, both being partakers of one Spirit. Formerly, the Spirit operated through the written word, through types and shadows, through laws and ordinances, reproving men of sin, and kindling their hopes of a better time; but now He operates especially through the Living Word, of whom all the Scripture testifies, and Who is the Way, the Truth, and the Life. He manifests Christ in His completed work to the heart of man, and quickens the believer into newness of life by breathing into him that eternal life that is in the Father, and in His Son Jesus Christ. Metaphysically, we cannot understand the nature of this agency, but theologically, and as a matter of revelation, we believe and thankfully receive it.

The last class of passages to which reference has to be made consists of those that seem to identify the Spirit of God with the results that He is producing in the heart and life of man. Thus we read of the spirit of sonship or adoption (Rom. 8:15); the spirit of meekness (I Cor. 4:21); the spirit of faith (II Cor. 4:13); the spirit of wisdom and revelation (Eph. 1:17); the spirit of truth (I John 4:6); and the spirit of holiness (Rom. 1:4). It is evident that these passages refer, not to the inherent characteristics of the Holy Spirit, but to those effects that He produces in the believer. They answer to a similar class of passages in the O.T. See, for example, Isa. 11:2.

5

Heart, Will,
Conscience, Understanding

The present chapter has for its subject a discussion of those elements in human nature that are the sources or centers of emotion, volition, deliberation, and spiritual apprehension. It is comparatively easy for the physiologist or anatomist to mark out the different organs of the human body, and to learn their structure and manifold uses. But the psychologist has a harder task to perform. He has to analyze and classify his own sensations and emotions, to determine so far as possible which are from the body and which from an immaterial source. He must attempt to compare his own mental constitution with the effects produced on and by the minds of others; he seeks to note how different classes of external entities appeal to and call forth distinct feelings, moving in various spheres of existence and touching finer or ruder chords of human sensibility, according to their nature and the aspect in which they are presented. The mental analyst is in danger of running to one of two extremes, and more especially so when applying his study to Scripture. He is sometimes inclined to construe the popular words that represent the inner life in a very loose and vague sense, using the one for the other as people do in their ordinary conversation—as though there were but one faculty of emotion and volition in man, receiving different names according to the different relationships it has to sustain. At other times he is tempted to exercise his powers of mental anatomy in arranging and classifying the different powers of the immaterial existence in several groups, assigning each to a separate faculty. Thus he makes the heart, the will, the conscience, and the understanding to be distinct members of a spiritual organism. Each of these approaches represents an aspect of truth, but each is imperfect if taken by itself. We are not in a position to grasp the subject of immaterial existence, and can only approach it relatively and in those aspects in which it exists in connection with bodily life.[1] As human beings we are, as it were, organized grains of dust floating on an ocean of spiritual existence that permeates our being, connects us with one another, and binds us to that higher sphere of life in which God dwells. In the spirit-world we live and breathe and know and feel and think and determine. But we understand little of its nature. And certainly we are not in a position to decide whether there is only one hidden agency at work in our bodies, taking many forms through the medium of the brain and nerves, or whether the nucleus of our conscious life is to be considered as composite in its original nature. In other words, we might ask whether human nature is like an Aeolian harp (which has many strings, and produces wild and plaintive music through the blind force of the wind) or whether it is like an organ, not only complex in itself but also played upon by a complex being, who gives expression to his own thought and feeling as he touches its keys.

The Bible does not discuss this subject. It makes use, however, of certain terms that require careful consideration, since they have stamped themselves on our popular and religious language and are sometimes used without consideration of the ideas they were originally intended to convey.

§1. *The Heart*

The general Hebrew word for the heart is Lêb (לֵב, 3820), answering to the Assyrian *libbu*. It is usually rendered καρδία (2588) in the LXX, but sometimes Greek words signifying the soul, the intellect, or the understanding are taken to represent it.

Two or three other words are occasionally translated *heart* in the A.V., e.g., **Nephesh** (5315), *the soul* (Exod. 23:9, et al.); **Me'îym** (מֵעִים, 4578), the *bowels* (Ps. 40:8); **Qîyr** (קִיר, 7023), the *wall* of the heart (Jer. 4:19); and **Qereb** (קֶרֶב, 7130), the *inner* or *middle part* (Jer. 9:8). Our

---

1. Physiology and psychology are now seen to be closely related, and the brain (which is never referred to in the Bible) is regarded as the medium as well as the seat of mental faculties.

translators might have adopted a similar rendering in John 7:38, which would then run thus: "out of his *heart* shall flow rivers of living water" (the heart representing the innermost part of the body). The R.V. has made no correction.

The heart (Lêb, 3820), according to Scripture, includes not only the motives, feelings, affections, and desires, but also the will, the aims, the principles, the thoughts, and the intellect of man. In fact, it embraces the whole inner man, the head never being regarded as the seat of intelligence. Hence we read of men being "wise hearted" (Exod. 31:6; 36:2); of wisdom being put into the heart (II Chron. 9:23); of the heart being awake (Eccles. 2:23; Song of Sol. 5:2); of the thoughts of the heart (Deut. 15:9); of words being laid up in the heart (I Sam. 21:12); and of mercy being written on the tablets of the heart (Prov. 3:3). In II Kings 5:26, Elisha says to Gehazi, "Went not my *heart* with thee [or after thee]?" Here a combination of knowledge and feeling is implied. There is also a beautiful expression in the Hebrew, "to speak to the heart," which we render "to speak comfortably or friendly" (Ruth 2:13; II Sam. 19:7; II Chron. 30:22; Isa. 40:2 ["Speak ye comfortably to Jerusalem"]; Hos. 2:14 ["will bring her into the wilderness and speak comfortably to her"]).

While it is the source of all action and the center of all thought and feeling, the heart is also described as receptive to influences both from the outer world and from God Himself. The wisdom of Solomon was "put in his heart" by God (II Chron. 9:23). When Saul turned from Samuel, "God gave him another heart" or "turned his heart into a new direction" (I Sam. 10:9). The LORD gave to Solomon "a wise and an understanding heart" (I Kings 3:12). He says concerning His people, "I will give them one heart, and one way, that they may fear me for ever. . . . I will put my fear in their hearts, that they shall not depart from me" (Jer. 32:39, 40). "I will give them one heart, and I will put a new spirit within you; and I will take the stony heart out of their flesh, and will give them an heart of flesh" (Ezek. 11:19; 36:26). Compare Ps. 51:10: "Create in me a clean heart, O God." The word is used in the N.T. in the same way as in the O.T.

§2. *The Hardening of the Heart*

The hardening of the heart is described in Scripture as the work of God. Pharaoh's case is by no means unique. It is a sample of the history of all those who neglect the opportunities that God gives them. Such neglect provokes Him to put in exercise that law to which the whole human race is subject—that moral impressions, if not acted on, become (subjectively) weaker and weaker, until at last the heart of man becomes altogether callous. In the case of Pharaoh three words are used to represent the hardening process. **Châzaq** (חָזַק, 2388), *to brace up* or *strengthen*,[2] points to the hardihood with which Pharaoh set himself to act in defiance against God, and closed all the avenues of his heart to those signs and wonders that were wrought by the hand of Moses. **Kâbêd** (כָּבֵד, 3513), *to be heavy, dull*, or *unimpressible*, denotes his insensibility and grossness of perception. **Qâshâh** (קָשָׁה, 7185), *to be harsh*, marks the restlessness, impatience, petulance, and irritability with which his course was characterized while he was resisting the urgent appeals, not of Moses only, but also of his own people. Each of these words is used under similar circumstances in other parts of the O.T. Thus **Châzaq** (2388) is found in Josh. 11:20: "It was of the LORD to harden their hearts." (Cf. Jer. 5:3; Ezek. 3:9.) It is usually rendered *to be strong, be courageous, hold fast, be valiant, stout, mighty.* **Kâbêd** (3513) is used in I Sam 6:6: "Wherefore then do ye *harden* your hearts, as the Egyptians and Pharaoh hardened their hearts?" It is also found in Ezek. 3:5, 6: "of a *hard* language." It is usually rendered *heavy.* **Qâshâh** (7185) is found in Exod. 18:26; Deut. 1:17; and 2:30, where we read, "The LORD thy God *hardened* his spirit, and made his heart obstinate, that he might deliver him into thy hand." See also Deut. 15:18 and 26:6: "The Egyptians laid upon us a *hard* bondage." Compare II Sam. 3:39; II Kings 2:10; 17:14; Neh. 9:16, 17, 29; Job 9:4; Ps. 60:3; 95:8; Prov. 28:14; 29:1; Isa. 8:21; 14:3; Jer. 19:15; Ezek. 3:7. The usual renderings are *hard, grievous, cruel, stiff.* It is to be noticed that in God's mission to Ezekiel, in the third chapter, the three words now mentioned occur together. Other words of similar meaning are **Qâshach** (קָשַׁח, 7188), which is found in Job 39:16 and Isa. 63:17, and **Teqêph** (תְּקֵף, 8631), which occurs in Dan. 5:20.

§3. *The Will*

The English word *will* is sometimes merely the sign of the future tense, while at other times it expresses the willingness of the agent.

---

2. This word is also used of God's bringing Israel out of Egypt "with a strong right hand." The firmness of the Creator overcame the firmness of the creature.

In the Hebrew, as in the Greek, those ideas are represented by different words, and in many passages it is important to notice the distinction.

'Âbâh (אָבָה, 14—Assyrian *Abitu*) represents the inclination that leads toward action, rather than the volition that immediately precedes it. In the LXX, 'Âbâh (14) is rendered both by βούλομαι (*1014*) and θέλω (*2309*). It is rendered *will* or *willing* in the following passages: Gen. 24:5, 8; Exod. 10:27 ("He *would* not let them go"); Lev. 26:21 ("If ye *will* not hearken unto me"); Deut. 1:26 ("Ye *would* not go up"); Deut. 2:30 (Sihon "*would* not let us pass by him"); 10:10 (the Lord "*would* not destroy thee"); 23:5; 25:7; 29:20; Josh. 24:10; Judg. 11:17; 19:10, 25; 20:13; I Sam. 15:9; 22:17; 26:23; 31:4; II Sam. 2:21; 6:10; 12:17; 13:14, 16, 25; 14:29; 23:16, 17; I Kings 22:49; II Kings 8:19; 13:23; 24:4; I Chron. 10:4; 11:18, 19; 19:19; II Chron. 21:7; Job 39:9; Ps. 81:11; Isa. 1:19 ("If ye *be willing*"); 28:12; 30:9, 15; 42:24; Ezek. 3:7 ("The house of Israel *will* not hearken unto thee, for they *will* not hearken unto me"); 20:8.

It is remarkable that these passages, with two exceptions (Isa. 1:19 and Job 39:9), are *negative*. Where they refer to the disobedience of Israel, they imply that the refusal to hearken to God's Word was voluntary, and that they were responsible for it. Where reference is made to the Divine action, it is implied that God is a moral Governor; His dealings with men are deliberate, and to some extent dependent on their obedience or disobedience.

In Hos. 13:10, 14, we read, "I *will* be thy king. . . . O death, I *will* be thy plagues; O grave, I *will* be thy destruction." The word for *will*, 'Ĕhîy (אֱהִי, 165), might probably be better rendered *where?* as in the margin and in the R.V.; and this rendering would identify the passage all the more closely with Paul's words in I Cor. 15:55.

Châphêts (חָפֵץ, 2654) *to delight*, is usually rendered θέλω (*2309*) or βούλομαι (*1014*) in the LXX. In the A.V., it is rendered *will* in Ruth 3:13 ("If he will not do the part of a kinsman to thee"); I Sam. 2:25; I Kings 13:33; I Chron. 28:9; Job 9:3; Prov. 21:1; 31:13.

This word is used in the phrase "there is a time for every *purpose*" (Eccles. 3:1, 17; 8:6); also in Eccles. 12:10, "The preacher sought to find out *acceptable* words." The Psalmist uses it when he says, "Let them be put to shame that *wish* me evil" (Ps. 40:14).

Châphêts (2654) is rendered *please* or *pleasure* in several passages (including Judg. 13:23; Job 21:21; 22:3; Ps. 5:4; 35:27; 115:3; Isa. 42:21; 53:10; Ezek. 18:23, 32; 33:11; Mal. 1:10).

It is rendered *favor* in II Sam. 20:11; Ps. 35:27; 41:11. In these passages there is no reference to what we call *favoritism,* i.e., the overlooking of the claims of some so as to gratify the wishes of special friends; it is simply recorded that pleasure was found in certain persons, whatever the ground of it might be.

It is often rendered *desire* (e.g., in I Sam. 18:25; Ps. 34:12; 40:6; 51:6, 16; Hos. 6:6). It is also rendered *delight* very frequently, as in I Sam. 15:22: "Hath the LORD as great delight in burnt offerings and sacrifices, as in obeying the voice of the LORD?" We also read in II Sam. 22:20, "He delivered me because he delighted in me." Compare Ps. 1:2; 22:8; 40:8; Isa. 1:11; 62:4 (**Chephtsîy-bâhh,** 2657—"My delight is in her").

On reviewing all the passages where the word **Châphêts** (2654) is used, the reader will probably come to the conclusion that its true meaning is not so much an intense pleasurable emotion as a favorable disposition, or the prompting of the heart to take a certain course of action from a sense of fitness. It is usually relative rather than absolute. It teaches us much about the Divine nature: that God is naturally disposed to look for obedience, trust, and holiness in those who were created after His own likeness; that He deals tenderly but uprightly with His creatures; that He confers life rather than death, if morally possible; that He administers judicial punishment where necessary; and that He has seen fit to inflict suffering on the Messiah. It also marks His unwillingness to be put off with ceremonial observances as a substitute for the devotion of the heart.

Râtsôwn (רָצוֹן, 7522), which properly means *good pleasure* or *acceptance,* is occasionally translated *will* (Gen. 49:6, "In their self-will they digged down a wall"; Lev. 1:3,[3] "of his own voluntary will"; 19:5, "At your own will"; 22:19, 29; Neh. 9:24, "as they would"; Esther 9:5; Ps. 40:8, "I delight to do thy will"; 143:10, "Teach me to do thy will"; Dan. 8:4, "He did according to his will"; 11:3, 16, 36). The word is less abstract than the previous ones. It sets forth a pleasurable emotion, whether leading to action or not. Both the substantive and the verb are used to represent that which is pleasant, delightful, acceptable, or approved of by God.

The LXX usually adopts θέλημα (2307), εὐδοκία (2107), or δεκτός (1184) as a rendering for this word.

---

3. Probably these passages in Leviticus ought to be translated otherwise. See chap. 16, §3.

It is interesting to observe what a number of passages there are in the N.T. in which reference is made to "the will of the Lord." God's good pleasure is everywhere regarded as the law whereby all things, human and Divine, are ordered. Christ is regarded as its embodiment and manifestation; and the Christian, being—by profession at least—one with Christ, is supposed to be conformed to that will in all things.

Θέλημα (2307), answering to **Râtsôwn** (7522), is that which God decides to have done because it is pleasing to Him; βουλή (1012), which answers to **Châphêts** (2654), marks His *disposition* rather than His counsel or purpose. The two words are found together in Eph. 1:11.[4] The latter word implies not so much that there has been a consideration of the circumstances that call for action, as that they are in accordance with the nature and attributes of God. The former points to the fact that the course of action determined on gives a real pleasure to Him.

§4. *Freedom of the Will*

Voluntary action, as opposed to that which is constrained or compulsory, is indicated by the word **Nâdab** (נָדַב, 5068), for which the LXX frequently uses προθυμέομαι (L-S 1481A—*to be ready, willing, eager to do*). **Nâdab** (5068) is applied to the offerings for the tabernacle that were given "willingly" (Exod. 25:2; 35:5, etc.), to the "freewill offerings" for Solomon's temple (I Chron. 28:21; 29:5), and to the "free offerings" in the days of Josiah (II Chron. 35:8).[5] In Lev. 7:16 and Ezek. 46:12 it is rendered *voluntary*. In Ps. 68:9 it is used of the "*plentiful* rain" that was sent freely or without stint on God's inheritance.

This word occurs in Ps. 54:6, "I will freely sacrifice unto thee"; in Hos. 14:4, "I will love them freely"; also in Ps. 51:12, "Uphold me with thy free spirit," i.e., "sustain in me an unconstrained spirit of devotion." In this last passage the LXX reads πνεύματι ἡγεμονικῷ (4151, L-S 763A), "with thy guiding or ruling spirit," the Hebrew reading followed being perhaps slightly different from our own.

In Ps. 110:3 we read, "Thy people shall be willing in the day of thy

4. Editor's note: Girdlestone's definitions of the two Greek words in question do not accord with the more carefully researched definitions of the standard lexicons of the Greek N.T.

5. In Assyrian, *nindabu* means a freewill offering (Sayce).

power." These words are sometimes taken as referring to God's "prevenient grace," and they have been cited by a few as justifying a man in sitting listlessly under God's Word, waiting till power comes on him from above. Such an interpretation is held in forgetfulness of the fact that God works through the will, not apart from it—that He *turns* the lock, but does not force it. The form of the word in this passage is the plural substantive, so that the literal rendering would be, "thy people shall be *freewill offerings. . . .*" Luther renders it, "thy people shall offer willingly" (see also R.V.); and the words seem to point to the fact that in the day of the Messiah's exaltation His people shall offer Him unconstrained service, yielding their bodies as living sacrifices to God, rendering Him a rational (as opposed to a *cere-monial*) service. (See Rom. 12:1, and compare the English Prayer Book Version of the Psalms.)

The word προθυμία (4288) is not often found in the N.T., but there is one passage, viz., II Cor. 8:11, 12, where it occurs, which calls for some slight elucidation. The A.V. runs thus: "Now therefore perform the doing of it; that as there was a readiness to will, so there may be a performance also out of that which ye have. For if there be first a willing mind, it is accepted according to that a man hath, and not according to that he hath not." The words *a readiness* in the first part of this passage, and *a willing mind* in the second, stand for the Greek word προθυμία (4288); so that the Apostle would say, "as there was a readiness to be willing [προθυμία τοῦ θέλειν—4288, 3588, 2309], so let there be a carrying out of that willingness by a contribution from what you possess; for where there is a real willingness, such a contribution is acceptable, even though small, because it is given according to what a man does possess, not according to what he does not." The word προθυμία (4288) here answers to **Nâdab** (5068), while the word θέλειν (2309) answers rather to **'Âbâh** (14). Paul did not accept the will (**'Âbâh**, 14) for the deed; but if what is given is given voluntarily (**Nâdab**, 5068), then he gladly accepted the gift in proportion to the means of the giver.

The word that marks volition, or that which immediately precedes action, is **Yâ'al** (יָאַל, 2974). The LXX generally represents this word by ἄρχομαι (756), *to begin*. We meet with it in Josh. 17:12: "The Canaanites *would* dwell in that land." Compare Judg. 1:27, 34, and Hos. 5:11. "He *willingly* walked after the commandment." It is rendered *assay* in I Sam. 17:39, "He assayed[6] to go." This implies that

---

6. The R.V. retains this spelling, instead of *essayed*.

David was on the verge of starting off (Vulgate, "he began to step out") in Saul's armor, but he had not proved it (and consequently took it off). Yâ'al (2974) is rendered *begin* in Deut. 1:5. In Gen. 18:27, 31, it is found in the expression "*I have taken upon me* to speak unto the Lord." All these passages exhibit the real meaning of the word as representing the volitional element in an act rather than the feelings, dispositions, or motives that have prompted it.

In a few passages Yâ'al (2974) is rendered *content,* where the word signifies that a certain effort of the will was necessary before the thing required was done. See Exod. 2:21; Josh. 7:7; Judg. 17:11; 19:6; II Kings 5:23; 6:3; Job 6:28. Where the sentence is in the form of a petition, it seems to answer to our use of the word *do* in the sentence, "Oh, *do* come!" In accordance with this sense, it is rendered *be pleased* in I Sam. 12:22; II Sam. 7:29; I Chron. 17:27; Job 6:9.

§5. Conscience

We look in vain for the word *conscience* in the O.T. except in the margin of Eccles. 10:20, where it represents part of the word Yâda' (יָדַע, 3045), *to know* (Assyrian, *idû*). In the Apocryphal books we meet with συνείδησις (4893) twice, viz., in Ecclesiasticus 10:20 where it is rendered *wittingly;* and in Wisdom of Solomon 17:11, where it seems to point to the constraining power of a sense of right. The verb συνείδω (4894) is used of *knowledge* in Lev. 5:1; also in Job 27:6, where the LXX reads οὐ γὰρ σύνοιδα ἐμαυτῷ ἄτοπα πράξας (3756, 1063, 4894, 1683, 824, 4238), "I am not conscious of having acted foolishly." These words have no Hebrew text answering to them, but they find an echo in the Apostle Paul's phrase, "I know nothing against myself" (οὐδὲν ἐμαυτῷ σύνοιδα—3762, 1683, 4894—I Cor. 4:4).

The verb συνείδω (4894) is also used to represent ordinary perception, without reference to the moral aspect of the thing perceived, in five passages in the books of the Maccabees.

Conscience, then, so far as the O.T. throws any light on it, is to be taken not as a separate faculty that enables a man to distinguish right and wrong, but as the exercise of *consciousness.* And it will be seen, by noting the passages in the N.T. in which the word occurs, that this meaning is generally adhered to there also. Omitting John 8:9, the reading of which is doubtful, we do not meet with the word συνείδησις (4893) until we arrive at the end of the Acts. Paul, standing before the council, says, "In all good conscience have I lived under the government of God unto this day" (Acts 23:1). These words are elucidated by the statement made before Felix: "In this I exercise myself, having [or to have] a conscience void of offense towards God and towards man continually" (Acts 24:16). He evidently signified that he was not conscious of living or aiming to live in any course that was wrong in the sight of God or really offensive to man. In exact accordance with these expressions, he writes to the Corinthians, "I am not conscious of anything against myself; yet am I not hereby justified, but he that judgeth me is the Lord" (I Cor. 4:4).

The same Apostle refers to his consciousness that what he said was spoken in sincerity (Rom. 9:1): "My conscience also bearing me witness." Compare Rom. 2:15; II Cor. 4:2; 5:11. In I Cor. 8:7 we read of those who are eating "with conscience of the idol"—that is, with a conscious feeling that they are eating what is offered to idols. Thus their conscience, i.e., their moral sense, being weak and susceptible, is defiled. See also verse 10.

The moral sensibility or conscience is referred to in I Cor. 10:25-29:

> Whatever is sold in the meat market eat, asking no questions because of consciousness; . . . not your own consciousness, but that of the weak brother who has not yet attained to that liberty and knowledge that enables you to disregard heathen superstitions [paraphrased].

When Paul is describing the end or sum and substance of the charge that Christ lays on men, he characterizes it as "love out of a pure heart, and a good conscience, and unfeigned faith" (I Tim. 1:5). By these words he means that there should be a conscious aim at that which is good in God's sight, and a faithfulness untainted by a particle of hypocrisy. Compare I Tim. 1:19, where faith and a good conscience are again joined together.

The passages in the Epistle to the Hebrews in which the word occurs are very interesting and important. From Heb. 9:9 we gather that the offerings under the O.T. could not make men "perfect as pertaining to the conscience," i.e., could not take away the sense of sin that hinders man from oneness with God. They did not take away sin, as a matter of fact; they could not, from the very nature of things. For if the effect of the Levitical dispensation had been to make men perfect, i.e., at one with God (see chap. 8, §2), then the offerings would not have needed repetition. If the worshipers had been purged once for all, they would have had no more consciousness of sins (Heb. 10:2). But "the blood of Christ" cleanses a man's consciousness from dead works, and enables him to serve the living God (Heb. 9:14). The heart is thus "sprinkled from an evil conscience" (10:22). In other words, the faithful acceptance of the sacrifice of Christ takes away that sense of sin that had been a bar between man and God, and enables a man to live no longer as a servant but as a son.

Peter says, "This is grace [A.V. thankworthy], if for conscience toward God [i.e., through consciousness of his duty and of his relationship to God in Christ] a man endure pains, suffering unjustly" (I Pet. 2:19). He urges that men should keep "a good conscience" (3:16). And he reminds them that it is not the external cleansing, the putting away of the filth of the flesh, that now saves us. Rather, it is the answer of a good conscience toward God, or, as we might render it, the seeking[7] unto God with a good conscience (I Pet. 3:21).

The verb συνείδω (4894), *to be conscious,* is used in only three passages in the N.T. (exclusive of that already mentioned in I Cor. 4:4): Acts 5:2; 12:12; 14:6.

Conscience was thus originally identical with consciousness, but while the latter word may be used by us with reference to external facts or to internal feelings, the former is now confined to the knowledge that a man has of the moral aspect of things. A good conscience, according to Scripture, is not only a sense of freedom from past guilt, but also a consciousness of purposing and doing that which is good in God's sight. It implies purity of motive and action. It is inconsistent with a deliberate course of sin or with departure from the living God, and it is closely connected with faith in Christ.

§6. *Words Marking Intelligence*

Coming to the words that designate man's intellectual capacities, we may begin with the word *wisdom.* This word generally answers in the A.V. to the Hebrew **Châkâm** (חָכָם, 2450). This is an important

---

7. Ἐπερώτημα εἰς Θεόν (1906, 1519, 2316). This passage has awakened much discussion. I am inclined to be guided by the fact that ἐπερωτάω (1905) sometimes answers to the meaning of **Dârash** (דָּרַשׁ, 1875), *to seek,* in the O.T. The Vulgate confirms this view by reading *interrogatio conscientiae bonae in Deum* ("the inquiry of a good conscience toward God"). Luther renders it "the contract [Bund] of a good conscience [Gewissen] with God." De Sacy takes it as "the engagement of the conscience to keep pure for God."

word in Scripture, and is used to represent the discernment of good and evil, prudence in secular matters, skill in arts, experience in Divine things, and even dexterity in magic. In its reflexive verbal form it signifies *to be wise in one's own eyes*, and hence *to outwit another*. Its general rendering in the LXX is σοφία (4678), which is used in the same largeness of sense in the N.T. See especially James 3:17. It is moral rather than intellectual; it is the adaptation of what we know to what we have (and ought) to do. In this sense the Lord Jesus grew in wisdom, i.e., in its exercise.

The understanding is most generally represented by the word Bîyn (בִּין, 995), *to perceive, to be intelligent*. This word, again, is used with many shades of meaning, such as *to consider, discern, feel, know, look, mark, perceive, view*. The LXX usually represents this word by σύνεσις (4907), but occasionally by ἐπιστήμη (L-S 660A—*understanding, skill*) and φρόνησις (5428).

Sâkal (שָׂכַל, 7919), *to look, to be knowing*, and hence *to prosper*, is used to represent a certain kind of wisdom in Gen. 3:6, and of various other aspects of wisdom in a good many other passages. The LXX renderings are instructive.

One word remains to be noticed, namely, Tûwshîyâh (תּוּשִׁיָּה, 8454). The LXX renderings for this word are quite variable. Some critics understand it as signifying *essentia* or existent being. Hence it is rendered *that which is* in Job 11:6; 26:3. It is rendered *substance* in Job 30:22. Compare the cognate Yêsh (יֵשׁ, 3426) in Prov. 8:21. In Isa. 28:29, it is translated *working*. In Job 5:12, we find the word *enterprise* adopted. The most general rendering, however, is *wisdom*, or *sound wisdom*. Thus we read in Job 6:13, "Is wisdom quite driven from me?" Prov. 2:7 says, "He layeth up sound wisdom for the righteous." Prov. 8:14 has this: "Counsel is mine, and sound wisdom." Micah 6:9 declares, "The Lord's voice crieth unto the city, and [the man of] wisdom shall see thy name." The margin has here, "Thy name shall see that which is."

6

Sin

The pictorial power of the Hebrew language is seldom exhibited more clearly than in connection with the various aspects of evil. Every word is a piece of philosophy; nay, it is a revelation. The observer of human affairs is painfully struck by the wearisomeness of life, and by the amount of toil and travail the children of men have to undergo to obtain a bare existence. He sees the hollowness, vanity, and unreality of much that seems bright and charming at first. He notes that human nature, in its personal and social aspects, is distorted and out of course; that the chain of love that ought to bind the great family in one has been snapped asunder; that isolation and desolation have taken the place of unity and happiness. He observes that the relationship between man and his Maker has become obscured, and that even when man knows the will of God there is something in his nature that prompts him to rebel against it. Lastly, he comes to the conviction that this state of things is not original, but is opposed to men's best instincts, and frustrates the original design of their creation.

The Hebrew Bible meets us with a full acknowledgment of these manifold aspects of human suffering. It blends wrongdoing and suffering to a remarkable degree, setting forth sin in its relation to God, to society, and to man's own self, depicting it in its negative aspect as iniquity or unrighteousness and in its positive aspect as rebellion and a breach of trust.

§1. Sin

The word translated *sin* throughout the O.T. (with very rare exceptions) is derived from the word Châṭâ' (חָטָא, 2398), which originally signified *to miss the mark* and answers to the Greek ἁμαρτάνω (264). This underscores the fact that all wrongdoing is a *failure* or a *coming short* of that aim that God intended all His children to reach.[1] If man was originally made in the image of God, it must have been implanted in him as a first principle that he should live as God lives. Every departure, therefore, from the law of Right is a coming short of the purpose for which man was made, and a missing of the goal that ought to be reached.

The word usually implies blameworthiness, and is used largely in confessions to express a conviction that wrong has been done either toward God or toward man. This wrong is not necessarily willful, for many sins were committed through negligence or ignorance (see Lev. 4:2; 5:15; Num. 15:28). Sin is not usually regarded in the O.T. as a condition (i.e., sinfulness) but as a definite act, whether of thought, word, or deed. The word was applied not only to moral evil and idolatry but also to breaches of ceremonial regulations.

The following are the only passages in which other words besides Châtâ' (2398) have been rendered *sin* by the translators of the A.V. In Lev. 4:13 and Num. 15:28, 29, we find the word **Shâgâh** (שָׁגָה, 7686), *to err;* in I Kings 17:18, Âvôn (עָוֹן, 5771), *vanity* or *iniquity;* in Prov. 10:12, 19, and 28:13, **Pesha'** (פֶּשַׁע, 6588), *rebellion* or *transgression.*

Châtâ' (2398) is occasionally rendered by some other word instead of *sin.* Thus it is rendered *fault* in Gen. 41:9 and Exod. 5:16; *trespass* in I Kings 8:31; *harm* in Lev. 5:16; *blame* in Gen. 43:9 and 44:32; *offend* in Gen. 20:9 and 40:1; I Kings 1:21; II Kings 18:14; Eccles. 10:4; Isa. 29:21; Jer. 37:18.

The verb has a peculiar meaning in the Piel or intensive stem or conjugation as is the case with several other verbs. In this stem it is rendered as follows: *to make reconciliation* (II Chron. 29:24); *to bear loss* (Gen. 31:39); *to offer for sin* (Leviticus, passim); *to cleanse from sin* (Exod. 29:36; Lev. 14:49, 52; Ezek. 43:20, 22, 23; 45:18); *to purge* or *purify* (Lev. 8:15; Num. 8:7, 21; 19:9, 12, 13, 17, 19, 20; 31:19, 20, 23); also in the familiar words of Ps. 51:7, "*Purge* me with hyssop and I shall be clean," and in Job 41:25, where we read of the Leviathan that "when he raiseth up himself, the mighty are afraid; by reason of breakings they *purify* themselves."

---

1. The word is used in its original sense in Judg. 20:16, where we read of "seven hundred chosen men left handed, every one of whom could sling stones at an hair's breadth, and not miss."

The LXX, which is generally very consistent in retaining the rendering ἁμαρτάνω (264), has in some ceremonial passages adopted renderings similar to those now noticed. Thus we find ἐξιλάσκομαι (L-S 594B) in II Chron. 29:24; Ezek. 43:22; 45:18; ἁγνίζω (48) in Num. 8:21; 19:12, 13; 31:19, 23; ἀφαγνίζω (L-S 285B) in Lev. 14:49, 52; Num. 19:12, 19, 20; 31:20; καθαρίζω (2511) in Exod. 29:36; Lev. 8:15; 9:15; ῥαντίζω (4472) in Ps. 51:7; ἱλασμός (2434) in Ezek. 44:27; ἐξιλασμός (L-S 594B) in Exod. 30:10; Ezek. 43:23; 45:19; ἅγνισμα (L-S 11B) in Num. 19:9; and ἁγνισμός (49) in Num. 8:7; 19:17.

§2. *Wrong*

The perversion or distortion of nature that is caused by evildoing is represented by the word 'Âvâh (עָוָה, 5753), *to be bent* or *crooked*. The original meaning of the word is found in these texts: Isa. 21:3, "I was *bowed down* at the hearing of it"; Lam. 3:9, "He hath made my ways *crooked*"; and perhaps in Ps. 38:6, where we read in the A.V., "I am *troubled*; I am bowed down greatly." The English word *wrong*, i.e., that which is wrung out of course, gives the same idea of evil and is taken as a translation of 'Âvâh (5753) in Esther 1:16. We also find the analogous word *perverseness* as a rendering in I Sam. 20:30; II Sam. 19:19; I Kings 8:47; Job 33:27; Prov. 12:8; Isa. 19:14; and Jer. 3:21. *Amiss* is found in II Chron. 6:37; and *iniquity* in II Sam. 7:14; Ps. 65:3; 106:6; Jer. 9:5; Ezek. 28:18; Dan. 4:27; 9:5; Mal. 2:6.

The chief renderings for 'Âvâh (5753) in the LXX are ἁμαρτία (266), ἀνομία (458), and ἀδικία (93), none of which quite coincide with the original in their primary meanings.

§3. *Travail*

That sin has made life a burden and has turned work into toil and travail is acknowledged by all, and this fact has found its place among the lessons contained in Hebrew words. The word 'Âmâl (עָמָל, 5999) sets forth labor in its toilsome aspect, and is well represented in the LXX by κόπος (2873), μόχθος (3449), and πόνος (4192). It is rendered *toil* in Gen. 41:51; *trouble* in Job 5:6, 7; *wearisome* in Job 7:3; *sorrow* in Job 3:10; Ps. 55:10; *pain* or *painful* (in its old sense, as involving labor) in Ps. 25:18; 73:16; and *labor* in Ps. 90:10 ("yet is their strength labour and sorrow"). This last rendering is constantly found in the Book of Ecclesiastes, which is devoted in great measure to a setting forth of the burdensomeness of an earthly existence. In Eccles. 4:6 Âmâl (5999) is rendered *travail*. This rendering has been adopted in Isa. 53:11, where we read of the Messiah that "he shall see [the fruits] of the travail of his soul, and shall be satisfied."

The passages hitherto noted do not trace the weariness of life to its source, but there are others in which this is not obscurely taught. In Isa. 10:1 and Hab. 1:3, Âmâl (5999) is rendered *grievousness;* in Num. 23:21, *perverseness* ("he hath not seen perverseness in Israel"); in Hab. 1:13, *iniquity* ("thou canst not look on iniquity"); in Job 4:8, *wickedness;* in Job 15:35, *mischief* ("they conceive mischief and bring forth vanity"). See also Ps. 7:14, 16; 10:7, 14; 94:20; 140:9; Prov. 24:2; Isa. 59:4—in all of which the same rendering is given and the same idea implied.

§4. *Iniquity*

The word Âval (עָוֶל, 5765) is thought to designate the want of integrity and rectitude that is the accompaniment, if not the essential part, of wrongdoing. This word in some of its forms reminds one of the word *evil* (cf. German, *übel*), and of the contracted word *ill.* The chief renderings for it in the LXX are ἀδικία (*93*) and ἀνομία (*458*), of which the first is probably the best. Âval (5765) is rendered *unjust* in Ps. 43:1; 82:2; Prov. 29:27; Isa. 26:10; Zeph. 3:5; *unrighteous* in Lev. 19:15, 35; Deut. 25:16; Job 27:7; Ps. 71:4; 92:15; *ungodly* in Job 16:11; *perverse* in Isa. 59:3; *wickedness* in twelve passages, including Ps. 89:22 ("The enemy shall not exact upon him, nor the son of wickedness afflict him").

Âval (5765) is also rendered *iniquity* in about thirty passages. *Iniquity,* taken in its original sense as a departure from that which is equal and right, is probably the most suitable rendering. The usage of the word is well illustrated by Mal. 2:6, where we read of Levi that "the law of truth was in his mouth, and iniquity was not found in his lips; he walked with me in peace and equity, and did turn many away from unrighteousness."

§5. *Transgression*

The idea of transgression, or crossing over the boundary of right and entering the forbidden land of wrong, is marked by the use of the word Âbar (עָבַר, 5674), *to cross over* (compare the Assyrian *ebiru,* "to cross"). Though used for the most part to describe acts in a morally neutral sense, it is rendered *transgress* in eighteen passages: e.g., Ps. 17:3; Hos. 6:7; 8:1.

§6. *Evil*

The word generally used for evil and wickedness is Ra' (רַע, 7451), which appears to signify *breaking up* or *ruin*. The LXX rendering for it is usually κακός (2556) or πονηρός (4190). It is one of those words that binds together in one the wicked deed and its consequences. It is *evil* as opposed to good in Gen. 2:17 et al. It is rendered *calamity* in Ps. 141:5; *distress* in Neh. 2:17; *adversity* in I Sam. 10:19; Ps. 94:13; Eccles. 7:14; *grief* in Neh. 2:10; Prov. 15:10; Eccles. 2:17; Jonah 4:6; *affliction* in Num. 11:11 and ten other passages; *misery* in Eccles. 8:6; *sad* in Gen. 40:7; Neh. 2:1, 2; Eccles. 7:3; *sorrow* in Gen. 44:29; Neh. 2:2; *trouble* in Ps. 41:1 and eight other passages; *sore* in Deut. 6:22 and eight other passages; *noisome* in Ezek. 14:15, 21; *hurt* in Gen. 26:29 and twenty-eight other passages; *heavy* in Prov. 25:20; *vex* in Num. 20:15 and II Sam. 12:18; *wretchedness* in Num. 11:15; also *harm, ill*, and *mischief* in almost every place where these words are found in the A.V.

These passages sometimes imply injury done to a person, but do not touch on its moral aspect. This is to be borne in mind as we read Isa. 45:7, "I create evil," and similar verses. In other cases, however, this element is introduced. In Judg. 11:27, we read, "I have not sinned against thee, but thou doest me wrong to war against me." Here the wrong or injury is regarded as an injustice. Again, in I Sam. 17:28 ("I know thy pride and the *naughtiness* of thy heart"), moral evil seems to be intended. The word is also rendered *naught* or *naughty* in II Kings 2:19; Prov. 20:14; Jer. 24:2. But in these passages *naughty* has its original sense of "good for nothing," a sense in which the word is still used in some parts of the English-speaking world. Perhaps this was all that was implied in Eliab's rude speech to David (I Sam. 17:28).

Ra' (7451) is rendered *wicked* a great many times; it is also frequently rendered *bad*, but in the latter class of passages that which is injurious is referred to rather than that which is morally evil. Ra' (7451), in fact, generally indicates the rough exterior of wrongdoing as a breach of harmony, and as a breaking up of what is good and desirable in man and in society. While the prominent characteristic of the godly is lovingkindness, one of the most marked features of the ungodly man is that his course is an injury both to himself and to everyone around him.

§7. *Rebellion*

Pâsha' (פָּשַׁע, 6586) signifies *to revolt* or *refuse subjection to rightful authority* (cf. Pesha', 6588, p. 92). It is very generally rendered *transgression*. The chief LXX renderings for it are ἀσέβεια (763), ἀδικία (93), and ἀνομία (458). We meet with the verb in the following texts: Ps. 51:13, "Then will I teach *transgressors* thy ways, and sinners shall be converted unto thee"; Prov. 28:21, "For a piece of bread a man will transgress [i.e., rebel]"; Isa. 43:27, "Thy teachers have transgressed against me."

Pâsha' (6586) is rendered *sin* in Prov. 10:12 ("Love covereth all sins"), where the contrast between the offense and the mercy is brought out very clearly by the use of the word. Again it is found in verse 19 ("In the multitude of words there wanteth not sin"). In II Kings 8:20, 22, it is used in its primary sense of the *revolt* of Edom and Libnah; in I Kings 12:19, of the *rebellion* of Israel against Judah (so also in other passages). We meet with the word in Job 34:37, where it is said of Job that "he addeth rebellion unto his sin." Lastly, it occurs in the opening of the prophecies of Isaiah: "I have nourished and brought up children, and they have rebelled against me" (Isa. 1:2).

§8. *Wickedness*

Râshâ' (רָשָׁע, 7563) is the word most generally rendered *wicked*[2] in the A.V. It is derived from Râsha' (רָשַׁע, 7561), which is supposed originally to refer to the *activity*, the *tossing*, and the *confusion* in which the wicked live, and the perpetual agitation that they cause to others. Thus Isaiah says (57:20, 21), "The wicked are like the troubled sea, when it cannot rest, whose waters cast up mire and dirt. There is no peace, saith my God, to the wicked." Job also (3:17) looks forward to the grave as the place "where the wicked cease

2. The word *wicked* is supposed by some etymologists to be connected with *quick*, and to mean *lively*; if this be its true significance, it answers admirably to Râshâ' (7563). See Dean Hoare's work on *English Roots*.

from troubling, and the weary are at rest." In the Book of Job the wicked are represented as triumphing for a time, but as finally put out into darkness. In the Psalms they are represented as busily occupied in disturbing the peace of others, and as trying to destroy them. They are frequently contrasted with the righteous; and their ways are fully described in Ezek. 18 and 33. If Kennicott's view of Isa. 53:9 could be substantiated, we should read of the Messiah, "he made his grave with the rich, but with the wicked was his death"; and the use of the word to mark the robbers or disturbers of the public peace would have been very appropriate.

Râshâ' (7563) is usually rendered ἀσεβής (765), *ungodly*, in the LXX, but ἄνομος (459) and ἁμαρτωλός (268) are found in several passages.

The *verb* in its Hiphil or causative form is generally taken as signifying *to condemn*, literally *to make wicked*, and hence *to deal with as wicked*. It is found in all but four passages where the word *condemn* occurs in the A.V.

§9. *Breach of Trust*

The word Ma'al (מַעַל, 4604) probably points to the unfaithfulness and treachery of sin. It represents wrongdoing as a breach of trust, whether between man and man or between man and God. It is rendered *trespass* about thirty times, *transgression* fifteen times, and *falsehood* in Job 21:34. In the first passage where it occurs (Lev. 5:15), it refers to the trespass committed in ignorance; in the second, to any sin committed against one's neighbor (6:2). In Josh. 7:1 and 22:20, it is used of Achan's sin; the building of the altar on the east of Jordan was also described by this word (Josh. 22:16). It is applied to Uzziah (II Chron 26:18); to Ahaz (28:22); to Manasseh (33:19); and to the people who married heathen wives (Ezra 9:2, 4; Neh. 13:27). It is also found in Prov. 16:10, where we read that "the king's mouth transgresseth not in judgment." The breach of trust denoted by this word was regarded by God in a very serious light. See Ezek. 14:13; 15:8; 18:24; 39:23. The reason for this is manifest. The persons guilty of sin in this particular aspect were chiefly persons in authority. A certain trust had been reposed in them, which they had abused. Much had been given to them, and much was required of them. The nation of Israel as a whole was put in a position of high privilege and consequent responsibility, hence their departure from the way of God was marked specially by this word as an act of unfaithfulness.

The word **Bâgad** (בָּגַד, 898), *to deal treacherously,* is sometimes used in the same sense.

§10. *Vanity*

The word most frequently rendered *iniquity* is **Âvôn** (עָוֹן, 5771)— Assyrian, *'annu.* Some critics connect this word with a root that signifies *desire;* others, with greater reason, hold that its original meaning is *nothingness.* Its connection with idolatry is noticeable (see chap. 27, ‡2), and originates in the fact that an *idol* is a thing of naught, a vain thing. In Amos 5:5 we read, "Bethel shall come to naught" (**Âvôn**, 5771). And turning to Hosea (4:15; 5:8; 10:5, 8), we find that Bethel, the House of God, is designated as **Bêyth-Âven** (1007), i.e., the *house of vanity,* because idols were worshiped there.

The word is rendered *vanity* in several passages: Job 15:35, "They conceive mischief and bring forth *vanity*"; Ps. 10:7, "Under his tongue is mischief and vanity"; Prov. 22:8, "He that soweth iniquity shall reap vanity." See also Isa. 41:29; 58:9; Jer. 4:14; Zech. 10:2.

The word **Âvôn** (5771) is to be found in Prov. 11:7 (*unjust*); Isa. 10:1; 55:7 (*unrighteous*); Ps. 90:10 (*sorrow*); Deut. 26:14 (*mourning*); Job 5:6 (*affliction*); Ps. 140:11 (*evil*); Prov. 17:4 (*false*); Ps. 36:4 (*mischief*).

Âvôn (5771) is rendered *wickedness* in a few passages, and *iniquity* in thirty-eight places. The most noticeable are these: Num. 23:21; I Sam. 15:23; Job 4:8; 21:19; 31:3; 34:22; Ps. 5:5; 6:8; Isa. 1:13; Micah 2:1.

On considering all these passages, we shall be led to the conclusion that the word **Âvôn** (5771) suggests not so much breach of law or injury done to another as a course of conduct that will in the end prove unprofitable to the doer. It presents the evil devices of man in their false, hollow, and unreal aspect. By the use of this word the inspired writers put a stamp of nothingness or unreality on every departure from the law of God, whether it consists of wrongdoing, evil devising, false speaking, or idolatrous worship.

The leading rendering of **Âvôn** (5771) in the LXX is ἀνομία (458); ἀδικία (93) is used several times, πόνος (4192) and κόπος (2873) occasionally.

§11. *Guilt*

We now come to a word about which there has been a good deal of difference of opinion, namely **Âshâm** (אָשָׁם, 817), the usual rendering of which in the LXX is πλημμέλεια (L-S 1418B), a *mistake,* and in the A.V. *trespass* or *guilt.*[3]

Some critics hold that while Châtâ' (2398) denotes sins of commission, Âshâm (817) designates sins of omission. Others have come to the conclusion that Châtâ' (2398) means sin in general, and Âshâm (817) sin against the Mosaic law. An examination of all the passages in which the word occurs leads to the conclusion that Âshâm (817) is used where a sin, moral or ceremonial, has been committed through error, negligence, or ignorance. A loose code of morality might permit such offenses to be passed by, but not so the law of Moses. An offense against the person of another *is* an offense, whether it be known or found out at the time or not. When it comes to our knowledge we are liable, i.e., we are to regard ourselves as having offended even though it has been unwittingly; and compensation must be made. So also when the offense is a breach of ceremonial law, or if it is an act of idolatry (for which the word Âshâm [817] is frequently used). When the matter is brought to a man's cognizance he is not to content himself with the excuse that he acted in error. Rather, he is to acknowledge himself as Âshâm (817), and is to offer an Âshâm (817) or *guilt-offering*[4] for his trespass.

In Lev. 4:13, we read,

> If the whole congregation of Israel sin through error [A.V. ignorance], and the thing be hid from the eyes of the assembly, and they have done somewhat against any of the commandments of the LORD concerning things which should not be done, and are guilty; when the sin, which they have sinned against it, is known, then the congregation shall offer a young bullock for the sin. . . .

See also verses 22 and 27. In these cases a commandment has been broken unwittingly; it afterwards comes to the knowledge of the offender, and he is Âshâm (817)—*guilty.*

In Lev. 5:2, 3, Moses declares, "If a soul touch any unclean thing . . . and if it be hidden from him; he also shall be unclean, and guilty. . . . when he knoweth it, he shall be guilty"; verse 4, "Or if a soul swear . . . and it be hid from him, when he knoweth of it, then he shall be guilty"; verses 5, 6, "And it shall be, when he shall be guilty

---

3. The English word *guilt* is probably derived from Anglo-Saxon *geldan,* to pay a fine.
4. See Chap. 16.

in one of these things, that he shall confess that he hath sinned in that thing: and he shall bring his trespass-offering unto the LORD. . . . Verse 15, "If a soul commit a trespass [Ma'al (מַעַל, 4604)], and sin through error [or ignorance], in the holy things of the LORD; then he shall bring for his trespass unto the LORD a ram . . . for a trespass-offering." Moreover, in verses 17–19 Moses declares,

> If a soul sin, and commit any of these things that are forbidden to be done by the commandments of the LORD; though he wist it not, yet he is guilty, and shall bear his iniquity. And he shall bring a ram . . . and the priest shall make an atonement for him concerning his ignorance wherein he erred and wist it not, and it shall be forgiven him.[5] It is a trespass offering: he hath certainly trespassed against the Lord.

It is unfortunate that unity of rendering has not been preserved in these passages, as there is nothing to show the English reader the connection between the words *guilty* and *trespass*. But see R.V. Consider and compare Gen. 42:21; Num. 5:6, 7; Judg. 21:22; I Chron. 21:3; II Chron. 19:10; 28:10, 13; Ezra 10:19; Ps. 69:5; Prov. 30:10; Jer. 2:3; 50:7; Ezek. 22:4; 25:12; Hos. 4:15; 5:15; 10:2 (cf. II Sam. 14:13).

It may be gathered from a consideration of these passages that while Châtâ' (2398) marks the peculiar nature of sin as a missing of the mark, Âshâm (817) implies a breach of commandment wrought without due consideration, which, when brought to the notice of the offender, calls for amends or atonement.

§12. *Words for Sin in the N.T.*

Most of the Greek words that have been referred to in the foregoing sections are to be found in the N.T. The original sense of ἁμαρτάνω (264) and Châtâ' (2398) seems to be referred to in a most important passage in the Epistle to the Romans (3:23), "For all have sinned, and come short of the glory of God." The sinner is one who has missed or come short of the mark. An important definition of sin is given by James: "Therefore to him that knoweth to do good, and doeth it not, to him it is sin" (4:17). It would seem to be implied

---

5. Is it not in some degree implied here that a man is, in a measure at least, responsible for his *ignorance?*

that where there is no knowledge of what is right or wrong there is no sin; and with this agree the words of our Lord to the Pharisees, "If ye were blind, ye should have no sin: but now ye say, We see; therefore your sin remaineth" (John 9:41). The profession of knowledge involved responsibility, and caused the Pharisees to be condemned, out of their own mouth, as sinners. Absolute ignorance is excusable even though it is a missing of the mark, but negligence is not (see Heb. 2:3).

The relationship of ἀνομία (458) to ἁμαρτία (266) is clearly shown in I John 3:4: "Whosoever committeth *sin* committeth *iniquity* [ἀνομίαν, 458]: and *sin* is *iniquity* [lawlessness—A.S.V.]." So again with regard to the connection existing between ἀδικία (93), *departure from right*, and ἁμαρτία (266), we read (I John 5:17), "All unrighteousness is sin." A similar relationship between ἀσέβεια (763) and ἁμαρτία (266) is implied in the juncture of ἀσεβεῖς (765) and ἁμαρτωλοὶ (268) in I Tim. 1:9; I Pet. 4:18; Jude 15. With regard to all these words, it is to be noticed that the N.T. leans on the O.T., and that the vivid teaching of the latter is taken for granted as authoritative by the writers of the Christian Scriptures.

The labor and wearisomeness of sin is not dwelt on in the N.T. But the words that imply it are usually found in a more noble sense, in connection with toil for Christ. With regard to κόπος (2873), one passage may be referred to as an illustration of this fact, namely, I Cor. 3:8, where we read that every minister shall be rewarded according to his own labor (κόπον, 2873). He shall be rewarded not by the results produced—this would have involved the use of the word ἔργον (2041)—but by the amount of labor expended; hence κόπος (2873) is used. A few verses further down ἔργον (2041) is used with great propriety, where we read that the fire shall test a man's work, of what sort it is. Here the point of the passage is that it is not the outward show or bulk, but the real value of the work done, that shall be the test of a man's faithfulness at the Great Day. The words κόπος (2873) and μόχθος (3449) are found together in II Cor. 11:27; I Thess. 2:9; II Thess. 3:8. While the former implies pains and labor, the latter signifies toil of such a sort as produces weariness. Where πόνος (4192) is used, it is generally to indicate a tax on one's physical strength, whether arising from toil or from pain. In Rev. 21:4 we are told that there shall be none of it in the new heaven and new earth. The etymological relationship between πόνος (4192-*toil*) and πονηρία (*4189-depravity*) is undoubted though no passages in the N.T. clearly refer to it, and the double use of the word 'Âmâl (5999) is exactly analogous to it. Πονηρία (*4189*) is often to be understood in the N.T. as signifying rapacity, which is the fruit of covetousness. It is also used of "evil spirits."

7
Repentance, Conversion, Amendment

The previous chapters of this book have been occupied with discussion on the names, and consequently on the nature and capacities, of God and of man, and also on the varied aspects of human sin. Attention is now to be called to some of the sacred words used to express the moral or spiritual process whereby man is restored to his true position. Two ideas are set forth in the O.T., and adopted in the N.T., in this connection: one marks the bringing of a man to *himself*, the other the bringing of a man *to God;* the first is ordinarily designated *repentance*, the second *conversion*.

§1. *Repentance*

Very diverse views have been held with respect to the meaning of the word *repentance*. Some take it to indicate a change of heart or thought (the German word *Sinnesänderung*—change of mind, recantation—is found in the Berlenburger Bible), others a change of aim or purpose, and others a change of life or conduct. With the exception of three passages—namely, I Kings 8:47; Ezek. 14:6; 18:30 (in which the Hebrew is Shûwb[1] [שׁוּב, 7725], and the Greek ἐπιστρέφω, 1994)—the English word *repent* is used in the A.V. of the O.T. to represent a form of the Hebrew Nâcham (נָחַם, 5162), from which the name of the prophet Nahum is derived. The original meaning of this word is generally understood to be *to draw a deep*

---

1. See below, §3.

breath; this is taken as the physical mode of giving expression to a deep feeling, either of relief or sorrow. The one aspect of **Nâcham** (5162) is represented by the Greek παρακαλέω (3870), the other by μετανοέω (3340) and μεταμέλομαι (3338).

Nâcham (5162) is rendered by μετανοέω (3340) in the following passages: I Sam. 15:29 ("The Strength of Israel will not lie nor repent: for he is not a man, that he should repent"); Jer. 4:28 ("I have purposed it, and will not repent"); Jer. 18:8 ("If that nation against whom I have pronounced turn from their evil, I will repent of the evil that I thought to do unto them"; cf. v. 10, where we read, "If it do evil in my sight, that it obey not my voice, then I will repent of the good wherewith I said I would benefit them"); Joel 2:13, 14 ("The Lord . . . repenteth him of the evil. Who knoweth if he will return and repent . . . ?"); Amos 7:3, 6 ("The Lord repented for this. It shall not be, saith the Lord"); Jonah 3:10 ("God repented of the evil that he had said he would do unto them; and he did it not"). See also Jonah 4:2; Zech. 8:14 ("I repented not").

All these passages refer to God's repentance. The two that remain refer to man's repentance: Jer. 8:6 ("No man repented him of his wickedness, saying, What have I done?"); Jer. 31:19 ("Surely after that I was turned, I repented; and after that I was instructed, I smote upon my thigh").

The LXX has μεταμέλομαι (3338) for **Nâcham** (5162) in the following passages: Gen. 6:7 ("It repenteth me that I have made them"); I Sam. 15:11 ("It repenteth me that I have set up Saul to be king"—see also v. 35); I Chron. 21:15 ("The Lord beheld, and he repented him of the evil, and said to the angel that destroyed, It is enough, stay now thine hand"); Ps. 106:45 ("He remembered for them his covenant, and repented according to the multitude of his mercies"); Ps. 110:4 ("The Lord hath sworn, and will not repent"); Jer. 20:16 ("Let that man be as the cities which the Lord overthrew, and repented not"); Hosea 11:8 ("Mine heart is turned within me, my repentings are kindled together").

In the following passages μεταμέλομαι (3338) is used in the LXX of *man's* repentance: Exod. 13:17 ("Lest peradventure the people repent when they see war, and they return to Egypt"); Ezek. 14:22 ("Ye shall repent [A.V., be comforted] concerning the evil that I have brought upon Jerusalem").

It is evident from a consideration of these passages that when we approach the subject of repentance in the N.T. we must not tie it down too strictly, either to one formal process or to one set time in a man's life. But we must understand by it such a state of deep feeling as leads to a change or amendment of life. The etymology and the classical usage of the words μετανοέω (*3340*) and μετα-μέλομαι (*3338*) must give way before the fact that these words were used by Greek-speaking Jews as representatives of the passive and reflexive stems of Nâcham (*5162*). It is hard indeed to find one expression in any language that can adequately represent the complex emotions implied by the word. When the word is used with reference to God there is implied an idea of change, and perhaps of sorrow, but not the consciousness of wrongdoing. When it is used with reference to man, sorrow arises from a sense of sin, a conviction of wrongdoing in its varied aspects fills the heart with bitterness, and change of purpose and of the outward life ensue. Also an undercurrent of *relief* accompanies the sorrow. For the penitent draws a deep breath as the sin, which has been leading him astray, shows itself to him in its true colors and gives way before the announcement of mercy.

There is a remarkable tract on Penitence[2] written by Moses Maimonides, in which the subject is treated not as a matter of feeling but of practice. Penitence is described as the condition of a man who, having once fallen into a sin, now abstains from it, although the inducements to return to it are as strong as ever. The Hebrew word that the writer adopts to represent this process is a noun derived from Shûwb (*7725*), *to turn*. But the first open step in this change is confession, which is to be expressed in words similar to the following: "O Lord, I have sinned; I have done wrong, and such things. Behold, I am sorry [Nâcham, *5162*], and am ashamed because of my misdeeds; and I will never commit any such offenses again." It is neither sorrow without change, nor change without sorrow. Rather, it is such a deep feeling of sorrow as gives rise to a determination to change, or, as the English Church Catechism has it, "repentance whereby we forsake sin."

The learned Rosenmüller defines repentance as the admission of wrongdoing followed by grief and leading to a wiser course: *"Post factum sapere, et de errore admisso ita dolere ut sapias."*[3] He holds

2. An edition of this tract, with a Latin translation by Mr. Clavering, was published in Oxford in 1705.
3. "To be wise after the deed, and by admitting error thus to grieve to the end that you may be wise."

to the Latin *resipiscere* (to recover one's senses) as the best rendering of the word; and this view has been very common since the days of Beza, from whom Rosenmüller takes his definition almost word for word. The distinction between μεταμέλεια (L-S 1114A), *regret*, and μετάνοια (*3341*), *reconsideration*, which Beza subscribed to, must not be pressed very far, because (as we have seen) these words are used in almost the same sense in the LXX.[4] Besides, as a matter of fact, the noun μεταμέλεια (L-S 1114A) does not occur in the N.T., and the verb μεταμέλομαι (*3338*) falls into the background. It is once used with respect to *God* (in Heb. 7:21, which quotes from Ps. 110:4) and four times of *man* (in Matt. 21:29, 32; 27:3; II Cor. 7:8). See the negative form in Rom. 11:29; II Cor. 7:10.

The objections to the Latin word *poenitentia* (repentance, penitence) as a rendering of μετάνοια (*3341*) were more forcibly expressed by Erasmus in his *Annotations*. But he wrote without at all taking into consideration the Hebrew and Judeo-Greek usage, whence we derive the word μετάνοια (*3341*). Because in his days the Roman sacrament of *penance* (i.e., satisfaction for sins committed *after* baptism) was called by the same name as *penitence* (or sorrow for sins committed either *before* or *after* baptism) he thought that some other word should be adopted. He called *poenitentia* a barbarism and a solecism. To him must be given the credit of pressing on his contemporaries the word *resipiscentia* (a change of mind, reformation, repentance), which had previously been adopted by Lactantius as the better of the two. Lucas Brugensis, however, well replies that *poenitentia* had a far wider meaning among Latin ecclesiastical writers than was usually supposed. It implied not only sorrow, but also a change for the better. While, on the other hand, μετάνοια (*3341*) had a wider meaning than *change;* for it included *sorrow* and compunction of heart.

In the Decrees of the Council of Trent, a careful distinction is drawn between the *poenitentia* that precedes baptism and that which follows it. The former is general, and consists of a sorrow for sin with a renunciation of wickedness. Here we have the complex idea of repentance evidently implied in the usage of the word,

4. The opinion here advanced has the support of Elsner. See also Archbishop Trench's discussions on the word. In his work *Synonyms of the N.T.* he is inclined to draw out the distinction between the two words above named, but in his work on the Authorized Version he rather disclaims Beza's *resipiscentia* (a change of mind, reformation, repentance).

though not in its etymology. The *poenitentia* that follows after baptism is not efficacious, according to the theory of the Church of Rome, without confession followed by sacerdotal absolution.[5]

When Martin Luther made his first translation of the N.T., he adopted the phrase *bessert euch*, "better yourselves" (a phrase answering to "amend your ways"), as a rendering for μετανοείτε (3340), *repent*. But after a few years he returned to the customary phrase of the country, *thut Busse*, a phrase meaning *Do penance* or *Be penitent*. Perhaps he was moved to this change by the feeling that moral amendment in the abstract was no equivalent for repentance, and tended rather to mislead. In seven passages he has *Reue, regret*; thus the "repentance not to be repented of" (Vulgate, *poenitentiam stabilem*—"repentance that stands firm") is rendered *eine Reue, die Niemand gereuet*, "a regret that no man regrets."

§2. *Comfort*

Where the word **Nâcham** (5162) signifies *to be comforted*, the LXX rendering is usually a form of παρακαλέω (3870). But the word *comfort* in its modern usage hardly conveys the etymological force that it ought to have. It originally signified support and encouragement quite as much as consolation. The Comforter or Advocate of the N.T. administers help and strength as well as peace and joy; and the being comforted often involves both a confirmation in the right course and also a relinquishing of a previous course.

The verb παρακαλέω (3870) in the N.T. generally signifies *to beseech* or *to encourage*. It represents an earnestness and urgency prompted by deep feeling. See, for example, Matt. 8:5, where the leper falls before Christ, "beseeching him" to cleanse him. In Rom. 12:1 Paul says, "I beseech you . . . by the mercies of God." Sometimes, however, it signifies to *cheer up*, as in II Cor. 1:4: "Who comforteth us in all our tribulations." Compare Matt. 5:4: "Blessed are they that mourn, for they shall be comforted."

The word παράκλητος (3875) occurs five times in the N.T. In four

---

5. Satisfaction, according to the Tridentine theology, consists of certain acts of self-denial, whether corporal suffering or otherwise, imposed on the penitent according to the judgment of the priest and the rules of the Church for the purpose of bringing men into greater conformity with Christ. For "if we *suffer* with him, we shall also be glorified together." These acts are considered to represent the "fruits meet for repentance" and to be accepted by God through Christ.

of these passages we have rendered it by the word *Comforter.* In the fifth, although we have our Lord's authority for adopting the same rendering in the one case as in the other,[6] we have rendered it *Advocate.* The Vulgate has *Paraclitus* (comforter, protector, defender, advocate) in John 14:16, and *Advocatus* (legal counselor, attorney, or advocate, and thus an intercessor) in I John 2:1; so Luther has *Tröster* (comforter, consoler) and *Fürsprecher* (legal advocate, intercessor). The word *Beistand* (helper, supporter, stand-by) adopted by De Wette and Van Ess gives rather the classical than the Judeo-Greek sense.

In Rom. 15:4, 5, we read of "patience and comfort" of the Scriptures, and of "the God of patience and consolation." The Apostle here beautifully represents the truth that the Scriptures are the *means* of conveying that patience and comfort of which God is the *source.* The R.V. has comfort in both verses.

§3. *Conversion*

Two words answer to the English word *conversion* in the O.T. Hâphak (הָפַךְ, 2015), *to turn,* is used in Isa. 60:5: "The abundance of the sea shall be converted unto thee." Shûwb (שׁוּב, 7725), *to return,* is the general word. It is found in several texts that address man's need for spiritual conversion: Ps. 51:13 ("Sinners shall be converted unto thee"); Ps. 19:7 ("The law of the LORD is perfect, converting [or restoring] the soul"); Isa. 1:27 ("Zion shall be redeemed with judgment, and her converts [or those belonging to her who return] with righteousness"); Isa. 6:10 ("Lest they see with their eyes, and hear with their ears, and understand with their heart, and convert and be healed"). In these passages, with the exception of Ps. 19:7, the word is used in the active stem and in an intransitive sense, and might be rendered *return.* It is frequently used with a second verb to give the sense of *again* or *back.*

The LXX usually renders Shûwb (7725) by ἐπιστρέφω (1994), which is the general word used to represent the turning of the heart to God, whether from Judaism, idolatry, or sin, in the N.T. (See, e.g., Gal. 4:9; I Thess. 1:9; James 5:19, 20.) The process called *conversion* or

---

6. "He shall give you *another* Comforter," implying that they had *one* already, even Himself. John in his first Epistle may well be supposed to have this passage in his mind when he uses the word παράκλητος (3875) of Christ.

turning to God is in reality a *re-turning*, or a turning back again to Him from whom sin has separated us, but whose we are by virtue of creation, preservation, and redemption. The form στρέφω (4762) is used in Matt. 18:3.

§4. *Amendment*

The idea of amendment or improvement has been sanctioned by our translators in a few passages. In II Chron. 34:10, where we read of the amending of the House of the LORD, the Hebrew word is **Châzaq** (חָזַק, 2388), *to be strong*. In the Book of Jeremiah (7:3, 5; 26:13; 35:15—"Amend your ways") we find **Yâṭab** (יָטַב, 3190), *to make good*. This word is used in a great variety of senses in the O.T. Thus it is said that "God saw all that he had made, and, behold, it was very good" (Gen. 1:31). In Exod. 2:2 Moses is called "a goodly child." The tents of Israel, too, are called "goodly" (Num. 24:5). It is used of a beautiful woman (II Sam. 11:2); of the fair daughters of men (Gen. 6:2); of fair houses (Isa. 5:9); of precious ointment (Ps. 133:2; Eccles. 7:1); of the idol ready for the soldering (Isa. 41:7); of welfare (Neh. 2:10); of prosperity (Deut. 23:6; Zech. 1:17); of wealth (Job 21:13); of a good dowry (Gen. 30:20); of the tree that was good for food (Gen. 3:6); and of a merry heart (I Sam. 25:36). The thought to be gathered from a consideration of these passages is that goodness is not an absolute moral quality, but signifies that which is agreeable or pleasing, whether to God or man. Hence the verb is rendered *to please*, or *to be pleasant in one's eyes* (Neh. 2:6; Ps. 69:31); *to find favor* (I Sam. 2:26; 29:6); *to be accepted* (Lev. 10:19; I Sam. 18:5). If this view be correct, we are to understand that when Jeremiah says "amend your ways" he does not mean "improve them" in the abstract, or with relation to what they were before; but rather, "make your course such as is agreeable to God, and do what is well pleasing in His sight."

There are several renderings for this word in the LXX, but ἀγαθός (18), καλός (2570), and χρηστός (5543) are the most common. Ἀγαθός (18) is generally but not always used of moral goodness (as opposed to πονηρία, 4189, wickedness) in the N.T., but the idea of what is pleasant in God's sight is implied. In the case of the word καλός (2570), the elements of fairness and nobleness underlie the idea of goodness.

Where χρηστός (5543) is used in the N.T., the idea of kindness or kindliness is specially introduced. Thus where the Lord says ὁ ζυγός μου χρηστός (*3588, 2218, 1473, 5543*—Matt. 11:30), we might render his words "my yoke is *kindly*"—something more than easy; this yoke is pleasing to the spiritual sense of the converted man. So of wine, we may read in Luke 5:39, "The old is more kindly." With this sense Luke 6:35 might read, "He is kind to the unthankful"; Rom. 2:4, "The kindness of God leadeth them to repentance"; I Cor. 15:33, "Evil communications corrupt kindly manners"; I Pet. 2:3, "If so be that ye have tasted that the Lord is kind" (quoted from Ps. 34:8).

8
Perfection

§1. *Words Signifying Perfection*

The moral relationship existing between ideas that at first sight appear utterly unconnected with one another is seldom more beautifully illustrated than in the choice of Hebrew words whereby the ideas of perfection or completeness are portrayed in Scripture.

A few passages may first be noticed in which there is some uncertainty as to the accuracy of our authorized translation. Thus, in II Chron. 24:13, the word Ârûwkâh (אֲרוּכָה, 724) is generally understood to signify *health*. But our own language testifies to a relationship here, for health is wholeness. In Jer. 23:20, where the A.V. reads, "Ye shall consider it *perfectly*," we might better render the word Bîynah (בִּינָה, 998) *intelligently.* When the Psalmist says (in Ps. 138:8), "The LORD will perfect that which concerneth me," he uses the word Gâmar (גָּמַר, 1584—Assyrian *gamru*), *to finish,* implying his confidence that God, having begun the good work, will bring it to a successful issue. So Ezra is described as a *perfect,* i.e., a *finished,* scribe (Ezra 7:6).

In Prov. 4:18, the A.V. reads, "The path of the just is as the shining light, that shineth more and more unto the perfect day." This verse is sometimes understood as if it meant that the way of the righteous is like the sun, the light of which keeps increasing in brightness until the noonday. But the word Kûwn (כּוּן, 3559) here rendered *perfect* properly means *to fix* or *establish,* and the truth taught is that the way of the righteous is like the dawning light, which increases more and more in steadiness and brightness until the full

111

sun arises and thus establishes the day (LXX, ἕως κατορθώσῃ ἡ ἡμερα—2193, L-S 930A, 3588, 2250—*until the day fully dawns*).

Two words, nearly related to each other, and both signifying *completion* or *a consummation*, namely, Kâlâh (כָּלָה, 3615—Assyrian *kalû*) and Kâlal (כָּלַל, 3634—Assyrian *kalâlu*), are found several times in the Scriptures. Thus in Job 11:7 we read, "Canst thou find out the Almighty unto *perfection* [i.e., *entirely*]?" Note also the following texts: Job 28:3, "He searcheth out all perfection," meaning that nothing is hid from Him; Ps. 50:2, "Out of Zion the perfection [i.e., the climax] of beauty God hath shined"; Ps. 119:96, "I have seen an end of all perfection [i.e., I have thoroughly examined the utmost limits of all things human], but thy commandments are exceeding broad"; Ps. 139:22, "I hate them with a perfect [i.e., a consummate] hatred"; Lam. 2:15, "Is this the city that men call the perfection of beauty?" See also Ezek. 16:14; 27:3, 4, 11; 28:12.

These two words are usually rendered συντελέω (4931), συντέλεια (4930), ἐξαναλίσκω (L-S 584A—*spend entirely, exhaust, destroy utterly*), παύω (3973), and ἐκλείπω (1587) by the LXX.

The word συντέλεια (4930) occurs six times in the N.T., and always in one phrase—συντέλεια τοῦ αἰῶνος (4930, 3588, 165), or τῶν αἰώνων (3588, 165), "the end of the world [age(s)]." Five of these passages are in Matthew's Gospel (13:39, 40, 49; 24:3; 28:20). In Heb. 9:26, we might render the words "now once on the completion of the ages [or dispensations]" (νῦν δε ἅπαξ ἐπὶ συντελείᾳ τῶν αἰώνων— 3568, 1161, 530, 1909, 4930, 3588, 165). The Vulgate, *consummatio saeculi*, "the consummation of the age," is an admirable rendering of the Greek, and well sustains the meaning of the Hebrew Kâlâh (3615). The German word for perfection or *completion*, *Vollkommenheit*, answers well to Kâlâh (3615) and συντελέω (4931), but it has not been retained in the passages now noted.

§2. *The Word* Shâlam

We now come to one of the most notable words used to represent the idea of perfection, namely, Shâlam (שָׁלַם, 7999). It is used of a perfect heart in fourteen passages. Its usual signification is *peace*, the name *Salem* (Shâlêm, 8004—early name for Jerusalem) being derived from it. Thus we read in Isa. 26:3, "Thou wilt keep him in perfect peace" (Shâlôwm Shâlôwm—7965, 7965). The root may have originally signified *oneness* or *wholeness*, and so *completeness*. Not only does it represent the ideas of peace and perfection, but also of compensation or recompense.[1]

The following renderings have also been given to the verb **Shâlam** (7999) in the A.V.: *to be ended, to be finished, to prosper, to make amends, to pay, to perform, to recompense, to repay, to requite, to make restitution, to restore, to reward.* In all these cases there is implied a bringing of some difficulty to a conclusion, a finishing off of some work, a clearing away—by payment or labor or suffering—of some charge.

In Prov. 11:31 we read, "the righteous shall be recompensed in the earth; much more the wicked and the sinner." Here we have for the righteous *recompense* or, according to the LXX, *salvation,* or, we might say, *peace* on earth. But the messenger of peace to the righteous conveys by implication a presage of wrath to the wicked. The LXX rendering of these words is adopted by Peter when he says, "If the righteous scarcely be saved, where shall the ungodly and the sinner appear?" (I Pet. 4:18).

The chief representatives of **Shâlam** (7999) in the LXX are ἀπο-δίδωμι (591), *to render;* ἀνταποδίδωμι (467), *to recompense;*[2] ἀποτίω (661), *to retaliate;* ὑγιαίνω (5198), *to be whole* or *in health;* εἰρήνη, (1515), *peace;* σωτήριον (4992), *salvation;* τέλειος (5046), *perfect;* and ὁλόκληρος (3648), *whole,* which last word is found in the phrase "whole stones" in Deut. 27:6 and Josh. 8:31.

§3. *The Word* Tâmam

The word **Tâmam** (תָּמַם, 8552), whence the name of the *Thummim* (8550—perfections) is derived, is best rendered by the words *unblemished, entire* (cf. Latin, *integer*), and *sincere.* Our translators render it, in one or other of its forms, *perfect, plain, undefiled, upright, integrity, simplicity, full, at a venture, without blemish, sincere, sound, without spot, whole, to be consumed, to be accomplished, to end, to fail, to be spent, to be wasted.*

The following are the most noteworthy passages in which it occurs: Gen. 6:9, "Noah was a just man, and perfect in his generation"; Gen. 17:1, "Walk before me, and be thou perfect" (Luther,

---

1. In Assyrian, *salâmu* means "to perfect or complete," *salimu* means "peace"; but the initial letters are slightly different, answering to שׁ and ס.

2. This word occurs as a rendering for **Shâlam** (7999) in Deut. 32:35: "I will repay, saith the LORD"—words twice quoted in the N.T. (see Rom. 12:19 and Heb. 10:30).

Fromm, i.e., *pious*); Lev. 22:21, "The sacrifice . . . shall be perfect to be accepted; there shall be no blemish therein"; Deut. 18:13, "Thou shalt be perfect with the LORD thy God"; Deut. 32:4, "He is the Rock, his work is perfect"; I Sam. 14:41, "Give a perfect lot" (R.V. Shew the right); II Sam. 22:31, "As for God, his way is perfect" (in verses 24 and 26 the same word is rendered *upright*); II Sam. 22:33, "He maketh my way perfect" (cf. Ps. 18:30, 32); Job 1:1, "That man was perfect and upright" (see v. 8; 2:3); Job 8:20, "Behold, God will not cast away a perfect man"; Job 9:20–22, "If I say I am perfect, it shall also prove me perverse. Though [if] I were perfect, yet would I not know my soul. . . . He destroyeth the perfect and the wicked"; (see also 22:3; 36:4; 37:16); Ps. 15:2, "He that walketh uprightly" (cf. Prov. 2:7; 10:9; Amos 5:10); Ps. 19:7, "The law of the LORD is perfect"; Ps. 37:37, "Mark the perfect man, and behold the upright." See also Ps. 64:4; 101:2, 6; Prov. 2:21; 11:5; Isa. 18:5; 47:9; Ezek. 28:15.

The LXX represents the Thummim (8550) three times by ἀλήθεια (225),[3] and once by τελείωσις (5050). The verb **Tâmam** (8552) is rendered ἐκλείπω (1587) and συντελέω (4931).

The adjectival form of the word is generally rendered ἄμωμος (299), *unblemished;* but τέλειος (5046) occurs in several passages, and ἄμεμπτος (273) in a few. In I Kings 6:22, we meet with the word συντέλεια (4930); and in Isa. 1:6, we find ὁλοκληρία (3647), *wholeness.*

§4. *Teaching of the N.T.*

The ideas included in the word **Shâlam** (7999) are prominent in the N.T. There is one remarkable passage in which perfection and oneness are combined together, namely, John 17:23, where the Lord Jesus prays with respect to His disciples that they may be "perfected in one," or, more literally, "completed into one." The same idea runs through the N.T.; the perfection of each part of the body depends upon the completeness of the whole, and vice versa (I John 4:2). Christ is "our peace" because He has made both (i.e., both Jew and Gentile) one, and has done away with the middle wall of partition. The twain He has created in Himself into one new man, so making

3. It was remarked by Hody that the rendering ἀλήθεια (225) for Thummim (8550) was a proof of the *Alexandrine* character of the early part of the LXX. Aelian tells us that Egyptian magistrates used to wear a carved sapphire stone round their neck, and that it was called ἀλήθεια (225). The Urim (224) and Thummim (8550) are *manifestation* and *truth* in the Greek, *doctrine* and *truth* in the Latin, *light* and *right* in the German.

peace, and has reconciled both in one body to God by means of the Cross (Eph. 2:14–16). There is one body, the Church, and one Spirit, in whom both Jew and Gentile have access to the Father through Christ. While the Gospel develops *individuality*, it represses *isolation*. The whole body of disciples (ὁ πάντες —3588, 3956—all) will become a complete man (Eph. 4:13). And every man is to be presented complete, not in himself, but in Christ Jesus (Col. 1:28). For from Christ, who is the Head, the whole body gets its sustenance (Eph. 4:16).

There are some passages in the N.T. in which the word τέλειος (5046) marks an advanced stage of development in spiritual things, and is applied to those who are "grown up," as opposed to those who are children and only partly informed. Perhaps we may read in this sense our Lord's words to the young man, "If thou wilt be perfect [or mature], go sell that thou hast" (Matt. 19:21). Consider also the following texts: I Cor. 2:6, "Though our preaching is foolishness in the eyes of the world, yet it is wisdom in the judgment of the mature"; I Cor. 14:20, "In understanding be [not children, but] mature"; Phil. 3:15, "As many as are mature, let us be thus minded"; Heb. 5:14, "Strong meat is for them that are mature" (i.e., that have emerged out of the state of infancy). In these passages the word answers to the Hebrew root **Kâlâh** (3615), rather than to **Shâlam** (7999).

The word τελείωσις (5050) occurs only twice in the N.T. The first passage is Luke 1:45, where it signifies the accomplishment of God's promises; the other is Heb. 7:11, where we read that if there had been τελείωσις (5050), *completeness*, by means of the Levitical priesthood, there would have been no necessity for the raising up of a priest after an order other than that of Aaron. The priest bore the τελείωσις (5050) or Thummim (8550) on his breastplate, but it was only the shadow of which Christ gives us the substance. Completeness is attainable only through the Savior. He himself was perfected[4] for the work of the priesthood through suffering (Heb. 2:10), and

---

4. Some render the word τελειόω (5048) *to consecrate* in this and other passages; and they have the LXX as authority for so doing. See, for example, Exod. 29:22, 26, 27, 31, 34, 36, where it answers to the Hebrew expression *to fill the hands,* i.e., to *consecrate;* τὰς χέρας (3588, 5495—*the hands*) is added in some cases, but not in others. But it must be borne in mind that in our Lord's case His being perfected through suffering was His consecration. In fact, the Levitical formal solemnity of consecration has given way to the process of learning obedience by the things suffered. By this means our Lord was constituted a perfect High Priest, one that could sympathize with all the troubles and temptations of His people in that He Himself had suffered, being tempted.

being thus perfected, He became the Author or Cause of eternal salvation to all that obey Him (5:9).

The word ἄμωμος (299), "free from blemish," is not only used of Christ, who offered Himself without spot to God (Heb. 9:14 and I Peter 1:19), but also of Christians, who are to be ἅγιοι (40), or separate from the evil of the world, and ἄμωμοι (299), or free from moral blemishes (Eph. 1:4; 5:27; Phil. 2:15; Col. 1:22; Jude 24; Rev. 14:5).

The word ἄμεμπτος (273) is used of blameless characters. It is applied in Luke 1:6 to Zacharias and Elizabeth, and in Phil. 3:6 to Saul the Pharisee. In Phil. 2:15 and I Thess. 3:13, it is set forth as the characteristic of the true Christian, and as applicable to the heart as well as to the outward life. Compare also the uses of the adverbial form in I Thess. 2:10 and 5:23. In Heb. 8:7, 8, it serves to mark the contrast between the two dispensations: "If the first had no fault to be found in it [ἄμεμπτος, 273], place would not have been sought for a second; [but this is not the case] for finding fault [μεμφόμενος 3201], he saith, Behold, the days come. . . ."

The word ὁλοκληρία (3647) is used of the wholeness or perfect soundness of the body in Acts 3:16. And the adjective (ὁλόκληρος, 3648) is used in James 1:4, where it is coupled with τέλειος (5046). It is also in I Thess. 5:23, where Paul prays for the saints, that their complete spirit, soul, and body may be preserved (so as to be) blameless at the appearing of Christ.

It will thus be seen that the standard of perfection set before all Christians in the N.T. is very high indeed, no room being left for any wrongdoing; but the promise of indispensable spiritual power is equally explicit (II Cor. 12:9).

9

Righteousness, Faith, Hope

The subjects discussed in the present chapter will be found to group themselves around three leading ideas that lie at the foundation of that which is right, as it is set before man in Scripture. First, we are given a conception of rectitude, or the keeping to a straight and even line, as opposed to depravity, which swerves from the appointed course. Second, we are presented with an idea of fixedness, stability, and realization of the Truth of God, as contrasted with that which is transient, uncertain, and illusory. And third, there is set forth a spirit of dependence on Him who is the Source of Right and Truth.

§1. *Uprightness*

The idea of rectitude or uprightness is presented by the word **Yâshâr** (יָשָׁר, 3477), whence the names *Jasher* (3477) and *Jeshurun* (3484) are derived. (In Assyrian, *esiru* is *to go straight*, and *isaru* is *upright*.) This word is found wherever the A.V. uses the word *equity*, except in Eccles. 2:21 and Isa. 59:14 (cf. Isa. 26:10 and 57:2), where other words of the same significance are used.

Yâshâr (3477) is rendered *just* in Prov. 29:10. It is rendered *righteous* in Num. 23:10: "Let me die the death of the righteous." See also Job 4:7; 23:7; Ps. 67:4; 96:10; 107:42; Prov. 2:7; 3:32; 14:19; 15:19; 28:10.

The LXX renders the verb **Yâshar** (יָשַׁר, 3474) by ἀρέσκω (700), κατευθύνω (2720), and κατορθόω (L-S 929B—*to set upright*). It is also rendered by ὀρθοτομέω (3718) in two passages, namely, Prov. 3:6 ("He shall *direct* your paths") and 11:5 ("The righteousness of the perfect shall *direct* his way"). The noun is usually rendered εὐθύς (2117), but we also find ὀρθός (3717), ἀληθινός (228), ἀρεστός (701), and δίκαιος (1342).

The verb κατευθύνω (2720) is used only three times in the N.T. (Luke 1:79; I Thess. 3:11; II Thess. 3:5), and on each occasion reference is made to the work of God in rightly directing the heart and ways of man. In II Tim. 2:15, where we meet with the word ὀρθοτομέω (3718), the A.V. renders the passage "rightly dividing the word of truth." Some commentators have illustrated the word in this passage by the work of the carpenter or the stonemason; but it is probable that the LXX is the best guide in the matter. If so, we may render it "rightly directing the word of truth," i.e., setting it forth in upright-ness. Compare Gossner's version, where we find *verfährt* (handling), and the Vulgate, *recte tractantem* (rightly handling). The work of the plowman gives a good illustration of Paul's meaning. See A.S.V. and compare Luke 9:62.

§2. Righteousness

The renderings *righteous* and *just* usually stand for some form of the word **Tsâdaq** (צָדַק, 6663), which originally signified *to be stiff* or *straight* and whence the names compounded with **Tsedek** (צֶדֶק, 6664) such as Zedekiah (6667—*Righteousness of Jehovah*) and Mel-chizedek (4442—*King of Righteousness*) are derived. It is rendered *lawful* in Isa. 49:24, *moderately* in Joel 2:23, and *right* in several passages. It is unfortunate that the English language should have grafted the Latin word *justice* (which is used in somewhat of a forensic sense) into a vocabulary that was already possessed of the good word *righteousness*, since it tends to create a distinction that has no existence in Scripture. This quality indeed may be viewed, according to Scripture, in two lights. First, in its relative aspect it implies conformity with the line or rule of God's law. Second, in its absolute aspect it is the exhibition of love to God and to one's neighbor, because love is the fulfilling of the law. But in neither of these senses does the word convey what we usually mean by justice. No distinction between the claims of justice and the claims of love is recognized in Scripture. To act in opposition to the principles of love to God and one's neighbor is to commit an injustice, because it is a departure from the course marked out by God in His law.

For a further discussion of the word and of its Greek representative δικαιοσύνη (1343), viewed in relation to the doctrine of justification, see Chapter 14, §1.

§3. *Judgment*

Mishpât (מִשְׁפָּט, 4941), which signifies the due administration of judgment (see Chap. 21, §2), is rendered *right* in the A.V. in the following passages: Gen. 18:25, "Shall not the Judge of all the earth do right?"; Job 34:6, "Should I lie against my right?"; Job 34:17, "Shall even he that hateth right govern?"; Job 35:2, "Thinkest thou this to be right?"; Ps. 9:4, "Thou hast maintained my right"; Prov. 12:5, "The thoughts of the righteous are right"; Prov. 16:8, "Better is a little with righteousness than great revenues without right"; Isa. 10:2, "To take away the right from the poor of my people." See also Isa. 32:7; Jer. 5:28; 17:11; 32:7, 8; Lam. 3:35; Ezek. 21:27.

Kâshêr (כָּשֵׁר, 3787), that which is fitting, is rendered *right* in the A.V. in Esther 8:5 and Eccles. 4:4. **Nâkôwn** (נָכוֹן—from Kûwn—כּוּן, 3559), *stability*, is found in Job 42:7, 8: Ps. 78:37. It is also found in Ps. 51:10, where we read, "renew a right [i.e., a stable] spirit within me"—a suitable prayer for one who had fallen through instability. The same word occurs in Ps. 5:9, where the A.V. reads, "There is no faithfulness in their mouth." Compare the use of the derivative **Kênîym** (כֵּנִים, from כֵּן, 3651) in the expression "we be all *true men*," i.e., men to be relied upon, in Gen. 42:11, 19, 31, and 34.

§4. *Truth*

The general Hebrew word for truth or truthfulness, and faith or faithfulness, is a derivative of the verb **Âman** (אָמַן, 539—Assyrian *amanu*), whence the word **Âmên** (אָמֵן, 543) draws its origin. **Âman** (539) in its simple active form signifies *to nurse* or *nourish up; in the* passive, *to be firm* or *established,* and hence *steadfast* (Prov. 11:13); and in the Hiphil or causative form, *to take as established,* and hence *to regard as true, to realize,* or *to believe.* The last is its most general rendering. The A.V. translates it *to have assurance* in Deut. 28:66 and *to trust* in Judg. 11:20; Job 4:18; 12:20; 15:15,31; Micah 7:5. A form of this word is translated *pillars* in II Kings 18:16 (cf. I Tim. 3:15, "the pillar and ground of the truth").

In Dan. 3:14, where the A.V. reads, "Is it *true,* O Shadrach?" another word (צְדָא, 6656) is used that signifies *purpose* or *intentionally.* In various places in Daniel (3:24; 6:12; 7:16, 19) **Yatstsîyb** (יַצִּיב, 3330), *to be firm* or *settled,* is rendered *true.*

The form **'Emeth** (אֱמֶת, 571—from 539) is usually rendered *truth,* but is translated *right* in Gen. 24:48; Neh. 9:33; Jer. 2:21. The form **'Ĕmûwnâh** (אֱמוּנָה, 530—from 539), generally rendered *faithfulness,* is found in Hab. 2:4,[1] where we read, "The just shall live by his faith." These words ought to be read in connection with the fifth verse of the first chapter, "I will work a work in your days which ye will not believe, though it be told you." **'Ĕmûwnâh** (530) is used of the steadiness of the hands of Moses in Exod. 17:12, and of the stability of the times in Isa. 33:6. In several other passages it is used of God's *faithfulness,* and it would have been well if this rendering had been adopted (instead of *truth*) in Deut. 32:4; Ps. 33:4; 96:13; 98:3; 100:5; 119:30. See also Prov. 12:17.

The LXX almost always adopts πιστεύω (4100), *to believe,* as the rendering for the causative form of **Âman** (539), as in Gen. 15:6 where it first occurs. The adjective is sometimes rendered πιστός (4103), *faithful;* and sometimes ἀληθινός (228), *real* or *true.* When these two Greek words come together in the N.T. as characterizing the glorified Son of God, they express the Hebrew word in all its fullness, and answer to the *Amen,* by which title He is also described.[2] The substantive is usually πίστις (4102), *faith,* but sometimes ἀλήθεια (225), *truth.*

§5. *Trust*

Passing from the idea of faith to that of trust, a few exceptional

---

1. This passage might be rendered "the righteous [man] shall live in his faithfulness." The note on the text in Poole's *Synopsis* is as follows: *"Qui bonus probusque est manebit constans in expectatione eorum quae dixi"* (translation: "the good and upright man will continue firm in the expectation of those things which I have declared"). Certainly faith, in this passage, is something more than a bare acquiescence in God's word. It is such a belief in the revealed word of God as brings the man into contact with the Divine life, and so breathes righteousness or conformity to God's law into his heart. It worketh, as Paul says, by love. Compare Bishop Lightfoot's *Excursus* on faith in his commentary on the Epistle to the Galatians.

2. See Rev. 3:14; also 19:11; 21:5; 22:6. **Âmên** (543) is usually rendered ἀληθῶς (230), *verily,* or γένοιτο (1096), *so be it,* in the LXX; and only three times do we find the word in its Greek form' Ἀμήν (281). Dr. Sayce points out that at the end of many Babylonian hymns we find *amanu.*

renderings in the A.V. may be noted in the first instance. In Ps. 22:8, "He trusted on the LORD," the word Gâlal (גָּלַל, 1556), *to roll*, is used. In Job 35:14, "Trust thou in him," the word is Chûwl (חוּל, 2342), *"stay* thou [or *wait* thou] upon him." Yâchal (יָחַל, 3176), *to hope*, occurs in Job 13:15, "Though he slay me, yet will I trust in him." It is also found in Isa. 51:5, "On mine arm shall they trust."

Châçâh (חָסָה, 2620), *to flee for refuge*, is rendered *trust* in the A.V. in above thirty passages, out of which number twenty-four occur in the Psalms. It is often used where God is compared to a rock or a shield, or where the saint is described as taking refuge "under the shadow of his wings." It is used in Ps. 2:12 ("Blessed are all they that put their trust in him"), where we are taught that the Son affords that same kind of shelter or protection that the Father gives. Compare Ps. 34:8, where the same words are applied to Jehovah. The word is also used in Ps. 118:8 ("It is better to trust in the LORD than to put any confidence in man"); Isa. 14:32; 57:13; Zeph. 3:12.

The most general word, however, to express trust is Bâṭach (בָּטַח, 982), *to confide in* or *lean upon*.[3] Here it is to be remarked that though we are in the habit of speaking of faith and trust as the same thing, the Hebrew has two distinct words for them; and so has the LXX. While 'Âman (539) answers to πιστεύω (4100), *to believe* or *realize*, Bâṭach (982), *to trust*, is never so rendered. Nor is the substantive derived from it ever rendered πίστις (4102). For the verb we generally find ἐλπίζω (1679), *to hope*, or πείθομαι (3982), *to be persuaded;* and for the noun we have ἐλπίς (1680), *hope*. The man who believes God is he who, having received a revelation from Him, realizes it, and acts on it as true. The man who trusts God is he who casts all his hopes for the present and future on God. It is the former quality, not the latter, that God regards as a condition of justification. Faith must precede hope, because a hope for the future that is not grounded on a present acceptance with God is no hope; and a sense of acceptance that is not accompanied with a living, working faith is an unreality.

§6. *Hope*

The words ordinarily rendered *hope* in the A.V. are Qâvâh (קָוָה, 6960—Assyrian *qû*) and Yâchal (יָחַל, 3176). The first, which is fre-

---

3. Dr. Sayce says that this root is replaced in Assyrian by *takalu*, e.g., *ina tukulli Assuri*, "in reliance on Assur."

quently used in the Psalms, signifies the straining of the mind in a certain direction in an expectant attitude. The second, which occurs several times in the Book of Job, signifies a long patient waiting. The former is generally rendered ὑπομένω (5278); the latter is usually rendered ἐλπίζω (1679), but often also ὑπομένω (5278).

§7. *Teaching of the N.T.*

We now approach the N.T. with a clear distinction between faith on the one hand, and trust and hope on the other. Faith is taking God at His word. Trust and patience and hope are the proper fruits of faith, manifesting in various forms that confidence the believer feels. A message comes to me from the Author of my existence; it may be a threat, a promise, or a command. If I take it as "yea and amen," that is *faith;* and the act that results is an act of 'Ĕmûwnâh (530) or *faithfulness* toward God. Faith, according to Scripture, seems to imply a word, message, or revelation. So the learned Romaine says in his *Life of Faith:*

> Faith signifies the believing the truth of the Word of God; it relates to some word spoken or to some promise made by Him, and it expresses the belief which a person who hears it has of its being true; he assents to it, relies upon it, and acts accordingly: this is faith.

Its fruit will vary according to the nature of the message received, and according to the circumstances of the receiver. It led Noah to build an ark, Abraham to offer up his son, Moses to refuse to be called the son of Pharaoh's daughter, the Israelites to march round the walls of Jericho. "I believe God that it shall be even as it has been told me"[4]—this is a picture of that process which the Bible calls faith. It is the expectation (ὑπόστασις, 5287) of things *hoped for,* because it accepts God's promises concerning the future as true; and it is the conviction (ἔλεγχος, 1650) of what is (*trusted,* but) not seen, because those who have it do not depend on the use of their senses, but are able to endure, "as seeing Him who is invisible" (see Heb. 11).

In the Gospels the Lord Jesus demands to be believed. He asks all men to take Him to be what He claimed to be. If they would only

4. Acts 27:25.

take Him as true, they would be in the way of receiving and entering into a new life. He said, "I am the Truth" (John 14:6). All that Israel had to believe under the old dispensation was summed up in Him. If they believed Moses, they would believe Him. If they rejected Him, they were doing dishonor to God. Sin sprang from a disbelief of God's word. Christ came to manifest, in a life of love and purity and in a death of self-sacrifice, what God had really said, and what His feelings toward man actually were. Those that accepted the truth, as it was revealed in Jesus Christ, entered into life.

The Book of Acts carries this teaching a stage further by exhibiting the special facts that were prominently put forward as things to be believed. These facts were the mission, the death, and the resurrection of Jesus Christ as the ground of pardon, the way of life, and the pledge of an inheritance beyond the grave.

The Epistles enter more fully into details, answer different questions, expound doctrines, apply sacred truths to the exigencies of daily life. But all is summed up in Christ; "Whosoever takes him to be true shall not be ashamed" (Rom. 9:33, quoted from Isa. 28:16).

The word *hope* barely exists in the Gospels, but it is frequently to be found in the later books of the N.T. In Rom. 15:12, the Apostle quotes from the LXX version of Isa. 11:10 the words, "In him shall the Gentiles hope."[5] He then pronounces this blessing: "Now the God of hope fill you with all joy and peace in believing." In the A.V. the point of the connection is missed by the substitution of the word *trust* for *hope* in the first part of the passage. But there is no objection to this rendering in itself; for though ἐλπίζω (1679) represents trust with reference to the future, while πείθομαι (3982) represents confidence with regard to the present, yet they are both renderings of one Hebrew word, as we have just seen, and cannot be separated by a very strong line.

In Acts 2:26, Peter quotes from Psalm 16 the words, "My flesh also shall rest [or dwell] in hope [κατασκηνώσει ἐπ' ἐλπίδι—2681, 1909, 1680]." This expression, "in hope," is repeated several times, being applied to Abraham (Rom. 4:18), to Christians (Acts 26:6; Rom. 5:2; Titus 1:2), to Gospel ministers (I Cor. 9:10), and to creation itself (Rom. 8:20). All hope is concentrated in Christ (I Tim. 1:1; Col. 1:27) and looks for the unseen realities of another world (Rom. 8:24), even the resurrection (Acts 24:15), eternal life (Titus 3:7), and glory (Rom.

5. Here the Hebrew word is Dârash (1875), *to seek.*

5:2). The word *hope* as used in ordinary conversation has an element of uncertainty in it, but the Christian's hope is absolute confidence. The two Greek renderings of the Hebrew word **Yâchal** (3176) named above (§6), ἐλπίς (1680) and ὑπομονή (5281), are found together in I Thess. 1:3.

10

Grace, Mercy, Love

The Bible is preeminently occupied in setting forth the gracious feelings with which God regards the children of men. It depicts the Divine emotions not in the abstract, but as manifested in action. It also teaches that those who have tasted of God's grace and love and mercy are bound to exercise the same dispositions towards their fellowmen. They thus become in reality children of God, and are conformed to the nature of Him from whom their new life is drawn.

§1. *Grace*

Grace is the free bestowal of kindness on one who has neither claim on our bounty, nor adequate compensation to make for it. Throughout the O.T., with the exception of Hos. 14:2, where the word rendered *graciously* signifies *goodness* (טוֹב, 2896), it stands for some form of Chânan (חָנַן, 2603), *to show favor.*[1] It is often coupled with Râcham (רָחַם, 7355), a word that signifies a tender feeling of pity. These three words answer to the Assyrian *thabu, 'annu, rêmu.* The adjectival form, Channûwn (חַנּוּן, 2587, from 2603), *gracious,* is used only of God, and denotes the action that springs from His free and unmerited love to His creatures. The verb is rendered *pity* in Prov. 19:17: "He that hath pity upon the poor lendeth unto the Lord." Here the writer is not speaking of commiseration, but rather of the kindly dealing of one who "hopes for nothing again." It is also

---

1. Hence the name *Jo-hanan* (3076, 3110—John—"Jehovah showed favor" or "whom Jehovah gave"), and its inverted form, *Hanan-iah* (2608—"favor [or gift] of Jehovah").

used in Job 19:21 and Prov. 28:8, where it might be rendered *deal graciously* (*with*). Other renderings for this word in the A.V. are *to be favorable, to be merciful,* and (in the causative form) to *beseech, supplicate,* and *pray.* The LXX has ἐλεήμων (*1655*) for the adjective, but χάρις (*5485*) for the noun. The Greek χάρις (*5485*), and the English *grace* or *favor,* well represent the word. Only we must be on our guard against the supposition that *grace* is an abstract quality; it is an active personal principle, showing itself in our dealings with those by whom we are surrounded.

The adverb *graciously* is usually rendered δωρεὰν (*1432*) in the LXX. This word reappears in the N.T.: Matt. 10:8, "Freely ye have received, freely give"; Rom. 3:24, "Being justified freely by his grace"; Rev. 22:17, "Let him take the water of life freely." A secondary meaning that the Greek adverb has received is *without a cause.* In this sense we meet with it in John 15:25, "They hated me without a cause," words quoted from Ps. 69:4; also in Gal. 2:21, "then Christ died in vain [or causelessly]." We occasionally use the English word *gratuitous* in this sense, as when we speak of a gratuitous insult.

The verbal form is rendered χαρίζομαι (*5483*) in the LXX. This word occurs several times in the N.T. to indicate an exhibition of free grace, whether in the form of healing (Luke 7:21), or of remitting a debt (Luke 7:42), or of the loosing of a prisoner (Acts 3:14), of making a gift (Rom. 8:32; I Cor. 2:12), or of pardon (II Cor. 2:10; Eph. 4:32). Χαριτόω (*5487*), *to deal graciously,* is not an O.T. word (though found in the Apocrypha), but occurs in Luke 1:28 and Eph. 1:6.

An act done with any expectation of a return from the object on which it is wrought, or one that is meted out as a matter of justice, recompense, or reward, is not an act of grace. This is specially noted in Rom. 11:6. Compare also the words of our Lord: "If ye love them that love you, what *grace* [A.V. and R.V. *thank*] have you?" (Luke 6:32; see also vv. 33, 34). So Peter says, "This is grace [A.V. thankworthy, R.V. acceptable], if a man through consciousness of God endure pains, suffering unjustly" (I Pet. 2:19).

In the great proportion of passages in which the word *grace* is found in the N.T., it signifies the unmerited operation of God in the heart of man, effected through the agency of the Holy Spirit. We have gradually come to speak of grace as an inherent quality in man, just as we talk of gifts; whereas it is in reality the communication of Divine goodness by the inworking of the Spirit and through the medium of Him who is "full of grace and truth."

§2. *Pity*

Râcham (7355) expresses a deep and tender feeling of compassion, such as is aroused by the sight of weakness or suffering in those who are dear to us or need our help. It is rendered *pity*[2] or *pitiful* in a few passages: Ps. 103:13, "Like as a father pitieth his children, so the LORD pitieth them that fear him"; Ps. 106:46, "He made them also to be pitied of all those that carried them captives"; Lam. 4:10, "The hands of the pitiful women have sodden [boiled] their own children." It is curious that the word *pitiful* should have had its meaning so altered in modern times as to be hardly understood in the passage last cited.

Râcham (7355) is rendered *mercy* several times, and is the origin of the word Ruhâmâh (רֻחָמָה, 7355), which occurs in Hos. 2:1. Jacob used it to express his strong feeling on sending Benjamin with his brothers into Egypt: "God Almighty give you mercy before the man, that he may send away your other brother, and Benjamin" (Gen. 43:14). It is an element in the character of God, who shows mercy on whom He will show mercy (Exod. 34:6; Deut. 4:31). Accordingly David says, "Let us fall now into the hands of God, for his mercies are abounding" (II Sam. 24:14). Mercy (Latin, *misericordia*) is really the same thing as pity, though the words have gradually assumed rather different senses.

Râcham (7355) also represents the beautiful expression *tender mercy* wherever it occurs. Thus the Psalmist prays, "According to the multitude of thy tender mercies blot out my transgressions" (Ps. 51:1). It is the only word rendered *mercy* (with two exceptions, Jer. 3:12 and Dan. 4:27) in the prophetical books of the O.T., being specially used in them to mark the tenderness with which God regards His people in their downcast condition. It is rendered *compassion* and *bowels of compassion* in nearly all passages where these expressions are found in the A.V. (with the exception of Exod. 2:6; I Sam. 23:21; II Chron. 36:15, 17; and Ezek. 16:5, where a less forceful word (חָמַל, 2550) is used. Râcham (7355) has twice been rendered *love*, in Ps. 18:1 and Dan. 1:9. With regard to the first of these passages—"I will love thee, O LORD, my strength"—the word seems at first sight out of place, because there can be no element of pity in man's love to God. But it expresses here the depth and tenderness

2. The English word *pity* is really *piety*.

of the Psalmist's feeling; and it may be observed that in this passage the word is not in the Piel or intensive stem (as in all other passages), but in the Qal, or simple active stem.

The most prominent rendering for **Râcham** (7355) in the LXX is οἰκτιρμός (3628). This word occurs five times in the N.T., twice as an attribute of God (Rom. 12:1 and II Cor. 1:3), and three times as a quality to be manifested in our dealings with one another (Phil. 2:1; Col. 3:12; see also Heb. 10:28).

§3. *Love*

The general word for love in the O.T. is **Âhab** (אָהַב, 157), from which it has been supposed that its Greek representative ἀγάπη (26) is derived; but compare **Âgab** (5689) below. It indicates desire, inclination, or affection, whether human or Divine. In Amos 4:5, it has been rendered by the weaker English word *like*. In a few passages the participial form has been rendered *friend:* II Sam. 19:6, "Thou lovest thine enemies, and hatest thy friends"; II Chron. 20:7 (cf. Isa. 41:8), "Thou gavest thy land to the seed of Abraham thy friend," an expression James singled out for comment in his Epistle (2:23); Zech. 13:6, "I was wounded in the house of my friends." See also Esther 5:10, 14; 6:13; Prov. 14:20; 27:6; Jer. 20:4, 6. In these passages intimacy and affection, the cleaving of soul to soul, is implied, and *lovers* rather than *acquaintances* are designated. Occasionally the LXX adopts φιλέω (5368) instead of ἀγαπάω (25), but never where God's love is concerned.

Other words pertaining to love in the A.V. are as follows: **Yᵉdîyd** (יָדִיד, 3039), whence the name *Jedidiah* (**Yᵉdîydᵉyâh**, 3041); **Reaʻ** (רֵעַ, 7453—Assyrian *rû*), a companion (Song of Sol. 1:9, 15; 2:10, 13; 5:2; 6:4; Jer. 3:1); **Âgab** (עָגַב, 5689), used of impure love, and rendered *doting* (in Ezek. 23:12; 33:31, 32); **Châshaq** (חָשַׁק, 2836), *to join together* (Ps. 91:14); **Dôwdîym** (דּוֹדִים, 1730—Assyrian *dadu*), the *impulse* of the heart, or of sexual affection (Prov. 7:18; Ezek. 16:8); and **Cheçed** (2617), *mercy.*

The Greek ἀγάπη (26) is in a measure consecrated by the fact that it makes its first appearance in the LXX, being apparently unknown to early classical authors. It is used in the N.T. to designate the essential nature of God, His regard for mankind, and also the most marked characteristic of the Divine life as manifested in Christ and in Christians. It is unfortunate that English, along with some other languages, should have accepted two renderings for this important word. The Latin word *charity* was introduced as an alternative for the good old Saxon word *love*, but it has arisen through fear lest spiritual love should be confused with sensuous affection. The Greek ἔρως (L-S 695B) is never used in the Bible except in Prov. 7:18 and 30:16.

The word φιλέω (*5368*) is rarely used in the N.T. But see I Cor. 16:22, and especially John 21:15–17, where the distinction between love and friendship is noticeable in the Greek, but is lost in the English and other versions.

§4. *Mercy*

We have now to consider the word Châçad (חָסַד, 2616), which is used in various forms to designate God's dealings with man, and also to indicate the mode in which men ought to deal with one another. The meaning of this word when used as a substantive (Cheçed, 2617) is made clear from the fact that the LXX has rendered it ἔλεος (*1656*), *mercy*, in 135 passages. The nature of the quality may be illustrated by the conduct of the Good Samaritan, "the one who shewed the mercy" (ὁ ποιήσας τὸ ἔλεος—*3588, 4160, 3588, 1656*) on him who was attacked by robbers (Luke 10:37). It is a practical exhibition of lovingkindness toward our fellowman, whose only claim may be misfortune and whom it is in our power to help, though perhaps at the expense of time, money, convenience, and even religious or national prejudice.

The general English renderings for the word in the A.V. are these: *kindness, mercy, pity, favor, goodness,* and *lovingkindness*. It is often found united with righteousness, faithfulness, truth, compassion, and other Divine qualities.

A few instances may be cited to illustrate its usage: Gen. 24:12, "O LORD God . . . shew kindness unto my master Abraham"; Gen. 24:27, "Blessed be the LORD God of my master Abraham, who hath not left my master destitute of his mercy [LXX δικαιοσύνη, *1343*] and truth"; Gen. 24:49, "If ye will deal kindly and truly with my master, tell me"; Gen. 39:21, "The LORD was with Joseph, and shewed him mercy"; Gen. 40:14, "Shew kindness unto me, and make mention of me unto Pharaoh"; Exod. 20:6, "Shewing mercy unto thousands of them that love me, and keep my commandments"; Num. 14:19, "Pardon, I beseech thee, the iniquity of this people according unto the greatness of thy mercy"; Josh. 2:12, "Swear unto me by the LORD, since I have shewed you kindness, that ye will also shew kindness unto my father's house"; Job 6:14, "To him that is afflicted pity should be shewed from his friend"; Job 10:12, "Thou hast granted me life and favor"; Ps. 5:7, "I will come into thy house in the multitude of thy mercy"; Ps. 6:4, "Oh save me for thy mercies' sake"; Ps. 13:5, "I have trusted in thy mercy"; Ps. 32:10, "He that trusteth in the LORD, mercy shall compass him about"; Ps. 89:33, "My lovingkindness will I not utterly take from him"; Ps. 89:49, "Lord, where are thy former lovingkindnesses?"; Ps. 119:159, "Quicken me, O LORD, according to thy lovingkindness" (cf. v. 88); Hos. 4:1, "There is no truth nor mercy"; Hos. 6:4, "Your goodness is as a morning dew" (the A.V. obscures the connection between this verse and the sixth, where the same word is found: "I desired mercy and not sacrifice"; see R.V. margin); Hos. 10:12, "Sow to yourselves in righteousness, reap in mercy"; Hos. 12:6, "Keep mercy and judgment"; Micah 6:8, "What doth the LORD require of thee, but to do justly, and to love mercy, and to walk humbly with thy God?"; Micah 7:18, "He delighteth in mercy"; Zech. 7:9, "Execute true judgment, and shew mercy and compassions every man to his brother."

These passages put the general signification of the word Cheçed (2617) beyond the shadow of a doubt. We now have to examine whether this meaning is to be enlarged or modified. The LXX adopts the rendering δικαιοσύνη (1343), righteousness, in Gen. 19:16 and some other places. We also find ἐλεημοσύνη (1654) and ἐλπίς (1680) in a few passages. In Isa. 40:6, where the word Cheçed (2617) is applied to the grace or goodliness of man that so soon fades away, the LXX has δόξα (1391), glory; and the passage is quoted by Peter in his first Epistle (1:24) according to this interpretation.

In the passages that remain to be considered, the adjectival form Châçîyd (2623) is found. This word must signify not only the reception but also the exercise of Cheçed (2617), just as Tsaddîyq (6662), righteous, signifies the reception and exercise of Tsedeq (6664), righteousness. If Cheçed (2617), then, means mercy, Châçîyd (2623) must mean merciful; and accordingly it is so translated in the A.V. in II Sam. 22:26 and in Ps. 18:25: "With the merciful thou wilt shew thyself merciful." The LXX, however, both in these passages and wherever the word Châçîyd (2623) is found, has adopted ὅσιος (3741), holy, as a rendering. This course has had a great influence upon other languages, as it has led translators to confound Châçîyd

(2623) and Qâdôwsh (6918), ὅσιος (3741) and ἅγιος (40), forgetting
that to a Jew the meaning of the Greek word ὅσιος (3741) would be
ruled by the fact that it was to be taken as an interpretation of the
Hebrew Châçîyd (2623), *merciful*. In the two passages just cited, the
A.V. retains the right rendering, but the Latin has *cum sancto* (*with
the saint* or *holy one*), and the German *Bei dem Heiligen* (*with the
holy ones* or *saints*). The Portuguese translator, D'Almeida, both here
and in almost all other places adopts the good word *Benigno* (*kindly*
or *benevolent one*), but he is quite an exception to the general
rule.

Our translators have followed the multitude in a large number of
instances. Thus in Ps. 145:17, we read, "The Lord is . . . holy in all his
works." Here the margin properly corrects the text by suggesting
merciful or *bountiful*. In Ps. 86:2 we read, "I am holy"; the margin
reads, "One whom thou favorest," but it would be better to read, "I
am merciful." The rendering *godly* has been adopted in Ps. 4:3, et
al.; and *saint* in II Chron. 6:41; Ps. 30:4, et al. This last rendering must
be regarded as unfortunate, because it serves to obliterate the real
meaning of the word and to confound it with another.

It has been held by distinguished scholars that Châçîyd (2623)
primarily signifies a *recipient* of mercy; but this meaning is not
always applicable, e.g., in Jer. 3:12, where God says of Himself, "I am
Châçîyd (2623)." *Here* it cannot mean, "I am a recipient of mercy";
our translators have rightly rendered the words, "I am merciful."
Nevertheless, the two aspects of mercy, its reception and its exercise,
are wonderfully blended in Scripture. The right and wholesome
effect of the enjoyment of God's lovingkindness is the exhibition of
the same spirit towards our fellows. God is everywhere described as
delighting in mercy—"his mercy endureth for ever"—but He requires that those to whom He shows it should, in their turn and
according to their opportunities, "love mercy" (cf. Micah 7:18 with
6:8).

It is a remarkable fact that the word Châçîyd (2623), when applied
to man, has usually a possessive pronoun affixed to it, so as to
indicate that the persons who are exercising this disposition belong
in a special sense to God. They are "his merciful ones" (A.V. "his
saints"). Merciful men may be very scarce (Ps. 12:1; Micah 7:2), but
wherever they are found they are regarded as God's own. "He hath
set apart him that is merciful for himself" (Ps. 4:3); and He gives His
special protection to those that are worthy of the name Châçîyd

(2623; Ps. 32:6; 37:28). They show their love to the Lord by hating evil (i.e., evil dealings against their neighbor), and the Lord, in His turn, preserves their souls (Ps. 97:10). When He comes to judgment He will gather to Himself those who are His merciful ones, and who have made a covenant with Him by sacrifice (Ps. 50:5); and they shall not only "rejoice in glory" (Ps. 149:5), but also shall have the honor of executing judgment on the nations (Ps. 149:9). In a word, mercy is the main characteristic of God's dealings with man, and hence it is to be looked for as the distinguishing mark of every child of God. "He that loveth is born of God." The *godly* are those who, having received mercy from Him, are exercising it for Him and as His representatives. It is owing to the fact, no doubt, that the word Châçîyd (2623) has been rendered ὅσιος (3741) in the LXX, that we find it represented by *sanctus* (adjective—*holy, sanctified*; noun— *saint*) in the Latin, and by *saint* or *godly* in the English; yet it is a serious evil that the primary meaning of the Hebrew word should almost have disappeared from the face of modern translations. The practical nature of godliness is thereby to some extent obscured, and the moral demand made upon man by his having become the object of Divine lovingkindness is thrown into the background.

It only remains to notice the application of the above remarks to one or two passages of importance in the O.T., and to observe their bearing on the interpretation of this word ὅσιος (3741) in the N.T.

In Deut. 33:8, Moses says, "Let thy Thummim and thy Urim be with thy Châçîyd (2623; ἀνδρὶ ὁσίῳ, 435, 3741—A.V. holy one) whom thou didst prove at Massah." The old Portuguese translator, D'Almeida, here has *amado* (beloved), with a note referring the word to Aaron. The same word is used of Aaron in Ps. 106:16, where he is called the Châçîyd (2623) of the Lord (A.V. "the saint of the Lord"). The context in Deut. 33 shows that reference is made to the slaughter of the Israelites by the House of Levi in the matter of Moab. The lesson we learn with regard to the word Châçîyd (2623) is that it does not betoken the weak "good nature" that some call *mercy*, but rather that devotion to God that produces the exercise of true lovingkindness toward man and that sometimes involves the taking of extreme and apparently harsh measures so as to prevent the spread of evil. In this respect man's mercy is to be like God's.

There are several passages relating to David and his seed in which the words Cheçed (2617) and Châçîyd (2623) occur; they need to be taken together in order that their whole force may be seen. In

II Sam. 7:14, 15, the Lord promises to David with respect to his son, "I will be his father, and he shall be my son. If he commit iniquity, I will chasten him with the rod of men, and with the stripes of the children of men: but my mercy shall not depart away from him" (cf. the parallel passage, I Chron. 17:13). This promise is referred to by Solomon at Gibeon in I Kings 3:6 and II Chron. 1:8. And at the dedication of the Temple he closed the service by the words, "O LORD God, turn not away the face of thine anointed; remember the mercies of David thy servant" (i.e., the mercies which thou hast promised to show unto David—II Chron. 6:42). On turning to Ps. 89, we find several references to these *mercies*. The Psalmist opens by saying "The mercies of Jehovah will I sing for ever"; "mercy," he continues in verse 2, "shall be built up for ever"; he then proceeds to speak of God's covenant and oath, which is faithful and sure and true, that David's seed should be established on the throne for evermore. After extolling the greatness of God, he continues (verse 14), "Righteousness and judgment are the establishment of thy throne: mercy and truth shall go before thy face." Returning to the covenant with David, the Psalmist sketches out its details, saying in verse 24, "My faithfulness and my mercy shall be with him"; and in verse 28, "My mercy will I keep for him for evermore"; and in verse 33, "Nevertheless my mercy [A.V. "my lovingkindness"] will I keep for him for evermore, and my covenant shall stand fast with him." Then the Psalmist breaks out in a lamentation on the troubles into which Israel was plunged, and cries out (v. 49), "Lord, where are thine original mercies [A.V. "thy former lovingkindnesses"], which thou swarest unto David in thy truth?" The Psalm concludes, as usual, with a note of thanksgiving.

We see here, first, that the word *mercy* seems to be used with peculiar significance in relation to God's promise to David and his seed; and secondly, that it is constantly introduced in connection with God's faithfulness or truth. In accordance with these passages we read in Isa. 55:3, "Incline your ear, and come unto me: hear, and your soul shall live; and I will make an everlasting covenant with you, even the mercies of David, which are sure [or faithful]. Behold, I have given him for a witness to the people, for a leader and lawgiver to the people."

The Apostle Paul, when addressing the Jews at Antioch, takes up these words as follows (Acts 13:32–35, 38):

We declare unto you glad tidings, how that the promise which was made unto the fathers, God hath fulfilled the same unto us their children, in that he hath raised up Jesus [again].[3] For it is written in the second psalm, Thou art my Son, this day have I begotten thee. And as concerning that he raised him up from the dead, no more to return to corruption, he said on this wise, I will give you the mercies of David which are faithful. Wherefore he saith also in another place, Thou shalt not suffer thy *merciful*[4] one [A.V. and R.V. "thine holy one"] to see corruption. . . . Be it known unto you therefore, that through this [risen Jesus] there is announced unto you forgiveness of sins.

With regard to the rendering of Ps. 16:10, we are so accustomed to the expression "thy Holy One," that it is not easy to make such a substitution as the sense requires. It may be noticed, however, that D'Almeida has "o teu Bem," *thy Good* or *Kind One;* the old Judeo-Spanish version of the Hebrew Scriptures published at Ferrara has "tu Bueno," which has the same meaning. The Spanish translator De Reyna, and also his reviser Valera, had "tu Misericordioso," *thy Merciful One*, although this excellent rendering has slipped out of modern editions.

The meaning of the word Châçîyd (2623) as representing mercy ought to be borne in mind in other passages where its representative ὅσιος (3741) occurs in the N.T. Thus in Heb. 7:26, the Lord should be described as "merciful and without malice," instead of "holy and harmless"; so in Rev. 15:4 and 16:5, the Lord's mercy, not His holiness, is specially referred to. The word ὅσιος (3741) is used of the Christian in I Tim. 2:8, where he is told to lift up "merciful hands, without wrath and contention"; and in Titus 1:8 it is said that God's steward should be merciful as well as righteous.

3. The R.V. rightly omits the word "again," and thus distinguishes the two "raisings up" of Jesus—first, on His entrance into the world; and secondly, on His resurrection.

4. The R.V. has strangely missed the point here.

11

Redemption and Salvation

Whatever theory one may hold as to the possibility or *a priori* probability of a Divine intervention in human affairs, the Bible is pledged to the fact that such an intervention has taken place. A study of its pages leads to the conclusion that it is as much in accordance with God's nature to help men out of the difficulties in which sin has involved them as it was to create them after His own likeness in the first instance. Nor will the student of the physical world fail to observe the analogy that here exists between nature and revelation; for if there be a *vis medicatrix naturae* (healing power of nature) that is called into play by the wounds, accidents, and diseases to which the body is subject, why should it be thought a thing incredible that the Father of our spirits should provide some means of restoration for those who have become a prey to evil passions, and who through temptation or self-will have become partakers of moral and material corruption?

The patriarchal and Mosaic economies appear to have been intended by the Divine Being to form a groundwork whereon a restorative work for the benefit of the human race might be built up in the fullness of time; and the pious Jew was trained up in the belief that amid all his sins and ignorances, his infirmities and misfortunes, he might look up to God and receive from Him those blessings that are summed up in the words *redemption* and *salvation.*

§1. *Redemption*

The word that specially indicates redemption is Gâ'al (גָּאַל, 1350), best known in the form Gô'êl (1350), *redeemer*.[1] Perhaps the original meaning of the word is *to demand back*, hence *to extricate*. It first appears in Gen. 48:16: "The angel which redeemed me from all evil bless the lads." In Exod. 6:6 and 15:13, it is used of God's redeeming Israel out of Egypt with an outstretched arm. We meet with it no more till we reach Leviticus 25 and 27, where it signifies the liberation of property from a charge, whether that charge was an ordinary debt or whether it had been incurred through a vow. The deliverance was to be effected in this case by payment or by exchange. In cases of poverty, where no payment was possible, the nearest of kin was made responsible for performing the work of redemption. Hence no doubt it came to pass that a kinsman came to be called by the name Gô'êl (1350), as he is in Num. 5:8; I Kings 16:11; and throughout the Book of Ruth. Compare Jer. 32:7, 8.

In the prophets the word is applied not only to the deliverance of God's people from captivity but to that more important and complete deliverance, of which all other historical interpositions of Divine grace are shadows. See Isa. 35:9; 41:14; 43:1, 14; 44:6, 22–24; 47:4; 48:17; 49:7, 26; 51:10; 52:3; 62:12; 63:4; Jer. 31:11.

One of the most important passages where the word occurs is in Isa. 59:20: "The Redeemer shall come to Zion, and unto them that turn from transgression in Jacob." Paul refers to these words as destined to have their fulfillment hereafter at the time of the complete salvation of Israel as a nation (Rom. 11:26).[2]

The word occurs once in Job, in the celebrated passage (19:25), "I know that my Redeemer liveth." Whatever view may be taken of this passage, whether we regard it as a prediction of the Messiah's coming, or as an intimation of the doctrine of the resurrection, or as referring to a temporal deliverance from disease and trouble, one point is clear: Job expresses his deep conviction that there is a living God who can and who will take his part, and shall indeed extricate him from all difficulties. This is the principle in which the Hebrew reader was to be trained.

---

1. Another word (גָּאַל, 1351), the same in spelling and sound, signifies *to defile* or *pollute*. Compare also the slightly different word (גָּעַל, 1602) that means *to loathe, reject with loathing, cast away*.

2. The text in Romans runs thus: "The Redeemer shall come from Zion, and shall turn away transgressions from Jacob." The LXX agrees in the latter part, but in the first part a different Hebrew reading must have been followed by Paul.

In Ps. 19:14, the Psalmist calls God his strength and his Redeemer. In Ps. 69:18, he appeals to God to draw nigh and redeem his soul. He uses the word again in a personal rather than a national sense, with reference to past or future deliverances, in Ps. 77:15; 78:35; 103:4; 106:10; 107:2. In Ps. 119:154, Gâ'al (1350) is rendered *deliver.*

Another application of the word was in the sense of avenging the blood of the slain. This is treated at length in Numbers 35, in connection with the subject of the cities of refuge. It is also referred to in Deut. 19:6, 12; Josh. 20:3, 5, 9; and II Sam. 14:11.

A remarkable combination of the senses of Gô'êl (1350) is to be found in Prov. 23:10, 11, "Remove not the old landmark; and enter not into the fields of the fatherless: for their redeemer is mighty; he shall plead their cause with thee." God takes the place of kinsman and also of avenger to the poor and helpless.

The idea of Gô'êl (1350) as the avenger of blood comes up again in Isa. 63:4, when the Mighty One in bloodstained garments says, "The day of vengeance is in mine heart, and the year of my redeemed is come." The word occurs again in verses 9 and 16 of the same chapter, where it rather signifies deliverance from captivity.

In most of the passages above enumerated *redemption* may be considered as synonymous with *deliverance,* but always with the idea more or less developed that the Redeemer enters into a certain relationship with the redeemed—allies Himself in some sense with them, and so claims the right of redemption. The truth thus set forth was doubtless intended to prepare the mind of God's people for the doctrine of the Incarnation. "Forasmuch as the children were partakers of flesh and blood, therefore *he* also took part in the same"; and having constituted Himself the kinsman of the human race, He fought their battle against "him who had the power of death," and delivered His people from bondage (see Heb. 2:14, 15).

The LXX generally renders Gâ'al (1350) by λυτρόω (3084), *to redeem;* but in fourteen passages we find ῥύομαι (4506), *to deliver;* and in ten, ἀγχιστεύω (L-S 17A), *to act the neighbor.* The verb ἀπολυτρόω (L-S 208B) is found in Zeph. 3:1 (A.V. *polluted*); λύτρον (3083) in Lev. 25:24, 51, 54; λυτρωτής (3086) in Lev. 25:31, 32; Ps. 18:15; 77:39.

In many of the passages above cited another word is used as a parallel to Gâ'al (1350), namely, Pâdâh (פָּדָה, 6299—Assyrian *padû,* "to spare"), which our translators have rendered by the words deliver, redeem, ransom,[3] and rescue. It is used in Exod. 13:13, 15, of the redemption of the firstborn, who were regarded as representatives of those who had been spared when the firstborn of Egypt were destroyed. This redemption extended to all unclean domesticated beasts, to all, that is to say, that were precluded from being offered as sacrifice (Num. 18:16, 17), and a set price was to be paid for their deliverance or quittance. Redemption money (A.V. *ransom*) is described in Exod. 21:30 as paid to make amends (Kôpher—כֹּפֶר, 3724) in certain cases of wrongdoing (see R.V.).

Pâdâh (6299) is often adopted to represent the deliverance of a servant from slavery, as in Exod. 21:8. It is also used of the people rescuing Jonathan from death in I Sam. 14:45.

This word is used in many texts, including the following: Ps. 31:5, "Into thine hand I commit my spirit: thou hast redeemed me, O LORD God of truth"; Ps. 34:22, "The LORD redeemeth the souls of his servants"; Ps. 49:7, 8, 15, "None can redeem his brother, nor give to God a ransom [Kôpher, 3724] for him: (for the redemption of their soul is precious, and it ceaseth for ever). . . . But God will redeem my soul from the power of the grave"; Ps. 130:7, 8, "With the LORD is plenteous redemption. And he shall redeem Israel from all his iniquities"; Isa. 1:27, "Zion shall be redeemed with judgment." The application of the word to Abraham, in Isa. 29:22, is remarkable: "Thus saith the LORD, who redeemed Abraham." It seems here to signify his call from the companionship of idolaters and his introduction into the covenant of promise.

From the passages that have now been cited, it will be gathered that the word Pâdâh (6299) is not used in the peculiar technical senses that Gâ'al (1350) expresses, but that it especially refers to the deliverance from *bondage*. The LXX generally represents it by λυτρόω (3084); five times we find ῥύομαι (4506), twice σώζω (4982), and once ἀπολυτρόω (L-S 208B).

The cognate form Pâda' (פְּדָע, 6308) is found in connection with Kâphar (3722) in Job 33:24, "Deliver him: I have found a ransom" (or mode of atonement); but we find Pâdâh (6299) in verse 28, "He will deliver his soul from going into the pit."

§2. N.T. Teaching on Redemption

In approaching the Greek words for redemption in the N.T., it is evident that we must not narrow our conceptions to one sole pro-

---

3. The English word *ransom* is only a contracted form of the word *redemption.*

cess of deliverance; for the O.T. has led us to look for redemption in many aspects. There may be *physical* deliverance, from disease or death; *social* deliverance, from conventional or legal barriers between man and man, between the sexes, between various classes of society or various nations of the world; and there may be *moral* and *spiritual* deliverance, from the power of evil in the heart and from the effects of that evil before God. Without pressing for a strong demarcation between ῥύομαι (*4506*), *to deliver,* and λυτρόω (*3084*), *to redeem,* we shall be prepared to find in both cases that the deliverance of man is costly, involving some gift or act of self-sacrifice on the part of the Redeemer. Nor shall we be surprised if we find that a certain identification is necessitated between the Deliverer and those whom He claims a right to deliver.

We find ῥύομαι (*4506*) in the sense of deliverance in the following passages:[4] Matt. 6:13, "Deliver us from evil"; Luke 1:74, "That we being delivered out of the hands of our enemies might serve him without fear" (connected with the coming of Christ); Rom. 7:24, "O wretched man that I am, who shall deliver me from the body of this death?" (but here note the answer, "through Jesus Christ"); Rom. 11:26, referring to Isa. 59:20, "The Redeemer (Gô'êl, 1350; or ὁ ῥυόμενος, *3588, 4506*) shall come *from* Zion" (see note on this passage on p. 136); Rom. 15:31, "That I may be delivered from them that are disobedient"; II Cor. 1:10, "Who delivered us from so great a death, and doth deliver: in whom we trust that he will yet deliver us"; Col. 1:13, "Who delivered us from the power of darkness, and translated us"; I Thess. 1:10, "Who delivers us from the wrath to come." See also II Thess. 3:2; II Tim. 3:11; 4:17, 18; II Pet. 2:7, 9.

The verb λυτρόω (*3084*) is used only three times in the N.T. In two of these passages there is evidently a reference to the cost or sacrifice that man's deliverance has involved. In Titus 2:14 we are told of Jesus Christ that He "gave himself for us, that he might redeem us from all iniquity." In I Pet. 1:18, 19, we read, "Ye were not redeemed from your vain manner of life with corruptible things, as silver and gold; but with the precious blood of Christ, as of a lamb without blemish and without spot." These passages may be compared with our Lord's own words found in Matt. 20:28 and Mark 10:45: "The

---

4. But it is to be remembered that while ῥύομαι (*4506*) occasionally stands for Gâ'al (1350) and Pâdâh (6299), it more generally represents the causative form of Nâtsal (נצל, 5337), *to rescue.*

Son of man came [i.e., identified himself with the human race], not to be ministered unto, but to minister, and to give his life a ransom [λύτρον, 3083] for many." Thus the Lord became the Kinsman of men, so as to have the right of redeeming them by the sacrifice of His own life. This truth was set forth in most striking words by the Apostle Paul, who says of the Savior (I Tim. 2:5, 6), "There is one mediator for God and men, the man Christ Jesus; who gave himself a ransom [ἀντίλυτρον, 487] for all, to be testified in due time."

Again, the two disciples, on the road to Emmaus, said of Jesus (Luke 24:21), "We trusted that *it had been he which should have redeemed* [λυτροῦσθαι, 3084] *Israel.*" By this expression they implied that a Redeemer was certainly coming, and that their hopes had been set upon Jesus of Nazareth as the person they were looking for. By the redemption of Israel perhaps they meant what the disciples described a few days afterward as the restoration of the kingdom to Israel. This redemption had been looked for with much eagerness among the Jews of that time, possibly owing to the study of Daniel's prophecy of Seventy Weeks. We have a glimpse of this expectation thirty years earlier in the prophetic song of Zacharias, which opens with these words (Luke 1:68): "Blessed be the Lord God of Israel, for he hath visited and redeemed [ἐποίησε λύτρωσιν—4160, 3085] his people, and hath raised up an horn of salvation for us in the house of his servant David." The word *redemption* here used by the aged priest appears to gather up in one all the blessings mentioned in the later portions of the song— light, pardon, peace, salvation, deliverance from the hand of enemies, and the power of serving God without fear, "in holiness and righteousness before him all the days of our life." Compare the words concerning the aged Anna (i.e., Hannah[5]) who went forth to speak of Him to all those who looked for redemption (λύτρωσιν, 3085) in Jerusalem (Luke 2:38).

The word λύτρωσις (3085) occurs once more, namely, in Heb. 9:12, where we read of Christ that "By his own blood he entered in once for all into the holy place [i.e., into the heavens], having obtained [or found] eternal redemption for us" (cf. Job 33:24).

The noun ἀπολύτρωσις (629), which does not exist in the LXX, occurs ten times in the N.T.; once in the Gospels, "Lift up your

---

5. It is a pity that the R.V. did not correct the spelling of this name as it did in the case of *alleluia.*

heads, for your redemption draweth nigh" (Luke 21:28). This passage evidently refers to a great future event, which shall constitute the final deliverance of Israel from desolation. The word is used with reference to a greater deliverance in Rom. 8:23, "Waiting for the adoption, to wit, the redemption of our body"; (see also in Eph. 1:13, 14; 4:30).

In several texts (Rom. 3:24; Eph. 1:7; Col. 1:14) redemption is apparently identified with present pardon and justification through the blood of Christ. But there is another passage that combines the present and future aspects of redemption in one, viz., Heb. 9:15. It is here stated that the death of Christ effects a redemption, or perhaps we might render it a *quittance* or *discharge* of the account of the transgressions incurred under the first covenant, that those who are called might receive the promise of eternal inheritance. In Heb. 11:35 the word is used with reference to that deliverance from death that the martyrs under the old dispensation might possibly have obtained at the cost of a denial of the faith.

The idea of purchase as connected with salvation is expressed still more strongly in the N.T. than in the O.T. by the use of the words ἀγοράζω (59) and ἐξαγοράζω (1805). The former of these is used several times in the Gospels in its ordinary sense. But in the later books we read, "Ye are [or *were*] bought with a price" (I Cor. 6:20 and 7:23); "Denying the Lord that bought them" (II Pet. 2:1); "Thou hast bought us for God by thy blood" (Rev. 5:9); "The hundred and forty-four thousand that are bought from the earth" (Rev. 14:3, 4).

The more complete form ἐξαγοράζω (1805) is found in Gal. 3:13: "Christ has bought us off from the curse." See also Gal. 4:5: "Made under the law, that he might buy off them that are under the law." It primarily refers to the special deliverance that Jews as such needed and obtained through the form and mode of Christ's death, so as to extricate them from the claims that the law of Moses would other-wise have established against them.

Another word is rendered *purchase* in the N.T., namely, περι-ποίησις (4047). The verb (περιποιέω, L-S 138A—*to acquire* [*in order to preserve*]) usually answers to the Hebrew Châyâh (חָיָה, 2421), *to make* or *keep alive*. It is also used in Isa. 43:21, where we read, "This people have I formed [or molded] for myself"; and the noun occurs in Mal. 3:17, where it signifies a peculiar treasure (A.V. *jewels*). The result of our being saved alive by God is that we become in a special sense His acquired property. Thus we may render Acts 20:28,

"Feed the church of God, which he hath acquired to himself by his own blood"; I Pet. 2:9, "An acquired people";[6] Eph. 1:14, "Until the redemption of the acquired property"; I Thess. 5:9, "For the acquisition of salvation"; II Thess. 2:14, "For the acquisition of glory."

§3. *Salvation*

The doctrine of salvation in the N.T. derives its name from a word that was ingrained in the history and language of Israel from the period of the deliverance of the people out of Egypt up to the time of their restoration from captivity. The word Yâsha' (יָשַׁע, 3467), *to save,* which generally answers to the Greek σώζω (4982), has given a name not only to Joshua, but to Jesus, who should save His people from their sins. Our translators have rendered Yâsha' (3467) by the words *save, help, preserve, rescue, defend,* and *deliver.*

Yâsha' (3467) is used of the deliverance of Israel from the Egyptians (Exod. 14:30; Isa. 43:3), and from other enemies (Num. 10:9; Deut. 20:4). The reference to this fact in I Sam. 10:19 is very striking: "Ye have this day rejected your God, who himself saved you out of all your adversities and your tribulations."

This salvation was often effected through the instrumentality of man. Thus the Lord said to Gideon, "Go in this thy might, and thou shalt save Israel from the hand of the Midianites: have not I sent thee?" (Judg. 6:14). Again, He says to Samuel concerning Saul, "Thou shalt anoint him to be captain over my people Israel, that he may save my people out of the hand of the Philistines" (I Sam. 9:16). Yet in such cases it was to be clearly understood that the work was God's, not man's; accordingly, Gideon's company was reduced in number, "lest Israel vaunt themselves against me, saying, My own hand hath saved me" (Judg. 7:2). Actuated by this conviction, Jonathan reminded his armorbearer that "there is no restraint to the Lord to save by many or by few" (I Sam. 14:6); and Saul, when appealing to the name of God, describes Him as the Lord who saveth Israel (I Sam. 14:39). In II Kings 13:5 we read that "the Lord gave Israel a saviour, so that they went out from under the hand of the Syrians." With this passage may be compared the words of Isaiah with regard to Egypt, "They shall cry unto the Lord because of the oppressors,

6. Thus a *peculiar* people, in the Bible, does not mean an eccentric or a strange people; it gives no excuse to people to affect *peculiarities.*

and he shall send them a saviour, and a great one, and he shall deliver them" (Isa. 19:20).

Over and above the national salvation depicted in these and many similar passages, there are numerous references in the O.T. to the fact that God exercises a saving care over individuals, especially over those who in their helplessness and trouble need and claim His protection. Eliphaz says of God, "He saveth the poor from the sword, from their mouth, and from the hand of the mighty" (Job 5:15); "He shall save the humble person" (22:29). The Psalmist says, "He saves the meek" (Ps. 76:9), the needy (72:4, 13), the contrite (34:18), the righteous (Prov. 28:18), but not the wicked (Ps. 18:41).

The principle on which this salvation from trouble is extended to man is simply the merciful disposition of God (Ps. 109:26) and His own honor (Isa. 37:35). He saves for His own Name's sake. He says emphatically, "I, even I, am the LORD; and beside me there is no saviour" (Isa. 43:11); "Look unto me, and be ye saved, all the ends of the earth: for I am God, and there is none else" (Isa. 45:22).

There is nothing in the word Yâsha' (3467) that indicates the mode or that limits the extent of salvation. It evidently includes Divinely bestowed deliverance from every class of spiritual and temporal evil to which mortal man is subjected. In Ps. 24:5, and elsewhere, it is set forth in connection with righteousness; in 25:5, with truth; in 40:10, with faithfulness; in 51:12, with joy; in 68:19, 20, with spiritual gifts; in 69:13, with the hearing of prayer; and in 79:9, with the forgiveness of sins.

The Messiah was to be the embodiment of the Divine help and salvation. His coming is thus proclaimed, "Behold, thy salvation cometh; behold, his reward is with him, and his work before him" (Isa. 62:11); "Behold, thy king cometh unto thee: he is just, and having salvation"[7] (Zech. 9:9); "Behold, your God will come with vengeance, even God with a recompence; he will come and save you" (Isa. 35:4).

It is to be noticed that Châyâh (חָיָה, 2421), *to save alive* or *make alive,* is used several times in the O.T., e.g., Gen. 12:12; Ezek. 3:18; 13:18, 19; 18:27. In these and other passages preservation in life is what is generally referred to. Compare I Pet. 3:18, which may be rendered "being kept alive in the spirit."

---

7. The word here is passive, and perhaps refers to the resurrection of Christ.

§4. *Teaching of the N.T. on Salvation*

The Greek representative of **Yâsha'** (3467) in the N.T. is σώζω (4982). We find it used of both temporal and spiritual deliverances, though the latter sense strongly predominates. *To be saved* and *to be made whole* are sometimes taken as renderings for the same word. Over and over again in this physical sense Christ "saved others," though He could not—the Jews supposed—"save Himself." There are also some passages in the Epistles that appear to refer to temporal salvation, while others are open to two interpretations.

The references in the N.T. to the "great salvation" wrought by Christ are very constant and most remarkable. Sometimes this salvation is identified with entrance into the kingdom of God (Mark 10:26; Luke 13:23); sometimes it is regarded as a present salvation (Luke 19:9; II Cor. 6:2); in other passages it is postponed till the Great Day (I Cor. 3:15), which is the day of the Lord Jesus Christ (I Cor. 5:5). It is everywhere set forth as attainable only through Him (John 10:9; Acts 4:12). It follows on repentance (II Cor. 7:10), on belief (Mark 16:16), on receiving the love of the truth (II Thess. 2:10), on public confession of Christ's resurrection (Rom. 10:9). In some passages salvation is deliverance from sins (Matt. 1:21); in others it appears to mean a continuous preservation from surrounding evil (II Tim. 4:18; Heb. 5:9); while in a third class of passages it is deliverance from the wrath to come (Rom. 5:9; 13:11; I Thess. 5:8; Heb. 9:28).

Being saved is brought several times into contrast with being lost. It is a present loss or perdition from which Christ comes to seek and to save in the first place. He is never represented as saving from final perdition those who deliberately reject His saving work here. His mission was essentially remedial and restorative. So long as He was on earth He restored health to the sick, sight to the blind, and cleanness to the leper; now that He has died, risen, and ascended into heaven, He restores the moral being of those who trust Him, not only by healing their backslidings and pardoning their offenses but also by giving them spiritual health and power to live unto God. Hereafter will come the restoration of the body and of the whole physical fabric of things connected with the body, together with the full development of spiritual life.

12

Atonement, Forgiveness, Acceptance

Moral actions are regarded in regarded in Scripture in two lights: first, they tend to influence the character of the agent; secondly, they affect his relations with his fellow beings, and also with God. Every breach of law, as a matter of fact, constitutes man an offender, and—if it be known or suspected—causes him to be regarded as such. This principle, with which we are all familiar in human affairs, is true, nay, it may be regarded as a truism, in things pertaining to God. And since the secrets of every heart are laid bare before Him, it follows that every evil motive, every cherished passion, every wrong word, and every evil deed awaken the Divine displeasure and call for judicial treatment at God's hands. As in man, however, there exist certain attributes that tend to compensate each other's action, so it is in God. Mercy rejoices against judgment, and the feelings of a Father exist in the bosom of Him whom we instinctively and rightly regard as a Moral Governor. God never forgets whereof we are made; He knows our frame, and remembers that we are but dust. And the sins into which we are often hurried through our fallen nature and our inherited constitution, through ignorance, through the force of circumstances, and through the machinations of the Evil One are weighed by Him in all their aspects. They are seen, if with a magisterial eye, yet through a medium of tender love and pity that has found its full expression and effect in the atonement.

§1. *The Hebrew Word for Atonement*

The Hebrew word whereby this doctrine is universally set forth in the O.T. is **Kâphar** (כָּפַר, 3722), the original meaning of which is supposed to be *to cover* or *shelter.* **Kâphâr** (כָּפָר, 3723), a noun formed from it answering to the modern Arabic *Khephr,* is sometimes used to signify a *village* as a place of shelter, e.g., Caper-naum (the village of Nahum). Another form of this word, **Kopher** (כֹּפֶר, 3724), usually rendered *ransom,* is transliterated *camphire* in Song of Sol. 1:14 and 4:13. In Gen. 6:14 the verb and noun are used, where God is represented as telling Noah *to pitch* the ark within and without with *pitch.*

Before referring to the passages in which the word has been rendered *to make atonement,* we may notice those in which other renderings have been adopted in the A.V. The following are the most important: Deut. 21:8, "They shall say, Be merciful, O LORD, unto thy people, whom thou hast redeemed, and lay not innocent blood unto thy people Israel's charge. And the blood *shall be forgiven* them"—i.e., the charge of having shed innocent blood shall be removed from them. I Sam. 3:14, "I have sworn . . . that the iniquity of Eli's house *shall* not *be purged* with sacrifice nor offering for ever." No sacrifice for sins of ignorance could cause God to change His determination in this case. It is not the eternal destiny of the individuals, but the official position of the family, that is here spoken of. II Chron. 30:18–20, "Hezekiah prayed for them, saying, The good LORD *pardon* every one that prepareth his heart to seek God, the LORD God of his fathers, though he be not cleansed according to the purification of the sanctuary." It is added that "the LORD hearkened to Hezekiah and healed the people." Here a ceremonial offense was committed, but, through the intercession of Hezekiah, the charge was done away with. Ps. 78:38, "He, being full of compassion, *forgave* their iniquity, and destroyed them not." In this case the charge was done away with, not because of man's innocence, but because of God's compassion. Ps. 79:9, "*Purge away* our sins, for thy name's sake." In this, as in other passages, the purgation is not the moral change, but the removal either of guilt or of the punishment that follows from guilt. The ground of appeal lies not in any latent goodness in the offender, but in the nature of God Himself. This is implied in the familiar but too little heeded phrase "for thy name's sake," which occurs so frequently in the O.T. Prov. 16:6, "By [or *in*] mercy and truth iniquity is *purged:* and by [or *in*] the fear of the LORD men depart from evil." This passage teaches that where a man departs from his evil courses and turns into the path of mercy and truth, God is ready to be gracious to him. (Compare Jer. 18:23.) Isa. 6:7, "Lo, this hath touched thy lips, and thine iniquity is taken away and thy sin *purged.*" Isa. 22:14, "Surely this iniquity shall not be *purged* from you till ye die." The men of whom this was said, and who had deliberately set themselves in opposition to God's revealed truth, would go into another world with their sins unpardoned. Isa. 27:9, "By this therefore shall the iniquity of Jacob be *purged;* and this is all the fruit to take away his sin." (Compare Num. 35:33; Deut. 32:43.) Isa. 28:18, "Your covenant with death shall be *disannulled.*" This use of the word **Kâphar** (3722) is interesting. To be disannulled is to be treated as nonexistent; and this is the way in which God covers sin. To use the vivid language of the Bible, He casts it behind His back. Ezek. 16:62, 63, "I will establish my covenant with thee; and thou shalt know that I am the LORD: that thou mayest remember, and be confounded, and never open thy mouth any more because of thy shame, when *I am pacified* toward thee for all that thou hast done." The pacification of God is literally the covering (by atonement) of the sins recorded against His people. Pacification, i.e., atonement, proceeds from Him only. See also Ps. 65:3; Isa. 47:11; Ezek. 43:20.

The word **Kâphar** (3722), in one or other of its forms, is rendered *atone* or *atonement* in about eighty passages, most of which are in the Levitical law. All men and all things human are represented in the law as needing atonement. Even when a priest, or an altar, or a temple was to be consecrated, there must be atonement made first.

And how was atonement wrought? A spotless victim had to be brought before the LORD to take the part of sinful man. Its death, after the sins of the offerer had been laid on its head, represented the fact that the innocent must suffer for the guilty. Then came the solemn mystery. The priest, God's agent, must take the blood of the victim and scatter it over God's altar. This process set forth the truth that God and the sinner must be brought into contact through means of Him whom priest and altar typified. The symbol was composite, or many-sided, and its various aspects can be realized and put together only when they are regarded in the light of Christ's death on the cross. It was not His life alone that made atonement, but His death, i.e., the giving up of His life. One of the ends and objects of His partaking of flesh and blood was that He might taste death. The people of Israel were frequently reminded that their hope lay in the death of a representative. This is brought out very clearly in Lev. 17:11, "The life [or soul] of the flesh is in the blood: and I have given it to you upon the altar to make an atonement for your lives; for it is the blood that maketh an atonement for[1] the life." When therefore the Son of God "poured out his soul unto death," shedding His lifeblood on behalf of the world, He gave substance and embodiment to the Divine disposition of mercy that was fore-shadowed in the Levitical law.

We now have to notice that the word **Kâphar** (3722) not only sets forth God's merciful disposition to shelter the sinner, and symbolizes the process whereby the shelter should be obtained, but also represents the act of the *priest* in making atonement for the sins of the people. An important conclusion may be drawn from this fact: that this Divinely appointed officer, when making atonement, was really representing not what man does in approaching God but what "God manifest in the flesh" does in sheltering man. The people might bring the sacrifices, but it was the priest alone that could take the blood and sprinkle it on the altar or on the mercyseat; and when he did so he was setting forth in a dim and shadowy figure the merciful provision of God for the pardon of the sinner. Atone-ment, then, was not something done by man to pacify or gratify God, nor was it something done by a third party with the intention of representing the sinner before God. But it is essentially the pro-duct of God's pardoning mercy, exhibited in figure through the agency of the priest's sprinkling of the blood and finally embodied in the work of Christ. "God was, in Christ, reconciling the world unto himself, not imputing their trespasses unto them" (II Cor. 5:19).

In accordance with the teaching of the O.T. on this subject, we have the doctrine of the Priesthood of Christ, the object of which was "to make atonement [A.V. *reconciliation*] for the sins of the peo-ple," plainly set forth in the Epistle to the Hebrews (2:17).

The fact that the priest in certain cases (e.g., Lev. 10:17) consumed the flesh of the atoning sin-offering may have symbolized the identi-fication between priest and victim that was to be accomplished when Christ offered Himself for our sins.

The application of the fire that was continually burning on the altar, together with incense, to make atonement in certain cases (e.g., Num. 16:46; Isa. 6:6, 7), seems intended to indicate that the

1. R.V. (?) "by reason of the life."

virtue of the atonement once made is continuous, and applicable to all cases.

The word *reconciliation* has been adopted by our translators instead of *atonement*, and must be considered as identical with it in Lev. 6:30; 8:15; 16:20; Ezek. 45:15, 17, 20; Dan. 9:24.

The form **Kôpher** (3724) has been rendered *satisfaction* in Num. 35:31, 32; *bribe* in I Sam. 12:3 and Amos 5:12; *sum of money* in Exod. 21:30; *ransom* in Exod. 30:12; Job 33:24; 36:18; Ps. 49:7; Prov. 6:35; 13:8; 21:18; and Isa. 43:3. The usage of the word in these passages, many of which were not ceremonial or symbolical, conveys an idea of *costliness* as an element in atonement, and thus allies it with redemption.[2]

The LXX has translated the verb **Kâphar** (3722) by ἐξιλάσκομαι (L-S 594B), and the noun generally by ἱλασμός (2434), *propitiation*; occasionally by καθαρισμός (2512), *cleansing*; and by λύτρον (3083), *ransom*, in six passages. The prevailing idea set forth both in the LXX and in other translations is that atonement is the doing away with a charge against a person, so that the accused may be received into the Divine favor and be freed from the consequences of wrongdoing. It should be added that *pacification, propitiation*, and such words are by no means adequate for the purpose of conveying the doctrine of atonement; they savor too much of heathenism and superstition, and lead to the supposition that man pacifies God, instead of teaching that God shelters man.

The name of the mercyseat, **Kappôreth** (כַּפֹּרֶת, 3727—cf. ἱλαστήριον, 2435), is derived from **Kâphar** (3722). The description of this remarkable object is to be found in Exod. 25:17-22, and its use is indicated in Lev. 16:13-15. It was the lid of the ark of the covenant, wherein was kept the law of God. Though made of pure gold, it needed to be sprinkled with blood by the high priest once a year. This lifeblood, shed to represent the punishment due to the Israelites for their sins, was thus brought (by means of sprinkling) into contact with the receptacle of the law.

The mercyseat is not only referred to as one of the Levitical "shadows" in Heb. 9:5, but is also identified with the atoning work of Christ in Rom. 3:25, where we read, "God hath set forth [Christ] to

---

2. The free offering of the jewels "as an *atonement* for the life" by those who had plundered the Midianites was a special case, and must not be regarded as pointing to an independent means of atonement; moreover, it is to be noticed that the gift was accepted by the priests not as an atonement, but as a memorial (Num. 31:50, 54).

be a propitiation [Luther, *zu einem Gnadenstuhl*—"for a mercyseat"] through faith in his blood."

§2. *N.T. Teaching on Atonement and Substitution*

The verb ἐξιλάσκομαι (L-S 594B) does not appear in the N.T., but both ἱλασμός (2434) and καθαρισμός (2512) are used of the atoning work of Christ (see I John 2:2; 4:10; Heb. 1:3). The word λύτρον (3083) is also applied by Christ to His own death, which was "a ransom for many" (λύτρον ἀντὶ πολλῶν—3083, 473, 4183), Matt. 20:28 and Mark 10:45. We have here strongly brought out the truth that the Divine interposition on behalf of sinful man was not a work that cost nothing; it called for no less an offering than the precious lifeblood of Christ, who was a "lamb without blemish and without spot." As it was an act of self-sacrifice on the Father's part to give His Son freely to bear and suffer what He deemed needful, so it was an act of self-sacrifice on the Son's part to drink the cup that His Father put into His hands. He was at once both a living and a dying sacrifice.

The truth set forth by our Lord in the above-named passages concerning the costliness of atonement is further illustrated by the words of the Apostle Paul in I Tim. 2:5, 6, "There is one God, and one mediator belonging to God and men, Christ Jesus, (himself) man; who gave himself *a ransom for all* [ἀντίλυτρον ὑπὲρ πάντων—487, 5228, 3956], to be testified in due time." The word μεσίτης (3316) here translated *mediator* is not to be found in the LXX; it seems to imply not so much what is ordinarily meant by a mediator as a *medium*, and so a *common ground*. Jesus Christ is a Being in whom Godhead and manhood meet, so that God and man are made one in Him, and are represented by Him. The Son of God, who is One in nature and attributes with the Father, took not only a human *body* but human *nature*, so that every child of Adam may claim Him as kinsman; and then gave Himself a ransom for all. Here Paul, not content with the word λύτρον (3083), adopts a composite word to make the passage still more emphatic, ἀντίλυτρον ὑπὲρ πάντων (487, 5228, 3956), *a substitutionary ransom on behalf of all*. What men could not do, that Christ Jesus did for them, in their place and on their behalf, by the will of God. The obedience of Christ, which culminated in His death, was thus devised, wrought, and accepted by God for the benefit of all men. It may not be needful to assert that He *suffered* what all men deserved to *suffer*, but he certainly *did* what all men were originally intended *to do*, viz., His Father's will in all its fullness. That will, in His case, required that He should suffer death for the sin of the world, destroying thereby the body of sin. By His resurrection He would open the kingdom of heaven to all believers.

The Hebrew preposition rendered by the word *for* in connection with the doctrine of acceptance and atonement does not mean *instead of*, but *over, on, because of*, or *on account of*. The preposition that properly marks *substitution* is never used in connection with the word **Kâphar** (3722). To make atonement for a sin is literally to cover *over* the sin. The preposition 'Al (עַל, 5921) is constantly used with verbs signifying *to cover* as in Hab. 2:14, "As the waters cover the sea." Be'ad (בְּעַד, 1157), *because of*, is used in some passages, as in Exod. 32:30. In one passage only does the strict idea of substitution, as distinguished from representation, appear in the O.T. in connection with sacrifice, namely, in Gen. 22:13, where we are told that Abraham offered up a ram *instead* of his son. The absence of this peculiar mode of expression from the Levitical law is significant; and it teaches us to be cautious in the use of language relative to the *transfer* of sins and of righteousness effected in the atonement. In connection with this point, the following weighty words from Archbishop Magee's work on the Atonement deserve consideration:

> The expression *to bear the sins of others* is familiarized to denote *the suffering evils inflicted on account of those sins*. I will not contend that this should be called suffering the *punishment* of those sins, because the idea of punishment cannot be abstracted from that of guilt; and in this respect I differ from many respectable authorities, and even from Dr. Blayney, who uses the word punishment in his translation. But it is evident that it is, notwithstanding, a judicial infliction; and it may perhaps be figuratively denominated *punishment*, if thereby be implied a reference to the actual transgressor, and be understood that suffering which was due to the offender himself; and which, if inflicted on him, would then take the name of punishment. In no other sense can the suffering inflicted on one on account of the transgressions of another be called a punishment; and in this light the bearing the punishment of another's sins is to be understood as bearing that which in relation to the sins and to the sinner admits the name of punishment, but with respect to the individual on whom

it is actually inflicted, abstractedly considered, can be viewed but in the light of suffering.

The same writer observes that

those that hold the doctrine of a vicarious punishment feel it not necessary to contend that the evil inflicted on the victim should be exactly the same in quality and degree with that denounced against the offender; it depending, they say, upon the will of the legislator what satisfaction he will accept in place of the punishment of the offender.

Once more, he remarks that "a strict vicarious substitution or literal equivalent is not contended for, no such notion belonging to the doctrine of the atonement."

To sum up the Scriptural view on this doctrine, we may say that atonement signifies *shelter by means of representation.* Applying this general definition to the case of *sin,* Scripture teaches that shelter for the sinner is secured through his being represented by Christ before the Father; and in order that he should be so represented, Christ became our kinsman and wrought out that perfect righteousness that man has failed to attain. Further, He endured death on the cross, and more than death—the hiding of His Father's countenance, which was the curse due to sin. Thus He who knew not sin was made (or dealt with as) sin for us, that we might be made the righteousness of God in Him. It is a real substitution, for what He did and suffered took the place of what we ought to have done and suffered.

The only time that the word *atonement* is used in the A.V. of the N.T. is in Rom. 5:11. Here it stands for the Greek καταλλαγή (2643), which ought to have been rendered *reconciliation* in accordance with the previous verse (see R.V.). It is to be remarked that καταλλαγή (2643) is never used of the atonement in the O.T. The verb καταλλάσσω (2644) is found in the following passages in II Maccabees: (1:5) "May God *be at one* with you"; (5:20) "The great Lord being *reconciled*"; (7:33) "He shall *be at one* with his servants"; (8:29) "They besought the merciful Lord *to be reconciled* with his servants." While these four Apocryphal passages speak of God's reconciliation to man, in the N.T. we read only of man's being reconciled to God. The minister of reconciliation has to beseech men to be reconciled to God (II Cor. 5:20), and in so doing he is expressing in words that which Christ expressed in deeds. For "God reconciled us to himself through Christ" (II Cor. 5:18). And the process by which He did it, namely, the death on the cross (Rom. 5:10), is available for the whole world (II Cor. 5:19; Rom. 11:15).

When we speak of Christ reconciling His Father to us,[3] we are not to imagine an angry Judge being propitiated by a benevolent Son; this would be an entire misrepresentation of the Christian faith. Rather we should regard the Son as sent by His Father to die for the sins of the world, in order that He might remove the bar that hindered the free action of Divine love on the heart of man. As the Father has committed the work of Judgment to the Son, so has He committed the work of Atonement; and the Son of Man is as much the Agent of His Father's will in the latter case as in the former.

§3. *Forgiveness*

Passing from the subject of atonement to that of forgiveness, we meet with the word Çâlach (סָלַח, 5545—Assyrian *sulû*), a term of great importance, because it is reserved especially to mark the pardon extended to the sinner by God. It is never used to denote that inferior kind and measure of forgiveness that is exercised by one man toward another. This word is used about forty-five times. The LXX sometimes renders it by ἀφίημι (863), *to remit*, but the usual rendering is ἵλεως εἰμι (2436, 1510) or ἱλάσκομαι (2433), *to be propitious*, the word used by the publican when he said, "God *be merciful* to me a sinner" (Luke 18:13).

Çâlach (5545) is to be found in the following (among other) passages: Exod. 34:9, "If now I have found grace in thy sight, O Lord, let my Lord, I pray thee, go among us; for it is a stiffnecked people; and pardon our iniquity and our sin, and take us for thine inheritance." Lev. 4:20, "The priest shall make an atonement for them [i.e., for the congregation when they had sinned through ignorance], and it shall be forgiven them" (see also vv. 26, 31, 35; 5:10, 16, 18). Num. 14:19, 20, "Pardon, I beseech thee, the iniquity of this people according unto the greatness of thy mercy, and as thou hast forgiven this people, from Egypt even until now. And the LORD said, I have pardoned according to thy word." In Deut. 29:20, with respect to the apostate and licentious man, it is said, "The LORD will not spare

---

3. See the second article of the Church of England.

him, but . . . the anger of the LORD and his jealousy shall smoke against that man, and all the curses that are written in this book shall lie upon him, and the LORD shall blot out his name from under heaven." I Kings 8:30, 39, "When thou hearest, forgive." II Kings 5:18, "The LORD pardon thy servant, that when my master goeth into the house of Rimmon to worship there, and he leaneth on my hand, and I bow myself in the house of Rimmon, the LORD pardon thy servant in this thing." II Kings 24:3, 4, "Surely at the commandment of the LORD came [this punishment] upon Judah, to remove them out of his sight, for the sins of Manasseh, according to all that he did; and also for the innocent blood that he shed . . . which the Lord would not pardon." Neh. 9:17, "Thou art a God ready to pardon" (lit., a God of pardons). Ps. 25:11, "For thy name's sake, O LORD, pardon mine iniquity; for it is great." Ps. 86:5, "Thou, LORD, art good, and ready to forgive." Ps. 103:3, "Who forgiveth all thine iniquities; who healeth all thy diseases." Ps. 130:4, "There is forgiveness [LXX ὁ ἱλασμός, 3588, 2434—the propitiation] with thee, that thou mayest be feared." Isa. 55:7, "Let the wicked forsake his way, and the unrighteous man his thoughts: and let him return unto the LORD, and he will have mercy upon him; and to our God, for he will abundantly pardon." Jer. 5:1, "Seek in the broad places [of Jerusalem] if ye can find a man, if there be any that executeth judgment, that seeketh the truth; and I will pardon it." Jer. 5:7, "How shall I pardon thee for this?" Jer. 31:34, "I will forgive their iniquity, and will remember their sin no more." Jer. 33:8, "I will cleanse them from all their iniquity, whereby they have sinned against me; and I will pardon all their iniquities, whereby they have sinned, and whereby they have transgressed against me." Jer. 36:3, "It may be that the house of Judah will hear all the evil that I purpose to do unto them; that they may return every man from his evil way; that I may forgive their iniquity and their sin." Jer. 50:20, "The iniquity of Israel shall be sought for, and there shall be none; and the sins of Judah, and they shall not be found; for I will pardon them whom I reserve." Lam. 3:42, "We have transgressed and rebelled: thou hast not pardoned." Dan. 9:9, "To the Lord our God belong mercies and forgivenesses, though we have rebelled against him." Amos 7:2, 3, "When [the grasshoppers] had made an end of eating the grass of the land, then I said, O Lord GOD, forgive, I beseech thee: by whom shall Jacob arise? for he is small. The LORD repented for this: It shall not be, saith the LORD."

It appears, on the whole, that the process represented by this word Çâlach (5545) is the Divine restoration of an offender into favor, whether through his own repentance or the intercession of another. Though not identical with atonement, the two are closely related. In fact, the covering of the sin and the forgiveness of the sinner can only be understood as two aspects of one truth; for both found their fullness in God's provision of mercy through Christ. The Apostle brings atonement and pardon closely together when he says, in summing up the symbolic value of the Levitical system, "Without shedding of blood [the preliminary to atonement] there is no forgiveness [ἄφεσις, 859]" (Heb. 9:22).

The words ἀφίημι (863) and ἄφεσις (859) are constantly used in the N.T. to denote the forgiveness of sins, whether by God or by man. One of the chief objects of the mission of Christ was that forgiveness of sins might be proclaimed through His name; and His death on the cross has been the means of obtaining it. See Matt. 26:28; Mark 1:4; Luke 1:77; 24:47; Acts 2:38; 5:31; 13:38; 26:18; Eph. 1:7; Col. 1:14.

§4. *Sin Bearing*

Nâsâ' (נשׂא, 5375—Assyrian *nasû*), *to bear*, though found in connection with the putting away of sin, is by no means confined to this purpose. It is used very frequently of the bearing of the ark, also of an armorbearer. It implies first the *lifting-up*; secondly, the *carrying*; and thirdly, the *taking away* of a burden. Nâsâ' (5375) is often used of the endurance of punishment, or of the incurring of responsibility. Thus, in Gen. 4:13, Cain says, "My punishment [or *fault*] is greater than I can bear." Here the LXX less correctly renders, "My fault is too great to be forgiven." (See also the Vulgate and Luther.) We also frequently meet with the expression, "He shall bear his iniquity," i.e., he shall incur the responsibility of his sin, as in Lev. 5:17, "He is guilty, and shall bear his iniquity." In some passages the stern consequence of a man having to bear his iniquity is plainly set forth. Thus, in Lev. 19:8, we read, "He shall bear his iniquity, because he hath profaned the hallowed things of the LORD; and that soul shall be cut off from among his people."

The word Nâsâ' (5375), however, is also used of the undertaking of the responsibilities or sins of others by substitution or representation. The high priest was to bear the name of Israel before God (Exod. 28:12). The scapegoat was to bear the iniquity of the people

(Lev. 16:22). In Lev. 10:17, the expression "to bear the iniquity of the congregation" is identified with the making of atonement for them before the LORD. A different Hebrew word, Çâbal (סָבַל, 5445), *to bear a burden* (rather than *to lift*), is used in Isa. 53:11: "He shall bear their iniquities." But in verse 12 the word Nâsâ' (5375) occurs, "He bore the sins of many," and the two Hebrew words are found together in verse 4. The expression is very instructive. Christ did not *drive* sins away; He *bore* them. Moreover, the emphatic personal pronoun is added. Compare I Pet. 2:24, "Who his own self bore our sins."

The transition from the vicarious bearing of sin to the idea of pardon is very natural, but it is remarkable that this transition should have been effected as early as the days of the patriarchs. Joseph's brethren use the word Nâsâ' (5375) when they say, "Forgive the trespass of the servants of the God of thy fathers" (Gen. 50:17). Pharaoh says, "Forgive, I pray thee, my sin only this once" (Exod. 10:17). Moses says to God (Exod. 32:32), "If thou wilt forgive their sin." Among God's attributes it is recorded that He forgives iniquity and transgression and sin (Exod. 34:7; Num. 14:18; Micah 7:18). Again, Moses intercedes, "Pardon the iniquity of this people" (Num. 14:19). Joshua uses the word of God, "He will not forgive your transgressions nor your sins" (Josh. 24:19). In some of these passages the English word *bear* or *put up with* might possibly express the meaning as well as the word *forgive*. Nâsâ' (5375) is also used in Ps. 25:18; 32:1, 5; 85:2; 99:8; Isa. 2:9; 33:24.

In other passages our translators have rendered Nâsâ' (5375) as *spare* or *pardon*. See Gen. 18:24; Exod. 23:21; I Sam. 15:25; Job 7:21; Isa. 44:21; Jer. 23:39; Lam. 3:17.

The usual Greek renderings for Nâsâ' (5375) are $\alpha \ddot{\iota} \rho \omega$ (*142*) and $\lambda \alpha \mu \beta \acute{\alpha} \nu \omega$ (*2983*), and these are reproduced in the N.T. Thus, in Matt. 8:17 we read that the Lord, in healing various people that came to Him, fulfilled the words of the prophet, "Himself bore our infirmities and carried our sorrows." Here the Greek $\dot{\alpha} \sigma \theta \epsilon \nu \epsilon \acute{\iota} \alpha s \ \dot{\eta} \mu \hat{\omega} \nu \ \ddot{\epsilon} \lambda \alpha \beta \epsilon$ (*769, 2257, 2983—bore our infirmities*) is not quoted from the LXX, but is a translation of the original words in Isa. 53:4.

In John 1:29 we have the words of John the Baptist, "Behold the Lamb of God, that taketh away the sins of the world." Here the word $\alpha \ddot{\iota} \rho \omega$ (*142*) answers to Nâsâ' (5375), and implies the lifting up or taking of a burden upon oneself, and consequently the delivering of others from it. This sentence seems to be referred to by the Apostle

John when he says concerning the Lord, "He was manifested that he might take away our sins" (I John 3:5).

The word ἀναφέρω (*399*), which occurs in the LXX in Isa. 53:11, is used of the offering of sacrifices in Heb. 7:27; 13:15; James 2:21; I Pet. 2:5. It is also twice used of the bearing of sin, i.e., the taking of the responsibility of the sin of others upon oneself: in Heb. 9:28, "Christ was once offered [προσφέρω, *4374*] to bear [ἀναφέρω, *399*] the sins of many"; and again, in I Pet. 2:24, "Who himself bore our sins in his own body on the tree, that we, being dead [ἀπογενόμενοι, *581*[4]] to sins, might live to righteousness."

§5. *Acceptance*

Several words are taken to represent the doctrine of the Divine acceptance of man. In Prov. 21:3, we read, "To do justice and judgment is more acceptable to the Lord than sacrifice." Here the word **Bâchar** (בָּחַר, *977*) signifies *to choose* or *select*, whether for work or for honor. This is the word used of the "chosen people," and answers to the word ἐκλεκτός (*1588*), *elect*, in the LXX and the N.T. In some passages the LXX has rendered it αἱρετίζω (*140*). It has been rendered *elect* in Isa. 42:1; 45:4, and 65:9, 22. In all these passages there is reference to either Israel or the Messiah.

In Lev. 10:19 we read, "Should it have been good [or pleasing—טוֹב, *2896*] in his sight?" Ps. 20:3 says, "[The Lord] remember all thy offerings, and accept thy burnt sacrifice." Here, as we read in the margin, the word for *accept* (דָּשֵׁן, *1878*) may signify either *make fat* or *turn to ashes*, the latter being the most probable. In Eccles. 12:10 we read, "The preacher sought to find out acceptable words." The word **Chêphets** (חֵפֶץ, *2656*) signifies *pleasant* or *desirable.*

In I Sam. 26:19, David says to Saul, "If the Lord have stirred thee up against me, let him accept an offering." Here the word *to smell* (רוּחַ, *7306*—Assyrian *ruhhu*) is used. Thus the passage may be compared with others, such as Gen. 8:21, where God is described as smelling a sweet savor, that is to say, being pleased with the offering and hence with the offerer.

Nâsâ' (נָשָׂא, *5375*), which has been discussed above, is frequently used to represent *acceptance* when used together with the word **Pânîym** (פָּנִים, *6440*), *face* or *person.* It occurs in Gen. 19:21, where

---

4. This word is unique, and marks *severance* rather than *death.*

the angel says to Lot, "I have accepted thee concerning this thing"; in Gen. 32:20, where Jacob says of Esau, "Perhaps he will accept of me"; and in Job 42:8, 9, when God says of Job, "Him will I accept." See also I Sam. 25:35; Job 13:8, 10; 32:21; 34:19; Ps. 82:2; Prov. 18:5; Mal. 1:8.

A noun, Se'êth (שְׂאֵת, 7613), formed from the verb Nâsâ' (5375) is used without the additional word *face* or *person* in Gen. 4:7: "If thou doest well, shalt thou not be accepted?" Perhaps the word might be rendered *excellency* (as in the margin), or *superiority*, rather than *acceptance*. Our translators have rendered it *dignity* in Gen. 49:3, *excellency* in Job 13:11, and *highness* in Job 31:23.

The most important word for acceptance is Râtsâh (רָצָה, 7521), *to be well pleased*. It is used of God's acceptance of Aaron's ministrations on behalf of Israel (Exod. 28:38; Deut. 33:11), and is applied to the Divine regard for the offerer who comes before God in the appointed way. Thus, we read in Lev. 1:4, "He shall put his hand upon the head of the burnt offering, and it shall be accepted for him (לוֹ), to make atonement for him." In verse 3 of the same chapter, instead of reading with the A.V. "of his own voluntary will," there is little doubt that we should read "for his acceptance"; and so in other passages. See R.V.

The following passages illustrate the usage of Râtsâh (7521): Lev. 7:18, "If any of the flesh of the sacrifice of his peace offerings be eaten at all on the third day, it shall not be accepted, neither shall it be imputed unto him that offereth it: it shall be an abomination, and the soul that eateth of it shall bear his iniquity" (cf. 19:7; 22:21; 23:11). II Sam. 24:23, "And Araunah said unto the king, The Lord thy God accept thee." Ps. 19:14, "Let the words of my mouth, and meditation of my heart, be acceptable in thy sight." Ps. 69:13, "As for me, my prayer is unto thee, O Lord, in an acceptable time," i.e., at a season agreeable to Thee (cf. Isa. 49:8). Ps. 119:108, "Accept, I beseech thee, the freewill offerings of my mouth." See also Prov. 10:32; Eccles. 9:7; Isa. 56:7; 58:5; 60:7; 61:2; Jer. 6:20; 14:10, 12; Ezek. 20:40, 41; 43:27; Hos. 8:13; Amos 5:22; Mal. 1:10, 13.

It is evident that by the Divine acceptance is to be understood the pleasure with which God welcomes into personal contact with Himself those who approach Him in His own appointed way, and in a spirit cognate to His own. An evildoer, as such, is not acceptable to God, even though he offers sacrifices. He must be sheltered by atonement, and must thus have the germ at least of a Divine life working in him if he would be regarded by God with pleasure.

The LXX frequently adopts εὐδοκέω (2106), *to be well pleased,* for Râtsâh (7521), especially in the Psalms. We also find προσδέχομαι (4327) and δέχομαι (1209), *to accept,* in several passages. The adjectival form is usually δεκτός (1184), and the substantive is εὐδοκία (2107) and θέλημα (2307).

In the utterance, "Thou art my beloved Son, in whom I am well pleased" (which is repeated in six passages in the N.T. in slightly different forms), there may be an implied reference to Isa. 42:1 ("Mine elect, in whom my soul delighteth"), where the word Râtsâh (7521) is found. If so, we might gather that the purport of the announcement was that Christ Jesus was accepted by God as the minister of the true sanctuary and as the offering for the sins of the world. It is more probable, however, that the Greek word here used answers rather to the Hebrew Châphêts (2654), and signifies that Christ is one in whom God takes pleasure.

The verb προσδέχομαι (4327) in the N.T. generally means either *to expect* or *to receive.* It is used in the passage, "This man receiveth sinners, and eateth with them" (Luke 15:2). In Phil. 4:18, Christian service is spoken of as "an acceptable sacrifice" (θυσία δεκτή—2378, 1184). That which is acceptable in God's sight is spoken of as εὐδοκία (2107) in Matt. 11:26 and Luke 10:21, "So it seemed good in thy sight"; compare also Eph. 1:9 and Phil. 2:13. In Eph. 1:5, the two Greek renderings of Râtsôwn (רָצוֹן, 7522) are combined in one phrase—"according to the *good pleasure* of his *will.*" In the angels' song (Luke 2:14), if we accept the reading "good will toward men," we must understand God's willingness to accept men; if we read "toward men of good will," we ought to understand His good will. Thus the meaning is practically the same; and, after all, we are dealing only with a Greek rendering of what must have been a Hebrew song.

With regard to the word θέλημα (2307), we have, in Heb. 10:7, a quotation from the Psalms that rules the meaning of the word in other passages: "Lo, I come . . . to do thy will, O God." Here θέλημα (2307) answers to Râtsôwn (7522), that which is acceptable in God's sight. "By the which will," continues the writer, "we are sanctified" (v. 10). Forasmuch as sacrifices of bulls and goats did not prove acceptable to God, the Divine Son came to do what would be acceptable. He substituted the offering of Himself for the types; and this offering being accepted by God, believers in Him were sanctified thereby (see Matt. 26:39). In Heb. 10:36, the responsibility of doing the will of God is laid on the believer; and so in Heb. 13:21, where we learn that what we do is wrought in us by God and is acceptable to Him through Jesus Christ. Compare Rom. 12:1.

On reviewing the passages of the N.T. in which the idea of acceptance is presented, they will be seen to confirm the view taken of the Hebrew word as signifying the favorable and pleasurable reception given to man by God. God's acceptance of the man who believes in His Son is not to be regarded as a mere fictitious theory; it is a solid fact, a spiritual reality. Just as men here below have pleasure in one another under certain circumstances, so the unseen Author of existence takes pleasure in those who fear Him, draws near to them when they draw near to Him, and in the Person of Christ "receiveth sinners, and eateth with them." It is indeed a mystery; but it is gloriously true, and will be more fully realized hereafter when the tabernacle of God shall be with men.

13

Purification, Baptism

One of the essential attributes of God is His *purity*. This truth is constantly set forth in Scripture, both in plain declarations and also in symbolical representations. "God is light, and in him is no darkness at all" (I John 1:5). In the remarkable vision recorded in Exod. 24:10, we read, "They saw the God of Israel: and there was under his feet as it were a paved work of a sapphire stone, and as it were the body[1] of heaven in his clearness." With this description we may compare the vision of the Divine glory that the Apostle John had: "Before the throne there was a sea of glass like unto crystal" (Rev. 4:6). What is compared in the one place to the brilliancy of the firmament,[2] is described in the other as an ocean of blazing crystal. That spotless purity that is the basis of the Divine character, and the atmosphere in which God exists, cannot indeed be adequately pictured forth by either of these figures. Even the heavens, though they declare His glory, are not pure in His sight (Job 25:5). The ethereal splendor of the noonday is turned to darkness in the presence of Him who is "the Father of lights." Saul of Tarsus knew well the dazzling brightness of an Eastern sun at midday, but when the Divine glory of the Sun of Righteousness shone round about him, he found it to be "above the brightness of the sun" (Acts 26:13).

The ideal condition of man is to be godlike, that is, to be pure and

---

1. Literally the *bone* of heaven, i.e., the very heaven *itself*. The Hebrews often used the word *bone*, as we use *marrow*, for the essence of a thing. Our word *bone* is literally *beon* or essence.

2. LXX, ὥσπερ εἶδος στερεώματος τοῦ οὐρανοῦ τῇ καθαρότητι (5618, 1491, 4733, 3588, 3772, 3588, 2514—"just as [the] appearance of [the] firmament [or arch] of heaven in [its] purity").

unpolluted in heart, word, and deed. But he fails to live up to this ideal. There is a fearful gulf between the purity of the Divine Being and that defilement which is, in greater or less degree, the sad inheritance of every child of Adam. How is this gulf to be spanned? Who is there that can bring a clean thing out of an unclean? "If I wash myself with snow water, and make my hands never so clean, yet shalt thou plunge me in the ditch" (Job 9:30, 31). "Though thou wash thee with nitre, and take thee much soap, yet thine iniquity is marked before me, saith the Lord God" (Jer. 2:22). But what man cannot do, God Himself has done, according to the Scriptures. He has opened a fountain for sin and for uncleanness.

§1. *Purification*

The process whereby moral impurity was to be done away with was typified or shadowed forth by the purifications of the Levitical ritual. The word that is in general use in the O.T. to express the process is Tâhêr (טָהֵר, 2891), which signifies, in the intensive form, *to make clear, bright,* or *shining,* and hence *to make* or *pronounce clean.* It is used of *clearness* in the passage quoted at the beginning of this chapter.

External purification was taken at a very early time as a symbol of internal cleansing. Thus Jacob says to his household, "Put away the strange gods that are among you, and be clean, and change your garments: and let us arise, and go up to Bethel" (Gen. 35:2, 3). The cleansing and the change of dress were evidently intended to set forth the resolution to put away those false gods by which their lives had been contaminated. Nor were the people of God peculiar in the use of this symbolical rite. It has been found in all ages and in almost all countries, especially where there is a hot climate. The word that is adopted for the purifications appointed by God is also used to express idolatrous purgations in Isa. 66:17. The purification in the gardens there spoken of was simply misdirected symbolism.

Among the elements used for ceremonial cleansing in the Levitical system, three are especially to be noticed, namely, *fire, water,* and *blood.* Precious metals taken from idolatrous nations were to be passed through the fire; this process, together with an application of water, was considered to have purged them of their defilement. Clothing and all things that could not abide the fire were to be made to go through the water; and the persons of those who had come in contact with the heathen were to be reckoned unclean until this process was accomplished (Num. 31:23, 24). Cleansing by blood was needed in various cases of ceremonial defilement; in fact, "almost all things are by the law purged with blood" (Heb. 9:22).

No instance of ceremonial cleansing is more fully detailed or more interesting than that of the leper. Here we have to distinguish between three processes, each of which was called by the same name. There was, first, the actual cure of the disease; secondly, the authoritative pronunciation by the priest; and, thirdly, the external washings, offerings, and other rites that signed and sealed the same, and gave the healed man admittance into the congregation. With regard to the cleansing away of the disease, we have no exact account in Scripture. Leprosy appears to have come and gone, no one knew how. It was regarded as incurable by human means, and was considered to be a special visitation from God. Hence it was often designated as *the plague* or *stroke*.[3] The cure of Naaman is thus described, "His flesh came again like unto the flesh of a little child, and he was *clean*" (II Kings 5:14). It was with reference to this actual cure that the leper said to the Lord Jesus, "Lord, if thou wilt, thou canst make me *clean*." What the waters of Jordan were appointed to do in the one case to indicate that salvation was of the Jews, the word and touch of Jesus of Nazareth did in the other to show that saving power was vested in Him. Second came the inspection by the priest. "Go, shew thyself to the priest." If he was satisfied, by the presence of certain symptoms clearly described in the Law, that the man before him was cured or "clean" (in the first sense of the term), then he "pronounced him clean"—literally, "cleansed him." The official and authoritative declaration of the fact is thus identified in language with the fact itself.[4] In order, however,

---

3. In the opinion of some scholars leprosy is referred to in Isa. 53:4, where we read, "yet we did esteem him stricken, smitten of God, and afflicted." Jerome's (Latin Vulgate) translation is, "et nos putavimus eum *quasi leprosum* et percussum a Deo et humiliatum," that is, "we regarded him as if he were leprous, smitten of God, and humbled."

4. This identification in language is well worth observing in connection with the form of Absolution in the Service for the Visitation of the Sick in the Church of England. In the General Absolution we read that God "hath given power and commandment to his ministers to declare and pronounce to his people, being penitent, the Absolution and Remission of their sins." In the Visitation Service, after the Priest or Presbyter has "moved the sick person to make a special confession of his sins, if he feel his conscience troubled with any weighty matter," he "shall absolve him," i.e., declare him absolved (see Hooker, *E.P.* Book VI.).

that the man thus doubly "cleansed" might be received into the congregation and restored to those privileges from which he had been debarred, it was needful that he should be "cleansed" in a third sense through the offering of certain gifts and the performance of sundry remarkable rites, including being sprinkled with blood and washed with water (see Lev. 13 and 14).

A few other leading instances of the use of the ceremonial word Tâhêr (2891) for purification may be noticed. It is used to distinguish the clean from the unclean beasts (Gen. 7:2, 8; 8:20; Lev. 20:25); to express the cleansing of the priests and Levites (Ezra 6:20); the cleansing of the people, the gates, and the walls of Jerusalem (Neh. 12:30; 13:9, 22, 30); of the land (Ezek. 39:12, 14, 16). It also represents the pure gold used in the construction of the tabernacle vessels, etc. (Exod. 25); the pure perfume (Exod. 30:35); the clean place where the ashes of the offerings were cast (Lev. 4:12; 6:11); and clean persons, who were to perform certain rites (Lev. 7:19; 10:10; 11:32, etc.).

When we turn to the Psalms and the Prophets, we find Tâhêr (2891) used several times in a moral and spiritual sense. The following are the most important passages: Ps. 12:6, "The words of the LORD are pure words: as silver tried in an earthen furnace, purified seven times." Ps. 19:9, "The fear of the LORD is clean, enduring for ever." Ps. 51:2, "Wash me throughly from mine iniquity, and cleanse me from my sin." Ps. 51:7, "Purge me with hyssop, and I shall be clean: wash me, and I shall be whiter than snow." Ps. 51:10, "Create in me a clean heart, O God; and renew a right spirit within me." Prov. 15:26, "The words of the pure are pleasant words." Prov. 22:11, "He that loveth pureness [or cleanness] of heart, for the grace of his lips the king shall be his friend." Jer. 13:27, "O Jerusalem! wilt thou not be made clean?" Jer. 33:8, "I will cleanse them from all their iniquity . . . and I will pardon all their iniquities." Ezek. 36:25, 33, "Then will I sprinkle clean water upon you, and ye shall be clean: from all your filthiness, and from all your idols, will I cleanse you. . . . In the day that I shall have cleansed you from all your iniquities I will also cause you to dwell in the cities." Ezek. 37:23, "I will save them out of all their dwellingplaces, wherein they have sinned, and will cleanse them." Mal. 1:11, "In every place incense shall be offered unto my name, and a pure offering"; this is in contrast with the polluted offering of verse 7. Mal. 3:3, "He shall sit as a refiner and purifier of silver: and he shall purify the sons of Levi, and purge them as gold and silver, that they may offer unto the Lord an offering in righteousness."

§2. *Purification according to the N.T.*

With the exception of a few passages, Ṭâhêr (2891) has been rendered by καθαρίζω (2511) in the LXX. The exceptions are as follows: in II Chron. 29:16, 18, and 30:17, 18, we find ἁγνίζω (48); in these passages reference is made to the cleansing or purification of the temple and the worshipers at the Feast of the Passover; ἀφαγνίζω (L-S 285B) occurs in Num. 8:6, 21, where the cleansing of the Levites is spoken of; βρέχω (1026) in Ezek. 22:24, where the prophet speaks of the land not being cleansed with rain; ἁγνεία (47) in II Chron. 30:19; ἁγνισμός (49) in Num. 8:7; δίκαιος (1342) in Prov. 30:12; and δόκιμος (1384) in II Chron. 9:17.

Tracing the Greek word καθαρίζω (2511) through the N.T., we find that the Levitical purifications marked by this word were fulfilled in Christ. He made a καθαρισμός (2512), or *purgation*, whereby our sins are done away (Heb. 1:3). His blood cleanses from all sin (I John 1:7). Consequently, "If we confess our sins, [God] is faithful and righteous to forgive us our sins, and to cleanse us from all iniquity" (I John 1:9). The blood of Christ, who through the Eternal Spirit offered Himself without spot to God, purges the conscience from dead works, so that the purged person is in a position to serve (λατρεύειν, 3000) the living God (Heb. 9:14). Christ loved the Church, and gave Himself for it, that He might sanctify and cleanse it with the washing of water by the Word (Eph. 5:26). He gave Himself for us, that he might redeem us from all iniquity, and purify unto Himself a peculiar people, zealous of good works (Titus 2:14).

In connection with these announcements we have the corresponding exhortations: "Let us cleanse ourselves from all filthiness of the flesh and spirit, perfecting holiness in the fear of God" (II Cor. 7:1); "Let us draw near with a true heart in full assurance of faith, having our hearts sprinkled from an evil conscience, and our bodies washed with pure water" (Heb. 10:22).

These passages teach that the offering of Christ is not only the pledge of pardon, but also the appointed means of cleansing for all who feel their moral pollution. The defilement of sin was to find its cure in that one great work. Nor were its benefits confined to Jews.

What God had cleansed was not to be regarded any longer as common or unclean. The middle wall of partition between Jew and Gentile was broken down. God made no difference between the two; He purified the hearts of both through faith (Acts 15:9).

The cleansing thus effected through Christ answers to all the aspects of the ceremonial cleansing of the O.T.: there is the actual moral change in the individual, the clean heart, the renewed spirit, the godly life; there is the changed social position, membership in the body of Christ becoming a reality; and there is the being pronounced and regarded as clean in the sight of God through the mediatorial agency of the High Priest.

§3. *Washing*

The Hebrew words for washing deserve attention from the fact that they too are used ceremonially and morally as well as literally.

Dûwach (דּוּחַ, 1740), *to cast off,* and hence *to purge from impurity,* is used only four times in the O.T. Twice it is rendered *wash* (II Chron. 4:6 and Ezek. 40:38). In each of these places reference is made to the putting off of the pollution contracted by the priests and Levites while preparing the animals for offering. The first of these passages may be thus understood: "He made also ten lavers, and put five on the right hand, and five on the left, to wash in them" (II Chron. 4:6). The defilement contracted by the operations connected with the burnt offering they cleansed in these lavers. The Levites washed in the lavers, and the priests in the larger vessel called *the sea.* The R.V. has failed to draw out the distinction.

Dûwach (1740) is used in a spiritual sense in Isa. 4:4: "When the Lord shall have washed away the filth of the daughters of Zion, and shall have purged the blood of Jerusalem from the midst thereof by the spirit of judgment, and by the spirit of burning." The other passage where the word occurs is Jer. 51:34. Here the LORD, identifying Himself with his people, says, "Nebuchadnezzar . . . hath devoured me, . . . he hath cast me out"—i.e., has treated me as if I were the offscouring of the earth.

Shâṭaph (שָׁטַף, 7857), *to flood, overflow,* or *pour copiously,* is used in I Kings 22:38 of the cleansing of Ahab's chariot;[5] in Job 14:19 of the

---

5. Different Hebrew words are used for the washing of Ahab's chariot and for the cleansing of his armor. Were the two washed at the same place? The chariot was washed

destruction of the surface of the land by floods of water; and in Ezek. 16:9 of the "thorough washing" that represented the care with which God dealt with His people Israel at their first beginning.

We now come to the two words that were in most ordinary use among the Jews, namely, **Kâbaç** (כָּבַס, 3526), for which the LXX has πλύνω (4150) or ἀποπλύνω (637), which was applied to the washing of garments; and **Râchats** (רָחַץ, 7364—Assyrian *rahatsu*), generally rendered νίπτω (3538) or λούω (3068), but in seven passages πλύνω (4150), which represented the bathing or washing of the body.

Kâbaç (3526) is the term applied to the *fuller*, and is supposed to refer in the first place to the treading whereby clothes were cleaned. This cleansing of garments was an important ceremonial action. We have already seen its meaning under a slightly different form in Gen. 35:2, where Jacob told his household to put away their false gods and *to change their garments;* evidently the latter action was taken as the external symbol of the former. Of the "divers washings" of the Levitical dispensation, some had to do with the *garments* and are described under the word **Kâbaç** (3526); while others had to do with the *flesh,* and are represented by **Râchats** (7364). The following come under the first head: the ceremonial cleansing of the garments before the people were allowed to approach Mount Sinai (Exod. 19:10, 14); the cleansing of the garment sprinkled with the blood of the offering (Lev. 6:27); the cleansing of men's clothing after leprosy or after contact with that which was pronounced unclean (Lev. 17:15); the cleansing of the Levites' clothing for their service (Num. 8:7), where it was connected with the sprinkling of "holy water" over their flesh.

Under the second head (**Râchats**, 7364—the washing of the flesh) come the washing or bathing of the body, the hands, and the feet generally; the washing of the sacrifices (Exod. 29:17); of the priests before their consecration, and also before their daily ministration (Exod. 29:4 and 30:19, 21); and the washing of the elders' hands over the beheaded heifer (Deut. 21:6). This word is also used figuratively in Job 29:6 and Ps. 58:10. In the triumphant expression, "Moab is my washpot" (Ps. 60:8 and 108:9), the image is taken from the laver for

---

in the pool of Samaria. But probably his armor was taken to be cleaned at his palace at Jezreel. Doubtless the dogs licked the blood that was rinsed from it at or near the pool of Jezreel according to the prophecy of Elijah, which otherwise would not have been literally fulfilled. But see R.V.

the cleansing of the body, not from the trough for the washing of garments.

Each of these expressions is applied to spiritual washing. The word Kâbaç (3526), which implies the cleansing of garments, is found in the four following passages: Ps. 51:2, "Wash me throughly from my sin"; Ps. 51:7, "Wash me, and I shall be whiter than snow"; Jer. 2:22, "Though thou wash thee with nitre, and take thee much soap, yet thine iniquity is marked before me, saith the Lord GOD"; Jer. 4:14, "O Jerusalem, wash thine heart from wickedness, that thou mayest be saved."

The word Râchats (7364), which signifies the washing of the body, is used in a spiritual sense in the following texts: Ps. 26:6, "I will wash my hands in innocency"; Ps. 73:13, "I have washed my hands in innocency"; Prov. 30:12, "There is a generation that are pure in their own eyes, and yet is not washed from their filthiness"; Isa. 1:16, "Wash you, make you clean"; Isa. 4:4, "When the Lord shall have washed away the filth of the daughters of Zion."

The word *wash*, whether applied to the body or to its clothing, is never used except with reference to *water*, and it appears to symbolize the purgation of the inclinations, the character, and the external life from moral pollution. Compare Heb. 10:22: "having our hearts sprinkled from an evil conscience, and our bodies washed with pure water."

In the N.T., νίπτω (3538) is used of washing the face (Matt. 6:17); the hands (Matt. 15:2); the eyes (John 9:7, 11, 15); and the feet (John 13:5, 6, 8, 10, 12, 14; I Tim. 5:10). The word λούω (3068) is used of the bathing of the body in Acts 9:37; 16:33; and II Pet. 2:22. In John 13:10 we read, "He that is bathed [λελουμένος, 3068] needeth not save to wash [νίψασθαι, 3538] his feet, but is clean every whit" (καθαρὸς ὅλος—2513, 3650—"all clean"). It is evident that our Lord here referred, in the first instance, to the well-known fact that after a complete bath a man needed only to cleanse away the impurity that he contracted in walking from it if he wished to be accounted entirely clean. The significance of the act to the disciples seems to have been that whereas they were in a measure clean *through the Word* that He had spoken to them, there was yet need that He should humble Himself still lower on their behalf in order to cleanse them in the sight of God. The act of washing their feet symbolized the humiliation of Him who took the form of a servant, and it set forth the necessity of yielding to His cleansing work as the only means of having part with Him in His future kingdom. Washing with water is also connected with the Word in Eph. 5:26. Here we read that Christ gave Himself (i.e., *died*) for His Church, that He might sanctify and cleanse it with the washing[6] of the water by the Word (τῷ λουτρῷ τοῦ ὕδατος ἐν ῥήματι—*3588, 3067, 3588, 5204, 1722, 4487*). Washing (λοῦτρον, *3067*) is also used as a symbol of regeneration in Titus 3:5. With these passages we may connect Acts 22:16, "Arise, and be baptized, and *wash away* [ἀπόλουσαι, *628*] thy sins"; and I Cor. 6:11, "Such were some of you, but ye are *washed*" (ἀπελούσασθε, *628*). In the Received Text of Rev. 1:5 we read, "Who washed us from our sins in his own blood." Others here read λύσαντι (*3089*, liberated) for λούσαντι (*3068*, washed).

The word πλύνω (*4150*), which is applied to the washing of garments, is used symbolically in Rev. 7:14.[7]

§4. *Purity*

Bârar (בָּרַר, *1305*—Assyrian *baru*), literally *to separate*, and hence *to manifest* or *make clean*, is sometimes used in the sense of cleansing. In David's hymn (II Sam. 22:21, 25, 27; Ps. 18:20, 24, 26) it is used in respect of the cleanness of his hands, i.e., his freedom from evil deeds. Job says, "If I make my hands never so clean, yet shalt thou plunge me in the ditch" (9:30); here the word is made the more emphatic by being used with **Zâkak** (*2141*—on which see discussion below). In Ps. 73:1 we read, "Truly God is good to Israel, even to such as are of a clean heart." The feminine adjective **Bârâh** (בָּרָה, *1249*, formed from *1305*) is used in the expression, "Fair as the moon and *clear* as the sun" in Song of Sol. 6:10. **Bârar** (*1305*) occurs also in Isa. 52:11: "Be ye *clean*, that bear the vessels of the LORD." These passages chiefly refer to moral purity, not to ceremonial cleanness, in which sense the word is never used. It evidently applies to the thoughts of the heart as well as to the outward actions, and it is sometimes used of that moral cleansing or purgation that consists of separating

---

6. The laver (כִּיּוֹר, *3595*) is rendered λουτήρ (L-S 1061B) in the LXX. The word λουτρόν (*3067*) only occurs in Song of Sol. 4:2 and 6:5 for **Rachtsâh** (רַחְצָה, *7367*) of the washing of sheep.

7. Editor's note: In two of the oldest Alexandrian MSS. (C. Sinaiticus, 4th cent. A.D., and C. Alexandrinus, 5th cent. A.D.), together with the Vulgate and the versions made from it, one finds in Rev. 22:14, "Blessed are they that wash their robes, that they may have a right to the tree of life." However, this reading is not supported by the Majority Text.

the evil from the good, the dross from the ore (see Ps. 24:4; Isa. 1:25; Ezek. 20:38; Dan. 11:35; 12:10). The word is used of "a pure language" in Zeph. 3:9, where perhaps clearness or plainness is what is referred to.

There are three roots closely connected together that all represent purity, cleanness, or freedom from pollution, namely (1) **Zâqaq** (זָקַק, 2212), which is used in Ps. 12:6 and Mal. 3:3; (2) **Zâkak** (זָכַךְ, 2141), which is found in Job 8:6; 11:4; 16:17 ("My prayer is pure"); 15:15 ("The heavens are not clean in his sight"); 33:9; Prov. 16:2; 20:11; 21:8; Lam. 4:7 ("Purer than snow"); also Exod. 27:20; 30:34; Lev. 24:4, 7; (3) **Zâkâh** (זָכָה, 2135), which we find in Job 15:14 ("What is man, that he should be clean?"); 25:4 ("How can he be clean that is born of a woman?"); Prov. 20:9 ("Who can say, I have made my heart clean, I am pure from my sin?"); Ps. 51:4 ("That thou mightest be clear when thou judgest"); 73:13 ("I have cleansed my heart in vain"); 119:9 ("Wherewithal shall a young man cleanse his way?"); Isa. 1:16 ("Wash you, make you clean").

These passages refer to moral purity and transparency of heart. They point to a character free from taint or sully as the object that man aims at, but which he fails to obtain by his own devices; and even at the best, that which seems perfectly pure in his sight is proved vile when seen in the light of God.

§5. *Sprinkling*

Two Hebrew words are rendered *to sprinkle* in the O.T. Zâraq (זָרַק, 2236) occurs thirty-five times, and is always so rendered, except in Isa. 28:25, where it is translated *scatter*, and II Chron. 34:4, where we find *strew*. It is curious that the LXX almost always renders it προσχέω (L-S 1531B), *to pour*,[8] giving the idea of shedding or scattering rather than sprinkling. The act set forth by this word was usually performed by means of a vessel, the name of which was derived from it, and which the LXX renders φιάλη (5357), a *phial* (A.V. *vial*). It is first applied to the scattering of the ashes of the furnace in Exod. 9:8; then to the pouring of the blood of the offering on the altar and on the people in Exod. 24:6, 8 (see also Exod. 29:16, 20; Lev. 1:5, 11; 3:2, 8, 13; 7:2, 14; 8:19, 24; 9:12, 18; 17:6; Num. 18:17; II Kings 16:13, 15;

---

8. This verb is not to be found in the N.T., but the noun derived from it (πρόσχυσις, 4378) is used in Heb. 11:28 of the *shedding* or *sprinkling* of the blood of the paschal lamb on the doorposts.

II Chron. 29:22; 30:16; 35:11). In Num. 19:13, 20, it is applied to the sprinkling of the water of separation; and in Job 2:12 to the sprinkling of dust on the head; in Isa. 28:25, to the scattering of cumin; and in Hos. 7:9, to the gray hairs which are *here and there* (margin, *sprinkled*) on the head.

The word is once used in a spiritual sense, namely, in Ezek. 36:25: "Then will I sprinkle clean water upon you, and ye shall be clean."

Nâzâh (הזָנָ, 5137) occurs twenty-four times, and is always rendered *to sprinkle*. It is not necessarily used in a ceremonial sense. The LXX renders it by ῥαίνω (L-S 1564A), ῥαντίζω (4472), and their compounds. It is applied to the priest's sprinkling of blood with the finger before the veil, or on the side of the altar, or on the mercyseat on the occasion of the sin offering (Lev. 4:6, 17; 5:9; 16:14, 15, 19). It is also applied to the sprinkling of the blood of the bird on the leper with hyssop (Lev. 14:7, 51); to the sprinkling of the water of purifying and separation (Num. 8:7; 19:21); and to the sprinkling of oil with the finger (Lev. 8:11, 30; 14:16, 27). The word is used with a spiritual significance in Isa. 52:15: "So shall he sprinkle many nations." It signifies *dropping*, while Zâraq (2236) marks *pouring forth*.

The sprinklings (ῥαντισμοί, 4473) specially referred to in the Epistle to the Hebrews are of two kinds: that which was performed with the ashes of a red heifer on persons who had contracted certain defilement (Heb. 9:13), and that which was performed with blood on the people and the Book in making the Old Covenant. There was also the sprinkling of blood on the tabernacle and various vessels connected with the sacred service (Heb. 9:19, 21). The substance of which these are the shadows is the sprinkling of the blood of Jesus, which speaks better things than that of Abel (Heb. 12:24).

Peter connects this "sprinkling of the blood of Jesus Christ" with obedience, and both of these with "sanctification of the Spirit" (I Pet. 1:2). This sprinkling has its effect both in the sight of God, where it signifies reconciliation, and on the conscience of man, which it purges from dead works to serve the living God (Heb. 9:14). Accordingly, the Christian is invited to approach God with a true heart sprinkled from an evil conscience (Heb. 10:22).

§6. *Baptism*

Many are the controversies that have gathered around the rite of baptism. Questions have been raised as to the mode of administration, as to the right age and condition of those to whom it is to be administered, as to the persons who may perform the ordinance, as to the privileges and responsibilities involved in it, as to the exact bearing of the symbol, and as to the nature of the nexus that exists between the sign and the thing signified. Only one of these questions need be discussed here. When our Lord gave orders to His followers to baptize, how would the word that He used be understood? Did it prescribe the exact mode in which the ordinance was to be administered? Or had it already arrived at that secondary or technical sense in which undoubtedly it has been largely used subsequently?

Classical authors have been diligently searched by contending parties with the hope of finding some solution of the question. But the more they have been scrutinized the more clearly has it appeared that the word βαπτίζω (907) has been used with very great latitude, and that it can be neither confined to its primary use of staining or dyeing nor restricted to the case of religious or ceremonial acts of cleansing.

The conclusion arrived at by a writer[9] who was himself a "Baptist," that is, one who holds to the practice of immersion, is as follows:

> The English translators did not translate the word *baptize*, and they acted wisely; for there is no one word in the English language which is an exact counterpart of the Greek word, *as the New Testament uses it*, containing the precise ideas of the Evangelist, neither less nor more. The difficulty, or rather the excellency, of the word is that it contains two ideas, inclusive of the whole doctrine of baptism. *Baptize* is a dyer's word, and signifies *to dip so as to colour*. Such as render the word *dip* give one true idea; but the word stood for two, and one is wanting in this rendering. This defect is in the German [New] Testament, Matt. 3:1: "In those days came John *der Täufer*"— John the Dipper; and the Dutch, "In those days came John *der Dooper*"—John the Dipper. This is the truth, but it is not the whole truth. The Anglo-Saxon [New] Testament adds another idea by naming John *le fulluhtere*—the fuller; and the Icelandic language translates Baptism, *skirn*, washing. These convey two ideas, *cleansing* by *washing*,

---

9. Mr. R. Robinson, of Cambridge, quoted by Elihu (a Baptist) in his Vindication of the Bible Society.

but neither do these accurately express the two ideas of the Greek *baptize*.[10]

As the question under discussion concerns a rite the performance of which has been held essential in all ages of Christianity, it certainly might have been supposed that this is one of the cases in which an examination of the early versions would decide the matter, but the search has led to no definite result. The old Latin version, indeed, rendered βαπτίζω (907) by *tingo,* that is, to *moisten, bathe, dye,* or *stain.* But Jerome adopted *baptizo,* a Latinized form of the Greek original, feeling, no doubt, that no Latin word could rightly convey its meaning. From the Latin Vulgate of Jerome the same word spread, through the influence of the church to which he belonged, into the Italian, Spanish, Portuguese, French, and English languages. The Syriac version has a very good word for dipping but never uses it for baptism, preferring a word that originally signifies *to stand,* which was adopted possibly from the position the catechumen took when the water was poured over him. In the Slavonic, modern Russian, and kindred languages, a term is used that is connected with *crossing* (i.e., making the sign of the cross over one), or possibly with *christening.* In Arabic and Persian, as also in Icelandic, we find words that signify washing or cleansing; and in Anglo-Saxon, as we have seen above, the word is almost the same. Wycliffe used *wash* and *baptize* indifferently; thus in Matt. 3:11 we read, "I *waishe* yhou in watir into pennance, but he that schal come after me is strenger than i, whos schoon y am not worthi to bere, he schal *baptise* you in the hooly Goost and fire." The German and kindred languages have been cited in favor of the rendering *dip,* but it has been shown by Dr. Henderson that there is a slight distinction between the words for *dip* and *baptize* in these languages; thus the German word for *dip* is generally *tauchen,* but the word for *baptize* is *taufen.* Moreover, in these languages the preposition following the verb is usually not *in* which would be expected if the verb answered to our English *dip,* but *with,* showing that the verb is used

10. An anonymous writer, quoted in the pamphlet from which this passage is extracted, says, "To *scrape* is the action employed when Paganini plays; but surely he would be offended if we were to use that homely word respecting his performance. In like manner, I think it would be bad grammar, and bad taste, to say *dip* instead of *baptize.*"

in a ceremonial rather than an etymological sense, for the administration of a cleansing rite.

It is evident that the versions of the Scriptures will not lead us to any definite conclusion, and we are thrown back once more on the Bible itself. Although the English word *baptize* does not occur in the O.T., yet on examining the LXX we find the Greek βαπτίζω (907) used twice in the canonical Scriptures, and twice in the Apocrypha. In Judith 12:7 we read, "She washed herself [ἐβαπτίζετο, 907] at the fountain of water." Apparently this was for ceremonial cleansing. In Sirach 34:25 we are told of one who was βαπτιζόμενος ἀπὸ νεκροῦ (907, 575, 3498), i.e., washed or bathed, in order to be cleansed from the ceremonial pollution that arises from contact with a dead body. This was done by sprinkling (Num. 8:7). In Isa. 21:4 the prophet says, "Fearfulness hath affrighted me," which the LXX renders ἡ ἀνομία μὲ βαπτίζει (3588, 458, 1473, 907—lit. "lawlessness baptizes me"). Here the word stands for the Hebrew Bâ'ath (בָּעַת, 1204), and seems to be used figuratively of one who was flooded, overwhelmed with evil.

The most important passage, however, where the word occurs is in the history of Naaman the Syrian in II Kings 5:14. Elisha had told the Syrian that if he would "wash" seven times in the Jordan he should be cleansed from the leprosy. Accordingly, he went and "dipped" (ἐβαπτίσατο, 907) seven times in the river. The Hebrew verb in this passage is Ṭâbal (טָבַל, 2881), *to dip*. It is the word used of Joseph's coat that was dipped in goat's blood (Gen. 37:31; the LXX has μολύνω, 3435, in the sense of *to stain*); of the priest's finger being dipped in blood (Lev. 4:6, 17; 9:9); of the living bird that was dipped in the blood of the slain bird (Lev. 14:6); of the finger being dipped in oil (Lev. 14:16); of hyssop being dipped in water (Num. 19:18); of the feet of the priests dipped in the brim of the water (Josh. 3:15); of Ruth dipping her morsel in the vinegar (Ruth 2:14); of Jonathan dipping the end of his rod in the honeycomb (I Sam. 14:27); of Hazael dipping a cloth in water (II Kings 8:15). We also meet with it in Job 9:30, 31, where we read, "If I wash myself with snow water, and make my hands never so clean, yet shalt thou plunge me in the ditch."

The meaning of the word Ṭâbal (2881) in these passages is clear and indubitable; it does not, however, follow that βαπτίζομαι (907) signifies *to dip* when adopted by the LXX in II Kings 5:14. In none of the passages above cited was the dipping effected for the purpose of *washing* the object dipped; in some quite the contrary; but in the case of Naaman the order was "Go, wash," where the word Râchats (7364) is used to signify the cleansing of the body (see §3); hence in this passage the verb Ṭâbal (2881) was used to express a process identical with the act of washing. Moreover, in none of the other passages is the word βαπτίζω (907) adopted as a rendering of Ṭâbal (2881); we always find either βάπτω (911)[11] or παραβάπτω (L-S 1304B). It may be concluded from this fact that the special word βαπτίζω (907) was used in the passage under consideration in order to show that Naaman's washing in the river Jordan was to be regarded as partaking of the nature of a symbolical or ceremonial cleansing.

On the whole, the usage of the word βαπτίζω (907) in the LXX cannot be said to decide whether the washing indicated by it must needs take place by a process of dipping (though this process would certainly be most in accordance with the passages referred to), or whether its requirements would be satisfied by having water poured over the person. Nor does the N.T. finally decide the matter. The word was used by the Jews in our Lord's time of ceremonial washing, rather than of mere dipping, as will be clearly seen by reference to Mark 7:4 and Luke 11:38, where the baptizing of the person is regarded as a sort of ritual observance; while in Mark 7:4 and 8, the baptism of cups and other vessels is spoken of in the same way.

The "divers baptisms" (A.V. "washings") spoken of in Heb. 9:10 may comprehend such observances as those just referred to, but they rather seem to indicate the various rites of purification that formed part of the Levitical system. These rites were of two kinds: there were those which a man had to perform for himself, and those which others were to administer to him. It is probably the last class of washings that is referred to here. They were performed by priests or other ceremonially clean persons, who poured or sprinkled oil, blood, water, or water impregnated with the ashes of a red heifer, on the persons who were to be purified. The application of the word βαπτισμοί (909) to these rites tends to confirm the view

11. The word βάπτω (911), *to dip* or *tinge*, is used only four times in the N.T. In Luke 16:24, it refers to dipping the tip of the finger in water; in John 13:26, it is twice used of dipping the sop; in Rev. 19:13, we read of "a vesture *dipped in blood*," but here it would be better to render the words, *stained with blood* (βεβαμμένον αἵματι—911, 129). The Vulgate rendering in this passage is "vestis *aspersa* sanguine" ("clothing having been sprinkled with blood.")

already indicated, that whatever the etymology and primary usage of the term *baptize* may have been, it had practically come to be used of *ceremonial washing* in our Lord's time, and that it was not exclusively or necessarily applied to *dipping*. If the true rendering of the expression $\beta\alpha\pi\tau\iota\sigma\mu\hat{\omega}\nu$ $\delta\iota\delta\alpha\chi\hat{\eta}\varsigma$ (909, 1322), in Heb. 6:2, be not "the doctrine of baptisms," as the A.V. has it, but "cleansings of teaching," i.e., the purging from old prejudices and superstitions through the teaching of the truth, then we have further confirmatory evidence in the same direction.

The exact mode in which John the Baptist administered the rite is not described in the N.T. The writers seem to take it for granted that such a description was not called for. Those who submitted to it acknowledged thereby their sorrow for their past sins and their determination to live a changed life, in order to prepare for the coming of Him who should fulfill the promise made by God to the fathers. A cleansing ordinance would suitably indicate the change of heart and life thus entered on.

When our Lord was baptized, it was not because He needed cleansing, but in order that He might give a personal sanction to the ordinance, submitting to it with the same humility as He evinced when falling in with other Jewish rites. The descent of the Spirit on Him immediately afterwards was intended not only to mark that He was "anointed to preach the gospel," but also to indicate that it was He who should *baptize* with the Holy Ghost, which He did when He "shed forth" the Spirit from on high at Pentecost like floods upon a dry ground. The use of the word in this connection suggests the symbolic action of sprinkling or effusion rather than of dipping.

The second baptism our Lord underwent (Matt. 20:22, 23; Luke 12:50) was no ceremony, but a solemn reality. He was to be perfected through sufferings, and the waves of trouble that poured on His soul were signified outwardly by the sweat that was "as it were great drops of blood falling down to the ground" (Luke 22:44).

The use of the word *baptize* thus leads to the conclusion that the act of dipping cannot be held as *essential* to Christian baptism unless it is proved to be so by the additional use of $\beta\acute{\alpha}\pi\tau\omega$ (911), or some such word, as an adjunct or an alternative. This, however, is confessedly not the case. Nor does the symbolic teaching connected with the rite suggest any other conclusion than that which we have now arrived at. Baptism is preeminently symbolic of cleansing, whether by the blood of Christ or by the inspiration of the Holy

Ghost; and so the ceremonial act is regarded by Peter as analogous with "the putting away of the filth of the flesh" (I Pet. 3:21). When a believer, or the child of a believer, is baptized, we are to understand that, by profession at least, he has become a disciple of Christ, and is one with Him by faith. He dies to sin, in union with the Captain of Salvation; he is buried with Him; he puts on the Lord Jesus Christ, as one puts on armor or clothing; he walks in newness of life; and he is admitted into the society or body of those who are similarly cleansed.

If this, the death to sin and the new birth to righteousness by the quickening power of the Spirit through faith in Christ Jesus, be indeed what is set forth in the rite of baptism, and if the word has gradually passed into this technical or ceremonial sense, then the exact mode in which the rite is administered, whether by immersion or effusion, is not a point of primary importance. Thus it may be left open to that discretion which has usually been permitted in non-essentials. Immersion ought not to be rigorously enforced; still less ought it to be rigorously denied. The ceremonial application of clean water to the person, as a symbol of the purifying efficacy of Christ's blood and of the quickening power of the Holy Spirit, and submission to the ordinance as a mark of discipleship to the Father, the Son, and the Holy Ghost—these are the grand points to be observed. The exact mode of administration is a matter of church order and discipline, concerning which there ought to be much forbearance and also considerable latitude for the carrying out of personal conviction. This is the case, theoretically at least, in the Church of England, as well as in some other Churches.

14

Justification

§1. Ideas Connected with the Word

The idea of justification appears to be in some measure legal or forensic rather than moral or psychological. It is frequently taken in Scripture to be the opposite of condemnation; and in some of its aspects it answers fairly to our word *acquittal*. But it has often been observed that human legal analogies are very inadequate for the purpose of representing the relation of the restored man to his God. Acquittal is the judicial declaration that an accused man is *not guilty* of a certain crime, so far as the law under which he has been tried is concerned. He may have committed the offense, but either it cannot be brought home to him by adequate testimony, or else the law under which he is tried has not provided for the charge laid against him. This, however, is a most imperfect representation of God's work in justifying, since it leaves out of sight the fact that His law is perfect and applicable to all cases, and that no outside testimony of man's guilt is necessary because God is acquainted with the very secrets of the heart. And what is still more important, it leaves out of sight the truth that is to be gathered from Scripture as a whole, that the process of Divine acquittal is so blended with the entrance of spiritual life into the person acquitted that, though they are theoretically distinct, one cannot be fully stated or even comprehended without reference to the other. The controversy between the Church of Rome and various Protestant bodies has arisen, in part at least, from the complexity of the relationship that thus exists between God and man.

Another difficulty has arisen in England from the poverty of our language. We have no one word that can convey the idea of *right-eousness* and that of *justification,* as they are set forth in Scripture. In this case, as in many others, we see the wisdom of God in select-ing Hebrew as the means of communication with His creatures, because here the ideas of *righteousness, justification,* and *acquittal* all cluster around one verbal root, and are thus seen to be parts of one whole.

The Hebrew verb that signifies *to be just* or *righteous* is Tsâdaq (צָדַק, 6663), which is supposed to convey originally an idea of straightness or stiffness (see chap. 9, §2).

The verb is once used in the Hithpael or reflexive stem in Gen. 44:16: "What shall we speak? or how shall we *clear ourselves?*" As a matter of fact, Judah and his brethren were innocent, but he asked this question under the impression that they were guilty. It is once used in the Niphal or passive in Dan. 8:14: "Thus shall the sanctuary be cleansed." It appears here to be used in a secondary or derived sense. Five times it occurs in the Piel or intensive: Job 32:2, "He justified his own soul rather than God"; Job 33:32, "If thou hast anything to say, answer me: speak, for I desire to justify thee"; Jer. 3:11, "The backsliding Israel hath justified her soul more than treacherous Judah"; Ezek. 16:51, 52, "Thou hast multiplied thine abominations more than they, and hast justified thy sisters in all thine abominations which thou hast done. . . . They are righteous in comparison with thee. Yea, be thou also confounded, and bear thy shame, in that thou hast justified thy sisters." The conduct of the inhabitants of Judah had been so much worse than that of Samaria or Sodom that they caused these nations to appear or to be accounted righteous in comparison.

Tsâdaq (6663) is used twelve times in the Hiphil or causative stem: Exod. 23:7, "I will not justify the wicked." This principle of the Divine action is laid down as an example to be imitated by the earthly judge in Deut. 25:1: "Then shall they justify the righteous and condemn the wicked." Absalom boasted (by implication) that he would exceed his father David in meting out justice if he were king in II Sam. 15:4: "Oh that I were made judge in the land, that every man which hath any suit or cause might come to me, and I would do him justice!" In dedicating the temple, Solomon suppli-cated God for the exercise of Divine justice in Israel (I Kings 8:32; II Chron. 6:23): "Judge thy servants, condemning the wicked, to bring his way upon his head; and justifying the righteous, to give him according to his righteousness." This passage is important as giving a fullness of meaning to the word *justification*, which otherwise might be missed. It is here not only acquittal, but the consequences of acquittal. Job says (27:5), "God forbid that I should justify you." Several other texts illustrate this fact. Ps. 82:3, "Do justice to the afflicted and needy." Prov. 17:15, "He that justifieth the wicked, and he that condemneth the just, even they both are abomination to the LORD." Isa. 5:23, "Woe unto them . . . which justify the wicked for reward, and take away the righteousness of the righteous from him." Isa. 50:8, "He is near that justifieth me; who will contend with me?" Isa. 53:11, "By his knowledge shall my righteous servant justify many; and it is he that shall bear their iniquities." This passage is usually explained as if "his knowledge" meant "the knowledge that others would have concerning him"; but there is no necessity to fall back on this explanation. The Messiah was to be "acquainted with grief"; moreover, he was to bear man's iniquities, and they became in some mysterious sense identified with Him. It was this that became the means of justifying many.[1] Dan. 12:3, "They that turn many to righteousness shall shine as the stars for ever and ever." Compare the teaching of the last verses of James' Epistle.

It remains to notice the passages where the verb is used in the active voice. They are as follows: Gen. 38:26, "She hath been more righteous than I." Job 4:17, "Shall a mortal man be more just than God?" Job 9:2, "How should man be just before God?" Job 9:15, "Though I were righteous I would not answer." Job 9:20, "If I justify myself [lit., if I be righteous], my own mouth shall condemn me." Job 10:15, "If I be righteous, yet will I not lift up my head." Job 11:2, "Should a man full of talk be justified [lit., be righteous]?" Job 13:18,

---

1. "No man, except Christ, has ever yet been able rightly to discern the nature and extent of sin; because only one whose penetrating gaze can apprehend the whole of the glory and worth of which God created humanity capable, the whole tenor of its downward way, and the high end it may yet attain; none but Jesus has ever sounded the whole extent of the aberrations, degradations, and disorder of our race. He, however, *has* sounded all these depths, His heart has been pierced with adequate sorrow for all that dishonouring of God's holy name, of which the beings, whose brother He became, were guilty; and consequently He has fully apprehended the righteous severity of Divine justice in connecting sin with death in its various forms. And because He has manifested the righteousness and justice of the Divine sentence, not in words only, but practically by His silent and holy endurance of its penalty, He has accomplished the purpose of Divine punishment, and has terminated it—on behalf of whom? on behalf of all those who by faith appropriate this His holy endurance of the Divine judgment as their own." *Essay on the Atonement*, by Wolfgang Friedrich Gess.

"Behold now, I have ordered my cause; I know that I shall be justified" (lit., that I am righteous). Job 15:14, "What is he that is born of woman, that he should be righteous?" Job 22:3, "Is it any pleasure to the Almighty that thou art righteous?" Job 25:4, "How can man be justified [lit., righteous] with God?" Job 33:12, "Behold, in this thou art not just." Job 34:5, "Job hath said, I am righteous." Job 35:7, "If thou be righteous, what givest thou him?" Job 40:8, "Wilt thou condemn me, that thou mayest be righteous?" Ps. 19:9, "The judgments of the Lord are true and righteous altogether." Ps. 51:4, "That thou mightest be justified [lit., be righteous] when thou speakest, and clear when thou judgest." Ps. 143:2, "Enter not into judgment with thy servant, O Lord: for in thy sight shall no man living be justified" (or righteous). Isa. 43:9, "Let them bring forth their witnesses, that they may be justified [or righteous]: or let them hear, and say, It is truth." Isa. 43:26, "Declare thou, that thou mayest be justified" (or righteous). Isa. 45:25, "In the Lord shall all the seed of Israel be justified [or righteous], and shall glory." Ezek. 16:52, "They are righteous in comparison with thee."

The passages cited above show that *justification* is a term applicable to something more than the discharge of an accused person uncondemned. As in our courts of law there are civil as well as criminal cases, so it was in ancient times; and a large number of the passages adduced seem to refer to trials of the former description in which some question of property, right, or inheritance was under discussion between two parties. The judge, by justifying one of the parties, decided that the property in question was to be regarded as his. Applying this aspect of the matter to the justification of man in the sight of God, we gather from Scripture that while through sin man has forfeited legal claim to any right or inheritance that God might have to bestow on His creatures, so through justification he is restored to his high position and regarded as an heir of God.

The adjective **Tsaddîyq** (6662) is almost always rendered δίκαιος (*1342*), *righteous,* in the LXX, and the substantives **Tsedeq** (6664) and **Tsᵉdâqâh** (6666) generally δικαιοσύνη (*1343*), *righteousness.* The word ἔλεος (*1656*), *mercy,* has been adopted in the following texts: Isa. 56:1, "My salvation is near to come, and my righteousness to be revealed"; also in Ezek. 18:19, 21, where we read of man doing "what is lawful and right." The righteousness of the law was specially manifested in mercy, so that the Greek translators were right in point of fact, though incorrect in their rendering in these passages.

In several passages the LXX has adopted ἐλεημοσύνη (1654), a word that has passed from its original meaning as the feeling of mercy or pity to the active development of that feeling in eleemosynary acts, or almsgiving. This is the case in Deut. 6:25, where our translation is, "It shall be our righteousness if we observe to do all these commandments." Here the LXX followed by the Vulgate and the translations made from it say, "There shall be mercy for us if we observe," etc. The passage literally translated would be, "There shall be righteousness for us," etc. Perhaps the LXX has preserved the true meaning of the passage, and certainly it is in accordance with the general tenor of God's Word. The same rendering is found in Deut. 24:13; Ps. 24:5; 33:5; 103:6; Isa. 1:27; 28:17; 59:16; Dan. 4:27; 9:16.

The verb Tsâdaq (6663) is rendered δικαιόω (1344), *to make righteous* or *to acquit,* almost everywhere by the LXX; but the various forms in which the verb is used were not capable of being accurately distinguished in the Greek. This difficulty has reappeared in at least one passage in the N.T. In Rev. 22:11, the words "He that is righteous let him *be righteous* still" are, if literally rendered, "He that is righteous let him be *justified* still"—a rendering adopted by the Latin Vulgate and found in most, if not all, versions made from that venerable work. This literal rendering is certainly very beautiful and instructive, though the usage of the LXX affords our translators some plea for departing from it. The R.V. has changed, but hardly improved, the rendering.

§2. *Righteousness in Relation to Justification*

The nature of righteousness, or conformity to the Divine law of love, has been pointed out in Chapter 9 but we must here notice its relationship with justification.

We read in Gen. 15:6, "Abraham believed God, and it was reckoned to him [for] righteousness." In this passage three words enter on the sacred pages for the first time—*belief, righteousness,* and *reckoning* or *imputation*—words that were destined to play a conspicuous part in Christian terminology. That element of Abraham's feeling and conduct toward God that we usually call *belief, faith,* or *faithfulness*[2] was regarded by God as a reason why he should be

2. See Chapter 9.

accepted as righteous or justified. Not only does all right action spring from belief in the Word of God, but also our heavenly Father justifies or acquits those persons who exercise it. Abraham's faith, according to the Hebrew text, "was reckoned unto him righteousness"; but the LXX, followed by the Apostle Paul, interprets this phrase as meaning *for* (εἰς, 1519), not "*as* [ὡς, 5316] righteousness."[3] It would follow that the passage does not teach us that Abraham's faith was regarded or estimated by God *as if it were* righteousness— the one quality being taken for the other—but that owing to the fact that he had faith in the promises, God accepted him, acquitted him from the charge of sin, pronounced him righteous, and conferred on him an inheritance. Thus as Paul says, Abraham was justified *by faith* (ἐκ πιστέως —1537, 4102), i.e., *owing to the fact that he had faith*. The ground on God's part and the method of justification are not touched by the word. It simply points to the aspect in which the Judge of all the earth regards the believer, and the way in which He deals with him.

It is not a little remarkable that the privilege thus granted to Abraham was accorded to another person in exactly the same terms, but apparently on a different ground. In Ps. 106:30, 31, we read, "Then stood up Phinehas, and executed judgment: and the plague was stayed. And that was counted unto him for[4] righteousness unto all generations for evermore." When we turn to the history (Num. 25) on which these verses are a comment, we find that Phinehas was zealous for God's sake against those who were committing whoredom and idolatry, going so far as to slay "a prince of a chief house among the Simeonites" together with the daughter of the "head over a people and of a chief house in Midian." What was it that prompted him to this bold and decided action, which atoned for the sins of the people? The prophet Malachi answers, speaking in God's name, "He feared me, and was afraid before my name. The law of truth was in his mouth, and iniquity was not found in his lips" (Mal. 2:5, 6). He "said unto his father and to his mother, I have

---

3. This important distinction, which has sometimes been neglected in controversy, has been observed in the Latin Vulgate—*ad* justitiam—"for righteousness"—and has been rendered thus by the following translators: Luther has "*zur* Gerechtigkeit"; De Sacy, "*à* justice"; D'Almeida, "*por* justiça." Beza, in his Latin version, made a mistake in putting *pro* justitia (in the place *of, instead of* righteousness) in Rom. 4:3, etc.

4. The Hebrew preposition *for* (ל) is inserted here, justifying the interpretation of the LXX in the passage previously discussed.

not seen him; neither did he acknowledge his brethren, nor knew his own children" (Deut. 33:9). He had respect to the unseen God, and despised the fear of man and the ties of kindred. In other words, he had *faith*, and his deed is of a class with many of those recorded in the eleventh chapter of Hebrews. It was his conviction of the truth of God's Word that caused him to be loyal when a whole nation seemed to be drifting into carnality and idolatry; and so "it was reckoned to him for righteousness."

The second passage in which the substantive occurs is Gen. 18:19, where God says of Abraham, "I know him, that he will command his children and his household after him, and they shall keep the way of the LORD, to do justice and judgment." Here justice (i.e., righteousness) seems to mark a course of action in conformity with the grand principle of right—loving God with all one's heart, and one's neighbor as oneself. This righteousness was not absolute, i.e., such as would commend Abraham to God as a rightful claimant of the inheritance of sonship, because, in that case, he would not have been said to have been justified by faith; it was therefore *relative*, and was the result of his faith in God (see Rom. 4:2-4, and cf. II Sam. 22:21).

Jacob appeals to this relative and practical principle in Gen. 30:33, with reference to his dealings with Laban (whether fairly or not), where he says, "So shall my righteousness answer for me in time to come, when it shall come for my hire before thy face." He implies that he had been honest, and more than honest; that he had borne losses that might fairly have gone to the account of Laban. This righteousness is something more than what we ordinarily mean by the word *justice*; it is not doing to others *as they have done to us*, but doing to them what we would like them to do to us if our respective positions were changed. It exceeds "the righteousness of the Scribes and Pharisees," which consisted in doing good either where a return was to be expected, or where the object was to make a fair show before men.

Another noteworthy passage is Deut. 9:4-6, where the people of Israel were guarded in the plainest terms from the supposition that they were being brought into Canaan on account of their own righteousness. They were thus trained in the idea that the inheritance was not to be regarded as a reward for human merit, but was to be received as a gift from the covenant-keeping God.

The expression, "O God of my righteousness," which is occasionally found in the Psalms, e.g., Ps. 4:1, has been diversely explained. Some critics suppose that it means, "O God, who art my righteous judge"; others, "O God, who justifies me."[5] But perhaps its explanation is more simple. As "the temple of God's holiness" in Ps. 138:2 signifies "God's holy temple," so the phrase "God of my righteousness" may mean "my righteous God." This conclusion is in harmony with the doctrine that God possesses in fullness Himself that righteousness which He bestows on man.

In Deut. 33:19 and Ps. 4:5 we read, "offer the sacrifices of righteousness." This cannot signify "substitute righteousness for sacrifices," but rather "offer righteous sacrifices"; that is, do not let your sacrifices be formal or impure, but bring them in a right spirit, in loving conformity with God's law. The form of the expression is exactly parallel to that which the A.V. translates "just balances" (lit., balances of righteousness) (Lev. 19:36; Job 31:6; Ezek. 45:10). That this is the right interpretation of the passage may be confirmed from a reference to Ps. 51:16, 17: "Thou desirest not sacrifice; else would I give it: thou delightest not in burnt offering. The sacrifices of God are a broken spirit: a broken and a contrite heart, O God, thou wilt not despise." Having said this, the Psalmist looks forward to a state of things when sacrifices should be once more acceptable: "Build thou the walls of Jerusalem. Then shalt thou be pleased with the sacrifices of righteousness, with burnt offerings and whole burnt offerings: then shall they offer young bullocks upon thine altar" (v. 20). Compare Mal. 3:3, where we are told that the Angel of the Covenant "shall purify the sons of Levi, and purge them as gold and silver, that they may offer unto the LORD an offering in righteousness." In all these passages the spirit of the offerers rather than the nature of the offering is described by the qualifying word *righteousness*.

In some passages in which God's righteousness is appealed to, it appears that its merciful aspect, as referred to so often by the LXX, is in the Psalmist's mind. Thus he says, "Lead me, O LORD, in thy righteousness" (Ps. 5:8); "Deliver me, in thy righteousness" (31:1). In these passages the writer throws himself on the revealed character of God as containing something more than abstract justice. There is

---

5. De Sacy renders it, "Dieu, *qui est le principe de ma justice*" ("O God, [you] who [are] the Source of my righteousness").

in Him an element of pity for the suffering, and of mercy for the fallen; there *must be*, for these principles have found expression in the law that He has prescribed for men's dealings with one another.

In Prov. 10:2 ("Righteousness delivereth from death") we have one of a class of passages very common in the O.T., pointing out the blessings that as a matter of fact follow from conformity to the will of God. When the prophet Ezekiel says (18:20), "The righteousness of the righteous shall be *upon* him, and the wickedness of the wicked shall be *upon* him," he teaches that a man is dealt with by God according to his own personal character and course of action, and that he must not delude himself with the idea that he can possess any hereditary immunity from evil.

Lastly, we read in Mal. 4:2 of a Being who is described as the Sun of Righteousness, who should rise with healing in His wings for those who fear the name of God. Just as the material sun in the heavens gives forth light and heat, and becomes a center of attraction for all other bodies that come within its gravitational sphere, so from the Messiah there was to issue healing power that should become an efficient remedy for all spiritual diseases and for physical corruption.

§3. N.T. Teaching on Justification and Righteousness

Turning now from the O.T. to the N.T., it is noticeable that the word *righteousness* is rare in the Gospels: Mark never employs it; Luke only once (four times in the Acts); John, twice; and Matthew, eight times at most. In the Epistles of Paul the word is used sixty-six times, and in various senses.

(1) There is one absolute and eternal standard of right that is of the essence of the nature of God; therefore we say that whatever He does must be right, because Right is summed up in Him.[6] With respect to this element in the character of God, Paul speaks of our own righteousness commending *God's righteousness* (Rom. 3:5). This is the only passage in Paul's Epistles in which the words are

---

6. The question is sometimes asked, Is a thing right because God does it; or does He do it because it is right? This is a metaphysical query far beyond the limits of the present work. Suffice it to say that if God has done a thing, it is certain to be right; and if a thing is certainly wrong, we may be sure that God does not approve of it. God and right, the Lawgiver and the law, are, so far as we can understand, not *two* but *one*.

put in the order, Θεοῦ δικαιοσύνη (*2316, 1343*); in all the others he—no doubt with a purpose—wrote, δικαιοσύνη Θεοῦ (*1343, 2316*).

(2) If we could obtain a thorough conformity with this Divine standard by the spiritual observance of the various principles and precepts contained in the law, we would be righteous even as He is righteous. But in this sense "There is none righteous, no, not one" (Rom. 3:10).

(3) Nevertheless, some have sought to establish their own righteousness by attempting to fulfill the letter of the law of Moses. This was the case with many of the Jews (Rom. 10:3), and it had been the aim of the Apostle Paul himself in his early days; so far, in fact, had he succeeded that he could say, "touching the righteousness which is of the law [I was] blameless," i.e., no fault could be found in me by those who measured me by the letter of the law (Phil. 3:6). Yet when the commandments contained in the law were opened up to him in their application to the thoughts of his heart,[7] he found that sin, though repressed, was not conquered: "Sin revived, and I died" (Rom. 7:9).

(4) One Being, however, has partaken of human nature, of whom God could say in the full meaning of the words, "Thou hast loved righteousness and hated iniquity" (Heb. 1:9). Jesus Christ is emphatically called "the Righteous One" (Acts 22:14; I John 2:1). He, in human nature, lived up to the perfect standard of the Divine law, so that His righteousness was of the same complexion and character as the righteousness of God.

(5) But Jesus Christ has become righteousness *to us* (I Cor. 1:30). Hence we read of those "who receive the gift of righteousness" (Rom. 5:17).

(6) This gift is made available to us—so far as *God's* part is concerned—by Christ's atoning death on the cross. God made Him, who knew not sin, to be sin (i.e., dealt with Him as sin should be dealt with), that we might become the righteousness of God in Him (II Cor. 5:21).

(7) The gift of God's righteousness is available to us—so far as *our* part is concerned—through faith. We must *yield* to it (Rom. 10:3). It is conferred "upon all them that believe." They are then "freely

7. A student of Luther's works will probably be led to the conclusion that there was no point in which he was more strong, more clear, and more excellent than in the application of the law of God to the whole man instead of confining it to external actions and so-called religious observances.

justified by his grace, through the redemption that is in Christ Jesus, whom God has set forth as a mercyseat [or propitiation], through faith in his blood" (Rom. 3:22, 24, 25). Hence it is called the righteousness *of faith.*

(8) Thus, by the term *the righteousness of God,* Paul generally intends that righteousness which comes up to God's standard, which flows from God to man when by faith he rests on Christ crucified as his ground of pardon and is united with Christ risen as the spring of his spiritual life.

(9) Lastly, the possession of it necessarily leads a man into practical conformity with the will of God, because it sets his heart in the right direction. It makes him a partaker of that Divine life which flows into him through the agency of the Holy Spirit of God. The Christian becomes in a practical sense "the righteousness of God in Christ" (II Cor. 5:21); being made free from sin, he is made servant to righteousness (Rom. 6:18). And he who has been hungering and thirsting after righteousness is filled out of the fullness that is in Christ Jesus our Lord.

The word *righteous* or *just* (δίκαιος, *1342*) is almost always taken in the N.T. to represent that upright and merciful character in conformity with law which we have already met with in the O.T.; and this is the case whether the word is applied to God the righteous Judge, to Jesus Christ "the Holy One and the Just," or to those who shall rise at "the resurrection of the just."

In the opening of the Epistle to the Romans, Paul takes as his text the words of Habakkuk (2:4), "a righteous man shall live by faith." From this passage he teaches that Divine life is not granted to a righteous man as a reward for his justice and obedience to the law of Moses. Rather it accrues to him by virtue of that faithfulness whereby he takes hold of Christ, and thus avails himself of the grace and righteousness of God. In this sense also are we to understand the words "by the obedience of one many shall be constituted righteous" (Rom. 5:19); it is not their own obedience that causes them to be righteous in God's sight, but through the work of Christ, who was "obedient unto [or, *up to*] death," they are accounted righteous before God.

Little needs to be added concerning the N.T. usage of the word *justify.* We have seen that it signifies a decision in a person's favor, and that it involves a consequent freedom from penalty and a claim to an inheritance. Paul sums up the whole matter very tersely in his speech at Antioch, where alone the word occurs in the Acts (13:39):

"Be it known unto you that through this [Jesus] is remission of sins proclaimed to you; and every one who believes in him is justified from all things, from which ye could not be justified under the law of Moses." Neither charge nor penalty exists for the believer. He is now justified in[8] Christ's blood (Rom. 5:9). His faith in the sacrifice of Christ is of such a nature as to identify him with Christ in his death to sin,[9] and thus "he that is dead [i.e., dead in this sense with Christ] is justified from sin" (Rom. 6:7, margin).

We see that to be justified, to be accounted righteous, and to have the gift of the righteousness of God, are three aspects of one and the same thing, and set forth most forcibly some of the benefits that we obtain through faith in Christ's offering of Himself.

§4. *Innocence*

The word **Nâqâh** (נָקָה, 5352—Assyrian *naqû*) signifies (in the passive) *to be cleansed* or *made free from pollution*, and so *to be guiltless, innocent,* and *unpunished*. It implies that a man's innocence with respect to a particular charge is established in the sight of others, so that the charge falls to the ground. The first passage in which it occurs is Gen. 24:8, 41, "Thou shalt be *clear* from this my oath."

We read (in Exod. 34:7; Num. 14:18; and Nah. 1:3) that "the LORD will by no means clear [the guilty]." These words, coming as they do after the representation of God as "forgiving iniquity and transgression and sin," are remarkable. They are illustrated by the following clause, "visiting the iniquity of the fathers upon the children, and upon the children's children, unto the third and to the fourth generation." They imply that, though God is ready to pardon sin, He by no means ignores or disregards it. The sinner is regarded as guilty in God's sight until the revealed way of removing that guilt is found and appealed to. The truth is also taught in the following

---

8. It is often hard to give an exact rendering to the preposition ἐν (1722, *in*), especially in Paul's Epistles. It marks position, relationship, or union. The expression "in Christ" usually signifies "by virtue of union with Christ by faith."

9. Christ died to sin once. He was crucified by sinners, and slain by wicked hands. The sin that slew Him was the sin of the world, summed up in one act of intense hatred of God and of goodness. He was constituted *accursed* under the law of Moses, not by wrongdoing, but by being fastened to a cross, and was further identified with sinners by being crucified between two thieves. All this was foreordained. He endured the cross and despised the shame because He knew that He, the innocent, was dying for a guilty world by the will of God.

passages where the word is used: Exod. 20:7 and Deut. 5:11, "The LORD will not hold him guiltless that taketh his name in vain." Num. 5:31, "Then shall the man be guiltless from iniquity," i.e., shall be acquitted from the charge of wrongdoing. Num. 32:22, "Then afterwards ye shall return and be guiltless before the LORD, and before Israel." Josh. 2:19, "His blood shall be upon his head, and we will be guiltless," i.e., with respect to the oath made to spare Rahab's kindred (cf. v. 17, where the same word is rendered *blameless*). I Sam. 26:9, "Who can stretch forth his hand against the LORD's anointed and be guiltless?" II Sam. 3:28, "I and my kingdom are guiltless before the LORD for ever from the blood of Abner, the son of Ner." II Sam. 14:9, "The woman of Tekoah said unto the king . . . The iniquity be on me and on my father's house: and the king and his throne be guiltless." I Kings 2:9, "Now therefore hold him not guiltless." Job 10:14, "If I sin, then thou markest me, and thou wilt not acquit me from mine iniquity." Every sin constitutes a distinct charge against a man in the sight of God, and it must be dealt with as such. Ps. 24:4, "He that hath clean hands and a pure heart"—clean hands are those which are innocent of bloodguiltiness. Joel 3:21, "I will cleanse their blood which I have not cleansed."

Some other renderings of the words may be noticed: Gen. 20:5, "In the integrity of my heart and in the innocency of my hands have I done this." Gen. 44:10, "Ye shall be blameless." Exod. 23:7, "The innocent and righteous slay thou not." Deut. 19:9, 10, "Thou shalt add three cities more for thee besides these three, that innocent blood be not shed in thy land, and so blood be upon thee." Deut. 19:13, "Thine eye shall not pity him, but thou shalt put away the guilt of innocent blood from Israel." Deut. 21:8, 9, "Lay not innocent blood to the charge of thy people Israel. . . . So shalt thou put away the guilt of innocent blood from among you." Deut. 27:25, "Cursed be he that taketh reward to slay an innocent person" (cf. I Sam. 19:5; II Kings 21:16; 24:4). Judg. 15:3, "Now shall I be more blameless than the Philistines." Job 4:7, "Remember, I pray thee, who ever perished, being innocent?" (see also Job 9:23, 28; 17:8; 22:19, 30; 27:17). Ps. 10:8, "He doth murder the innocent" (see Ps. 15:5; 94:21; 106:38; Prov. 1:11; 6:17; Isa. 59:7; Jer. 2:34; 7:6; 19:4; 22:3, 17; 26:15; Joel 3:19; Jonah 1:14). Ps. 19:13, "Keep back thy servant also from presumptuous sins; let them not have dominion over me: then shall I be upright, and I shall be innocent from the great transgression." Ps. 26:6, "I will wash my hands in innocency: so will I compass thine altar" (see 73:13).

Prov. 6:29, "Whosoever toucheth [his neighbour's wife] shall not be innocent" (see 11:21; 16:5; 17:5; 19:5, 9; 28:20; Jer. 2:35). Jer. 25:29; 49:12, "Should ye be utterly unpunished? Ye shall not be unpunished." Jer. 30:11; 46:28, "I will correct thee in measure, and will not leave thee altogether unpunished."

The above are almost all the passages in which the word Nâqâh (5352) occurs. It generally appears to signify proved innocence from specified charges, whether those charges are brought by God or man. The offenses, if committed, were punishable; but when they have not been committed, if that innocence can be made clear, the person against whom the charge is made goes off free from blame and punishment. It is evident that the innocence implied by this word is from one point of view not such a perfect state as what is called justification; for while the former leaves one in the negative position of not having done certain things, the latter advances a step further and constitutes one upright in the sight of God. Where Nâqâh (5352) is used, man is regarded as actually clear from a charge; where Tsâdaq (6663) is used, man is regarded as having obtained deliverance from condemnation, and as being thus entitled to a certain inheritance.

In the Piel or intensive stem, the word is only used in *negative* sentences, with the exception of Ps. 19:12, "*Cleanse* thou me from my hidden faults," i.e., hold me guiltless.

The LXX renders Nâqâh (5352) by ἀθωόω (or ἀθῷος, L-S 34A), καθαρίζω (2511), καθαρός εἰμί (2513, 1510), and, in a few passages, by ἀναίτιος (338) and δίκαιος (1342).

§5. *Imputation*

With the exception of I Sam. 22:15, where the word Sûwm (שׂוּם, 7760—Assyrian *samu*), signifying *to set, place*, or *appoint*, is used, the idea of imputation is always represented by Châshab (חָשַׁב, 2803). This word is largely used, and in slightly different senses. Our translators have rendered it by the word *think* thirty-seven times; *imagine* twelve times; *devise* thirty times; and *purpose* ten times. Hence it may be gathered that it signifies a mental process whereby some course is planned or conceived. Thus, it is applied to the *cunning* workmen who contrived the various parts of the tabernacle, and refers not so much to their skill in manipulating their materials as to their inspired genius in devising the arrangements. It is rendered *find out* in II Chron. 2:14, where we read of a certain person employed on the temple who was skillful to grave any manner of graving, and to "find out"—i.e., picture up in the imagination— "every device which shall be put to him." It is used in Gen. 50:20, where Joseph says to his brethren, "God meant it [i.e., planned it] for good, to bring to pass, as it is this day, to save much people alive." In Dan. 11:24, 25, the word is repeated in order to give it emphasis, where we read, "He shall forecast his devices against the strongholds. . . . they shall forecast devices against him." A similar use of the word in its doubled form is in Jer. 49:30, "The king of Babylon hath taken counsel against you, and hath conceived a purpose against you."

It is easy to see that a word that represents this process of the thought or imagination may be applied in various senses. Thus it is rendered *regard,* i.e., *pay attention to,* in Isa. 13:17 and 33:8. It is also used to express the estimation in which one person is held by another. Thus Job says (18:3), "Wherefore are we counted as beasts and reputed as vile in thy sight?" Compare Job 13:24; 19:15; 33:10; 41:27, 29; Isa. 29:16, 17; 53:3, 4; Lam. 4:2. The Anakim "were accounted giants" (Deut. 2:11, 20); silver "was nothing accounted of in the days of Solomon" (I Kings 10:21; II Chron. 9:20); "Cease ye from man, whose breath is in his nostrils: for wherein is he to be accounted of?" (Isa. 2:22).

The following passages may be adduced in further illustration of the meaning of the word: Gen. 31:15, "Are we not counted of him strangers? for he hath sold us, and hath quite devoured also our money." Lev. 25:31, "The houses of the villages which have no walls shall be counted as the fields of the country," i.e., shall be dealt with on the same principle as the fields. Num. 18:27, "Your heave offering shall be reckoned unto you as the corn of the threshingfloor, and the fullness of the winepress." Num. 18:30, "When ye have heaved the best thereof, then it shall be counted unto the Levites as the increase of the threshingfloor, and as the increase of the winepress." Josh. 13:3, "From Sihor . . . unto the borders of Ekron . . . which is counted to the Canaanite." II Sam. 4:2, "Beeroth also was reckoned to Benjamin." II Sam. 19:19, "Let not my lord impute iniquity unto me, neither do thou remember that which thy servant did perversely." Neh. 13:13, "They were counted faithful." Ps. 44:22, "We are counted as sheep for the slaughter." Ps. 88:4, "I am counted with them that go down into the pit." Prov. 17:28, "Even a fool, when he holdeth his peace, is counted wise." Prov. 27:14, "He that blesseth his friend with a loud voice, rising early in the morning, it shall be counted a curse to him." Isa. 40:15, 17, "The nations are counted by him as the small dust in the balance . . . they are counted less than nothing, and vanity." Hos. 8:12, "I have written to him the great things of my law, but they were counted as a strange thing."

In all these passages a mental process is involved whereby a certain thing or a course of action is subjected to a sort of estimation as to value or position. It is not an artificial proceeding, a mere fancy, but a distinct judgment, founded either on the nature of things or on the mind of him who is passing certain things under review.

Sometimes the word is used in our ordinary sense of *reckoning*— that is to say, to represent the arithmetical process of counting up—e.g., Lev. 25:27; 27:18; II Kings 12:15.

A few passages remain to be noticed, and they are important from their theological meaning:

Gen. 15:6, Abraham "believed in the LORD, and he counted it to him [for] righteousness." God reckoned him as righteous on the ground of his faith.

Lev. 7:18, "It shall not be accepted, neither shall it be imputed." The offering shall not be reckoned as having been made.

Lev. 17:4, "Blood shall be imputed to that man; he hath shed blood; and that man shall be cut off from among his people."

Ps. 106:31, "Then stood up Phinehas and executed judgment [P.B., prayed] . . . and that was counted unto him for righteousness." The *faith* of Phinehas, which moved him to act, caused God to regard him as righteous.

Ps. 32:2, "Blessed is the man unto whom the LORD imputeth not iniquity, and in whose spirit there is no guile." This nonimputation of iniquity is regarded by Paul as identical with imputation of righteousness (Rom. 4:6).

The word **Châshab** (2803) is generally rendered $\lambda o\gamma i\zeta o\mu\alpha\iota$ (3049) in the LXX, and the use of this word in the N.T. exactly accords with what we have gathered from the O.T.[10] There are several samples of the ordinary use of the word. Thus, in Rom. 6:11, we read, "Reckon

10. In Mark 15:28, the words "he was reckoned among transgressors" are quoted from Isa. 53:12, where, however, the Hebrew word is not **Châshab** (2803), but **Mânâh** (4487), *to number.*

yourselves dead indeed to sin," that is, regard yourselves in this aspect. In I Cor. 13:5, the words, "[charity] thinketh no evil," might perhaps be rendered "doth not impute evil," that is to say, "doth not take account of injuries done to it." A few verses below we read, "I thought as a child," by which we are to understand, "I took account of things as a child does." In Phil. 3:13 the Apostle says, "I reckon not myself to have attained," that is, "I do not regard myself as having attained." In the more distinctly doctrinal sense, we have in Rom. 2:26: "If the uncircumcision keep the righteousness of the law, shall not his uncircumcision be reckoned as circumcision ($\epsilon i s$ $\pi \epsilon \rho \iota \tau o \mu \dot{\eta} \nu$ — 1519, 4061)?" II Cor. 5:19, "God was in Christ, reconciling the world unto himself, not imputing their trespasses unto them." In Rom. 4:3, the words concerning Abraham in Gen. 15:6 are introduced and discussed at some length, the passage from Ps. 32 being also quoted in confirmation of the Apostle's argument. In verse 4 stress is especially laid on the fact that the reckoning of Abraham's faith for righteousness was not a matter of justice due to Abraham, but was a work of grace springing out of God's free love.

We see therefore that *to reckon, to impute,* and to account are one and the same thing, and that the word is used in Scripture to indicate what may be called a mental process whereby the love and mercy that exist in the Divine nature, and that were embodied in Christ, are brought to bear on the case of every individual who believes in (and acts on) the Word of God. There is nothing unnatural or artificial about the imputation of righteousness by faith. On the contrary, it commends itself to man's deepest convictions.

15

Sanctification, Anointing

§1. *Sanctify, Sacred, Holy*

Few religious words are more prominent in the Hebrew Scriptures than those which spring from the root **Qâdash** (קָדַשׁ, 6942— Assyrian *qadasu*), which is used in some form or other to represent a being set apart for the work of God. It generally answers to the Greek ἁγιάζω (37) and ἅγιος (40). Perhaps the English word *sacred* represents the idea more nearly than *holy*, which is the general rendering in the A.V. The terms *sanctification* and *holiness* are now used so frequently to represent moral and spiritual qualities that they hardly convey to the reader the idea of *position* or *relationship* as existing between God and some person or thing consecrated to Him. Yet this appears to be the real meaning of the word.[1]

(1) The word **Qâdash** (6942) is applied to places, e.g., to the camp of Israel (Deut. 23:14); to the hill of Zion (Ps. 2:6, etc.); to the ground where God manifested Himself to Moses (Exod. 3:5); to the city of Jerusalem[2] (Neh. 11:1; cf. Matt. 4:5); to heaven (Ps. 20:6); to the "Holy Land" (Zech. 2:12); to the tabernacle (Exod. 29:43); to the temple (I Kings 9:3); to the inner part of the temple or tabernacle, commonly

---

1. In accordance with the above view, Dr. Henderson renders Jer. 1:5 thus: "Before thou camest forth from the womb I *separated* thee." And in his note he says, "When Jehovah declares that He had sanctified the prophet before his birth, the meaning is not that He had cleansed him from the pollution of original sin, or that He had regenerated him by His Spirit, but that He had separated him in His eternal counsel to the work in which He was to be engaged." The Apostle Paul, he adds, uses language very nearly parallel when he says of God that He *separated him* (ἀφορίσας, 873) from his mother's womb. See Gal. 1:15; Rom. 1:1; Acts 13:2.

2. Jerusalem is still called in Arabic *El Khuds*, i.e., The Holy.

called the sanctuary or the Holy of Holies (Exod. 25:8); to the king's "chapel" (Amos 7:13); to the altar (Exod. 29:36); and consequently, as our Lord reminded the Jews,[3] to the gifts (Exod. 28:38) and offerings (Exod. 29:27) that were placed thereon; also to a house or field set apart for God (Lev. 27:14, 16).

(2) The word is applied to times, e.g., to the Sabbath (Gen. 2:3; Exod. 20:8, 11); to a day set apart as a fast (Joel 1:14); to the fiftieth year (Lev. 25:10).

(3) It is applied to persons, e.g., to the firstborn (Exod. 13:2); to the priests (Exod. 28:41); to the people (Deut. 7:6); to the assembly of the people (Ps. 89:7; Joel 2:16); to a man of God (II Kings 4:9); to Jeremiah *sanctified* in the womb (Jer. 1:5); to the guests at a sacrificial feast (Zeph. 1:7, margin); and to the saints or people dedicated to God, whether angels or men (Job 5:1; 15:15; Ps. 16:3; 34:9; Isa. 4:3; Dan. 4:13; 7:18, 21, 22, 25, 27; 8:13, 24; Zech. 14:5).

The point involved in every case is relation or contact with God. Thus the Sabbath day was holy because God rested thereon, and it was to be set apart by Israel as a sign that He had sanctified or set apart the people to Himself (Exod. 31:13); the mountain of the Lord was to be called holy because He would dwell there (Zech. 8:3); the *sanctuary* was to be made that the Lord might dwell among the people (Exod. 25:8); the firstborn, by being hallowed or set apart, were regarded by God as His own (Num. 3:13); and even the censers in which sinful men offered incense to God became hallowed by that very act (Num. 16:38).

God Himself was regarded as holy, i.e., as a Being who from His nature, position, and attributes is to be set apart and revered as distinct from all others. Israel was to separate itself from the world and the things of the world because God was thus separated; they were to be holy, for He was holy (Lev. 11:44; 19:2; 20:7, 26; 21:8). Joshua says, "Ye cannot serve the Lord, for he is an holy God [i.e., a God set apart and distinct from all other beings]; he is a jealous God, he will not forgive [or put up with] your transgressions nor your sins" (Josh. 24:19). In accordance with this teaching, the Lord was to be *sanctified*, i.e., regarded as occupying a unique position both morally and as regards His essential nature. Thus we read in Lev. 10:3, "I will be sanctified in them that come nigh me"; I Sam. 6:20, "Who is

3. Matt. 23:17.

able to stand before this holy LORD God?" Ps. 111:9, "Holy and rever-
end is his name"; Isa. 6:3, "Holy, holy, holy is the LORD of Hosts"; Isa.
8:13, 14, "Sanctify the LORD of Hosts himself,[4] and let him be your
fear, and let him be your dread, and he shall be for a sanctuary"; Isa.
29:23, "They shall sanctify my name, and sanctify the Holy One of
Jacob," i.e., the Being whom Jacob sanctified or set apart as his God.
In harmony with these passages, we find the LORD several times
described as "the Holy One of Israel," i.e., the Being to whom alone
Israel gave special and peculiar honor (II Kings 19:22; Ps. 71:22; Isa.
10:17; 49:7). In Ezek. 11:16 the LORD says, "Although I have cast them
far off among the heathen, and although I have scattered them
among the countries, yet will I be unto them as a sanctuary for a
little time [A.V. *as a little sanctuary*] in the countries whither they
shall come"; that is to say, "Although they will have no temple for a
little while, yet I will be with them, and they shall learn to reverence
me"; thus God Himself took the place of the *sanctuary* built by
Solomon (I Chron. 22:18, 19). The holy temple of the Lord represented His Presence, but that Presence could go with the people
into captivity even though the temple were to be destroyed.

The Spirit of God is called Holy in Ps. 51:11, "Take not thy holy
Spirit from me"; Isa. 63:10, 11, "They rebelled and vexed his holy
Spirit. . . . Where is he that put his holy Spirit within him?" Compare
the expression "the spirit of the holy gods" (Dan. 4:8, 9).

In all these passages it is implied that He whom Israel was to
worship was to be regarded as entirely separate from all other
beings, and also as pure from every thought and deed of evil. What a
contrast with the theology of heathendom!

The process of setting apart for sacred uses that is described by
the words *dedication* and *consecration* is also represented by
Qâdash (6942). See, for example, Judg. 17:3; II Sam. 8:11; II Kings
10:20; I Chron. 18:11; II Chron. 31:6. It was also used to denote the
setting apart of certain people for warfare, as in Jer. 51:27, "Prepare
the nations against her"; Joel 3:9, "Prepare war"; Micah 3:5, "They
even prepare war against him."

In II Sam. 11:4 Qâdash (6942) is rendered *purify*, to signify doing
away with ceremonial defilement. But the same word is also used
in Deut. 22:9, where we read, "Thou shalt not sow thy vineyard with

---

4. This passage is quoted in I Peter 3:15. Compare also the words of the Lord's Prayer
(Matt. 6:9), "Hallowed [or sanctified] be thy Name."

divers seeds: lest the fruit of thy seed which thou hast sown, and the fruit of thy vineyard, be defiled"; and in Job 36:14, "Their life is among the unclean." In these passages we have samples of the use of the word Qâdash (6942) in an opposite sense to the true one.

The familiar expression "beauty of holiness" is found in I Chron. 16:29; II Chron. 20:21; Ps. 29:2; 96:9; 110:3. Other suggested renderings are "the glorious sanctuary" and "holy array." The word rendered *beauty* frequently means majesty or excellency, and probably points to the glory of God rather than to the garments of man.

In Exod. 28:36 and Jer. 31:40, as well as other passages, we meet with the expression "Holiness to the Lord," or as it is sometimes rendered, "Holiness of the Lord," or "Holy to the Lord." This expression indicates that the object thus inscribed is dedicated to God.

The word *holy* is sometimes opposed to the unholy or profane (חל, 2455, from חָלַל, 2490; βέβηλος, 952), as in Lev. 10:10 and Ezek. 44:23, where the latter word signifies that which is devoted to ordinary uses. It also occurs in connection with the separation of the Nazarite in Num. 6:5, 8; and of the "holy seed" of Israel as compared with the Canaanites (Ezra 9:2). It was set forth as of the greatest importance that Israel should regard itself as a *separate people*. In this respect the Nazarite from the days of Joseph onward (Gen. 49:26) was a type of the whole nation. They were "a peculiar treasure" (Exod. 19:5; Deut. 14:2; 26:18; Ps. 135:4), redeemed by God for His own purposes (Exod. 33:15, 16); ordained to keep His law (Lev. 20:7, 8), and to live to His praise and glory (Lev. 20:24–26).

With regard to the mode in which ceremonial sanctification[5] was accomplished, we find it varying according to the circumstances of the case. When Aaron and his sons were hallowed or sanctified for the priesthood, "Moses took of the anointing oil, and of the blood which was upon his garments, and upon his son's garments with him." The A.V. has unfortunately rendered Qâdash (6942) *consecrate* instead of *hallow* in Exod. 28:3; 30:30; Josh. 6:19; II Chron. 26:18; 29:33; 31:6; Ezra 3:5.

The word used for consecration in Num. 6:9, 12, is Nâzar (נָזַר, 5144), *to separate*, and is rightly used of the *Nazarite* (נָזִיר, 5139) or

---

5. The technical act of consecration was a different process. It was literally the *filling of the hand*, part of the sacrifice being put into the hand and waved, and then borne to the altar.

separated person. Another form of this word is rendered *crown* in several passages, perhaps because the wearing of a crown was a special mark of distinction or separation. It is used of the golden crown on the High Priest's miter, on which the words "Holiness to the LORD" were written (Exod. 39:30); and of the "crown of the anointing oil" that separated him for the work of God (Lev. 21:12); it was the mark of the anointed king (Ps. 89:38, 39; 132:17, 18); and in Zech. 9:16 we are told that the Lord's people shall be "as the stones of a crown, lifted up as an ensign on his land." In most of the passages in which this word occurs, the LXX renders it ἁγίασμα (L-S 9A).

Chânak (חָנַךְ, 2596), *to initiate* or *inaugurate*, is used in Num. 7:10, 11, 84, 88, of the dedication of the altar; in I Kings 8:63 and II Chron. 7:5, 9, of the dedicating of the house of the LORD; in Ezra 6:16, 17, with reference to the rebuilt temple; in Neh. 12:27 of the wall of Jerusalem; and in Dan. 3:2, 3, of the dedication of the image that Nebuchadnezzar set up. This word is applied to the training or dedication of children in Prov. 22:6; see also Gen. 14:14.

The word *ordain* occurs seventeen times in the O.T., and represents eleven different Hebrew words. In some of these passages there is a reference to the appointment of rites and of religious or secular officers, but nothing in the words used indicates any peculiarities in the *mode* of appointment.

§2. *Teaching of the N.T. on Sanctification*

We now turn to the N.T. in order to trace the usage of the word ἁγιάζω (37), the Greek representative of **Qâdash** (6942). First, it is applied to the sanctification and consecration of the Son by the Father in John 10:36. Compare John 17:19: "In their behalf I sanctify myself," i.e., set myself apart for the special work of God. The Lord was *set apart* from the foundation of the world for the work of redemption, and His incarnation, temptations, and sufferings were the processes whereby His atoning death was prepared for and rendered valid.

Second, the sanctification of Christians is referred to as the work of the Father in John 17:17: "Sanctify them *in* [or *by*] thy truth." See also I Thess. 5:23 and Jude 1. But while the Father is the source, the Son is the agent; for His object in sanctifying Himself was that they also might be sanctified by the truth. Compare I Cor. 1:2; Eph. 5:26.

In Heb. 2:11 we read of Christ and Christians, that "both he that sanctifieth and they who are sanctified are all of one [i.e., from one source]: for which cause he is not ashamed to call them brethren."

The means whereby the Christian is sanctified is the blood, i.e., the offering of the lifeblood of Christ (Heb. 9:14; 10:10, 14).

In Rom. 15:16, the agency of the Holy Spirit is mentioned in connection with sanctification. Here reference is made to the power whereby the Apostle Paul's ministrations were effective in preaching to the Gentiles, and presenting them as an offering to God.

In II Tim. 2:21, the man who is purged from iniquity is compared to a sanctified vessel. The sanctification of food, i.e., its being regarded as free from ceremonial pollution, is referred to in I Tim. 4:5 as accomplished by means of the word of God and prayer. In I Cor. 7:14, we are told that "the unbelieving husband is sanctified by the wife, and the unbelieving wife is sanctified by the husband: else were your children unclean; but now are they holy." According to this passage, we are to understand that the marriage tie extends sanctity or sacredness from the husband to the wife, or from the wife to the husband, and so to the children. In these passages we have the idea of sacredness, affecting the *position* and *use* rather than the *nature* of that to which it refers. The preposition that is generally the connecting link between the object sanctified and that which sanctifies it is not *by* or *with*, but *in*. This seems to imply that sanctification takes place through the *contact* of one object with another. The gift by being placed on the altar becomes in a ceremonial sense *one* with it. The Christian is sanctified by becoming one with Christ, faith in His blood being that which makes both one; and Christ is sanctified in that He is one with the Father. We find the preposition ἐν (1722) with ἁγιάζω (37) in the following passages of the LXX: Exod. 29:43; Lev. 10:3; Num 20:13; Deut. 32:51; Ezek. 20:41; 28:22, 25; 36:23; 38:16; 39:27; 44:19.

The noun ἁγιασμός (38) occurs ten times in the N.T., and would best be rendered *sanctification*. The passages are as follows: Rom. 6:19, "Yield your members servants to righteousness unto holiness," i.e., with a view to sanctification; so also verse 22. I Cor. 1:30, "Christ Jesus is made unto us . . . sanctification," i.e., a means or ground of it. I Thess. 4:3, 4, 7, "This is the will of God, even your sanctification . . . that every one of you should know how to possess his vessel in sanctification and honor. . . . For God hath not called us unto uncleanness, but *in sanctification*." The A.V., by rendering the last two words *"unto holiness,"* obscures the connection of the verses.

II Thess. 2:13, "God hath chosen you to salvation in sanctification of [the] spirit."[6] I Tim. 2:15, "If they continue in faith and charity and sanctification with sobriety." Heb. 12:14, "Follow after sanctification, without which no man shall see God." I Pet. 1:2, "In sanctification of [the] spirit."[7] Thus, true sanctification involves the separation of the spirit from all that is impure and polluting, and a renunciation of the sins toward which the desires of the flesh and of the mind lead us.

While ἀγιασμός (38) may be regarded as the process of sanctification, ἁγιότης (41) and ἁγιωσύνη (42) are rather the result of the process. The former occurs in I Cor. 1:30 and Heb. 12:10; the latter in Rom. 1:4; II Cor. 7:1; and I Thess. 3:13. These passages, if examined, will show that the quality of holiness, or perfect freedom from pollution and impurity, is essential to the nature of God, was exhibited by His Son Jesus Christ, and is imparted to the Christian in proportion to his faith.

The adjective ἅγιος (40), *holy*, is used nearly a hundred times with reference to the Holy Spirit of God—that Spirit who was in Christ without measure, and who is now imparted to all who trust Him. Again, both in consequence of the indwelling of the Holy Spirit and because of their professed separation from evil and dedication to God, all Christians are regarded as ἅγιοι (40), *holy ones* or *saints*. The word is also applied to Christ, who was the holy one of God; and our Lord applies it to His "holy Father," and to the "holy angels." We find it used in a more ceremonial sense of the holy city Jerusalem (Matt. 27:53), and the holy place (Matt. 24:15); of the covenant with Abraham (Luke 1:72); of the Scriptures (Rom. 1:2); of the law and commandment (Rom. 7:12); of a kiss (Rom. 16:16); and of food that was separated from ordinary uses, and was therefore not to be cast to the dogs (Matt. 7:6).

The word ἁγνεία (47), which is found in Gal. 5:22 (in some MSS.), as well as I Tim. 4:12 and 5:2, answers very well to our word *purity*, in its double sense of chastity and freedom from wrong motives.

The verb ἁγνίζω (48) is used with reference to ceremonial purifications in John 11:55; Acts 21:24, 26; and 24:18. It is also used in a spiritual sense in three passages: James 4:8, "Purify your hearts, ye double-minded"; I Peter 1:22, "Seeing ye have purified your souls in

---

6. There is no article here in the Greek, so that the expression possibly signifies the sanctification of a man's own spirit, or, in a general sense, *spiritual sanctification* as opposed to that which is *external* or *ceremonial*. R.V. retains the article.

7. See footnote 6.

brethren, love one another with a pure heart fervently"; I John 3:3, "He that hath this hope in Him [i.e., not in himself, but in Christ] purifieth himself, even as He is pure."

The adjective ἁγνός (53) occurs eight times in the N.T. in the sense of moral chastity and purity. And ἁγνότης (54) which is derived from it and is peculiar to the N.T., is found in II Cor. 6:6, and, according to some MSS., in II Cor. 11:2. The adverb ἁγνῶς (55) occurs in Phil. 1:16.

§3. *Anointing*

In considering the ceremonial anointing of the O.T., we have to do with only one word, **Mâshach** (מָשַׁח, 4886), from which the name Messiah is derived, and which is almost always rendered χρίω (5548) in the LXX. Other words, indeed, are used, but not in a ceremonial sense. Among passages where such occur, two may be noted: the first is Isa. 10:27, "The yoke shall be destroyed because of the anointing," or literally, "from the face of the oil"; the other is Zech. 4:14, "These are the two anointed ones [lit., sons of oil or brightness] that stand by the Lord of the whole earth."

Mâshach (4886) is first used of the anointing of the pillar at Bethel (Gen. 28:18; 31:13), and it does not occur again till Exod. 25:6, where "the anointing oil" is spoken of. We next meet with it in connection with the consecration and sanctification of Aaron (Exod. 28:41). The anointing came *after* the offering of atoning victims in Aaron's case, as in the case of the altar (Exod. 29:36). The tabernacle, the ark, the table, and various vessels were to be anointed (Exod. 30:26–28). They were then regarded as sanctified or set apart, and whatever touched them had this sanctification communicated to it. The unleavened wafers and some other meat offerings were to be anointed (Lev. 2:4). In all these cases the unction was the mode of setting apart or sanctifying.

The anointing of a king is first mentioned in the parable of Jotham (Judg. 9:8, 15). It next occurs in the inspired hymn of Hannah (I Sam. 2:10), "He shall give strength unto his king, and exalt the horn of his anointed." Saul was anointed captain over God's people, that he might save them out of the hand of the Philistines (I Sam. 9:16). Various references are found to the Lord's anointed, that is to say, the king, both in the historical and poetical books. The following are the most important: Ps. 2:2, "The rulers take counsel together, against the LORD, and against his anointed"; 18:50, "He sheweth mercy to his anointed, to David, and to his seed for evermore"; 20:6, "Now know I that the LORD saveth his anointed"; 45:7, "God hath anointed thee with the oil of gladness above thy fellows"; 92:10, "I shall be anointed with fresh oil."

The reference in Ps. 105:15, "Touch not mine *anointed* [ones], and do my prophets no harm," is thought to be to the priests (compare Hab. 3:13). The meaning of the phrase "anoint the shield" (Isa. 21:5) is doubtful. In Isa. 45:1, Cyrus is called the LORD's anointed, because he was appointed king for a special purpose. In Isa. 61:1, the word receives a larger meaning, and teaches that the holy oil wherewith the priest and king and the vessels of the tabernacle were anointed was a symbol of the Holy Spirit. For we read, "The Spirit of the Lord GOD is upon me, because he hath anointed me to preach good tidings unto the meek."

In Ezek. 28:14, the king of Tyrus is described as "the anointed cherub." Some here translate the word *extended* instead of anointed; but compare Isa. 45:1. In Dan. 9:24, we are told that "seventy weeks is determined . . . to anoint the Most Holy," i.e., either the Most Holy Being or the Most Holy Place. In Amos 6:6 the word appears to be used of personal decoration with oil, and not of the ceremonial anointing. If this be the case, it is the only place in the whole O.T. in which the word is so used. Possibly there is a reference here to the abuse of holy things, a view that would be most in accordance with the accusations implied in the two previous verses.

The verb χρίω (5548) is used five times in the N.T. In four of these passages it refers to the anointing of Christ by His Father: Luke 4:18, which is quoted from Isa. 61:1; Heb. 1:9, quoted from Ps. 45:7; Acts 4:27, where it is used with special reference to the quotation from the second Psalm that immediately precedes it; and Acts 10:38, where we are told that God anointed Jesus with the Spirit. What, then, is the idea that we ought to connect with the name *Christ* or *Messiah?* It points to One who is King by Divine authority, and signifies that God would set His mark on Him by giving Him the Holy Ghost without measure. Perhaps also it teaches that the ministrations of the prophet, priest, altar, and tabernacle with all its vessels were foreshadowings of the work that He was to accomplish.

The anointing of Christians is spoken of in II Cor. 1:21, where we are told that "He who hath anointed us is God." In accordance with this fact, John three times in his first Epistle reminds those to whom he writes that they have a *chrism* or *unction* from the Holy One (I John 2:20, 27). This chrism includes not only the special temporary gifts of the Spirit, but also that indwelling and working presence of the Holy Ghost which the Christian receives from the Father through the Son.

The anointing of the sick is described by a different Greek word, namely, ἀλείφω (218). It was a medical rather than a ceremonial act, and was performed by friction or rubbing, not by pouring. So far from James's words (5:14) discouraging the use of medical help, they order it. The same word is used of the anointing of the head and of the body for purposes of decoration or preservation.

16

Offerings, Altar

Few elements in the Mosaic dispensation are more interesting to the Christian student than the system of offerings therein prescribed. The practice of slaying animals for a religious purpose appears to have been called into existence at a very early stage of human history. But the Levitical system claims to have been elaborated under Divine direction during the sojourning in the wilderness, and that with a fullness of detail that must arrest the attention of every reader. If it be true that even in earthly matters "coming events cast their shadows before," much more is it to be expected that when the Author of all existence was about to make a special intervention in the affairs of men He would not only intimate His purpose to some of those whom He was about to benefit, but would also prefigure the course that He was about to adopt. The system of offerings appointed to Israel may be regarded as a book of pictures sketched in shadowy outline, indicating to God's people the work that was to be accomplished by Divine grace when the fullness of the time should have come.

§1. *The Korban*

The word Qârbân (קָרְבָּן, 7133—Assyrian *Kurbannu*), with which we are familiar from its occurrence in the N.T. (Mark 7:11), is used for the offering in about seventy passages in the O.T. It is not restricted to any sacrifice in particular, but represents the various ways in which the offerer found a way of approach and acceptance. We might almost render it *a way of access.* The verb Qârab (קָרַב, 7126), whence it is derived, signifies *to approach* or *draw near,* and is often used of man's entrance into the presence of the living God (so also in Assyrian). It is no ordinary nearness that is represented by it, but rather that of the closest and most intimate kind (see, e.g., Num. 16:9; Ps. 65:4; Jer. 30:21). The very word just used (*intimate*) reminds us of the meaning of the word in its adjectival form **Qereb** (קֶרֶב, 7130), as applied to the innermost part of the body. In the noun form **Qârôwb** (קָרוֹב, 7138) it signifies a *near neighbor* or a *kinsman*. Another noun form, **Qᵉrâb** (קְרָב, 7128), is used of close hand-to-hand conflict, and hence is rendered *battle* or *war* in nine passages in the O.T. (so also in Assyrian).

Qorbân (7133) is also rendered *sacrifice* in Lev. 27:11, and *oblation* ten times in Leviticus, and twice in Numbers. It would be better to have a uniform rendering in these passages. The verb in its causative form is rendered *offer* more than fifty times in Leviticus, and twenty-five times in Numbers. It occurs in a nonsacrificial sense in Judg. 3:18, where we read of Ehud's offering a present to Eglon (also in I Chron. 16:1; II Chron. 35:12, et al.).

The LXX renders the verb ἐγγίζω (*1448*), προσφέρω (*4374*), προσ-έρχομαι (*4334*), προσάγω (*4317*); and the noun always δῶρον (*1435*).

The verb **Nâgash** (נָגַשׁ, 5066) has much the same meaning as **Qârab** (7126), and is applied to the presentation of offerings (Amos 5:25; Mal. 1:7, 8, 11, 13; 3:3). This word is coupled with **Qârab** (7126) in Jer. 30:21: "Their noble [A.V. nobles] shall be from themselves, and their ruler shall issue from amidst them, and I *will cause him to draw near* (**Qârab**, 7126), and he shall *approach* (**Nâgash**, 5066) unto me."

§2. N.T. Teaching

We find ἐγγίζω (*1448*) used once in the N.T. in a special sense in Heb. 7:19, "The bringing in of a better hope, by which *we draw near* unto God."

The word προσφέρω (*4374*) is used of the offering of gifts of many kinds. Thus we meet with it in Matt. 2:11 with respect to the offerings made by the Wise Men; in Matt. 5:23 of the offering or gift on the altar, where reference is evidently made to the ordinary offerings prescribed under the name in Leviticus. In several texts (Matt. 8:4; Mark 1:44; Luke 5:14) it is applied to the offering to be made by the cleansed leper. In John 16:2 we read, "Whosoever killeth you will think that he offereth religious service to God" (λατρείαν προσφέρειν τῷ θεῷ—*2999, 4374, 3588, 2316*). The only Epistle in which the word occurs is Hebrews, in which it is found twenty times, and, with one exception,[1] always in a sacrificial or religious sense. Thus it is said of the Lord Jesus that He offered Himself without blemish to God through the Eternal Spirit (Heb. 9:14), and that He was once for all offered to bear the sins of many (9:28).

The word προσέρχομαι (4334) is used of the sinner's approach to God on the basis of an offering (Heb. 4:16; 7:25; 10:1, 22; 11:6).

There is one remarkable passage in which προσάγω (4317) is used, namely, I Pet. 3:18: "Christ died, the just for the unjust, that he might bring us to God." Here the Vulgate rendering is striking, "that he might offer us to God," the offering being the means of the sinner's approach. The noun προσαγωγή (4318), derived from this verb, is used of the access or way of approach that the Christian obtains through Christ (Rom. 5:2; Eph. 2:18; 3:12).

In Matthew's Gospel we find δῶρον (1435) for a sacrificial gift several times; and Mark 7:11 specially interprets Qorbân (7133) by this word. In the Epistle to the Hebrews this word is put side by side with θυσίαι (2378), sacrifices.

The general lesson that we gain from the frequent and remarkable use of the word Qorbân (7133) in the Levitical law, and of its Greek representatives in the N.T., is that a way of access to God is made open not through the efforts of man, but through the good will and ordinance of our heavenly Father; for He has caused us to come near to himself in and through His Son Jesus Christ.

§3. Burnt-Offering

The word generally rendered burnt-offering[2] in the A.V. is 'Ôlâh (עֹלָה, 5930). The verb 'Âlâh (5927), from which it is derived, is rendered to burn (Exod. 27:20; Lev. 2:12; 24:2) and to offer in a few other passages. But the original meaning of the word in the Qal or active stem is to ascend; hence in the Hiphil or causative stem it signifies to make to ascend, or cause to go up. Some scholars have held that the best rendering for 'Ôlâh (5930) would be altar-offering, because the offering was lifted up and placed on the altar. This interpreta-

---

1. Namely, Heb. 12:7, "God deals with you [ὑμῖν προσφέρεται—4771, 4374] as with sons." The word is here in the middle voice, and signifies entrance into a certain relationship.

2. This is one of a large class of expressions in which a hyphen ought to be introduced. The R.V. is no better than the A.V. in this respect.

tion, however, has not been generally accepted. The Vulgate rendering (derived from the Greek) *holocausta*, "That which is wholly burnt," and the German *Brandopfer*, signifying *burnt-offering*, fall in with our own rendering, but they are descriptions rather than translations. The fact that flame *ascends*, and that "the sparks fly *upward*," furnishes us with the true solution of the name. The 'Ôlâh (5930), when turned into a cloud of smoke by the action of the fire, ascended into the heavens, and was gradually dispersed amidst the upper air. While beholding this striking sight, the offerer, who had identified himself with the victim by the pressure of his hands, realized his acceptance by God, who dwells in the heavens. The best rendering of the word would be *an ascending-offering*. Arias Montanus rendered it *ascensio* (an ascent).

The word is used frequently, both in the Levitical ritual and in the historical books. Its first occurrence is in Gen. 8:20, where Noah is said to have offered burnt-offerings on the altar. We next meet with it in Gen. 22:2–13, where Abraham is told to offer up Isaac as a burnt-offering. It is also used in Job 1:5 and 42:8, where the patriarch is described as offering for his sons, and where his friends are ordered to make an offering. The Levitical law, however, drew a clearer distinction between the two. The word is first used in connection with the people of Israel in Exod. 24:5. In this important passage we are told that Moses "sent young men of the children of Israel, which offered burnt-offerings and sacrificed peace-offerings unto the LORD"—the first kind being wholly burnt, and the last eaten. It was with the blood of these offerings that the people and the book of the Covenant were sprinkled. This transaction was previous to the appointment of the Aaronic priesthood. The making of the Covenant was a national, not a sacerdotal work. Moreover, it had not to do directly *with sin*, for neither the burnt-offering nor the peace-offering were sin-offerings; they represented acceptance rather than pardon (though these were closely related).

Passing by the historical books, we find 'Ôlâh (5930) used in a few other passages (Ps. 51:19; 66:15; Isa. 57:6; 66:3; Ezek. 43:18, 24; Amos 5:22).

The most general renderings for the verb 'Âlâh (5927) in the LXX are ἀναβαίνω (305), ἀναφέρω (399), ἀναβιβάζω (307), and ἀνάγω (321); the noun 'Ôlâh (5930) is almost always rendered either ὁλοκαύτωμα (3646), or ὁλοκαύτωσις (L-S 1217B), i.e., *that which is wholly burnt*.

Kâlîyl (כָּלִיל, 3632), that which is *complete*, is used of the whole burnt-offering (Lev. 6:22, 23; Deut. 33:10; I Sam. 7:9; Ps. 51:19).

On examining the N.T., we do not find the substantive applied directly to Christ through its Greek representatives, but the idea of ascending or going up, from which the burnt-offering received its Hebrew name and which is so fully sustained in the Greek verbs abovementioned, reappears in relation to the Lord's work in various ways that we shall briefly notice.

With regard to the word ἀναβαίνω (305), it may be deemed fanciful to refer to our Lord's expression, "Behold, we *go up* to Jerusalem" (see Matt. 20:18; Mark 10:32, 33; Luke 18:31; 19:28), because it was the ordinary and natural phrase to use when describing a journey to that city which was the Crown of the Holy Land. Yet it may be noticed that no site could be more aptly marked out as the altar of earth on which the Great Offering should be consummated. It had probably been the scene of sacrifice as early as the time of Abraham. It lies "beautiful for situation, the joy of the whole earth," 2400 feet above the Mediterranean (which washes the western shore of the land) and 3700 feet above the Dead Sea (which lies in leaden solitude in a cleft between the torrid mountains of Judah and the long purple wall of Moab).

Our Lord's ascension or "going up" to His Father in heaven is described by the word ἀναβαίνω (305) in John 20:17 and Eph. 4:9, 10.

The sacrificial word ἀναφέρω (399) is also used of our Lord's being "carried up" into heaven in Luke 24:51. It is applied to His offering of Himself in Heb. 7:27. It is also adopted with reference to the offering up of a sacrifice of praise (Heb. 13:15), and of spiritual sacrifices that are acceptable to God through Christ (I Pet. 2:5).

The word ἀνάγω (321) is used only twice in the Epistles, Rom. 10:7 and Heb. 13:20, in both of which passages it is adopted to express the bringing of Christ up from the dead—an essential element in the Lord's appointed work.

It may be gathered from these passages that while the slaying of the victim (which was to be a male without blemish) represented Christ's devotion of Himself to death, and while the pouring forth of the blood on the altar foreshadowed the atonement wrought by virtue of His death, the ascent of the slain animal in the form of a cloud of smoke into the heavens typified the bringing of Christ up from the grave and His ascension to the right hand of God. But since the offerer, by pressing his hand on the victim before slaying it in the presence of God, identified himself with it, he must be considered as symbolically going through the same process as it had to undergo. So also the Christian, identifying himself with his Savior by faith, is "crucified with Christ," dies with Him, is buried with Him, rises with Him under the influence of the Spirit of life, and is seated with Him in heavenly places, His life of devotion being compared to an offering made by fire, an odor of a sweet savor to God.

§4. *The Meat or Meal Offering*

The general Hebrew word for a *gift*, whether to God (Gen. 4:3) or to man (Gen. 32:13) is Minchâh (מִנְחָה, 4503). It is also the word that our translators have rendered *meat-offering*—*meat* being here used in its old sense of *food*, and not signifying *flesh*. The LXX has θυσία (2378, *sacrifice*) for it in 140 places, and δῶρον (1435, *gift*) in 32 places.[3] Minchâh (4503) is the word used of the offerings of Cain and Abel in Gen. 4:3–5, in which passage it is not restricted to its Levitical use as an unbloody sacrifice. It is first rendered *meat-offering* in Lev. 2:1, where it is described as a mixture of flour, oil, and frankincense—the flour being the essential part, the oil and frankincense being added that it might burn with a sweet savor. The word is used of the *jealousy-offering* in Num. 5:15, 18, 25, 26. It is also to be found in the following passages: Num. 16:15, "Respect thou not their offering." I Sam. 2:17, "Men abhorred the offering of the LORD"; verse 29, "Wherefore kick ye at my sacrifice, and at mine offering?" I Sam. 3:14, "The iniquity of Eli's house shall not be purged with sacrifice nor offering for ever." I Sam. 26:19, "If the LORD have stirred thee up against me let him accept [or smell] an offering." I Chron. 16:29 (cf. Ps. 96:8), "Bring an offering, and come before him." Ps. 20:3, "Remember all thy offerings." Isa. 43:23, "I have not caused thee to serve with an offering." Isa. 66:20, "They shall bring all your brethren for an offering unto the LORD out of all nations . . . as the children of Israel bring an offering in a clean vessel into the house of the LORD." Jer. 41:5, "There came certain from Shechem, from Shiloh, and from Samaria, even fourscore men, having their beards shaven, and their clothes rent, and having cut themselves, with offerings and incense

---

3. The Assyrian word is *manitu*. The LXX also occasionally reproduces the original word in the form μαναά. The Vulgate adopts *munus* (present, gift) and *oblatio* (oblation, offering, sacrifice) as renderings; and Luther has *Opfer* (offering, sacrifice) and *Speisopfer* (food-offering). Meat is literally that which we chew or grind.

[or rather *frankincense*] in their hand, to bring them to the house of the LORD." Amos 5:25, "Have ye offered unto me sacrifices and offerings in the wilderness forty years?" Zeph. 3:10, "From beyond the rivers of Ethiopia my suppliants, even the daughters of my dispersed, shall bring mine offering." Mal. 1:10, "Neither will I accept an offering at your hand"; see also verse 11, "In every place incense shall be offered unto my name, and a pure offering." Mal. 3:3, 4, "He shall purify the sons of Levi . . . that they may offer . . . an offering in righteousness. Then shall the offering of Judah and Jerusalem be pleasant unto the LORD, as in the days of old."

Minchâh (4503) is rendered *gift* in Ps. 45:12; *sacrifice* in I Kings 18:29, 36, the time of the offering of the (evening) sacrifice;[4] Ps. 141:2, "Let my prayer be set forth before thee as incense; and the lifting up of my hands as the evening sacrifice"; *oblation* in Isa. 1:13; 66:3; Jer. 14:12.

The Minchâh (4503), which was closely connected with the 'Ôlâh (5930), must be regarded as a token of love, gratitude, and thanksgiving to God, who is Himself the Giver of all good gifts. It was an acknowledgment on the part of man that "the earth is the LORD's and the fullness thereof." Part of it was called the *memorial*[5] and was burned with fire, and the rest was eaten by the priest and his family, not by the offerer.

§5. *The Sacrificial Feast*

We now come to the word Zebach[6] (זֶבַח, 2077), which (together with the verb Zâbach [זָבַח, 2076] from which it is derived) is generally rendered *sacrifice* in English, and θυσία (2378), θύω (2380), and θυσιάζω (L-S 812B) in the LXX. We certainly need greater uniformity of rendering for the Levitical terms than we possess at present. If the word *sacrifice* had been confined to the Zebach (2077), instead of being occasionally applied to the Minchâh (4503), the Qorbân (7133), the 'Ishsheh (801), the Chag (2282) or *feast* (Ps. 118:27 and Isa. 29:1), the Tôwdâh (8426) or *praise* (Jer. 17:26 and 33:11), and the verbs

---

4. The word *evening* is inserted in italics both here and in some other places. (Cf. II Kings 16:15; Ps. 141:2; Ezek. 9:4, 5; Dan. 9:21.) Reference is supposed to be made to the offering of a lamb every evening, prescribed in Num. 28:8. The lamb itself was an 'Ôlâh (5930), but no doubt it was accompanied by a Minchâh (4503).

5. The meaning is plain from Ps. 20:3, "[God] remember all thy Minchâhs [4503]."

6. Assyrian *zibû*; but *naqu* usually represents the word.

'Âsâh (6213) and Qâṭar (6999), present controversies might have assumed a very much milder form. The R.V. unfortunately does not help us much here.

The idea of a sacrifice is instinctively connected in our minds with that of a priest;[7] but this is a mistake. The verb Zâbach (2076) properly means to slay an animal for the purpose of food, and accordingly it is rendered *kill* or *slay* in Deut. 12:15, 21; I Sam. 28:24; II Chron. 18:2; and Ezek. 34:3. Although the verb has been also rendered *to offer* in thirty-seven passages (usually where the kindred substantive is found with it), yet in these passages it does not represent the act of the priest as such. Rather, it is the act of a lay offerer, e.g., the head of the family, who presented and slew the animal before God's sanctuary. The word is generally used in connection with a sacred feast in which the family or nation that offered the sacrifice (through their heads or representatives) proceeded to partake of the flesh of the victims, entering thereby into communion with God. Thus the Zebach (2077) or *sacrifice* was utterly distinct from the 'Ôlâh (5930) or *ascending-offering*, which was wholly burned or turned into smoke, and from the *sin-offering*, which was partly burned and partly eaten by the priest.

The various ceremonies connected with the sacrifice are described in Lev. 17:5-7 and other passages. A man brought an unblemished animal to the door of the sacred tent, pressed his hands on its head, and slew it. The priest, who in this and all other things acted on God's behalf, took the blood, which represented the life of the animal (and therefore the life of the offerer), and shed it forth on the altar as an atonement. He also burned the fat—to represent the fact that the richness or goodness of animal life proceeded from God, and was due to Him. A certain fixed portion of the flesh was then given to the priest, to be eaten by himself and his family, and the rest was eaten by the offerer and his household. Whether the feast was public or private, and whether the animal was offered by the elders of the nation or by the head of a family, these ceremonies were appointed in order to symbolize the union between God and man, who were thus made partakers of the same food. If it was impossible to perform the full rites connected with the sacrifice through distance from the "tabernacle of the congregation," or from the place that God should subsequently choose to

7. In some French translations of the Bible a priest is called *sacrificateur* (sacrificer).

put His name there, i.e., the temple,[8] one point at any rate was to be observed: the blood of the slain animal was to be poured on the earth and covered with dust (v. 13).

There can be little doubt that the rites connected with the **Zebach** (2077) were designed to produce a moral effect on the children of Israel. Every time that they slew an unblemished animal for food they were reminded of God's merciful disposition toward them; they were thus stimulated to live in conformity with His law and to deal mercifully with their poorer brethren. Nor can it be doubted that the death of the animal, followed by the sprinkling of the blood and the burning of the fat, would impress the pious Israelite with a recollection of the fact that sin brought death into the world, and that he himself had sinned. He would thus have what the Scripture calls "a broken spirit" (Ps. 51:17); and his sacrifice would be a strong call to *righteousness* (Ps. 4:5), to *obedience* (I Sam. 15:22), to *joy* (27:6), and to *mercy* (Hos. 6:6). Where the sacrifice had not this spirit, it lost all its value and significance.

The connection between the **Zebach** (2077) and the making of a covenant is brought out in various parts of Scripture, the sharing in food being a symbol of the oneness of the eaters. See, for example, Gen. 31:54 and Ps. 50:5. The Passover and the peace-offering, which were special kinds of **Zebach** (2077), are referred to below.

§6. *The Altar*

The Hebrew name for an *altar,* Mizbêach (מִזְבֵּחַ, 4196), is derived from **Zâbach** (2076) and is literally *a place of slaughter.* It is rendered θυσιαστήριον (2379) in the LXX, except where a heathen altar is referred to, and then the Greek word βωμός (1041) is adopted.[9] The primary idea that a Hebrew would attach to an altar would depend on his view of the word **Zâbach** (2076). According to Levitical usage, it would be the appointed place on which the blood of slain beasts was to be sprinkled and their fat to be burned. In a short but

8. See II Sam. 7:1 and I Kings 8:16, 29, where we have direct and unimpeachable references to Deut. 12:10, 11, et al.

9. The name 'Ărîy'el (740—Isa. 29:1, 2; Ezek. 43:15, 26) is supposed by some to mean "altar of God," an Arabic root akin to the Latin *ara* (altar) being produced in support of the translation; but this is doubtful.

interesting essay on the Jewish altar by David Mill,[10] it is noticed that the Rabbinical writers used to regard it not only as God's table[11] (see Mal. 1:7), but also as a symbol of mediation. Accordingly, they called it a *Paraclete* (פרקליט, Παρακλητος), i.e., an intercessor. It was regarded as a center for mediation, peacemaking, expiation, and sanctification. Whatever was burned on the altar was considered to be consumed by God, a guarantee that the offerer was accepted by Him.

It seems probable from the general use of Mizbêach (4196) for an altar that in the Patriarchal age the animals that were offered to the Lord as burnt-offerings were laid on the altar and sacrificed (i.e., slain) there. The account of the burnt-offering in Gen. 22 exactly falls in with this supposition. In this matter, however, as in many others, the law of Moses departed from the earlier practice while retaining the principal features of the system.

§7. *Altar and Sacrifice in the N.T.*

The word θύω (2380) is used in the N.T. both with respect to the slaying of the Passover Lamb and to the killing of animals for the purpose of food (e.g., Luke 15:23; Acts 10:13). The noun θυσία (2378) occurs several times in the N.T. with reference to Levitical rites, e.g., I Cor. 10:18; to the Christian life of self-sacrifice (Rom. 12:1; Phil. 2:17; 4:18; Heb. 13:16; and I Pet. 2:5); and to the sacrifice of Christ on the cross (Eph. 5:2; Heb. 9:26; 10:12).

The altar, θυσιαστήριον (2379), is mentioned in about twenty passages, in most of which the Jewish altar is referred to. In I Cor. 10:18, Paul reminds the Corinthians that in the case of Israel those who eat the sacrifices become in so doing partakers of (or with) the altar. By this he means that while the altar (which represented God) had part of the victim, the sacrificer had another part; thus the sacrificial victim being consumed partly by God and partly by man forms a bond of union between the One and the other.

In Heb. 13:10, the writer points out that there were certain offer-

---

10. David Mill was Reland's successor as Oriental Professor at Utrecht, where his *Dissertationes Selectae* were published.

11. The table was not provided in the Levitical law, but is referred to in Ezek. 40:39. It served a different purpose from the altar. The animal was slain and cut up on the table, but its blood was sprinkled, its fat burned, and, in the case of the 'Ôlâh (5930), all the pieces were burned on the altar.

ings of which neither priest not offerer might eat. They were not burned (i.e., turned to smoke on the altar), but were entirely consumed,[12] so that there was no communion with the altar or with God in these cases. "We Jews," the writer seems to say, "have an altar with which neither the offerer nor the priests who minister in the tabernacle have a right to share. Where part of the blood of the victim was brought into the Holy Place as a sin-offering by the high priest on the great Day of Atonement, it was sprinkled on and before the mercyseat or place of propitiation. In this case none of the body was eaten, the whole being utterly consumed in a clean place outside the camp." He then applies this feature in the Levitical law to the Christian dispensation, and shows that we are in an analogous position. Christ's blood is presented in the Holy Place now as an atonement for us. His body, therefore, is to be devoted to consumption outside the camp. But what is His body? *"We Christians,"* he implies, "are the body of Christ; and as His crucifixion literally happened outside the city walls, so we are to go forth to Him bearing His reproach, sharing the ill-treatment He received, being mocked and jeered at by the world as it passes by, having no continuing city here, but seeking that city which is to come."

§8. *Technical Sense of the Word "Do"*

The word Âsâh (עָשָׂה, 6213), *to do*, which usually allies itself in meaning with the words with which it stands connected, has among its extended significations an application to offerings. It is rendered *offer* in forty passages, most of which are in Leviticus and Numbers, e.g., Lev. 5:10: "He shall offer the second for a burnt-offering, according to the ordinance, and the priest shall make an atonement for him." Sometimes it refers to the service of the priest, and sometimes

12. It is important to notice that throughout the Levitical ritual two distinct words are used to represent *burning*. Qâtar (קָטַר, 6999), which properly means *to turn into smoke or vapor*, is used of the burning of the 'Ôlâh (5930), of the memorial portion of the Minchâh (4503), and of the fat of the Zebach (2077), all of which were intended as offerings for God's good pleasure and not for sin. This burning took place on the altar at the door of the tabernacle. Sâraph (שָׂרַף, 8313—Assyrian *sarapu*), *to consume* or *burn up*, is used of the burning of the bodies of certain sin-offerings. Nothing is said of their smoke ascending as a sweet savor to God, because they represent "the body of sin," an object that is by no means pleasing in His sight. This is the aspect of the matter presented by the sin-offering that the priest offered for himself, and still more emphatically by the offering of the goat for the sins of the people on the great Day of Atonement. Ordinary sin-offerings were eaten by the priest.

to the action of him who brings the offering and appoints what particular animal he will offer. Naaman, the Syrian, is represented as using the word in II Kings 5:17; and it is used of Jehu's offering in the house of Baal, II Kings 10:24, 25. We also find it in Ps. 66:15: "I will offer bullocks with goats."

The word first occurs in this sense in Exod. 10:25, where Moses says, "Thou must give us also sacrifices and burnt-offerings, that we may sacrifice unto the LORD our God." In Exod. 29:36 it is regularly introduced into the Levitical system: "Thou shalt offer every day a bullock for a sin-offering for atonement"; verses 38, 39, "Thou shalt offer . . . two lambs of the first year day by day continually. The one lamb thou shalt offer in the morning; and the other lamb thou shalt offer at even." See also Lev. 14:19, 30; 15:15, 30; 23:12, 19; Num. 6:11, 16, 17; 15:3, 14, 24; 28:4, 8, 20, 21, 23, 24, 31. The word is used of *preparing* or arranging the animal or meat-offering or drink-offering in Num. 15:5, 6, 8, 12; Judg. 13:15, 16; Ezek. 43:25, 27; 45:17, 23, 24; 46:7, 12–15. It may be added that 'Âsâh (6213) is used of the making or ordaining of feasts in Judg. 14:10; I Kings 3:15; 12:32; Ezra 3:4; 6:19; Neh. 8:18; Esther 2:18; 5:8.

The Greek rendering in these passages is invariably ποιέω (*4160*), *to do*, or *make*[13]; the Vulgate usually has *facere* (*to make* or *do*), but sometimes *offerre* (*to bring before, offer*); and Luther usually has *machen* (*to make* or *do*), but occasionally *opfern* (*to sacrifice, offer up*).

It has been supposed by some commentators that our Lord used the word ποιέω (*4160*) in a sacrificial sense when He said, "*Do this* in remembrance of me" (Luke 22:19). It seems most reasonable to suppose that the word is to be taken here in that ceremonial sense in which it is frequently found in the O.T. The question, however, remains to be asked, to what special religious rite was the Lord referring? When He said "Do this," He must at least have meant "Keep this rite"; but did He mean "Offer this bread and wine as an offering," or was there some special Mosaic rite to which the words would bear reference? In answering this question it must be remembered that our Lord was approaching His death, and was instituting an ordinance that bore a direct relationship to it, so that whenever it is duly observed we "shew forth the Lord's death." Also

13. This use of the word ποιέω (*4160*) must not be forgotten in the interpretation of such a passage as II Cor. 5:21, "He made him [to be] sin on our behalf."

it must be granted that the giving up of the Savior's life upon the cross was preeminently vicarious and redemptive, and that in it all the offerings of the old dispensation had their fulfillment. What objection, therefore, can lie against the conclusion that the Lord meant, "Perform this sacrificial rite"; and that while the blood of bulls and goats, together with various meat and drink-offerings, *prefigured* the Lord's death, the simple elements of bread and wine were to take their place for all time to come as *memorials* of the same? But even if we adopted the expression "offer this" as a rendering, would this imply that the offerer was in any sense a *priest?* Certainly not, because the Hebrew and Greek words for *do* are used of the *people* as well as of the *priests;* see, for examples of this usage, Lev. 23:12, 19; Deut. 12:27; I Kings 8:64; II Kings 5:17; II Chron. 7:7; Ps. 66:15. Again, would the expression "offer this" give additional force to the arguments by which the theory of transubstantiation is upheld? Certainly not. On the contrary, though the offerings under the old dispensation foreshadowed the Lord's atoning offering in its various aspects, yet they were not identical with it, so that the Christian offering (if such an expression may be permitted for the sake of argument) would by analogy be at most a representation of the same—the breaking of the bread setting forth the laceration of the body, and the pouring out of the wine setting forth the shedding of the blood.[14]

It has been observed, however, that wherever the word *do* is used in a sacrificial sense in the O.T., there lies in the context some noun substantive that indicates the nature of the rite. This, then, we must look for in the N.T. when investigating the ceremonial significance of the expression before us.

Our Lord was at a Passover Supper, and at the table were the lamb and also the bread and wine, which were the regular adjuncts of the feast. It was not the lamb, however, that He took as the basis of His new rite. If it had been so, then there might have been a clearer connection between the Lord's Supper and the O.T. animal sacrifices. It was the unleavened bread and the wine that He took in His hands, calling the one His body and the other His blood.[15] We

14. Wine is called "the *blood* of grapes" in Gen. 49:11, et al.

15. Our Lord did not say τοῦτο γίγνεται (3778, 1096), "this has become or is turned into," but τοῦτό ἐστιν (3778, 1510), which in ritual connection can only mean "this represents or stands for." The Roman Church, in advocating the doctrine of transubstantiation, departs from the literal sense of Scripture.

may hence gather that it was the *nutritious* efficacy of His sacrifice to which the Lord was specially referring when He instituted His Supper: "The strengthening and refreshing of our souls by the body and blood of Christ, as our bodies are (strengthened and refreshed) by the bread and wine." It may therefore be inferred that when the Savior said "Do this," He did not mean "Offer this atoning victim," but "Keep this memorial communion feast."

That this is a just view of our Lord's words will be seen more clearly when it is considered that the *keeping* of the Passover feast was constantly spoken of in the O.T. as à *doing*, the words Âsâh (6213) and ποιέω (4160) being almost invariably used with respect to it. Instances are as follows: Exod. 12:48, "Will keep the passover to the Lord." Num. 9:2, "Let the children of Israel also keep the passover." Num. 9:3, "Ye shall keep it in his appointed season." Num. 9:4, "That they should keep the passover." Num. 9:5, "And they kept the passover." Num. 9:6, "That they could not keep the passover." Num. 9:10, "Yet shall he keep the passover." Num. 9:11, "At even they shall keep it." Num. 9:12, "According to all the ordinances of the passover they shall keep it." Num. 9:13, "Forbeareth to keep the passover." Num. 9:14a, "If a stranger shall sojourn . . . and will keep the passover." Num. 9:14b, "According to the ordinance of the passover . . . so shall he do." II Chron. 30:1, 2, 5, "To keep the passover." II Chron. 30:3, "They could not keep it." II Chron. 30:13, "To keep the feast of unleavened bread." II Chron. 35:18, "Neither did all the kings of Israel keep such a passover as Josiah kept." Ezra 6:19, "And kept the passover."

In all these passages the word *do* or *keep* answers to that which our Lord used when He said "Do this." Compare Matt. 26:18, where our Lord definitely uses it of the Passover. It can hardly be doubted, then, that His words had direct reference to the Passover feast. The institution was necessarily proleptic, and anticipated His death. The Passover lamb was to be slain; the sacrifice on the cross fulfilled *this* part of the paschal celebration. Thenceforward the death of Christ on the cross was to be not only the means of atonement and pardon, but also the source of spiritual sustenance.

The faithful realization and the personal appropriation of what is meant by "Christ crucified" is the appointed means for sustaining and stimulating in the heart that Divine life which flows from God to the believer and enables him to walk even as Christ walked. Thus the *memorial* is a real *feast*, and the ordinance furnishes a special opportunity for feeding on Christ in the heart by faith as a means of renewing spiritual life in all its aspects.

§9. *To Slay a Victim*

Shâchat (שָׁחַט, 7819—Assyrian *sakhatu*), *to kill* or *slay*, is first found in Gen. 22:10: "And Abraham stretched forth his hand and took the knife to slay his son." The only other place in Genesis where it occurs is in chap. 37:31, "And they took Joseph's coat, and killed a kid of the goats, and dipped the coat in the blood." It is used of the killing of the Passover Lamb in Exod. 12:6, etc., and in the directions for sacrifices it constantly occurs. It is rendered *offer* in Exod. 34:25: "Thou shalt not offer the blood of any sacrifice with leaven."

In Judg. 12:6, it is applied to the slaughter of *men*; also in I Kings 18:40, where the slaughter of the priests of Baal is referred to (see also II Kings 10:7, 14; 25:7; Jer. 39:6; 41:7; 52:10). In Isa. 57:5, the slaughter of children in the valleys was probably sacrificial, to propitiate false gods (as in Ezek. 23:39, and perhaps Hos. 5:2).

The general rendering for the word in the LXX is σφάζω (4969), but in a few passages we find θύω (2380).

According to the Received Text, in Rev. 5:6 we read of a lamb as it were slain (ἐσφαγμένον, 4969); the fruits, if not the outward marks, of sacrifice abiding in the exalted Savior (cf. Rev. 5:9, 12; 13:8).

§10. *The Passover*

Pâcach (פָּסַח, 6452) gives its name to the Peçach (6453), the *Paschal* or *Passover feast*.[16] It is used of the angel passing over the houses of Israel in Exod. 12:13, 23, and 27, and it occurs perhaps with significant reference to the great deliverance from Egypt in Isa. 31:5: "As birds flying, so will the LORD of hosts defend Jerusalem; defending also he will deliver it; and passing over he will preserve it." It is not a little remarkable that the word means not only *to leap*, and hence *to pass over*, but also *to limp*. It is the only word rendered *lame* in the O.T., and is also found in I Kings 18:21, when Elijah says, "How long *halt ye* between two opinions?" In verse 26 it occurs in the Piel or

---

16. Dr. Geddes gravely proposed that this word should be translated *skip-offering*. But *leap-offering* would be more exact; compare to the word *leap-year*.

intensive stem, with reference to the priests of Baal *leaping* on the altar.

The Paschal feast is $\pi\acute{\alpha}\sigma\chi\alpha$ (3957) in the LXX, except in the books of Chronicles, where the variant form $\phi\alpha\sigma\acute{\epsilon}\kappa$ is adopted.

While the whole Gospel narrative points to the relationship between Christ and the Paschal lamb, there is only one passage in the N.T. that definitely asserts it. But that single sentence is clear enough, "Christ our passover is sacrificed [i.e., slain] for us" (I Cor. 5:7).

§11. *The Peace-Offering*

The *peace-offering* is always **Shelem** (8002), from **Shâlam** (שָׁלַם, 7999—Assyrian *sulmannu*). It has been noticed in a previous chapter that this word has various meanings (see Chap. 8). It conveys the idea of *completeness* or *perfection*, and also of *compensation*, as well as that of *peace*. The verb is used of the *payment of vows* and praises to the LORD (e.g., in Ps. 50:14; 56:12; 76:11; 116:14; Isa. 19:21; Jonah 2:9; Nah. 1:15). This fact may give a clue to the real nature of the **Shelem** (8002). It was a special kind of **Zebach** (2077), or sacrificial feast, occasioned by some particular event in family life that called for a thankful acknowledgment of God's goodness, and a rendering to Him of what return was due and possible. It might be rendered *recompense-offering*. The ceremonial offering of the **Zebach** (2077) of the Shelem (8002—A.V. sacrifice of the peace-offering) was ordained by God so as to unite religious worship with the enjoyment of domestic happiness. It is remarkable that **Shelem** (8002) is used only in the plural. The LXX renders it by $\epsilon\grave{\iota}\rho\eta\nu\iota\kappa\grave{\alpha}$ (1516) and $\theta\upsilon\sigma\acute{\iota}\alpha$ $\sigma\omega\tau\eta\rho\acute{\iota}\upsilon$ (2378, 4992).

§12. *The Sin-Offering*

The *sin-offering* is always **Chattâ'th** (חַטָּאת, 2403), for which the LXX has $\pi\epsilon\rho\grave{\iota}$ $\acute{\alpha}\mu\alpha\rho\tau\acute{\iota}\alpha\varsigma$ (4012, 266—*for* [*the removing or destroying of*] *sin*). The verb **Châtâ'** (חָטָא, 2398), whence it derives its name, signifies *to sin*, but in the Piel stem *to cleanse* or *purge*, or *to offer for sin*, as in Lev. 6:26 and 9:15; also in Ps. 51:7, "*Purge* me with hyssop, and I shall be clean." It is used of *purification* in Num. 19:9, 17; see also Job 41:25. The main peculiarities of the sin-offering have been referred to above in Chap. 6. But it may be added that while the 'Ôlâh (5930) (an offering of devotion) went *upward*, both the blood and the flesh being placed on the altar and turned to smoke, the sin-offering, which was mystically identified with sin, went *downward*. The blood was poured down at the side of the altar; the animal, if not eaten by the priest, was burned up on the ground. And as there was nothing pleasing to God in the sin that it represented, the smoke is not described as rising up to God as a sweet odor.

The identification of Christ with the sin-offering ($\pi\epsilon\rho\grave{\iota}$ $\dot{\alpha}\mu\alpha\rho\tau\acute{\iota}\alpha\varsigma$ — 4012, 266) seems clear from Rom. 8:3, where we are told that "God sending his Son in the likeness of sinful flesh [or of flesh which is the seat of sin], and for sin [i.e., as a sin-offering], condemned sin in the flesh." The flesh, which had been the seat of sin in all other persons, was the seat of righteousness in Christ. In all the points in which the Apostle Paul (in the previous chapters) had shown the flesh to be wanting, Christ proved more than conqueror. His members were instruments of righteousness, His feet were swift to go on errands of mercy, His words were sweeter than honey and the honeycomb, His heart was pure from all taint of sin. Hence the force of His own question (John 8:46, R.V.), "Which of you convicteth me *of sin* [$\pi\epsilon\rho\grave{\iota}$ $\dot{\alpha}\mu\alpha\rho\tau\acute{\iota}\alpha\varsigma$ — 4012, 266]?" And thus we behold the efficacy of His being a sin-offering ($\pi\epsilon\rho\grave{\iota}$ $\dot{\alpha}\mu\alpha\rho\tau\acute{\iota}\alpha\varsigma$ — *for sin*) His life in the flesh was a practical condemnation of sin and a victory over it; and His death as a sin-offering was, by the will of God, the means of imparting that victory to all who are one with Him by faith.

In II Cor. 5:21 we read, in confirmation of the passage just commented on, that God made Him who knew not sin (experientially) to be sin for us. God identified Him with sin, dealt with Him as sin deserves to be dealt with, and thus fulfilled in Him that of which the sin-offering of the O.T. was a type.

The phrase $\pi\epsilon\rho\grave{\iota}$ $\dot{\alpha}\mu\alpha\rho\tau\acute{\iota}\alpha\varsigma$ or $\pi\epsilon\rho\grave{\iota}$ $\dot{\alpha}\mu\alpha\rho\tau\acute{\iota}\omega\nu$ (4012, 266) is also used with reference to the type or antitype in Gal. 1:4; Heb. 10:6, 12, 18, 26; 13:11; I Peter 3:18; I John 2:2; 4:10.

§13. *The Trespass-Offering*

The *trespass-offering*[17] is 'Âshâm (אָשָׁם, 817). Here, as in the case of the sin-offering, the offense and the sacrifice are identical in name.

---

17. If *trespass* is the right word for 'Âshâm (817), the word *guilt* should be changed; but if on the whole *guilt* gives the best idea, it would be best to render the word here the guilt-offering; otherwise the English reader loses the connection between the offense and the offering.

The exact nature of the trespass or guilt indicated by this word has already been discussed (see Chap. 6). The trespass-offering of the Philistines, mentioned several times in I Sam. 6, is called βάσανος (931), *torment*, in the LXX; but the general rendering is πλημμέλεια (L-S 1418B), a *discord* or *mistake*. In Isa. 53:10, where the A.V. and R.V. read "Thou shalt make his soul *an offering for sin*," Âshâm (817) is used, thus extending the efficacy of Christ's sacrifice to the class of sin designated by this Hebrew word. The LXX, however, renders the wording περὶ ἁμαρτίας (4012, 266). It also occurs in Prov. 14:9: "Fools make a mock at sin." These words have received various renderings. We might translate it, "Fools scorn the trespass-offering," or perhaps, "As for fools, [God] scorneth their trespass-offering; but among the upright there is acceptance." See R.V.

§14. *Fire-Offering*

The offering made by fire is 'Ishsheh (אִשֶּׁה, 801—Assyrian *isatu*), from 'Êsh (אֵשׁ, 784), *fire*. It is used freely from Exodus to I Samuel, but never later. It is generally rendered κάρπωμα (L-S 880A), *fruit* or *offering*, in the LXX, but sometimes ὁλοκαύτωμα (3646), or that which is wholly burned. In one passage 'Ishsheh (801) is used with reference to a sacrifice that was not burned at all (Lev. 24:7–9).

§15. *Drink-Offering*

The *drink-offering* is Neçek (נֶסֶךְ, 5262—Assyrian *nasaku*), from Nâçak (5258), *to pour out*. The LXX always renders it σπόνδη (L-S 1629B). The use of the verb Nâçak (5258) in Ps. 2:6 is remarkable: "I have poured out [as a drink-offering?] my king upon my holy hill of Zion." Compare Prov. 8:23, where wisdom is described as "poured out from everlasting." The word *set* adopted by the A.V. is intelligible, but hardly adequate. The verb σπένδομαι (4689) is twice used by the Apostle Paul of himself as ready to be *poured forth* as an offering (Phil. 2:17; II Tim. 4:6).

§16. *Incense*

The burning of perfume or incense is always expressed by the word Qâtar (קָטַר, 6999), *to burn* or *turn into smoke*, the incense being called Qᵉṭôreth (7004). In the Hiphil or causative stem, the verb is used of the burning of animal sacrifices (see p. 215, note). In the Piel or intensive stem it is rendered *offer*, in connection with incense (Num. 16:40; I Chron. 6:49; Jer. 11:12, 17; 32:29; Amos 4:5). The word θυμιάω (2370) is generally adopted for it in the LXX. See Rev. 5:8; 8:3, 4; 18:13, for the use of this word in the N.T. We must distinguish *incense* from *frankincense* (L^ebôwnâh, 3828), which was one of its components. The R.V. has corrected the six places where they are confused by the A.V. (Isa. 43:23; 60:6; 66:3; Jer. 6:20; 17:26; 41:5).

§17. *The Freewill-Offering*

The *freewill-offering* is always that which is given willingly, bountifully, liberally, or as a prince would give. The word N^edâbâh (נְדָבָה, 5071—Assyrian *nindabu*) refers not to the nature of the offering or to the external mode in which it is offered, but to the motive and spirit of the offerer. The most usual rendering in the LXX is ἑκούσιος (1595). The verb occurs in Exod. 35:29, "The children of Israel brought a willing offering unto the Lord"; 36:3, "They brought yet unto him free offerings every morning."[18] In Lev. 7:16 it is called "a voluntary offering." In Judg. 5:2, 9, in Deborah's song the people are praised for offering themselves willingly. The word occurs again in I Chron. 29:6, 9, 14, 17, with reference to the offerings made for the construction of the temple; also in II Chron. 17:11; Ezra 1:6; 2:68; 3:5; 7:15, 16; Neh. 11:2. *Free offerings* are also referred to in Ps. 54:6; 110:3; 119:108; Amos 4:5. It is used of the rain as a free gift of God in Ps. 68:9; and of His free love in Hos. 14:4.

§18. *The Wave-Offering and Heave-Offering*

The *wave-offering*, T^enûwphâh (תְּנוּפָה, 8573), was supposed to be shaken to and fro, while the *heave-offering*, T^erûwmâh (תְּרוּמָה, 8641), was elevated. The LXX usually has ἀφαίρεμα (L-S 285B), ἀφόρισμα (L-S 292B), or ἐπίθεμα (L-S 633B) for the wave-offering, and ἀπαρχή (L-S 180B), *first-fruits*, for the heave-offering. The verb Nûwph (נוּף, 5130), which gives the name to the wave-offering, is rendered *to wave* in many places in the A.V. In II Kings 5:11, Naaman expresses

---

18. It is important to notice that when in Lev. 1:3 and elsewhere the A.V. reads, "He shall offer it of his own *voluntary will*," an entirely different word is used. These passages ought to be rendered, "He shall offer it *for his acceptance.*"

his supposition that Elisha would "strike his hand over the place," or as our margin has it, "move his hand up and down." Compare Isa. 30:28, where we read of God's "sifting the nations with the sieve of vanity." It is rendered *shake* in Isa. 10:15, et al. The word is found in Ps. 68:9: "Thou didst send [i.e., sift out from the clouds] a gracious rain upon thine inheritance." In Exod. 20:25; Deut. 27:5; and Josh. 8:31, the *lifting up* (i.e., the *movement to and fro*) of the graving tool is spoken of.

The noun is rendered *oblation* in II Chron. 31:14; Isa. 40:20; and Ezek. 44:30; it is rendered *offering* in Exod. 25:2, et al.

17

Word, Law, Covenant

It was observed by the late Dr. McCaul[1] that "whether we take the Hebrew Scriptures as true or not, it is an incontrovertible fact that the fundamental idea of the Hebrew religion is that Jehovah is a God who reveals Himself to His creatures; that He has not left the human race to grope their way to the regions of religion or morality as they best can, but that from the beginning He has taken His children by the hand, cared for their welfare, made known to them His will, and marked out for them the way to happiness." In accordance with this undeniable fact, the Divine Being is represented as speaking by word of mouth with His creatures.

Under the general title "the Word of the Lord" in the O.T. we find not only the law of the ten commandments (literally, *the ten words*) uttered by the Divine voice on Mount Sinai, but also all the promises, warnings, precepts, prophecies, revelations of the Divine character, and messages of mercy that proceeded from God through the medium of "holy men of old." In the Psalms and prophetical books the whole body of revealed truth, including all historical manifestations of God's righteous and merciful rule, appears to be referred to as the Word of the Lord. Occasionally the utterance of speech on God's part is taken as identical with the exertion of His power, as when we read that "By the word of the Lord were the heavens made" (Ps. 33:6); and again, "Man doth not live by bread alone, but by every word that proceedeth out of the mouth of God" (Deut. 8:3); and again, "He sent his word and healed them" (Ps. 107:20). Throughout Scripture a distinction is drawn between *the will of God* and the

---

1. See his essay on "Prophecy" in *Aids to Faith*.

expression of that will or *the Word of God*. He was not content with willing that there should be light, but He *said*, "Let there be light," and there was light. Thus without the Word was not anything made that was made (see John 1:3).

The mode of transmitting the message from God to man was by no means uniform. God said to Moses, "Who hath made man's mouth? or who maketh the dumb, or deaf, or the seeing, or the blind? have not I the LORD? Now therefore go, and I will be with thy mouth, and teach thee what thou shalt say" (Exod. 4:11, 12). A little further we learn that Moses was to transmit the Divine message to his brother Aaron, and that he was to pass it on to the people; thus Moses was to be to Aaron in the place of God. This would imply the suggestion of the substance of what was to be said, though not necessarily the dictation of the words. In the remarkable instance of Jeremiah's prophecy (Jer. 36) God spoke the words to Jeremiah, and he dictated them to Baruch, who wrote them down. In the vision in which Ezekiel received his special appointment as a messenger from God to Israel, he is directed to eat the roll on which the woes to be inflicted on the people were recorded. Having thus made the message his own, he was to go forth with the words "Thus saith the Lord GOD."

§1. *The Word*

The most ordinary Hebrew terms setting forth the Divine utterances are Âmar (אָמַר, 559), *to say*, and Dâbar[2] (דָּבַר, 1696), *to speak*. The former refers rather to the mode of revelation, and the latter to the substance. Hence the noun Dâbâr (1697) is frequently rendered *thing*, as in Gen. 15:1 and 19:8; compare Luke 1:37. Millâh (מִלָּה, 4405, 4406) has also been rendered *word* in thirty passages, nineteen of which are in Job and seven in Daniel. It is used in II Sam. 23:2, "The spirit of the LORD spake by me, and his word was in my tongue"; Ps. 19:4, "Their words unto the end of the world." In the LXX the verb Âmar (559) is generally rendered ἔπω (2036) and λέγω (3004), and its noun forms 'Êmer (אֶמֶר, 561) and 'Ômer (אֹמֶר, 562) are usually rendered by ῥῆμα (4487) and λόγιον (3051); Dâbar (1696) is generally rendered λαλέω (2980), and the noun Dâbâr (1697) generally by λόγος (3056), sometimes ῥῆμα (4487), and in thirty-five passages

2. Whence Debîyr (דְּבִיר, 1687), *oracle*, is derived. See I Kings 6:5 and later passages.

πρᾶγμα (4229). **Millâh** (4405, 4406) is rendered λόγος (3056) and ῥῆμα (4487); and **Nâ'am** (נָאַם, 5001), *to utter* or *assert*, which is rare in the earlier books and frequent in the later, is rendered λέγω (3004). **Peh** (פֶּה, 6310), *mouth*, is rendered *word* in Gen. 41:40 and fourteen other passages.

In the N.T. "the word of God" frequently stands for the truths contained in the O.T.; but it often stands for "the Gospel," i.e., the story of the life, teaching, death, resurrection, ascension, and second coming of Christ, together with their bearing on human life and destiny.

Christ Himself is called *the Word*, both at the beginning of John's Gospel and elsewhere; and though it is supposed by some that this title was given to Him by the Evangelist with special reference to the philosophical theology current in his time, the usage of the O.T. is quite enough to justify and to suggest it.

The LXX usage of ῥῆμα (4487) and λόγος (3056) does not justify a profound distinction between these words in the N.T. The first, perhaps, stands for the utterance, and the second for the drift and reason of what is uttered. See I Pet. 1:23, 25, where they are combined.

§2. *The Law*

The general word for *Law* is **Tôwrâh** (תּוֹרָה, 8451—Assyrian *toretu*, the law of the gods). By this word the Pentateuch is universally described among the Jews to the present day. The verb **Yârâh** (יָרָה, 3384) whence it is derived signifies *to project*, and hence *to point out* or *teach*. The law of God is that which points out or indicates His will to man. It is not an arbitrary rule, still less is it a subjective impulse; it is rather to be regarded as a course of guidance from above. The verb and noun are found together in Exod. 24:12: "I will give thee a law, and commandments which I have written; that thou mayest teach them." It is generally, though imperfectly, represented in the LXX by the word νόμος (3551).

Tôwrâh (8451) has been rendered *law* in all places but one, namely, II Sam. 7:19, "The *manner* [8452] of man," literally, "The law of the man." In the parallel passage (I Chron. 17:17), **Tôwr** (תּוֹר, 8448), which is evidently the same word, is rendered *estate*.

Tôwrâh (8451) is first found in Gen. 26:5 in connection with Abraham's loyalty to God. It frequently signifies ritual, custom, or prescriptive right. It is applied to specific ordinances, to groups of regulations and instructions, and to the books that contain them.

The word Dâth (דָּת, 1881, 1882), an *edict*, is used as part of a compound word in Deut. 33:2: "From his right hand went a fiery-law for them." This term is frequently adopted in Ezra, Esther, and Daniel. Chôq (חֹק, 2706), a *statute* or *decree*, is frequently used, either in its masculine or feminine form, for the Divine statutes. It is rendered *law* in the following passages: Gen. 47:26, "Joseph made it a law over the land of Egypt unto this day." Gen. 49:10, "The sceptre shall not depart from Judah, nor a lawgiver [Piel participle of חָקַק, 2710, from which Chôq, 2706, is derived] from between his feet, until Shiloh come." Num. 21:18, "The princes digged the well, the nobles of the people digged it, by the direction of the lawgiver [2710]." Deut. 33:21, "He provided the first part for himself, because there, in a portion of the lawgiver [2710], was he seated." I Chron. 16:17; Ps. 105:10, "He confirmed the same to Jacob for a law, and to Israel for an everlasting covenant." Ps. 60:7; 108:8, "Judah is my lawgiver" (a passage interesting in connection with Gen. 49:10, cited above). Ps. 94:20, "Shall the throne of iniquity have fellowship with thee, which frameth mischief by a law?" Prov. 31:5, "It is not for kings to drink wine . . . lest they forget the law, and pervert the judgment of any of the afflicted." Isa. 33:22, "The LORD is our judge, the LORD is our lawgiver, the LORD is our king; he will save us."

The most usual renderings of Chôq (2706) in the LXX are δικαίωμα (1345), πρόσταγμα (L-S 1525B), and νόμιμον (L-S 1179B).

In Isa. 49:24, "the lawful captive" is literally "the captivity of the righteous"; in Jer. 32:11 a word is used that signifies *commandment;* in Ezra 7:24, *lawful* means *permissible;* while judgment is the literal rendering in Lev. 24:22; Ps. 81:4; Ezek. 18:5, 19, 21, 27; 33:14, 16, 19 ("lawful and right").

§3. *Commandment*

The most general word for *command* or *commandment* is some form of Tsâvâh (צָוָה, 6680), which appears to signify literally *to set up* or *appoint.* It is largely used from Gen. 2:16 onward, and applies to any order, human or Divine. The general Greek renderings are ἐντέλλομαι (1781), προστάττω (4367), and ἐντολή (1785).

'Âmar (אָמַר, 559), *to speak,* is rendered *command* in Exod. 8:27 and forty-four other passages; and Dâbar (דָּבַר, 1696), *to speak,* is so rendered twenty times. What is spoken either by the Lord or by anyone of high authority is naturally looked on as a commandment. With God, to speak is to command; and with man, to hear ought to be to obey.[3] Âmar (559) is used in Job 9:7, where we read that God "commandeth the sun and it riseth not"—the laws of nature, their continuance, and their cessation, being equally regarded as the utterance of the Divine word. So God "commandeth and raiseth the stormy wind" (Ps. 107:25); "He sendeth forth his commandment upon earth: his word runneth very swiftly" (Ps. 147:15).

Peh (פֶּה, 6310), *mouth*, is rendered *commandment* in Gen. 45:21 and Exod. 17:1, as well as thirty-two other passages. It is possibly an Egyptian idiom, and may be compared with the use of *mouth* as signifying *self* in Coptic. It occurs in Job 39:27, "Doth the eagle mount up at thy command?"; in Prov. 8:29, "He gave to the sea his decree that the waters should not pass his commandment"; Eccles. 8:2, "Keep the king's commandment"; Lam. 1:18, "I have rebelled against his commandment."

§4. *Charge or Precept*

The word Piqqûwd (פִּקּוּד, 6490—Assyrian *paqadu*) is properly a *charge*. It is found only in the plural, and is always rendered *precepts* except in Ps. 103:18 and 111:7. The general renderings of the verb are ἐπισκέπτομαι (1980), *to visit*, ἐκδικέω (1556), *to avenge*, and καθίστημι (2525), *to appoint*. It is used of *visitation*, whether for purposes of mercy or for purposes of chastisement. The substantive in the feminine form, Pᵉquddâh (6486—answering to ἐπίσκεψις, L-S 656B, or ἐπισκοπή, 1984), is found in the former sense in Jer. 27:22; but in the latter sense in Isa. 10:3; 29:6; Jer. 6:15; 11:23; 23:12; 48:44. In these cases the context plainly decides the matter; and though it is noticeable that the instances of the *noun* being used of judgment preponderate, if the passages where the verb is used were also cited this would not be the case.

But the word has a further sense. It is often rendered ἐντολή (1785) and δικαίωμα (1345), and signifies a *charge*. Sometimes it denotes the oversight or care that a responsible person is enjoined to take. Thus we read in Num. 4:16 that Eleazar had the *oversight* (ἐπισκοπή, 1984) of all the tabernacle. It was put in his charge, and

---

3. The ordinary word for *obedience* in the O.T. literally signifies *hearing*.

he was responsible for its safekeeping. In Ps. 109:8 we read, "Let another take his *office*" (ἐπισκοπή, 1984), i.e., let another perform the duties which are laid on him. It is a pity that this passage has not been translated more literally where it is quoted in the N.T., in Acts 1:20, where we read, "His *bishoprick* let another take." The margin here very properly has *office* or *charge*. While it is true that a *bishopric* is an ἐπισκοπή (1984), not only etymologically but really, yet it does not follow that an ἐπισκοπή (1984) is a modern *bishopric*. This rendering, like many others, has come to us from the Latin Vulgate. It was accepted by Wycliffe and Tyndale without hesitation. See R.V.

The word ἐπίσκοπος (1985) answers to another form of **Pâkad** (6485), viz., the noun **Pâqîyd** (6496), and indicates the persons who have a charge or responsibility laid on them, whether for military, civil, or religious purposes. The following are among the passages in which it occurs: Num. 31:14, "Moses was wroth with the officers of the host"; Ju.lg. 9:28, "Is not Abimelech the son of Jerubbaal? and Zebul his officer?" II Chron. 34:12, "The men did the work faithfully; and the overseers of them were Jahath and Obadiah"; verse 17, "They have delivered the money into the hand of the overseers and to the hand of the workmen." See also Neh. 11:9, 14.

§5. *Combination of Words in Psalm 119*

In reading Psalm 119 we are struck with the constant recurrence of various titles by which God's revelation of Right is described. In the first nine verses we find eight different titles given to the truth of God.[4] They are as follows:

(1) The law or **Tôwrâh** (8451).

(2) The word.

(3) The commandments.

(4) The statutes.

(5) The precepts, **Piqqûwdîym** (6490).

(6) The ways. The word used throughout this Psalm for *way* is 'Ôrach (אֹרַח, 734), a *course, journey,* or *pilgrimage*; while in other parts of the Scripture **Derek** (דֶּרֶךְ, 1870), a *path*, is the expression used. Either word implies that man's course of life, thought, and

---

4. Compare Ps. 19:7–9, in which five words are used to designate God's law, namely, *decree, testimony, statutes, commandments,* and *judgments*.

desire ought to be brought into harmony and made coincident with God's.

(7) The judgments. The word **Mishpât** (מִשְׁפָּט, 4941) is used twenty-one times in the Psalm, and seems to point to rules of righteous administration.

(8) The testimonies. The word for *testimony* is derived from 'Ûwd (עוּד, 5749), *to bear witness*. It is used fourteen times in this Psalm, and in various other parts of the O.T. The law of God is His testimony, because it is His own affirmation concerning His nature, attributes, and consequent demands.

With exquisite beauty and with inspired depth of thought the writer of Psalm 119 draws out these varied aspects of the Divine Truth, and presents the law of God in every light in which the experience of a godly man can regard it. Certainly no student of the Psalms can doubt that the pious Israelite found the revealed will of God anything but a heavy burden or an intolerable yoke. Yet whosoever trusted in the Most High soon learned to take pleasure in God's commandments, and to realize their breadth and spirituality; and he was thus enabled to love God's law as well as to long for His salvation.

§6. *Teaching of the N.T.*

The word νόμος (3551) is very frequently used of the law of Moses, ,which is regarded, both in the O.T. and N.T., as *one*, though containing many ἐντολαί (1785) or specified commandments (see Matt. 22:36). This law is also called the law of the LORD, because, though it was given by Moses (John 1:17) and by the disposition of angels (Acts 7:53), it really represented the will of the Lord God (Luke 2:23).

In the four Gospels and Acts the law is referred to fifty times, and generally in the sense now mentioned; in some passages, however, it specially designates the books of Moses, according to the ordinary Jewish mode of dividing the O.T.

In Rom. 2:14 we have another sense of the word introduced. The heathen nations "have not [the[5]] law." But if it should be found that they do the things of the law (i.e., act on those great principles

5. There is no definite article here, and hence some critics have doubted whether the reference is made to the law of Moses, or whether the principle of *law* in the abstract is to be understood. But this is probably one of the cases in which the absence of the article ought not to be pressed.

which lie at the root of the whole Mosaic legislation), then, though they "have not [the] law," they become a law to themselves, inasmuch as they show forth in their outer life the results that the law aimed at producing, and which were written not indeed on external tables, but on their hearts. Moreover, their consciousness and the r inmost convictions, which lead them to disapprove of one course of action and approve of another, will bear witness with these outward results in the Day when God shall form a judicial estimate of the secrets of the heart.

With regard to the persons thus described, Paul says again, in verses 26, 27, that the uncircumcision, i.e., the Gentiles, who accomplish the law, will be reckoned as true Jews, and will judge those Jews who have the letter of the law and circumcision, but who nevertheless are transgressors.

In Rom. 5:14, Paul says that up to the time that the law was given, i.e., from Adam to Moses, sin was in the world (and among the heathen nations that have not heard of Christ's salvation sin is still in the world; nor did the command that all men everywhere should repent go forth till the Day of Pentecost); but sin is not reckoned where there is no law; and yet death, the fruit and penalty of sin, reigned all this time, even on those whose sins were committed under far less aggravated circumstances than the transgression of Adam. Hence we are left to infer that there is some law that all the heathen have transgressed, and that in all the children of men there has been such a departure from God as has justified Him in inflicting death. Sin was in them, though not in the form of rebellion against the law of Moses.

In other passages the word νόμος (3551) rather signifies *order* or *principle*. This is sometimes the case with Dâbâr (1697), *word*, in the O.T., as in the familiar sentence, "Thou art a priest for ever after the order of Melchizedek."[6] In Rom. 3:27, Paul asks, "On what principle [A.V. by what law] is a man accounted righteous? on the principle of works? no; on the principle of faith." So again in Rom. 8:2, "The binding principle of the spirit of life in Christ Jesus hath made me free from the binding principle of sin and death."

In Rom. 7:2 the word is used in two senses: the married woman is bound by *law* (i.e., by the law of Moses) to her living husband; but if

---

6. Some render these words, "after *my word*, O Melchizedek."

the husband dies she is liberated[7] from the *bond* or *tie* that had existed between the two parties. So, carrying out the parallel, we may understand verse 6: Now we are liberated from the bond that connected us with the flesh, sin, and the letter of the law, for we have been identified through faith with the death of Christ—a death whereby sin was overcome, the flesh was made an instrument of good instead of evil, and the letter of the law had its complete fulfillment and consequent abolition.

When Paul said, "I was living without the law once" (Rom. 7:9), he seems to be referring to a part of his previous history during which sin lay dormant in him. But when the commandment came—i.e., some special commandment of the law that went against Paul's manner of life and natural dispositions—sin burst forth into a new life,[8] while I died, i.e., trespassed and so brought death on myself. And the commandment in question, which if I had kept it would have kept me in the way of life, proved practically a means of leading me to death. For sin, receiving an impetus (ἀφορμήν, *874*) from the commandment, deceived me (as it is the way of all sin to do; see Gen. 3:13; I Tim. 2:14; James 1:14), and made use of the law of God to slay me. Perhaps Paul's reference in Gal. 2:19 to a point in his past history may be explained in the same way. "I through the law died to the law, that I might live to Christ"; i.e., the law taught me my sinfulness and led me to believe in Christ, and accordingly I did what all converted Jews must do—I died to the law, identifying myself with Christ in His death, that I might live no longer to myself, but to Him who died for me. The words διὰ νόμου (*1223, 3551*) might, however, be explained by a similar phrase in Rom. 2:27 (διὰ γράμματος—*1223, 1121*), as "although I had the law," or "in spite of the law."

We find δικαίωμα (*1345*) ten times in the N.T. In seven of these passages it conveys the O.T. word *precept* (Luke 1:6; Rom. 1:32; 2:26; 8:4 [A.V. the righteousness of the law]; Heb. 9:1, 10; Rev. 15:4). In Rev. 19:8, we are obliged to render the word "the *righteousness* of the

---

7. The word κατηργήται (*2673*) is not an easy word to translate. It signifies a complete abolition of that relationship which had previously existed.

8. The word ἀνέζησε (*326*) seems to imply that he had felt its power before, but that he had, as he thought, quite overcome it, so that he supposed it was dead. He had brought himself into complete harmony with the law as he imagined, but suddenly a special commandment in the law was pressed upon his attention, and brought out the old Adam in renewed vigor.

saints"; (A.V. justification); verse 18, "by one righteousness" (A.V. by the righteousness of one).

The words ἐντέλλεσθαι (*1781*) and ἐντολή (*1785*) are used of the charges contained in the law. They are also applied to the orders given by Christ Himself, the new Lawgiver; see Matt. 28:20; John 15:14, 17; Acts 1:2; 13:47. The latter class of passages shows that the Lord laid great stress on the keeping of His commandments. The ἐντολή (*1785*) spoken of in various verses of Rom. 7 was doubtless some portion of the Mosaic commandments; but the "holy commandment" of II Pet. 2:21 must be referred to the charge laid down by our Lord; see also II Pet. 3:2.

The verb ἐπισκέπτομαι (*1980*) is used ten times in the N.T., and generally, if not always, signifies *visitation* for purposes of mercy. The kindred term ἐπισκοπέω (*1983*) is used in Heb. 12:15 and I Pet. 5:2, and denotes responsibility and watchfulness rather than rule. The Lord is called the Shepherd and Watcher over our souls or lives, I Pet. 2:25. The Apostles had a charge of the same kind, though more limited (Acts 1:20); and the Ephesian elders are told to take heed to the flock over which the Holy Ghost had appointed them as watchers (Acts 20:28). The word ἐπίσκοπος (*1985*), which is found in these two places, gradually assumed a more technical sense, and stood for the *whole* office, of which this careful watching was only a part (I Tim. 3:1, 2; and Titus 1:7).[9]

The word ἐπισκοπή (*1984*) occurs in Luke 19:44, where the Lord spoke of the doom that was coming on Jerusalem, because she knew not the time of her *visitation*. This was the visitation of God's mercy and grace in the Person of Christ, of whom it is said that "He came unto his own [things or property], and his own [people] received him not." Compare Luke 1:68, 78, with John 1:11. There is another day of visitation yet to come, in which the mercy of God in Christ will be more gloriously manifested. See I Pet. 2:12.

---

9. It has been said that "in the incumbent of a large London parish, with curates, Scripture readers, district visitors, lay agents, and Sunday school teachers, dependent on his piety, zeal, vigour, ability, and force of character, for direction, stimulus, encouragement, superintendence and tone, we seem to have the best representative now in existence of the Primitive Bishop." See *Church Missionary Intelligencer* for April 1871; and on the whole subject of the Primitive Christian ministry consult Dr. Lightfoot's Essay in his *Commentary on the Epistle to the Philippians*.

§7. *Covenant*

The Hebrew word for *covenant* is always B^erîyth (בְּרִית, 1285). This word is rendered διαθήκη (*1242*) in the LXX in every passage where it occurs, except Deut. 9:15, where it is rendered μαρτύριον (*3142*), *testimony,* and I Kings 11:11, where it is rendered ἐντολή (*1785*), *commandment.*

The word διαθήκη (*1242*) is confined to this one use in the LXX, with the exception of four passages: Exod. 31:7 and Lev. 26:11, where it may represent a different Hebrew reading from that which we now possess; also Deut. 9:5, where it stands for a *word;* and Zech. 11:14, where it is used of the *brotherhood* (אַחֲוָה, 264—Assyrian *akhutu*) between Judah and Israel.

Translators have found much difficulty in giving a uniform rendering to the word B^erîyth (1285) even in the O.T. Expressions answering to the words *alliance, bond, compact, covenant, disposition,* and *treaty* have been resorted to, but none of them are perfectly satisfactory, and for this reason: that while they represent the nature of a covenant between man and man, none of them are adequate for the purpose of setting forth the nature of God's gracious dealings with man. The translators of the LXX evidently felt the difficulty, and instead of using συνθήκη (L-S 1717A), which would be the natural word for a covenant, used διαθήκη (*1242*), which means a legal *disposition,* and hence a *testament.*[10] The Syriac version transliterates the Greek word. The Arabic substitutes 'ahad, a *compact.* The Spanish translator De Reyna, after discussing in the Preface to his Bible the words *Concierto* (good order and arrangement of things— cf. II Sam. 23:5; bargain, agreement, or contract), *Pacto* (compact, contract, covenant, pact), and *Alliança* (alliance, agreement, covenant), comes to the conclusion that none of them are good, because what is needed is a word that signifies an agreement "made in conjunction with a solemn ceremony of death[11] of some animal" (*hecho con solemne rito de muerte de algun animal*). On the whole, however, he thought it better to use a word that was an imperfect representation of B^erîyth (1285) than to reproduce the word and thus convey no sense at all.

10. *Testamentum,* literally something attested or borne witness to, but always used of a will whereby we dispose of our goods.

11. The idea of bloodshedding in connection with the Abrahamic covenant was sustained in the memory of Israel by the rite of circumcision. See Acts 7:8.

The Lord Jesus is called the mediator of the New Covenant, because He is the medium wherein the Disposition of God is carried into effect, whether as regards the individual or the race as a whole (Heb. 8:6; 9:15; 12:24). The inheritance that was given by *promise* to Christ (Gal. 3:16) was conveyed by *covenant* (through His blood-shedding) to all believers (Gal. 3:17, 29), who are made *one* with Him by faith; and it is this union of God with man, and of man with God, in Christ, that is summed up in the N.T. sense of the word Berîyth (1285).

The crucial passage in the N.T. in Heb. 9:17, which the R.V. renders, "A testament is of force where there has been death: for doth it ever avail while he that made it liveth?" This rendering does not go far to reduce the difficulty. The real point that the passage brings out is that the victim represents the makers of the covenant, i.e., the contracting parties, and they could be united representatively in the victim only by means of its death. So in the death of Christ man and God are made one. It is a covenant, not a last will and testament, that is in the writer's mind.

18
Worship, Praise, Preach

Two classes of words are put together in this chapter. *First,* there are those adopted in Scripture to set forth man's public and private expression of his dependence on God, and of his thankfulness to the Being who "giveth to all men liberally and upbraideth not." Prayer and praise are uniformly regarded in Scripture as actions well-pleasing to God. They are based on an acknowledgment of His Personality, of His greatness, and of His power and willingness to interfere in the temporal and spiritual affairs of men. *Secondly,* there are the words by which the Hebrews set forth the mode of conveying truth from man to man. In each case there is something of that pictorial power to which attention has been called in previous chapters.

§1. *Worship*

The word *worship* is the general representative of the Hebrew **Shâchâh** (שָׁחָה, 7812), and of the Greek προσκυνέω (4352). The following are the only exceptions: the Aramaic word Çᵉgîd (סְגִד, 5457) is used in Dan. 2:46, where we read that the king Nebuchadnezzar prostrated himself before Daniel, and commanded sweet odors and an oblation should be offered to him; it is also used throughout the third chapter for the prostration or worship that was to be offered to the image of gold. Âtsab (עֲצַב, 6087) is found in Jer. 44:19, where it appears to signify the fashioning of cakes as images of "the queen of heaven." The words "did we make her cakes to worship her?" might be rendered "did we make her cakes to represent her?" In II Kings

237

10 the word used for the *worshipers* of Baal is ʿEbed (עֶבֶד, 5650), which signifies a *servant* or *slave*.

Shâchâh (7812) originally signified *prostration* as a mark of respect, and is applied in Scripture not only to God and to false gods but also to men, just as the English word *worship* is used of the husband's reverence for his wife in the marriage service of the English Church, and is a title of respect for a civil magistrate. Shâchâh (7812) is also rendered in the A.V. by the words *bow, stoop, crouch, fall down, beseech humbly, make obeisance,* and *do reverence.* It is used of Abraham's reverent prostration before his three angelic visitors (Gen. 18:2), and of his obeisance before the Hittites (Gen. 23:7, 12); it occurs in the blessing that Isaac gave to Jacob, "Let nations bow down to thee: let thy mother's sons bow down to thee" (Gen. 27:29); Jacob himself bows down or prostrates himself seven times on meeting Esau (Gen. 33:3, 6, 7); Joseph dreams that he receives this worship from his parents and brethren (Gen. 37:10), and he *does* receive it (Gen. 42:6). See also Gen. 48:12; 49:8; Exod. 11:8; Ruth 2:10; I Sam. 20:41; 24:8.

In Gen. 47:31 we read that Israel bowed himself (worshiped or prostrated himself) on the bed's head, or, according to the LXX, as quoted in Heb. 11:21, on the top of his staff. Various explanations are given of this statement. The difference between the LXX and the Hebrew depends not on the letters, but on the vowel points. On comparing the passage with others in which the same verb is used with the same preposition in Hebrew and the LXX, it will be seen that the top of the rod was not that which he *leaned* on, as might seem to be implied by the italics in the A.V., but that which he *touched with his forehead* in the act of prostration. The only question that remains is whether the worship thus offered was directed to Joseph in fulfillment of the dream and in reverence for his high office, or whether it was directed to God in accordance with whose promise Jacob exacted an oath from Joseph concerning the transmission of his bones to Canaan, or, finally, whether by faith he saw in Joseph a type or foreshadowing of the true deliverer of the people. De Sacy, in his French version, gives an interpretation to which Calvin is very much inclined also. Bearing in mind the Egyptian custom of carrying a staff of authority, such as may still be seen graven on the walls of the ancient temples, he holds that Jacob bowed to the staff that Joseph bore in his hand, and thereby recognized his son's secular authority and fulfilled the dream of Joseph.

Turning to the more directly religious use of the word Shâchâh (7812), it may be observed that the worship of God was to be carried out by the people themselves, and was not done for them by the priest. It was not only to consist of outward prostration, such as the heathen offered to their false gods, but was to be accompanied by the devotion of the heart. The annual keeping of the three feasts was considered a mark of worship (I Sam. 1:3). See also I Sam. 15:25; II Sam. 12:20; II Kings 18:22; Ps. 5:7; 29:2; 132:7; 138:2; Isa. 27:13.

Reverent worship was to be offered in later days to the Messiah, as seems evident from Ps. 22:27, "All the kindreds of the nations shall worship before thee"; verse 29, "All they that be fat upon earth shall eat and worship; all they that go down to the dust shall bow before him"; Ps. 45:11, "He is thy LORD; and worship thou him"; Isa. 49:7, "Thus saith the LORD . . . to him whom man despiseth, to him whom the nation abhorreth, to a servant of rulers, kings shall see and arise, princes also shall worship, because of the LORD."

With regard to the heathen, the prophet's assurance is not only that their old worship is evil, but that "men shall worship [God], every one from his [own] place, even all the isles of the heathen" (Zeph. 2:11). Each man, whether in this mountain or in that, was to render true allegiance to God. And this prediction is fully consistent with others that speak of all peoples going up to Jerusalem and to the temple of the LORD to worship, as in Isa. 66:20–23; Ezek. 46:2–9; Zech. 14:16, 17.

§2. N.T. Teaching

The witness of the N.T. is very interesting in connection with the prophetic passages cited above. We find, for instance, that our Lord received worship from the Magi (Matt. 2:8, 11), from the leper (Matt. 8:2), from the ruler (Matt. 9:18), from His disciples after He had calmed the storm (Matt. 14:33), from the Canaanitish woman (Matt. 15:25), from Salome (Matt. 20:20), from the blind man (John 9:38), and from His disciples after His resurrection (Matt. 28:9, 17). It has been thought that this was only civil worship, and that it was paid to Jesus as a mark of respect or gratitude. But was it so in all cases? Did not the man whose eyes had been opened by Jesus Christ mean something more than civil worship when he prostrated himself before Him on hearing that He was the Son of God? Did not the disciples mean something more than civil worship when they

bowed before their risen Lord? And it may be fairly asked whether
the Lord would have permitted it to be paid to Him unless He were
worthy to receive it? Surely not. He would have said, as Peter did to
Cornelius when he fell at his feet and worshiped, "Stand up, for I
also am a man" (Acts 10:26). He would have said, as the angel did to
the Apostle John, when acting in the same way, "See thou do it not,
for I am thy fellow servant . . . : worship God" (Rev. 19:10; 22:9). The
truth is that in receiving worship from men, the Lord Jesus Christ
was assuming to Himself the right of the First Begotten, of whom
the Lord had said, "Let all the angels of God worship him" (Heb. 1:6).
Compare Rev. 5:11–14, where there is an ascription of blessing and
honor, and glory, and power forever and ever to Him who sits on the
throne, *and to the Lamb.*

Various instances of worship or adoration are found in the N.T. in
addition to the passages now referred to. When Satan tempted the
Lord to fall down and worship him, the answer given from Deut.
6:13 was this: "Thou shalt worship the LORD thy God, and him only
shalt thou serve." Evidently stress is here laid on the word *worship,*
and yet when we turn to the Hebrew and to the LXX in the passage
in question, we find the words, "Thou shalt fear," etc. Worship, then,
is regarded by our Lord as the expression of reverential fear; and
what Satan called for was recognized as an act of that kind which
should only be offered to God.

In our Lord's conversation with the woman of Samaria, the word
$\pi\rho\sigma\kappa\nu\nu\epsilon\omega$ (4352) occurs nine times in the course of five verses, and
the true principle of worship is clearly enunciated. The spirituality
of worship, however, was not intended to supersede all external
forms in religion, as may be shown by the fact that the worship of
God, as manifested in outward prostration, is referred to in later
times (see I Cor. 14:25; Rev. 4:10; 5:14; 19:10). The movements of the
body may therefore still be allowed to represent outwardly the
feelings of the spirit. External ceremonial is not done away with in
the present dispensation, though its relative importance is considerably reduced, and every place is hallowed ground.

The word $\sigma\epsilon\beta\omega\mu\alpha\iota$ (4576), answering to Yârê' (יָרֵא, 3372), *to fear,* is
occasionally found in the LXX; it is used several times in the Acts
(never in the Epistles), generally with reference to outsiders who
had been led to look with reverence on the God of Israel. See Acts
13:43, 50; 16:14; 17:4, 17; 18:7, 13; 19:27.

The word $\delta\delta\xi\alpha$ (1391) is used in Luke 14:10, where the A.V. says,

..1 shalt thou have worship in the presence of them that sit at .neat with thee." This rendering is as old as Coverdale, but Tyndale's rendering *praise* is better, and *glory* would be still more literal. See R.V.

§3. *Prayer*

Twelve Hebrew words have been rendered by the English word *pray* in the O.T. Two are interjections, namely, 'Ânnâ' (אָנָּא, 577) and Nâ' (נָא, 4994); the former is found in Gen. 50:17, and the latter in Gen. 12:13; 18:4; and Judg. 9:38. Chânan (חָנַן, 2603), *to be gracious*, when used in the reflexive or causative sense, signifies *to seek the favor of another*. See, for example, II Chron. 6:37.

Pâlal (פָּלַל, 6419), in the reflexive, "to cause another to intervene or arbitrate in one's case," is found very frequently, and is generally represented by the Greek προσεύχομαι (4336). This word conveys a very *objective* idea about prayer. It shows that men were not in the habit of praying merely as a relief to their feelings, but in order to ask another Being, wiser and mightier than they, to take up their cause.

In Job 22:27 and 33:26, the word 'Âthar (עָתַר, 6279), *to entreat*, is used. In Job 21:15 a different word is used, namely, Pâga' (פָּגַע, 6293), which signifies *to meet*: "What profit shall we have if we meet[1] him" (to supplicate his mercy)? In Isa. 26:16 we read, "LORD, in trouble have they visited thee, they poured out a prayer when thy chastening was upon them." Here Lâchash (לָחַשׁ, 3907), *to whisper*, is used, in order to convey the idea of the secret and sorrowful sighing of the oppressed. This word is usually rendered *enchantment*.

Shâ'al (שָׁאַל, 7592—Assyrian *sâlu*), *to ask*, whether in the sense of inquiry or petition (whence the name of *Saul* is derived) occurs in Ps. 122:6, where it is adopted for the sake of alliteration, "Pray for the peace of Jerusalem"; Sîychâh (שִׂיחָה, 7881), *meditation* or *complaint*, is used in Job 15:4; Ps. 55:17; 64:1.

In Ezra 6:10 we find Tselâ' (צְלָא, 6739), *to request*; in Dan. 6:11, Be'âh (בְּעָה, 1156), *to seek*; and in Dan. 9:13 a composite phrase is

---

1. This word is used in Isa. 47:3, "I will not meet thee as a man"; Isa. 64:5, "Thou meetest him that rejoiceth." Also in Isa. 53:6 (Hiphil), "The LORD hath laid [margin, "made to meet"] on him the iniquity of us all"; and in verse 12, "He made intercession for the transgressors." The Christ was to be as it were a common meeting-ground between God and the sinner.

adopted, which probably means *to conciliate the face of a person*, and hence *to pray* with some prospect of success.

With regard to the act of prayer as represented by the word προσεύχομαι (4336) in the N.T., it may be noticed in passing that it is never used in John's Gospel or Epistles. Prayer was to be offered "in spirit" (Eph. 6:18).[2] It appears to have been generally directed to God the Father. The only exception is Acts 1:24, where the disciples are apparently described as praying to their ascended Master. Compare Acts 7:59, where Stephen appealed to the Lord Jesus.

§4. *Praise and Blessing*

The praises of God are set forth very largely in the O.T., and are represented by two or three words. The most general is **Hâlal** (הָלַל, 1984—Assyrian *ellu*, "bright"), whence comes the word *Hallelu-jah*,[3] "Praise ye the LORD." Its original meaning is *to shine*, then *to make clear*, and afterwards *to exclaim in a loud tone*. It is perhaps something more than a coincidence that the Greek δοξάζω (1392), *to glorify*, which is often used of the praise of God, should also refer in the first instance to the making clear, bright, or shining. The LXX rendering for **Hâlal** (1984), however, is not δοξάζω (1392), but αἰνέω (134), ἐπαινέω (1867), or καυχάομαι (2744).

Another word largely used in the Psalms, and from which the Hebrew name for a psalm is derived, is **Zâmar** (זָמַר, 2167), *to sing*. Originally it meant *to pluck*, or *prune* (as a vine). It came to signify *to play* (by plucking) *a musical instrument* or *to sing so accompanied*. With the exception of the Book of Psalms, it is only found in Judg. 5:3 and II Sam. 22:50. This word is rendered ψάλλω (5567) in the LXX, whence the English *psalm*. See Rom.15:9; I Cor. 14:15; Eph. 5:19; and James 5:13.

Bârak (בָּרַךְ, 1288—Assyrian *baraku*), *to bless* (whence the name B[e]râkâh [1294] in II Chron. 20:26), literally, *to kneel*, is translated *praise* in Judg. 5:2 and Ps. 72:15; and it is to be noticed that blessing signifies not only the act of a superior to an inferior, but also the

---

2. A.V. "in *the* Spirit." There is no article in the Greek; the words therefore seem an exact parallel to our Lord's description of worship, that it is to be "in spirit and in truth." But see Jude 20.

3. This word is sometimes spelled *alleluia* in modern hymnals, in imitation of the mode of spelling that found favor in medieval times. The letter H ought certainly to be restored at both ends.

expression of grateful praise proceeding from the inferior and ascending to the superior. The usual Greek translation of this word is εὐλογέω (2127).

Bârak (1288) is the word used in the important promise, "In thy seed shall all the families of the earth be blessed." This promise was uttered on five different occasions; in three passages (Gen. 12:3; 18:18; 28:14) the verb is used in the Niphal or passive stem; in the other two, however (Gen. 22:18 and 26:4), the Hithpael or reflexive stem is adopted, so that we might render it, "In thy seed shall all the nations of the earth bless themselves." The same is the case in Deut. 29:19; Jer. 4:2; Ps. 72:17; and Isa. 65:16. But, after all, the difference is not so great, for while the passive signifies that the blessing is a gift of God, the Hithpael appears to signify that the blessing received from God produces fruit in the life; and those who bless themselves in God indicate by this expression that they acknowledge their blessings to be summed up in Him.

Yâdâh (יָדָה, 3034), *to set forth*, or *confess publicly*, whether in the way of praise or otherwise, whence the name *Judah* (יְהוּדָה, 3063), is found in a great many passages, the first instances being in Gen. 29:35 and 49:8. It occurs chiefly in the Psalms. The verb is generally rendered ἐξομολογέω (1843) in the LXX, the noun αἴνεσις (133).

The only other word to be noticed is **Shâbach** (שָׁבַח, 7623), *to praise* and *commend*, which is used four times in the Psalms, once in Ecclesiastes (4:2), and five times in Daniel (שְׁבַח, 7624).

The verb αἰνέω (134) is used in the N.T. only with reference to the praise of God; but the compound ἐπαινέω (1867) is not so restricted. The verb καυχάομαι (2744) occurs very infrequently in Paul's Epistles, but is not found in any other book of the N.T. except in James 1:9 and 4:16. When used in a good sense, it signifies that sort of boasting or rejoicing that manifests itself in giving praise to God. While εὐχαριστία (2169) is the rendering of thanks to God, εὐλογία (2129) generally signifies in the N.T. the bestowing of blessing on man. There is, however, a close relationship between these acts. When our Lord broke the bread and distributed it through the disciples among the five thousand, He *gave thanks* (εὐχαριστήσας, 2168—John 6:11); but Matthew (14:19) tells us that on the same occasion He *blessed* (εὐλόγησε, 2127). Again, at the Last Supper, we read that when He had *given thanks*, He broke the bread (Luke 22:19; I Cor. 11:24), and also taking the cup when He had *given thanks* He gave it to them (Mark 14:23). But we are also told that He *blessed* and broke the bread (Mark 14:22), and the cup is described as the cup of *blessing* which we bless (I Cor. 10:16). Thus the giving of thanks to God is the means of conferring a blessing on men. It is true that the word *bless,* when used with God as its object, signifies the praising of Him or speaking good of His name. But still the relationship just pointed out really exists, and may fairly be gathered from the word.

The word εὐλογητός (2128), *blessed,* is used only of God and of Christ; but εὐλογημένος (2127) is used more generally. The verb is often used to express the blessing promised to Abraham and conveyed to the faithful in Christ.

The word ἐξομολογέω (1843) is used in the N.T. of an open or public confession, whether of sins[4] (Matt. 3:6; Mark 1:5; Acts 19:18; James 5:16), or of the praise of God (Matt. 11:25; Luke 10:21; Rom. 14:11; 15:9; Phil. 2:11; Rev. 3:5). The use of the word in Luke 22:6 implies that Judas made an open avowal before the priests that he would betray the Lord.

§5. *Preaching*

The word *preach* means either *to tell good tidings* or *to proclaim.* The first idea is represented by **Bâsar** (בָּשַׂר, 1319), εὐαγγελίζω (2097), *to evangelize;* the second by **Qârâ'** (קָרָא, 7121—Assyrian *qaru*), κηρύσσω (2784). **Bâsar** (1319) is used in Isa. 61:1, "To preach good tidings to the meek"; and in the same verse **Qârâ'** (7121) is rendered *proclaim*—"to proclaim liberty to the captives." **Bâsar** (1319) is rendered *preach* in one other passage, namely, Ps. 40:9: "I have preached righteousness in the great congregation." Here the use of the word is important. It was not a mere proclamation of righteousness, but the announcing of good tidings concerning righteousness that the Psalmist refers to; and this point is confirmed and expounded by the following verse (v. 10), where we read, "I have not hid thy righteousness within my heart; I have declared thy

---

4. Only three kinds of confession are recognized in Scripture: (1) secret confession to God, which is followed by pardon from Him; (2) confession to our neighbor when we have injured him; and (3) public confession before the congregation where a public offense has been committed. In the lapse of time it was found that these public confessions sometimes created scandals, and private confessions were allowed to take their place; but these have gradually grown into a system, called, indeed, the confessional, but which is not, properly speaking, so much open confession as secret examination.

faithfulness and thy salvation: I have not concealed thy lovingkindness and thy truth from the great congregation."

This word is translated *publish* in I Sam. 31:9 and II Sam. 1:20; also in Ps. 68:11, where we read, "The Lord gave the word: great was the company of those that published it" (Prayer Book version, "Great was the company of the preachers"). The word is here in the feminine gender, and reference is made to the bands of women who proclaimed the good tidings of a victory. An instance of this custom may be found in I Sam. 18:6, 7. The same word is used in I Chron. 16:23; Ps. 96:2; and Isa. 60:5, 6.

Bâsar (1319) is only once used where evil tidings were to be given, namely, in I Sam. 4:17, where we read that "the messenger answered and said, Israel is fled before the Philistines."

Qâra' (7121), *to call* or *proclaim*, is rendered *preach* in Neh. 6:7, "Thou hast also appointed prophets to preach [i.e., proclaim] of thee at Jerusalem, saying, There is a king in Judah"; Jonah 3:2, "Arise, go unto Nineveh, that great city, and preach unto it the preaching that I bid thee." It is usually rendered *to call, cry, name, bid, invite, proclaim, publish*. It also signifies *to read aloud*, the only kind of reading ever referred to in the O.T. In this sense it is used more than thirty times. Hence the name *Karaite*, as applied to that sect of Jews which confines its teaching to that which may be gained from the reading of the O.T. Another extra-Biblical word derived from **Qâra'** (7121) is **Q^ere**, the word that signifies what is to be read as opposed to **K^ethiyb** (from כָּתַב, 3789), what is written in those passages of the Hebrew Scriptures in which MSS. differ. Another sense in which the word **Qârâ'** (7121) is frequently used is *to be named;* also *to invoke*, or *call* upon the name of the LORD, as in Gen. 4:26, which our translators have rendered, "Then began men to call upon the name of the LORD" (margin, "to call themselves by the name of the LORD"). Luther renders it, "Then began men *to preach concerning the name of the LORD.*"[5]

In I Kings 8:43 we find **Qârâ'** (7121) used in both its senses. "Hear thou in heaven thy dwelling place, and do according to all that the stranger calleth to thee for: that all the peoples of the earth may know thy name, to fear thee, as do thy people Israel; and that they

---

5. "*Zu predigen von des Herrn Namen.*" The LXX has ἐπικάλεισθαι (1941—*to call upon*).

may know that this house, which I have builded, is called by thy name."

The LXX usually retained the distinction between these two aspects of the verb Qârâ', (7121), which is represented by προσκαλέω (4341). In the active and passive voices this Greek word is always used for *to name* and *to be named;* but in the middle voice it signifies *to invoke* or *call on* a person. Instances of the former sense will be found in Num. 21:3, "He called the name of the place Hormah"; Deut. 15:2, "It is called the LORD's release"; Isa. 43:7, "Every one that is called by my name"; Dan. 9:18, "Behold the city which is called by thy name"; Amos 9:12, "All the heathen that are called by my name." The middle voice is adopted in the following passages: Gen. 12:8, "He builded an altar unto Jehovah, and called upon the name of Jehovah"; Deut. 4:7, "What nation is there so great, who hath God so nigh unto them, as Jehovah our God is in all things that we call upon him for?" See also Prov. 21:13; Isa. 55:6; 64:7; Jonah 1:6; Zech. 13:9.

The word rendered Preacher in the Book of Ecclesiastes is Qôheleth (קֹהֶלֶת, 6953), which is rendered ἐκκλησιάστης (L-S 509A) in the LXX, whence we have derived the name of the book. It is generally supposed to signify one who convokes an assembly, from Kâhal (6950—see Chap. 19). The noun (6953) is in the feminine form, perhaps to mark dignity or office. Some critics, however, connect the word with a cognate Arabic root, and translate it *the Penitent.*

The verb κηρύσσω (2784), *to proclaim*, is found about sixty times in the N.T., and κήρυγμα (2782) eight times. It is used of the public reading of the law of Moses (Acts 15:21), and of the declaration of the gospel of Christ. Where this word is used, more stress is laid on the publicity of the proclamation than on the nature of the news itself. It has been observed that it is this word, not εὐαγγελίζομαι (2097), which is found in I Pet. 3:19, a passage that is usually considered to refer to the notification of the fulfillment of the Divine purposes in Christ, made to a special portion of the spirits of the departed.[6]

§6. *Teaching*

Twelve Hebrew words are used to convey the idea of teaching in the O.T. In Deut. 6:7, "Thou shalt teach them diligently unto thy

---

6. In I Peter 4:6 the word εὐαγγελίζομαι (2097) is used. See Alford's note.

children," the word **Shânan** (שָׁנַן, 8150), *to whet* or *sharpen*, is used. Here the idea seems to be not so much the sharpening of the children's understanding as the plying of the Divine statutes to and fro in their hearts, and the setting forth of God's truth in all its aspects. In II Chron. 30:22, where we are told that the Levites "taught the good knowledge of the LORD," the word **Sâkal** (שָׂכַל, 7919— Assyrian *sukhallu*, "intelligence"), *to make wise,*[7] is used, to mark the fact that the Levites were not content with superficial teaching. The same word is found in Prov. 16:23: "The heart of the wise teacheth his mouth." In Isa. 43:27, "Thy teachers have transgressed against me," the marginal rendering *interpreters* is probably the best, reference being made to the expositors (מְלִיצִים, from לוּץ, 3887) of the law. In Prov. 31:1 and Ezek. 23:48, **Yâçar** (יָסַר, 3256), *to chasten,* is used, a word that answers to the Greek παιδεύω (*3811*) by which it is usually rendered, the instruction often involving chastisement. In Ps. 105:22 we find **Châkam** (חָכַם, 2449), a word often heard in a modern Jewish school and cognate with the Arabic *hakim, a wise man.* In Exod. 18:20 the word used is **Zâhar** (זָהַר, 2094), *to illuminate,* and hence *to warn.* Thus the analogy of spiritual and intellectual light was set before Israel at the beginning of their history. This is the word rendered *shine* in Dan. 12:3.

'Âlaph (אָלַף, 502), a verb connected with the first letter of the Hebrew alphabet, is found in Job 33:33, "I shall teach thee wisdom," and 35:11, "[God] teacheth us more than the beasts of the earth, and maketh us wiser than the fowls of heaven." It is also found in Job 15:5: "Thy mouth uttereth [margin, teacheth] thine iniquity." Compare Prov. 22:25: "Lest thou learn his ways." Evil, like good, has its alphabet. **Dâbar** (דָּבַר, 1696), *to speak* or *to broach a subject,* is used in Jer. 28:16 (cf. 29:32): "Thou hast taught rebellion against the LORD." The so-called prophetic utterances of Hananiah had really been rebellious words. **Bîyn** (בִּין, 995), *to make to understand,* is found in I Chron. 25:8, where the teacher is put in contrast, or rather in company, with the scholar. It also occurs in II Chron. 35:3 and Neh. 8:9, with reference to the teaching of the Levites. **Yâda'** (יָדַע, 3045—

7. This word, which is almost always used in the Hiphil stem, seems to signify sometimes the receiving and sometimes the giving of instruction. In Dan. 12:3, the words "they that *be wise*" might be rendered "they *that teach.*" Sâkal (7919) has sometimes been rendered *prosper,* as in Jer. 23:5, "A king shall reign and prosper"; but it may here signify *do wisely,* or *give instruction.* The title of several of the Psalms, *Maschil,* is derived from it. The LXX usually renders it συνίημι (4920) and σύνεσις (4907).

Assyrian *idu*), *to make to know,* is used in Deut. 4:9, and Judg. 8:16, "He taught the men of Succoth," i.e., gave them a lesson that they would not readily forget. Compare II Chron. 23:13; Ezra 7:25; Job 32:7; 37:19; Ps. 90:12; Prov. 9:9; and Isa. 40:13.

Lâmad (לָמַד, 3925—Assyrian *lamadu*), whence the name *Talmud* is derived, is frequently used; it signifies *to chastise,* and hence *to teach,* and is rendered διδάσκω (*1321*) and μανθάνω (*3129*). Also **Yârâh** (יָרָה, 3384), *to cast forth,* hence *to guide* or *direct,* is applied to teaching several times. The *master* and the *scholar* in Mal. 2:12 are literally the *awakener* and the *answerer.* It is the teacher's business to awaken thought in the heart of the pupil, and it is the scholar's business to answer to the test to which his understanding is put.

19

Temple, Tabernacle, Congregation, Church

The identification in name between a building set apart for sacred purposes and the worshipers who meet therein may be traced back to the days of Moses, perhaps to an earlier period. The people of Israel were to be a spiritual house, and God was to dwell among them, as in a tabernacle. In the N.T. Christians are described in almost the same terms.

§1. *Temple*

The ordinary Hebrew name for the temple was **Hêykâl** (הֵיכָל, 1964—Assyrian *ekallu*, palace). This word, however, does not necessarily denote a sacred edifice. It is translated *palace*[1] in I Kings 21:1; II Kings 20:18; Ps. 45:15; Isa. 13:22; 39:7; 44:28, et al. It ought also to have been so translated in Hos. 8:14, where we read in the A.V., "Israel hath forgotten his Maker, and buildeth temples." The context shows that palaces are here referred to (see R.V.). In these passages the LXX usually adopts the rendering οἶκος (3624), *house*. The **Hêykâl** (1964) was evidently regarded as the king's house, the dwellingplace of one who is highly exalted. The more general word for a palace (אַרְמוֹן, 759) is never used of the temple, as it signifies a fortress rather than a dwellingplace. This word first occurs in I Kings 16:18 and II Kings 15:25, where the palace, i.e., the fortified part of the king's

---

1. The word *palace* is derived from the name of one of the seven hills on which Rome was built (*Palatium*).

house, is referred to. Before the temple was built the tabernacle was regarded as God's Hêykâl (1964—I Sam. 1:9; 3:3; II Sam. 22:7), though a curtained tent might seem unworthy of such a title. The general Greek rendering for the word Hêykâl (1964), when applied to the temple, is ναός (3485). Another word rendered temple is Bayith (כַּיִת, 1004—Assyrian bitu), a *house*. This is the only word used for a house in the O.T., except in Ps. 83:12, where we find the word Neʾowth (נְאוֹת, plural of נָאָה, 4999), which signifies *pastures* or *pleasant places;* and in Job 1:3, where not a house, but a household of servants (עֲבֻדָּה, 5657), is really spoken of. Bayith (1004) is rendered *temple* in II Kings 11:10, 11, 13; I Chron. 6:10; 10:10; II Chron. 23:10; 35:20.

The sanctuary is literally that which is holy (קֹדֶשׁ, 6944), or, in other words, that which is set apart for sacred uses (see Chap. 15).

§2. *Tabernacle*

The usual word for a tabernacle is ʾÔhel (אֹהֶל, 168), which properly means a *tent*. Another word frequently rendered *tent* is Mishkân (מִשְׁכָּן, 4908—Assyrian *maskamu*), the ordinary word for a *dwelling-place*,[2] which is found in Song of Solomon 1:8, "Beside the shepherds' tents." Qubbâh (קֻבָּה, 6898—Assyrian *qubbu*), a *dome* or *vault* (compare the modern Arabic *qubbet*), is found in Num. 25:8, where we read, "He went after the man of Israel into the tent." Çukkah (סֻכָּה, 5521—Assyrian *sukku*), a *booth* (whence the plural name *Succoth*), is used by Uriah in II Sam. 11:11, where he says, "The ark, and Israel, and Judah, abide in tents." Machǎneh (מַחֲנֶה, 4264) is a *camp*, or *company*, hence the name Mahanaim (4266, two hosts). See Gen. 32:2, 7, 8, 10, 21, and compare I Chron. 12:22; II Chron 14:13; 31:2; Song of Sol. 6:13. It is translated *tent* in Num. 13:19; I Sam. 17:53; II Kings 7:16; Zech. 14:15; and also in II Chron. 31:2, where it is applied in the plural form to the temple of God.

The LXX has various renderings for ʾÔhel (168), but the most general are σκηνή (4633), σκήνωμα (4638), and οἶκος (3624). Mishkân

2. These words are found together in Exod. 26:7, the covering (ʾÔhel, 168) on the tabernacle (Mishkân, 4908), and in other passages. The Mishkân (4908) is evidently the structure as a whole, regarded as the *Shekinah* (from שָׁכַן, 7931) or dwellingplace of God, while the ʾÔhel (168) was the awning of goat's hair. The word the A.V. and R.V. perversely render the *door* of the tabernacle is not a door at all, but an opening or entrance.

(4908), a *dwellingplace*, which stands for the same Greek word, is rendered *tabernacle* in about 120 passages in the A.V.

Where the Feast of Tabernacles is referred to, Çukkah (5521) is used. It probably means a *place of shade* or *shelter*, hence a *booth*, *tent*, or *pavilion*. The rendering *cottage* in Isa. 1:8 is hardly accurate. In Job 36:29 we read, "Can any one understand the spreadings of the clouds, or the noise of his tabernacle?" Here reference is made to the heavens, either as God's place of shelter—His hiding place—or to the clouds as a shade for the earth.[3] The word is used again in Ps. 76:2, "In Salem is his *tabernacle*, and his dwellingplace in Zion." See also Isa. 4:6.

In Amos 5:26, "Ye have borne the tabernacle of Moloch," there may be reference to a movable tent in which the images of false gods were placed. The marginal rendering, "*Siccuth* your king," is endorsed by the Masoretic punctuation, is accepted by Luther and by the R.V., and may be illustrated by the name of the Assyrian god *Sakkut*. But the quotation in Stephen's speech (Acts 7:43) follows the LXX, and is confirmed by the implied contrast with another tabernacle of which we read in Amos 9:11, where the same word is used: "I will raise up the tabernacle of David that is fallen down, and will close up the breaches thereof." With this passage may be compared the complaint of Jeremiah concerning the temple at Jerusalem: "[God] hath violently taken away his tabernacle [σκήνωμα, 4638], as if it were a garden: he hath destroyed his places of assembly: the LORD hath caused the solemn feasts and sabbaths to be forgotten in Zion" (Lam. 2:6). The word for *tabernacle* here, Sôk (שׂךְ, 7900), though spelled differently, is from a cognate root. Some render it *hedge* or *fence*, but perhaps it signifies *shelter* or *covering*, and so is applicable to the "tabernacle of David."

§3. *Congregation*

The general word for congregation is Qâhâl (קָהָל, 6951). It properly signifies an *assembly* or *assemblage*, and is applied to all sorts of gatherings, whether for war, for complaint, for listening to instruction, or for any similar purpose.

---

3. Compare its use in II Sam. 22:12, "He made darkness pavilions round about him"; also Ps. 18:11, "His pavilion round about him were dark waters and thick clouds of the skies."

The verb is first used of the gathering of the people against Moses (Exod. 32:1); compare Num. 16:3, 19 (the LXX has συνίστημι, 4921, in each case). In Num. 20:2 the LXX has συναθροίζω (4867) to mark the tumultuous nature of the gathering; in verse 4 the congregation is συναγωγή (4864); and in verse 8 the verb ἐκκλησιάζω (L-S 509A) is used, while the Hebrew word is the same throughout. Gatherings for wicked purposes are referred to in Gen. 49:6; Prov. 5:14; and Ps. 26:5.

The first passage of special interest in which the noun occurs is Gen. 28:3, where Isaac says to Jacob, "God Almighty bless thee, and make thee fruitful, and multiply thee, that thou mayest be an assemblage of peoples"[4] (εἰς συναγωγὰς ἐθνῶν—1519, 4864, 1484). In Gen. 35:11 this blessing is repeated by God Himself, "I am God Almighty: be fruitful and multiply; a nation and a company of nations shall be of thee"; and Jacob, when an old man, cited the words of the blessing in his conversation with Joseph, "I will make of thee a multitude of peoples" (48:4). The word *multitude* is unfortunate. The R.V. has *company*.

The congregation or assembly of Israel, which is so often spoken of in the O.T., is sometimes referred to as συναγωγή (4864, synagogue), sometimes as ἐκκλησία (1577, ecclesia), in the LXX. Once, where the judicial function of the congregation is referred to, the LXX renders the word συνέδριον (4892, whence the word Sanhedrin), namely, in Prov. 26:26, "His wickedness shall be shewed before the congregation."

The assembly or congregation of Israel is well defined in Josh. 8:35: "There was not a word of all that Moses commanded, which Joshua did not read before all the congregation of Israel, with the women, and the little ones, and the strangers that were conversant among them." The congregation, then, properly meant all the male adults of the nation. In Ezra 2:64, 65, "the whole congregation" was numbered at 42,360, exclusive of manservants and maidservants. In Ezra 10:1 we read of "a congregation of men, women, and children." In Neh. 8:2 we are told of "a congregation both of men and women." In Joel 2:16 the prophet says, "Gather the people, sanctify [i.e., call with sacred solemnity] the congregation, assemble the elders, gather the children, and those that suck the breasts."

---

4. The words 'Am (עַם, 5971) and Gôwy (גּוֹי, 1471) had not yet received their differentiated and technical meaning. See Chap. 22.

Israel was regarded as a vast family, the women and children forming an integral portion of it, except for public or judicial purposes, and none excluded except through willful disobedience of the law of Moses, or (for a time) through ceremonial uncleanness. This great family was addressed, both by Moses and the prophets, in the *singular* number, as if they might be regarded as one, in spite of their diversities of age, circumstances, and dwellingplaces. This fact illustrates the teaching of the N.T., where we find that there was one Person who concentrated in Himself the fulfillment of much that had been spoken to Israel in its corporate capacity, and became in His turn a center of unity to a spiritual Israel, gathering together into one all the children of God that were scattered abroad (John 11:52).

The first great assembly of Israel was at the giving of the Law at Mount Sinai. The reference to it in Deut. 18:16 is interesting from its connection with the prophecy concerning Him who was to build up a new *ecclesia:*

> The Lord thy God will raise up unto thee a Prophet, from the midst of thee, of thy brethren, like unto me; unto him ye shall hearken. According to all that thou desiredst of the Lord thy God in Horeb in the day of the assembly [ἐκκλησία, 1577], saying, Let me not hear again the voice of the Lord my God, neither let me see this great fire any more, that I die not. And the Lord said unto me, They have well spoken that which they have spoken. I will raise them up a Prophet from among their brethren like unto thee, and will put my words in his mouth; and he shall speak unto them all that I shall command him (Deut. 18:15–18).

The assembly on the occasion here referred to was a representative assembly, but the whole of Israel, even all their generations, were regarded as pledged by what was then transacted. This is brought out clearly, both in Exodus and Deuteronomy. Thus in Deut. 4:10, 11, we read, "The Lord said unto me, Gather me the people together, and I will make them hear my words. . . . And ye came near and stood under the mountain." In Deut. 5:22, after recapitulating the commandments, Moses says, "These words the Lord spake unto all your assembly in the mount. . . . And it came to pass, when ye heard the voice . . . that ye came near unto me, even all the heads of your tribes and your elders." What the representatives did was evidently regarded as done by the whole people, and not by one generation only, for in Deut. 5:3 we read, "The LORD made not this covenant with our fathers [only], but with us, even us [also], who are all of us here this day." And yet the actual generation of men with whom the covenant was originally made had passed away.

Although theoretically "the congregation of Israel" signified the whole people of Israel, yet for practical purposes they were represented by elders. Other examples will be found in I Kings 8:1–3, and II Chron. 5:2, 3. The same was probably the case in the gathering (Qâhâl, 6951) of all the congregation at the entrances of the tabernacle for the observance of special national ceremonies. See Lev. 8:3, 4.

In Lev. 4:13, 14, 21, the whole congregation is described as having sinned; a national offense had been committed, and a national sin-offering was to be offered. Accordingly, the elders of the congregation in their representative capacity laid their hands on the head of the bullock that was to be offered, to signify the transmission of the nation's evil deed to the atoning victim.

The gatherings at religious feasts are probably referred to in Ps. 22:22, 25; 26:12; 35:18; 40:9, 10; 68:26; 107:32; 149:1.

Being "cut off from the congregation of Israel" and being forbidden to enter it (Num. 19:20; Deut. 23:1) seem to have implied severance from the privileges, religious and social, that the nation as such enjoyed. In some places, however, it was synonymous with death. In Prov. 21:16 we read of "the congregation [συναγωγή—4864] of the dead," a striking picture of that vast gathering which is being daily enlarged as men are "gathered to their fathers," and that remains an integral portion of the family of man.

In Ps. 58:1—where we read, "Do ye indeed speak righteousness, O congregation?"—the word used is 'Êlem (אֵלֶם, 482), which signifies either *to bind into a sheaf*, or *to be dumb*. The former meaning would present a very suitable symbol of a congregation, but the latter meaning, "ye dumb folk," would also give good sense. See R.V.

In Ps. 68:10 the Psalmist says, "Thy congregation shall dwell therein"; and in 74:19, "Forget not the congregation of thy poor for ever." Here the word Chay (חַי, 2416) is used, which means a *living being*. Translators have not been agreed as to its meaning here, but our version gives a fair sense. In some versions we here find the strange rendering, "Thy beasts shall dwell therein."

Besides Qâhâl (6951), an *assemblage*, there is another word that occurs about 150 times in the O.T., with almost the same breadth of meaning, namely, 'Êdâh (עֵדָה, 5712). This word first appears in Exod. 12:3, and is almost always rendered *congregation*. It is frequently used in the early books, but rarely in the later. While Qâhâl (6951) generally refers to the *representative* gathering, 'Êdâh (5712) often signifies an informal massing of the people. 'Êdâh (5712) is used of the company of Korah (Num. 16:5; Ps. 106:17); in Judg. 14:8 it is used of a swarm of bees; in Ps. 68:30, of a multitude of bulls. It occurs only three times in the prophets (Jer. 6:18; 30:20; and Hos. 7:12), while Qâhâl (6951) occurs twenty-two times, chiefly in Ezekiel. The LXX usually has συναγωγή (4864) as a rendering for 'Êdâh (5712).

The word 'Êdâh (5712) not only signifies *congregation*, but also *witness* or *testimony*, and in another form ('Êdûwth, 5715) it is used of "the ark of the testimony." This chest was so called because it contained the tables of that Law which testified to God's character and attributes (Exod. 25:21, 22). The same form is used in connection with the tent that contained the ark, which was consequently called the tent or tabernacle of the testimony or of witness in Exod. 38:21; Num. 1:50, 53; 10:11; 17:7, 8; 18:2; and II Chron. 24:6.

Wherever we read of "the tabernacle of the congregation," the word Môw'êd (מוֹעֵד, 4150) is used. It is generally supposed that this word is derived from Yâ'ad (יָעַד, 3259), *to appoint*, and, in the passive, *to meet* or *make an appointment*. This verb is used of God's meeting Moses and communing with him from above the mercyseat in Exod. 25:22; and in Exod. 29:42, 43, it is apparently adopted to explain the true meaning of the word Môw'êd (4150), for we here read,

> This shall be a continual burnt offering throughout your generations, at the door [i.e., opening] of the tabernacle of the *congregation* before the LORD where I will meet you, to speak there unto thee. And there I will meet with the children of Israel, and the tabernacle shall be sanctified by my glory.

See also Exod. 30:6, 36, where the same Hebrew words are used in the same relationship. The "tabernacle of the *congregation*" was therefore the appointed place of meeting between God and Israel; they were brought near together in that Holy Place, just as God and man are said to be brought near together in the Body of Christ, which is the true Tabernacle not made with hands.

The LXX has almost always rendered this expression by the words σκηνή τοῦ μαρτυρίου (4633, 3588, 3142), "the tent of witness," thus connecting the word Môw'êd (4150) with 'Êdâh (5712), which has been discussed above. There is a good deal to be said in favor of this view of the matter, for the roots of the words are cognate, if not the same. See Acts 7:44; Rev. 15:5.

The word Môw'êd (4150) is also used to represent seasons (Gen. 1:14), appointed times (Gen. 18:14), feasts (Lev. 23:2), and solemnities (Deut. 31:10). In all these renderings, which frequently recur in the O.T., there is an idea of some *time* or *place* appointed by God.

What, then, was the tabernacle of the congregation? Not the tent or collection of tents in which the congregation of Israel dwelled, but the tent or tabernacle in the most sacred part of which the ark of the testimony was placed and that was set apart as the dwelling-place of God, the center whence issued the promises, warnings, and commands of the Most High. The R.V. rightly renders it "the tent of meeting."

§4. *Convocation*

The word used in the expression "a holy convocation" is **Miqrâ'** (מִקְרָא, 4744), from **Qârâ'** (קָרָא, 7121), *to call* or *convoke*. See Exod. 12:16; Lev. 23:2, et al.; and compare Num. 10:2. The sabbaths and feast days were occasions for this convocation. The word has been rendered *assembly* in Isa. 1:13 and 4:5. It seems to imply that assemblies were convened on these days for purposes of public worship, or for the reading and exposition of the Law. It may be, however, that the word answers to our word *institution* or *solemnity,* and signified that the days so designated were intended to be kept free from secular work and to be regarded as sacred by Divine command. The LXX usually has κλητὴ ἁγία (2822, 40), which, according to N.T. usage, might be rendered *called to be holy;* compare the κλητοὶ ἁγίοι (2822, 40) of Paul's Epistles (A.V. "called to be saints").

§5. *N.T. Teaching on the Temple and Tabernacle*

The most notable words that we have been considering reappear in the N.T., sometimes with a more spiritual significance. While the literal ναός (*3485*) or *temple* was built by Solomon, it was reserved for Christ, the true Son of David, to build the spiritual ναός (3485), which is composed of living stones based on Him as their foundation. The first hint in the N.T. that there should be such a spiritual temple is in John 2:19, where the Lord says, "Destroy this temple,[5] and in three days I will raise it up." He spoke, however, as the Evangelist tells us, of the temple of His body; but His body was itself a figure of that organism of which all Christians form a part, so that His resurrection was regarded as the rising of the Head, the First-fruits, while the Body is to be raised hereafter. This idea of the living Temple is touched on by the Apostle Paul several times (see I Cor. 3:16, 17; 6:19; II Cor. 6:16; Eph. 2:21); each Christian is regarded as a dwellingplace of the Holy Ghost, and, when viewed in connection with others, he is described as a living[6] stone in the great Temple of which Christ is the foundation and the chief cornerstone (I Pet. 2:5). Every Christian, whether Jew or Gentile, whether bond or free, is built up and "fitly framed" in harmony with the rest; and each community of Christians may be regarded as a chamber (κατοικητήριον, 2732—Eph. 2:22) in the great edifice.

In the Epistle to the Hebrews the σκηνή (4633) or *tabernacle* of the Mosaic dispensation is contrasted with that which the Lord pitched, of which Christ was the minister (Heb. 8:2). And in Rev. 21:3 we read, with respect to the same heavenly tabernacle, that hereafter it shall be set up among men.

The σκήνωμα (4638) is twice mentioned by the Apostle Peter as a symbol of the earthly body, or dwellingplace for the soul (II Pet. 1:13, 14). In this sense Paul uses the form σκῆνος (4636) in II Cor. 5:1, 4, where he speaks of "our earthly house of this tabernacle" being dissolved.

Besides the references to the temple as the house (οἶκος, 3624) of God in the N.T., we have the identification of the Church, i.e., the Body of believers, with the House of God in I Tim. 3:15 and I Pet. 4:17; while in Heb. 3 a comparison is instituted between the faithfulness of Moses as a servant over his house, i.e., the house of Israel that was committed to his charge by God, and the faithfulness of Christ

---

5. We have to distinguish between the ναός (3485), which is the Temple proper, and the ἱερόν (2411), or sacred precincts and courts. The latter is never referred to in a spiritual sense in the Epistles.

6. It seems unfortunate that the word translated *living* in the one verse should be rendered *lively* in the other, the very object of the Apostle being to show the oneness of nature between Christ and believers.

the Son of God in taking charge of those who believe in Him and who thus constitute His house. In Heb. 10:21 He is called a High Priest over the house of God, which is not a material but a spiritual house. See I Pet. 3:5.

The word συναγωγή (4864) in the N.T. is generally used of the building rather than of those that assemble in it. There are, however, a few passages in which the synagogue meant the judicial and religious assembly. See, for instance, Mark 13:9; Luke 21:12; and Acts 13:43.[7] In James 2:2 the word is apparently applied to the Christian place of meeting, where they were not to forsake the assembling of themselves together (Heb. 10:25).

§6. *The Ecclesia*

To the Christian the word *ecclesia* (ἐκκλησία, 1577) is far more important than the word *synagogue*. On examining the Gospels we find the word only in Matt. 16:18 and 18:17. The former passage revealed Christ's intention to supersede the *ecclesia*[8] of the O.T. dispensation by one that should be peculiarly His own and that should last forever. The latter points to the functions that this new body, or some local section of it, was to exercise through its representatives in cases of dispute between man and man (compare I Cor. 6:1).

When we pass to the Acts and Epistles, we find that Christians are formed into *ecclesiae*, or congregating bodies, in every town to which the Apostles went. All these smaller organizations were regarded as local representatives of a great spiritual and spotless *ecclesia* or Body, the Head of which was invisible, being at the right hand of God (Eph. 1:22). Membership in the *ecclesia* of Christ was obtained by faith in Him, and was sealed and signified by baptism.

Believers in Christ are regarded as one Body. They have one Master, one faith, one baptism, one God and Father. Originally they continued steadfast in the Apostles' teaching, and in fellowship (i.e.,

7. Compare also the technical word ἀποσυνάγωγος (656—John 9:22, et al.).

8. There have been various controversies as to the right rendering of this word. In many versions it has been reproduced without any attempt at translation. Others, like ourselves, have taken the word Κυριάκη (2960), *the Lord's household*, to represent it. Tyndale rightly translated the word *congregation* or *assembly*, thus retaining the relationship between the O.T. and the N.T. Luther's word *Gemeine*, "community," is a very good one.

sharing their goods with one another), and in breaking bread, and in prayers (Acts 2:42). As time went on there would be different local arrangements, different places of meeting, "diversities of administrations," but the word of the Apostolic body, as representing the teaching of Christ, was to be supreme. Christ was over all, and the Spirit was in all. This unity was to embrace not only *belief*, but also *life*. If anyone preached a false gospel, he was to be regarded as *anathema*, i.e., as one accursed. And if anyone did not love the Lord Jesus Christ, he too was to be regarded as *anathema*. Those that loved God and their brethren and walked worthy of their profession showed thereby that they were truly born of God, and were really members of the one Body in which the Spirit of Christ dwelled. But those whose religion consisted only of profession and talk and did not deny themselves for their brother's good were regarded as having a name that they lived, while really dead.

The fact that this body was called the *ecclesia* of Christ shows that it answers in some respects to the *ecclesia* of the O.T., the Israel of God. Believers in Christ are delivered out of a bondage worse than that of Egypt. They have a Leader greater than Moses, a Priest higher than Aaron, an atoning offering more precious than the blood of bulls or of goats, a tabernacle more lasting than of witness. They have the true Manna or Bread of Life to eat, and the true Rock supplies them with the Water of Life. From the hands of One higher than Joshua they hope to receive their promised inheritance, and one greater than David is their King. They are divided into many generations, and distributed through all parts of the world, yet they are *one*. And wherever Christ is loved and honored as Savior and Leader, wherever He is trusted as Priest and Sacrifice, wherever He is obeyed as King and hoped in as the Giver of an everlasting habitation, *there* are members of the one great *ecclesia*, the Holy Catholic Church.

The various local communities referred to as churches in the N.T. may be regarded as nurseries for the true Church of which Christ is the Head. An *ecclesia* was first formed in Jerusalem, and afterwards in every large town to which the Gospel came. Each *ecclesia* had its elders, who may be regarded, according to the analogy of the O.T., as its representatives, and who, like the elders of the Jewish *ecclesia*, had to exercise spiritual and prophetical, though not sacerdotal, functions.[9] The various *ecclesiae* formed through the Roman world

9. See Chap. 20.

were confederate Churches bound together by the common ties of Apostolic teaching and unity of Spirit, Jerusalem being still regarded as the Mother Church. There might be many places of meeting or *ecclesiae* in one city, but they were not independent of one another; such an event as the arrival of an Apostle would bring them all together as one brotherhood. As the Word of God grew and multiplied, it extended into the more outlying country districts, and the Churches thus formed were affiliated with the city communities, and thus what we may call dioceses were formed, all, however, acting in harmony with the directions that emanated from the Apostolic body at Jerusalem. When this venerable city was destroyed, the local center of unity vanished. About the same time the Apostles and their coadjutors passed away. But they left their writings behind, and these letters and authorized narratives of our Lord's history were received as the utterances of the Spirit of Christ, and took the same place in the Christian system that the Scriptures of the O.T. had occupied in the Jewish Church.

How, in the lapse of ages, Rome gradually assumed to itself both the authority of the Apostles and the local dignity that originally belonged to Jerusalem is a matter of history that need not here be touched on. It may be observed, however, that all schisms *in* the various Churches (or *from* them) arose partly from the fact that, as generations passed away, the churches lost something of that vital hold of simple Apostolic truth that they originally possessed, and partly because it does not seem (human speaking) possible that there should be on earth anything approaching to a perfect Church. There have always been offenses, heresies, false teachers, and false professors, and there will be to the end of this dispensation. Every attempt to form a new community on the Apostolic model has ended in the same way. A root of bitterness has sprung up again in spite of all precautions. Men have learned over and over again by sad experience that they must be content to put up with an imperfect organization and with indifferent teachers, while they have been also led to see that, amid all human imperfections, the true Head of the Church remains "the same yesterday, today, and forever," ministering grace to all that love Him in sincerity and truth.

The word *ecclesia* is used in other senses besides that now discussed in a few passages of the N.T. Thus, in Acts 19:32, 39, 41, a civil assembly is called by this name. In I Cor. 14 the *ecclesia* appears to be the assembly of Christians for Divine worship, answering to one of the senses of συναγωγή (4864) noted above. In Heb. 12:23 we read of the ἐκκλησία (1577) of the firstborn, whose names are written in heaven. Reference is here made perhaps to the true Israel of the old dispensation, that is, to the congregation[10] or *ecclesia* in the wilderness with whom God was pleased,[11] to those who did not bow the knee to Baal, and to those "who feared the LORD," and "spake often one to another." Others suppose that the *ecclesia* of Christ is here referred to; they hold that the Church is a representative body, and that the world at large will reap the fruit of the faith and love of the spiritual firstborn.

10. Acts 7:38. The A.V. here most unfortunately renders ἐκκλησία (1577) *church* instead of *congregation*. See R.V., margin.

11. Heb. 3:16, *"Some* did provoke . . . but not *all."* There was a Church within a Church, Jews who were Jews inwardly, Israelites indeed, a remnant according to the election of grace. Rom. 2:29; 11:4, 5; Mal. 3:16. Israel is called God's firstborn in Exod. 4:22.

20

Prophet, Priest, Elder, Minister

It has always been part of the system of the Divine government to employ *men* as instruments for the conveyance of heavenly truth and blessing to the world at large. Whether it be as the announcers of the revealed message, as the writers of the inspired Scripture, as the official representatives of God in matters relating to the atonement, or as teachers and guides of the people, human instruments have been employed, human voices have been heard, "the pen of a man" has been used, the agent has been "taken from among men," the treasure has been conveyed in "earthen vessels." There has, indeed, been a constant tendency in those that have been selected for these important services to constitute themselves into a caste and to assume to themselves powers and rights that God never gave them; and by a natural reaction, many persons, resenting such claims, have thrown discredit on sacred offices, and have sought to break through the distinctions that God Himself has marked out.

The practical advantages of a settled order of ministry are denied by comparatively few. But how many there are who differ, and that hotly, concerning the names, relative positions, and spiritual powers of the ministry! Metaphysical questions have intruded themselves to add to the entanglement. Not only has the nature of the special prophetic gifts of the O.T. and N.T. been earnestly investigated, but such points as the following are raised. Does the grace of God's Spirit come directly to each member of the Church, or only through certain privileged persons? Does the spiritual efficacy of baptism and the Lord's Supper depend on the presence and superintendence of a person who has received special gifts by the laying on of hands? Are the spiritual gifts referred to in the N.T. transmitted through episcopal consecration, or are they vested in the Holy Catholic church as a body, to be exercised through such representatives as may be appointed from time to time by the Christians of each locality? Is a threefold order of ministry—bishops, presbyters, and deacons—essential to the exercise of such gifts? Is episcopal succession from the Apostles' days, by a continuous laying on of hands, necessary in order to convey these gifts?

The animosity raised by such questions is endless. We need over and over again to be reminded that the great object of the ministry is not that men should set themselves up as a privileged caste but that they should lead others to Christ, while the object of Christ in dispensing His gifts to men is to make them conformable to the will of God. Whatever helps promote that conformity, whether it be the faithful use of the Lord's Supper, reading and meditating on Scripture, public prayer and preaching, or private spiritual intercourse between man and man, that is to be regarded as a *gift*, and as a means whereby the life of God penetrates the soul.

§1. *The Prophet*

The general name for a *prophet* in the O.T. is Nâbîy'[1] (נָבִיא, 5030). The original meaning of this word is uncertain; but it is generally supposed to signify the bubbling up of the Divine message, as water issues from a hidden fountain. It is used both of prediction, properly so called, and of the announcement of a Divine message with regard to the past or present; also of the utterance of songs of praise. It is applied to messengers of false gods (e.g., "the prophets of Baal"), and to a man who acts as the mouthpiece of another, as when the LORD says to Moses (Exod. 7:1), "Aaron thy brother shall be thy prophet." The first passage in which the word occurs is Gen. 20:7, where it is used of Abraham. In Deut. 18:15, 18, the title is applied to the Messiah, who was to have God's words in His mouth and who thus became the Mediator of the New Covenant, taking a position analogous in some respects to that of Moses. The LXX almost always adopts the rendering προφητεύω (4395) and προφήτης (4396) for Nâbîy' (5030).

In Micah 2:6, 11, the word Nâtaph (נָטַף, 5197), *to drop*, is used.

---

1. In Assyrian the *Nabû* proclaimed the will of the gods; hence *Nabû* or *Nebo* (?annap) "the prophet-god." The predicter of the future was the *asipu* (cf. אָשֵׁף, 825).

Some commentators suppose that it is adopted as a word of contempt. It is used, however, of a discourse distilling in drops in the following passages: Job 29:22, "My speech dropped upon them"; Prov. 5:3, "The lips of a strange woman drop as an honeycomb"; Song of Sol. 4:11, "Thy lips, O my spouse, drop as the honeycomb"; 5:13, "His lips, like lilies, dropping sweet smelling myrrh"; Ezek. 20:46, "Drop thy word towards the south"; 21:2, "Drop thy word towards the holy places"; Amos 7:16, "Drop not thy word against the house of Isaac."

The word Massâ' (מַשָּׂא, 4853), a *burden*, is used in Prov. 30:1 and 31:1, where the A.V. renders it *prophecy*. By a *burden* we are to understand the message laid on the mind of the prophet, and by him pressed on the attention of the people. The message of the LORD ought not to have been regarded as a burden by the people (see Jer. 23:33–38); but it could not fail to be realized as such by the prophets, who at times felt heavily laden with the weight of their message. See Jer. 20:9, and compare Nah. 1:1; Hab. 1:1; and Mal. 1:1.

In Hos. 9:7 the prophet is described as the "man of the spirit," or the "spiritual man," an expression that reminds us of the Apostle Peter's declaration that "holy men of old spake as they were moved by the Holy Ghost."

§2. *The Seer*

The *seer* is Chôzeh (חֹזֶה, 2374—Assyrian *khazu*), one who sees a vision, not with the eye of sense but with the spiritual and intellectual faculties. This term is usually (but not always) found in passages that refer to visions vouchsafed by God.

Chôzeh (2374) is rendered *prophet* only once, namely, in Isa. 30:10: "Which say to the prophets, Prophesy not unto us right things, speak unto us smooth things, prophesy deceits." Various cognate nouns (nos. 2376, 2377, 2378, 2380, and 2384 in Strong and Gesenius) are used of *visions* in most passages where they are mentioned. The verb Châzâh (חָזָה, 2372) is frequently found in the same sense, as in Exod. 24:11, "They saw God," where it explains and somewhat modifies the fact recorded in the previous verse in which the ordinary word for *sight* is used. Again, it is used in Num. 24:4, 16, where Balaam speaks of himself as seeing the vision of the Almighty, falling into a trance, but having his eyes open. In II Sam. 24:11 it is used of

Gad, David's *seer;* see also II Kings 17:13; I Chron. 21:9; 25:5; 29:29; II Chron. 9:29; 33:18, 19; 35:15.

The verb is used of spiritual apprehension in Job 24:1; 27:12; 34:32; 36:25.

In Ps. 63:2 two words are used, the first being the more general one, the second that which we are now considering. The Psalmist expresses his longing to *see,* Râ'âh (רָאָה, 7200), God's power and glory as he *has seen* (Châzah, 2372) God in the sanctuary. He wished to see face to face that Being whom now he only saw through a glass darkly.

Châzâh (2372) is used in Isa. 13:1, and similar passages, of the burden or vision the prophet saw. It occurs in Isa. 33:17, "Thine eyes shall see the king in his beauty," and implies that there would be something more in that beatific vision than what would be presented to the outer eye. It is used of false visions in Ezek. 13:6, 7, 8, 9, 16; compare I Kings 22:22. It is also used by Amos, Micah, and Habakkuk of their visions, and by Daniel in reference to dreams.

In some passages the word is found in a more general sense, as in Ps. 58:8, 10; Prov. 22:29; 24:32; 29:20; Song of Sol. 6:13; Isa. 48:6; and 57:8.

The more general word Râ'âh (רָאָה, 7200), *to see,* is used of prophetic or spiritual sight in a few passages, two of which have been already referred to. It represents the *visions* mentioned in Gen. 46:2; Num. 12:6; I Sam. 3:15; II Chron. 26:5; Isa. 28:7; Ezek. 1:1; 8:3, 4; 11:24; 40:2; 43:3; and Dan. 8:16, 27.

§3. *N.T. Use of the Word Prophet*

The words προφήτης (4396) and προφητεύω (4395) are used in the N.T. not only with respect to the prophets of the O.T., but also with reference to those persons who prophesy in Christ's name (Matt. 7:22) under the new dispensation. The prophecy of Zacharias (Luke 1:67) is an inspired hymn gathering together the O.T. predictions, and announcing that they were about to be fulfilled in Christ. The prophecy of Caiaphas (John 11:51) was an utterance capable of a meaning beyond that which was in the mind of the speaker, and it was intended by Him who overrules all things to have this double significance. When the Jews blindfolded the Lord and smote Him with their hands, they said, "Prophesy unto us, thou Christ, Who is he that smote thee?" (Matt. 26:68; Mark 14:65; Luke 22:64), implying that prophecy is the utterance of that which cannot be discovered by such means of knowledge as are ordinarily available. Among the special gifts of Pentecost, we find that both men and women were to prophesy (Acts 2:17), and the utterance of the wonderful works of God is said to have been a fulfillment of the prediction. Prayer, preaching, and singing all seem to be expressions of prophecy. It was also related to the gift of tongues. See Acts 19:6; 21:9; Rom. 12:6; I Cor. 11:4, 5; 12:10, 14 passim; I Thess. 5:20; I Tim. 1:18; 4:14; Rev. 10:11; 11:3.

Both John the Baptist and the Lord Jesus were regarded by many among the Jews as prophets (Matt. 21:11, 26, 46), and rightly so, for John was "more than a prophet," while the Lord was "the prophet who should come into the world" (John 6:14; Acts 3:22, 23). The Apostles are coupled with prophets sent by Christ in Luke 11:49 (Cf. Matt. 23:34, where *wise men* are substituted for Apostles). See also Acts 11:27; 13:1; 15:32; 21:10; I Cor. 12:28; Eph. 2:20; 3:5; 4:11; Rev. 18:20; 22:9.

There is no office in the Church at the present time quite analogous to the prophetic. This gift, in some of its aspects, must be classed along with others that were called into existence by the will of God for a special time and purpose, its object being the directing and strengthening of the faith of the infant Church. The Church was thus provided for temporarily, as every newborn child is, until God saw fit to leave His people to those less obtrusive but more permanent operations of the Spirit that are referred to in passages such as Gal. 5:22, 23.

§4. *The Priest*

The Hebrew name for a *priest* is Kôhên (כֹּהֵן, 3548) throughout the O.T., with the exception of three passages, where a word derived from Kâmar (כָּמַר, 3648), which means *to make hot* or *black,* is used, namely, II Kings 23:5; Hos. 10:5; and Zeph. 1:4. In these passages idolatrous priests are referred to.

The original meaning of the word Kôhên (3548) is lost in obscurity. In I Kings 4:5 the A.V. renders it *principal officer* (compare the marginal rendering of verse 2); in II Sam. 8:18 and 20:26 it has been rendered *chief ruler* (margin, *princes*). David's own sons were thus designated, but it seems impossible now to decide what duties were involved under this name. In Job 12:19 it is rendered *princes.*

Possibly the usage of the word in the passages now quoted is a remnant of its original signification, at a time when one man combined in Himself the priestly and the kingly office.

The Greek ἱερεὺς (2409) and the Latin *sacerdos* (priest) are far better (because more indefinite) renderings of Kôhên (3548) than either the French *sacrificateur* or the English *priest*, which last confused two things kept carefully distinct both in the O.T. and N.T.

The verb **Kâhan** (כָּהַן, 3547), *to minister in the priest's office*, is used several times in Scripture. In one passage it is rendered *to deck;* the bridegroom decks himself with ornaments, as the priest clothes himself with his special robes of office (Isa. 61:10). The LXX is very uniform in the use of ἱερεὺς (2409) for the noun and ἱερατεύω (2407) for the verb. Only once is λειτουργέω (3008), *to minister,* used for it, namely, in II Chron. 11:14.

The word Kôhên (3548) is not confined as a title to the priests of the Levitical order. It is applied to Melchizedek, to Potipherah (Gen. 41:45), to the priests of Midian (Exod. 3:1), and to the priests who conducted idolatrous worship. Moses is included among God's priests in Ps. 99:6.

The verb ἱερατεύω (2407) is used only once in the N.T., namely, where Zacharias is described as "executing the priest's office" (Luke 1:8). In the following verse ἱερατεία (2405) is found, and it occurs again in Heb. 7:5. In I Peter 2:5, 9, we meet with ἱεράτευμα (2406), which is used of Christians, regarded as a *holy priesthood,* and also as a *royal priesthood,* the last expression being an adaptation of the title given (conditionally) to Israel in Exod. 19:6, where the words "kingdom of priests" are rendered "royal priesthood" in the LXX. Compare Rev. 1:6; 5:10; 20:6. The word ἱερουργέω (2418), not ἱερατεύω (2407), is used in Rom. 15:16, and means the performance of sacred duties, not necessarily the exercise of sacerdotal functions.

It is remarkable that the word ἱερεὺς (2409) occurs nowhere through the whole range of the Epistles, except in the Epistle to the Hebrews, where the contrast between Christ's priestly work and that of Aaron is drawn out. If the ministry of the Christian Church were intended to occupy a position at all analogous to that of the Levitical priesthood, can it be doubted that the Epistle to the Hebrews would have contained some notification of the fact? But the minister is kept comparatively out of sight (except where matters of order were concerned) and attention is concentrated on One who cannot be seen with the outward eye, but who is our one and only High Priest, acting in our interests "within the veil." Sacerdotal terms were freely used of the ministry in the next ages of the Church. This is not to be wondered at when we remember that to Greeks and Romans sacerdotalism was almost identified with religion. Their usage does not imply that they saw any real analogy between the *Jewish* and the Christian ministry, though it does imply that the latter took the place of the *heathen* priesthood.

§5. *The Elder*

The *elder* is always **Zâqên** (זָקֵן, 2205), literally an *old man,* and is represented in the LXX by πρεσβύτερος (4245), *presbyter.* The word is frequently used in each language to express old age, for which in the LXX πρεσβύτης (4246) is also used; but gradually it was restricted to an official sense. The first intimation of such a sense is in Gen. 50:7, where we read that "Joseph went up to bury his father: and with him went up all the servants of Pharaoh, the elders of his house, and all the elders of the land of Egypt." The office was in those days a natural, social, and civil one. In Exod. 17:5 the elders are again referred to as lay representatives of the people. So again in Exod. 18:12; 19:7; 24:1, 9.

In Num. 11:16 the LORD says to Moses, "Gather unto me seventy men of the elders of Israel, whom thou knowest to be the elders of the people, and officers over them; and bring them unto the tabernacle of the congregation, that they may stand there with me." These men represented the various tribes of Israel, and were quite distinct from the Levites and priests (Josh. 24:1; I Kings 8:1–3). They acted on behalf of Israel on great occasions, whether civil or religious, and in the first instance their appointment was sanctioned by an outpouring of the Spirit on them, as we read in Num. 11:25:

> And the LORD came down in a cloud, and spake unto [Moses], and took of the spirit that was upon him, and gave it unto the seventy elders: and it came to pass, that, when the spirit rested upon them, they prophesied, and did not cease.

It was on the occasion now referred to that there remained two of the men in the camp, Eldad and Medad: "and the spirit rested upon them, and they were of them that were written, but went not out unto the tabernacle: and they prophesied in the camp." When

Joshua, in his eagerness, wished Moses to forbid them, the lawgiver gave that noble and remarkable answer, "Enviest thou [i.e., art thou jealous] for my sake? Would God that all the LORD's people were prophets, and that the LORD would put his spirit upon them!" (Num. 11:26–29). This passage implies that the outpouring of the Spirit on the presbyters caused them to become prophets, constituting them a *spiritual*, though not a sacerdotal, order.

The word is rendered *ancients* in Isa. 3:14; 24:23. The latter passage is one of peculiar interest. We here read that "the LORD of hosts shall reign in Mount Zion, and Jerusalem, and before his ancients gloriously," or (as it is in the margin) "there shall be glory before his ancients." Are not these *ancients* or *elders* the same as those whom the Apostle John saw in vision (Rev. 4:4) before the throne of God, giving glory to God and to the Lamb? May they not be taken as the representatives of all God's people?

§6. *The Office of Elder in the N.T.*

The importance of a right judgment of the position and functions of these elders cannot well be overrated when we come to discuss the nature of the analogous office of presbyter in the N.T. On the one hand, the elder was neither a priest nor a Levite, but a representative of the people; on the other hand, he had special duties and responsibilities in consequence of this position, and he also had special grace conferred on him (in the first instance, at least) to enable him to perform those duties aright.

The word *presbytery,* $\pi\rho\epsilon\sigma\beta\upsilon\tau\epsilon\rho\iota\sigma\nu$ (4244), is used three times in the N.T.: twice of the Sanhedrin (Luke 22:26; Acts 22:5), and once of the gathering of Christian elders who laid their hands on Timothy (I Tim. 4:14).[2]

Christian presbyters or elders are first named in Acts 11:30, where reference is made to the elders in Judea or Jerusalem. Paul appointed elders, apparently by the laying on of hands, and after nomination by the people, in every church he founded (Acts 14:23).

---

2. Paul himself laid hands also on Timothy (II Tim. 1:6), but perhaps at a different time and with a different object. It may be observed that the great Apostle of the Gentiles was formally appointed to his missionary work not by apostolic ordination but by the laying on of the hands of the ministers at Antioch (Acts 13:3), although he had previously received a mission, accompanied by the special gifts of the Holy Spirit, by the laying on of hands by Ananias.

We find these elders in conclave with the apostles in Acts 15, and we have a most instructive address illustrating their office and work in Acts 20:17–38.

Elders are not mentioned in the Epistles until we reach the First Epistle to Timothy, though they are probably the persons referred to in I Thess. 5:12.[3] It seems strange that they are not in the list of gifted persons mentioned in Eph. 4:11; but this may be accounted for by the fact that the work of an elder, *as such*, did not call for extraordinary gifts, and was to be carried on long after those gifts had ceased. They may, however, have been included under the name *prophets*. From the First Epistle to Timothy we learn the character and position of the elder, while from Titus 1:5 it would appear that the system of appointing elders in every city where there was a church was still sustained. Both Peter and John describe themselves by this title (II John 1; III John 1; I Peter 5:1).

The advice to the elders given by Peter falls in exactly with the exhortations given by Paul to those of Ephesus. James also doubtless refers to those who held the rank of elder in the Church, in the remarkable passage (5:14) in which he speaks of healing the sick by the medical use of oil in connection with the pardon of sin.

According to the analogy of the O.T., the elders would be spiritual but nonsacerdotal representatives and leaders of the various local communities that are feeders to the one Church (see Chap. 19). They would exercise their spiritual and ministerial functions in the name of the congregation, being counselors and helpers, guides and feeders of the flock over which the Holy Ghost had appointed them. Many of them at first were no doubt possessed of the gifts of prophecy and tongues, and were selected for the responsible position they held either because of their age, wisdom, and piety or because of the special gifts they possessed. But they no more held the peculiar position of the Kôhên (3548) or *priest* than did the elders under the O.T. dispensation. Although they would naturally take the chief part in the administration of the Lord's Supper, this was not a sacerdotal act. Just as the Passover supper was administered in every family by the head of the household, so the Lord's Supper is administered by the presbyter as leader of a community, but not as a *sacerdos* (Latin, *priest*), and at a *table*, not at an *altar*. See Chapter 16, §7.

3. Compare the προϊστάμενοι (4291) here with the προεστῶτες πρεσβύτεροι (4291, 4245) in I Tim. 5:17.

§7. *The Ministry*

The *minister* in the O.T. is **Shârêth** (שָׁרֵת, 8335), a word the LXX has almost always rendered λειτουργός (*3011*).[4] The office of minister was not necessarily sacred, but it was always honorable. The minister differed from the servant or slave in that the latter performed what we call menial duties, or at any rate was expected to toil for his master, whereas the former was a person in attendance on a king, prince, or great personage to render such honorable service as would be acceptable. In this sense Joseph was minister to Potiphar (Gen. 39:4), and afterwards was in attendance on the prisoners in behalf of the governor of the prison (Gen. 40:4). So, too, Joshua ministered to Moses, Samuel to Eli, and Abishag to David.

The word is constantly used of the ministrations of the priests and Levites, especially of the latter, and signifies that they were fulfilling high functions in respect of that unseen Being in whose honor they were employed. The term is equally applicable to angels, who are described in the Epistle to the Hebrews as ministering spirits (πνεύματα λειτουργικά—*4151, 3010*) sent forth by their Heavenly Master to minister to them who should be heirs of salvation.

In Ezek. 20:32 the heathen are said to serve or minister to wood and stone. Here the use of the word **Shârêth** (8335) is ironical. They are engaged in ministrations, but to whom? To the King of kings? No, to blocks of wood and stone.

The words λειτουργός (*3011*), λειτουργία (*3009*), and λειτουργέω (*3008*) are used of Christian ministrations several times in the N.T. In some of these passages they denote a ministering in worldly things. See Rom. 15:27; II Cor. 9:12; Phil. 2:25, 30. In Rom. 13:6 those in civil authority are honored by this title when described as God's *ministers.*

In Phil. 2:17 and Rom. 15:16 the work of the Christian ministry, properly so called, is spoken of in terms derived from the sacerdotal and ministerial system of the old dispensation. But when these passages are carefully examined, they will not be found to justify the claims that have sometimes been made by the ministerial order in later times. In Phil. 2:17 Paul describes himself as ready to be offered like a libation on the sacrifice and ministry of his convert's faith (cf. II Tim. 4:6), that is to say, that he might be sacrificed on

---

4. The verb is rendered διακονέω (*1247*) only in Esther 1:10; 2:2; 6:3.

their behalf. In Rom. 15:16 he speaks of himself as ministering the Gospel of God, that the offering up of the Gentiles might be regarded by God as an acceptable sacrifice, being sanctified by the Holy Ghost. In each of these cases the sacrifices are *persons;* and the passages are closely related to Rom. 12:1, where Christians are directed to offer their bodies as living sacrifices. But there is no reference whatsoever to what is now sometimes called "the Christian sacrifice."

§8. *Service*

With regard to the word *serve* or *service,* the LXX often keeps up a distinction that is not to be found in the Hebrew. It has both δουλεία (1397), which is *bond service,* and which may or may not be used in a religious sense; and λατρεία (2999), *sacred service,* a word only used in a religious sense, but not confined to the priesthood. For these two renderings the Hebrew has only one word, 'Âbad[5] (עָבַד, 5647), which is used of every kind of service, good and bad, whether exercised toward man, idols, or God. The distinction that is sometimes drawn between the words *douleia* and *latreia,* in connection with the worship of God and of created beings, cannot be substantiated by reference to the O.T.

The verb δουλεύω (1398), as well as the noun δοῦλος (1401), is frequently used in the N.T. of the service due from every Christian to God and to Christ (see, for example, Col. 3:24; I Thess. 1:9), whether that service take the form of ministry or not.

Λατρεία (2999) is used of that religious service of Christians that consists in self-dedication to God (Rom. 12:1; Phil. 3:3; Heb. 9:14; 12:28). Paul uses it of his own life of service in Acts 24:14; 26:7; 27:23; Rom. 1:9; II Tim. 1:3. It is also used to indicate the ceaseless employment of God's servants in heaven (Rev. 7:15; 22:3).

Διάκονος (1249) (whence the word *deacon*) and kindred forms are used in the N.T. in a general and nontechnical sense of all kinds of ministry or service for the good of others. See Matt. 20:18; John 12:2, 25. It is not applied to the seven so-called deacons, and only gradually grew up into a technical sense. See Phil. 1:1 and I Tim. 3:8, 12.

---

5. The Assyrian replaces *ebed* (slave) by *ardu.*

21
King, Judge, Punish

§1. *Kings and Rulers*

The Hebrew words translated *king* and *kingdom* in the A.V. are connected with the root **Mâlak** (מָלַךְ, 4427—Assyrian *malaku*), which appears in various proper names such as Ebed-Melech and Milcom. The verb is generally rendered *reign* (in Ezek. 20:33, *rule*).

Another word often used in the same sense is **Mâshal** (מָשַׁל, 4910—Assyrian *masalu*), which refers not so much to the office as to the government that that office implies. It is generally rendered *rule*, sometimes *reign* or *dominion*, and occasionally *govern* as in Gen. 1:18, where the heavenly bodies are described as governing the day and the night.

Shâlaṭ (שָׁלַט, 7980—Assyrian *saladhu*), *to get the mastery*, is used with much force in Ps. 119:133, "Let not any iniquity have dominion over me." It is also rendered *dominion* nine times in Daniel, and *rule* fourteen times in the same book. This word is used of Joseph when he is described as "the governor of Egypt" (Gen. 42:6). **Sheleṭ** (7982), which is derived from it, signifies a *shield*, and is rendered *ruler* in Hos. 4:18; and **Sholṭân** (7985—Assyrian *sildhannu*), which reminds us of the modern word *Sultan*, is rendered *dominion* in Dan. 4:3 and thirteen other times in the Aramaic section of Daniel.

Nâgîyd (נָגִיד, 5057), a *leader* or *guide*, is generally translated *prince* or *captain*, and is used of a *ruler* several times, especially in the books of Chronicles. See Isa. 55:4; Dan. 9:26, and 11:22.

Pechâh (פֶּחָה, 6346—Assyrian *pikhu*), a *satrap* or *pasha*, is used for a *governor* chiefly in the later historical books, also in Hag. 1:1, 14; 2:2, 21; and Mal. 1:8.

Sar (שַׂר, 8269—Assyrian *sarru,* king), a *chief captain* in the army, is the title given to the captain of the LORD's hosts in Josh. 5:14, 15. It is applied to judges or rulers of the tribes (Exod. 18:21), who are usually called *princes* in the A.V. in the later books. It is used of government in Ps. 68:27; Isa. 1:23; 32:1; Jer. 1:18; 52:10; also in Isa. 9:6, 7, where the Messiah is called "the prince of peace," and where it is said that "the government shall be upon his shoulders . . . and of the increase of his government and peace there shall be no end." The Messiah is also called the *prince* (**Sar,** 8269) in Dan. 8:11, 25; 10:13, 21; and 12:1.

Bâ'al (בַּעַל, 1166—Assyrian *bilu*), *to be lord, husband,* or *master,* is used of having dominion in I Chron. 4:22 and Isa. 26:13 ("Other lords beside thee have had dominion over us"). This word is found in the remarkable declaration in Isa. 54:5, "Thy Maker is thy husband." See Hos. 2:16.

Yâd (יָד, 3027—Assyrian *idu*), the *hand,* or instrument of power, is used of lordship in I Chron. 18:3 and II Chron. 21:8. In Gen. 27:40 ("When thou shalt have the dominion") the word **Rûwd** (רוּד, 7300) is used, the meaning of which is uncertain, but the cognate word **Râdâh** (רָדָה, 7287—Assyrian *radu*) is frequently used for *rule.* It also occurs in Jer. 2:31 and Hos. 11:12.

In Job 38:33 ("Canst thou set the dominion thereof in the earth?") the word used is supposed to signify rule or empire, and to be connected with the name of an officer or overseer, **Shôṭêr** (שֹׁטֵר, 7860—Assyrian *sadhir,* writer), of whom we read in Exod. 5:6; Deut. 1:15; 16:18; I Chron. 26:29; and Prov. 6:7.

Nâshaq (נָשַׁק, 5401), *to kiss,* whether as a mark of respect (Ps. 2:12) or otherwise, is rendered *rule* in Gen. 41:40, where the margin has *"be armed or kiss"* (see R.V.). The word is sometimes applied to armor because it fits closely and is folded together; it is also applied to the wings of the living creatures that touched one another (Ezek. 3:13).

In Prov. 25:28 ("He that hath no rule over his own spirit") the word **Ma'tsar** (מַעְצָר, 4623) signifies *self-restraint.* In II Kings 25:22 and I Chron. 26:32 we find the word **Pâqad** (פָּקַד, 6485—Assyrian *paqadu*), *to visit* or *superintend;* in Deut. 1:13, **Rô'sh** (רֹאשׁ, 7218—Assyrian *risu*), the *head;* in Isa. 1:10; 3:6, 7; and 22:3, **Qâtsîyn** (קָצִין, 7101), a *captain;* in Judg. 5:3; Ps. 2:2, and four other passages, the rulers or princes are described by the word **Râzan** (רָזַן, 7336), which perhaps answers to *august.* **Âlaph** (אָלַף, 502), *to lead* or *teach,* is used in Zech. 9:7; 12:5, 6; and **Châbash** (חָבַשׁ, 2280), *to bind* (usually for the purpose of hearing), in Job 34:17. Nâchâh (נָחָה, 5148), *to lead,* occurs in Ps. 67:4; and Châqaq (חָקַק, 2710), *to decree* (lit. *to engrave,* as in Job 19:24; Isa. 22:16; and 49:16), is rendered *governor* in Judg. 5:9, 14. Compare Gen. 49:10 (*lawgiver*). Nâsîy' (נָשִׂיא, 5387), a *captain* or *prince* (lit. one who *bears* responsibility, or who *holds aloft* an ensign), is often used of God's leading His people, and is rendered *ruler* or *governor* a few times in the Pentateuch and in II Chron. 1:2.

§2. *Judgment and Condemnation*

The words *judgment* and *condemnation* signify two very different things, yet they are sometimes confused by the Bible reader.[1] Shâphat (שָׁפַט, 8199—Assyrian *sapadhu*) is the general word for the administration of justice. It is once rendered *condemn* in the A.V., namely, in Ps. 109:31, and here the margin points to the true rendering. The usual word for *condemnation,* as has been shown elsewhere, is Râsha' (רְשַׁע, 7561), which in the Piel stem signifies *to account* or *deal with as wicked.* It is used in this sense sixteen times, and is the exact opposite of the Hiphil form of Tsâdaq (צָדַק, 6663), *to account* or *deal with as righteous.* In Ps. 109:7, "let him be condemned" is literally "let him go out as wicked." In II Chron. 36:3 and Amos 2:8 the word 'Ânash (עָנַשׁ, 6064) signifies *to be fined* or *mulcted.*

Coming now to the subject of judgment, we must distinguish the various shades of meaning that the word possesses. When the Psalmist prays, "Teach me good judgment" (Ps. 119:66), he uses a word that signifies *taste* or *discrimination* (טַעַם, 2940), and asks for a keen moral and spiritual perception such as is referred to by the writer of the Epistle to the Hebrews when he speaks of those who "by reason of use have their senses exercised to discern both good and evil" (Heb. 5:14).

In Gen. 31:37 Jacob says, "Set thy goods before my brethren and thy brethren, that they may judge [יָכַח, 3198] betwixt us both," that is, "that they may decide which of us is right." On the word 'Ĕlôhîym (אֱלֹהִים, 430), which is rendered *judges* in a few texts (Exod. 21:6; 22:8; and I Sam. 2:25), see Chapter 2. In Jer. 51:47, 52, "I will do judgment

---

1. The German language uses *richten* for various aspects of the administration of justice, and *urteilen* specifically for the giving of a judicial decision; but many languages are not able to mark this important distinction.

upon the graven images of Babylon," the word for *visitation* (פָּקַד, 6485) is used. See Chapter 17, §4.

Pâlal (פָּלַל, 6419), when used judicially, points to arbitration between two parties. It is rendered *judge* in I Sam. 2:25, "If one man sin against another, the judge ['Ĕlôhîym, 430] shall *judge* him" (or arbitrate between the one and the other); Ps. 106:30, "Then stood up Phinehas and *executed judgment*, and so the plague was stayed." The Prayer Book version reads, "Then stood up Phinehas and prayed" (i.e., sought the arbitration of God). See also Exod. 21:22; Deut. 32:31; Job 31:11, 28; Isa. 16:3; 28:7; Ezek. 16:52; 28:23.

Dîyn (דִּין, 1777—Assyrian *danu*), *to judge*, whence the name *Dan*, implies a settlement of what is right where there is a charge on a person, and so it comes to signify the decision of a cause. It is rendered *judge* in more than thirty passages. It is a *judicial* word, while Shâphaṭ (8199) is rather *administrative*. The one would mark the act whereby men's position and destiny are decided; the other would point to the mode in which men would be governed and their affairs administered.

Dîyn (1777) is found in the following passages: Gen. 15:14, "The nation whom they shall serve will I judge." Gen. 49:16, "Dan shall judge his people." Deut. 32:36, "The LORD shall judge his people." Ezra 7:25, 26 (Aramaic portion), "Set *magistrates* [Shaphᵉṭiyn, 8200] and judges [Dayyânîyn, 1782], which may judge [Dîyn, 1778] all the people that are beyond the river, all such as know the laws of thy God; and teach ye them that know them not. And whosoever will not do the law of thy God, and the law of the king, let judgment [Dîynah, 1780] be executed speedily upon him, whether it be unto death, or to banishment, or to confiscation of goods, or to imprisonment." Ps. 50:4, "He shall call to the heavens from above, and to the earth, that he may judge his people." Ps. 54:1, "Judge me by thy strength." Dan. 7:10, "The judgment was set and the books opened." Dan. 7:22, "Judgment was given to the saints of the most High; and the time came that the saints possessed the kingdom." Dan. 7:26, "The judgment shall sit, and they shall take away his dominion." See also Gen. 30:6; I Sam. 2:10; Esther 1:13; Job 19:29; 35:14; 36:17, 31; Ps. 68:5; 76:8; 96:10; 110:6; 135:14; Prov. 20:8; Isa. 3:13; 10:2; Jer. 22:16; Dan. 4:37; Zech. 3:7.

Shâphaṭ (8199) is the root of the name for the *judges* (Shôphᵉṭîym, 8199) who were raised up from time to time to be rulers over the land, to defend the people from enemies, to save them from their oppressors, to teach them the truth, to uphold them in the right course. It is in this general meaning that the word is usually found in the O.T. It is therefore not out of place that it should be rendered *defend* in Ps. 82:3; *deliver* in I Sam. 23:14; and *rule* in Ruth 1:1. The two words Shâphaṭ (8199) and Dîyn (1777) are found side by side in some places, e.g., I Sam. 24:15; Ps. 7:8; 9:8; 72:2; and Jer. 5:28. But this by no means proves that their meanings are identical. Shâphaṭ (8199) and Dîyn (1777) are rendered in the LXX κρίνω (2919), διακρίνω (1252), δικάζω (L-S 428B), and ἐκδικέω (1556). The word κατακρίνω (2632) barely exists in the LXX, but is found several times in the N.T. See, for example, Rom. 8:1, 34; I Cor. 11:32. The *judge* is κριτής (2923) or δικαστής (1348); and the *judgment* is κρῖμα (2917), κρίσις (2920), δικαιοσύνη (1343), δικαίωμα (1345).

§3. *Judgment in the N.T.*

Turning to the N.T., we may distinguish three kinds of judgment, namely: first, self-judgment, or the discrimination of one's own character; secondly, the Great Assize, when the destiny of each shall be assigned; and, thirdly, the administration of the world in righteousness.

It must be noticed, however, that κρίνω (2919) is sometimes used of an adverse judgment, as in John 3:17, 18, "God sent not his son into the world to condemn [κρίνειν, 2919] the world . . . he that believeth is not condemned (κρίνεται, 2919) . . . he that believeth not is condemned already" (ἤδη κέκριται, 2235, 2919); John 16:11, "Now is the ruler of this world condemned" (κέκριται, 2919); II Thess. 2:12, "That all might be condemned." In these passages the R.V. uses the word *judge*.

In other passages κρίνω (2919) means *to decide* or *form an estimate*, whether favorable or the contrary, as in Matt. 7:1, "Judge not [i.e., form no hard estimate of others], that ye be not judged" [i.e., that a hard estimate be not formed of you]. Compare Rom. 2:1; Luke 7:43, "Thou hast formed a right estimate"; Acts 16:15, "If ye have judged me to be faithful"; Rom. 14:5, "One judgeth one day above another"; James 4:11, "He that judgeth his brother sets himself up as a judicial interpreter of the law."

Occasionally there is reference to judicial administration. Thus, in Acts 17:31 it is said that God is about to judge the world in righteousness in the person of the Man whom He has ordained;

Matt. 19:28, "Ye . . . shall sit on twelve thrones, judging the twelve tribes of Israel"; I Cor. 6:2, "The saints shall judge the world"; I Cor. 6:3, "We shall judge angels."

God is described, under the name κριτής (2923), as the Judge of all (Heb. 12:23), as the righteous Judge (II Tim. 4:8), and as the one lawgiver (and judge), who is able to save and to destroy (James 4:12); while the Lord Jesus is called the Judge of quick and dead (Acts 10:42).

The word κρῖμα (2917) occurs nearly thirty times in the N.T., usually in the sense of condemnation. In the wider sense of administrative justice we may refer to the following passages: John 9:39, "For judgment am I come into this world, that they which see not may see, and that they which see may be made blind"; Rom. 11:33, "How unsearchable are his judgments"; Rev. 20:4, "I saw thrones, and they sat on them, and judgment was given unto them."

The word κρίσις (2920) is found in about fifty places in the N.T. Sometimes it signifies the formation of a right estimate of another's character and doings, as in Matt. 23:23, where it is joined with mercy and faith; Luke 11:42, where it is coupled with love. Accordingly, our Lord says to the Jews, "Judge not according to appearance, but judge righteous [or just] judgment" (John 7:24). He says of His own judgment, or mode of estimating and dealing with others, that it is righteous, and just, and true (John 8:16). An estimate of the character and work of all men is to be formed by Christ; and the period in which this work will be accomplished is described as the Day of Judgment.

The word κρίσις (2920) is sometimes used in the sense of condemnation, as in Matt. 23:33 and John 5:24, while in John 5:29 a contrast is drawn between those that rise to life and those that rise to condemnation. Judgment, however, is the better word.

§4. *Punishment and Vengeance*

The moral relationship between sin and punishment is illustrated by the fact that the latter is expressed by the words **Châtâ'** (חָטָא, 2398) and **'Âvôn** (עָוֹן, 5771—See Chap. 6, §1) in Gen. 4:13; Lev. 26:41, 43; I Sam. 28:10; Lam. 3:39; 4:6, 22; Zech. 14:19. **Yâçar** (יָסַר, 3256), *to chastise,* is found in Lev. 26:18: "If ye will not yet for all this hearken unto me, then I will punish you seven times more for your sins." **Nâkâh** (נָכָה, 5221), *to smite,* is used in Lev. 26:24; **Nâqam** (נָקַם, 5358), *to* *avenge,* in Exod. 21:20, 21; Râ'a' (רָעַע, 7489), *to bring evil,* in Zech. 8:14; 'Ânash (עָנַשׁ, 6064), *to amerce* or *fine,* five times in the Book of Proverbs. In the remaining passages, all of which are in the prophetical books, Pâqad (פָּקַד, 6485), *to visit,* is used, punishment being regarded as a visitation from God.

The avenging of the blood of the slain is referred to under the word Gâ'al (גָּאַל, 1350) in Num. 35:12, et al. From the earliest period of human history God is represented as taking the part of the injured, of the oppressed, and even of the slain. Their cries ascend into His ears; their blood calls to Him even from the ground. Thus the Redeemer is necessarily an avenger, and must exercise retributive justice. Shâphaṭ (8199), *to judge,* is used in this sense in II Sam. 18:19, 31. For a similar reason, perhaps, Yâsha' (יָשַׁע, 3467), *to save,* is rendered *to avenge* in I Sam. 25:26, 31, 33. The R.F. offers a marginal correction in the first of these verses.

In Deut. 32:42 ("The beginning of revenges upon the enemy"), and in Judges 5:2 ("Praise ye the LORD for the avenging of Israel"), a word is used that is derived from Pâra' (פָּרַע, 6544), *to strip.*

The most usual word for avenging is Nâqam (נָקַם, 5358). It first appears in Gen. 4:15, "Vengeance shall be taken on him [or rather *for* him, i.e., for Cain] sevenfold." Compare verse 24, "If Cain shall be avenged sevenfold, truly Lamech seventy and seven fold." The word is used altogether about seventy-five times in the O.T. Personal and private revenge was forbidden to Israel: "Thou shalt not avenge nor bear any grudge against the children of thy people, but thou shalt love thy neighbor as thyself" (Lev. 19:18). The children of Israel were always taught to leave vengeance in God's hand, as He would avenge the blood of His servants, and would take their part against their enemies. See, for example, Deut. 32:35, 43; Ps. 18:47; 94:1; Jer. 11:20; Nah. 1:2. The Lord's vengeance is regarded as *retribution,* but not as *retaliation;* it is set forth not as an *evil passion,* but rather as the righteous and unerring *vindication* of His own people and of His own course of action to the discomfiture of those who had set themselves in opposition to Him. He metes it out with Justice, and on such a *day* or at such a time as seems fitting to Him. See Isa. 34:8; 61:2; 63:4; Jer. 46:10; 51:6.

The words ἐκδικέω (1556) and ἐκδίκησις (1557) stand occasionally both for Shâphaṭ (8199) and also for Nâqam (5358). They imply the visitation of due penalty on the criminal, whether by the hand of the human judge (Luke 18:3; Acts 7:24; Rom. 13:4; I Peter 2:14), or by the agency of God (Luke 18:7, 8; 21:22; I Thess. 4:6; II Thess. 1:8; Rev. 6:10; 19:2).

There is no place given in the N.T., any more than there is in the O.T., for the avenging of personal injuries. On the contrary, the feeling of revenge is studiously condemned. Where the magistrate is not called upon to vindicate the sufferer, there God will step in. "Vengeance belongeth unto me, saith the Lord" (Rom. 12:19; Heb. 10:30).[2]

2. These words are quoted from Deut. 32:35, and are translated from the Hebrew, not from the LXX, which reads ἐν ἡμέρᾳ ἐκδικήσεως (1722, 2250, 1557) instead of ἐμοὶ ἐκδίκησις (1698, 1557).

22

Nation, People

§1. *Gentile or Heathen*

The only word rendered either *Gentile* or *heathen* in the O.T. is Gôwy (גּוֹי, 1471); it is generally used in the plural number, and after the time of Moses was generally used of outside nations. Gôwy (1471) is translated *nation* in all passages where the A.V. has adopted this word, with the exception of about thirty-five. In ten passages it is rendered *people*. In nineteen out of twenty places in which the word is found, the LXX has adopted ἔθνος (1484) as a rendering, and hence is derived the English word *heathen*. The first passage in which Gôwy (1471) appears is Gen. 10:5, where the historian, writing of the children of Japheth, says, "By these were the isles of the Gentiles divided in their lands; every one after his tongue, after their families, in their nations." The word for *isles* may perhaps be used here in the more extended sense of *territories*.

The word Gôwyim (1471) frequently occurs in connection with the promises made to Abraham. His seed was to inherit Canaan, which was at that time possessed by Gôwyim (1471). He was to be the father of many Gôwyim (1471), and in him and his seed were all the Gôwyim (1471) of the earth to be blessed.

Where the word has been rendered *people* it will always be found to be in the singular number, and in these cases it usually refers to Israel. There is, however, one exception, namely, Zech. 12:3, where we read of all the people (i.e., nations) of the earth being "gathered against Jerusalem."

Throughout the historical books, the Psalms, and the prophets, the word Gôwyim (1471) primarily signifies those nations that lived in the immediate neighborhood of the Jewish people; they were regarded as enemies, as ignorant of the truth, and sometimes as tyrants. Yet gleams of brighter and better days for them appear on the pages of Scripture from time to time. The Gôwyim (1471) were to seek after the Messiah, the son of Jesse (Isa. 11:10). God's chosen One was to minister judgment to them (Isa. 42:1). He was to be not only a covenant to the *people* (of Israel) but also a light to the Gôwyim (1471—42:6), and a salvation to the ends of the earth (49:6). In Isa. 60:16 and elsewhere, the Gôwyim (1471) are described as contributing to the glorification of the regenerated Israel; while in other places we read of them as agents in punishing Israel (Jer. 4:7). Their idolatry was fearful, and their abominations were great (II Kings 16:3). Their triumph over Israel and their ignorant fury against Israel's king are denounced in strong terms. But, after all, they are to be God's inheritance; they are told to rejoice in His coming to judge the earth, and all nations whom God has made are to come and worship before Him.

§2. *The People*

If Gôwy (1471) denotes a *nation* regarded from without, 'Am (עַם, 5971) signifies a *people* as viewed by one of themselves. Sometimes it is used in the familiar and domestic way in which we speak of *folk*, a rendering it has received in Gen. 33:15. In the LXX it is generally rendered λαός (2992). It is often brought into direct relationship or contrast with Gôwy (1471). Thus Moses, speaking to God concerning Israel, says, "This nation [Gôwy, 1471] is thy people ['Am, 5971]" (Exod. 33:13). It is used by the later O.T. writers to distinguish Israel as God's people, and to mark them off from the surrounding Gôwyim (1471). Yet the prophets give a hope that the Gôwyim (1471) who had not been an 'Am (5971) should become the people of God through Divine mercy. Thus in Ps. 18:43 we read, "Thou hast made me the head of the heathen [Gôwyim, 1471]: a people ['Am, 5971] whom I have not known shall serve me." This will come to pass when God shall be recognized as holding rule as "King of the Gôwyim" (1471—see Jer. 10:7). Compare Hos. 1:9, 10, and 2:23.

A word that occupies a less definite position than either Gôwy (1471) or 'Am (5971) is Leôm (לְאֹם, 3816), a *race*. It is generally found in the plural. It is used frequently in the Psalms and Isaiah, and two or three times in earlier and later books. It first appears in Gen. 25:23:

"Two races shall be separated from thy loins; the one race shall be stronger than the other race." See also Hab. 2:11 and Jer. 51:58, which is quoted from it. This word is applied sometimes to Israel, and sometimes to other nations. 'Ummah (אֻמָּה, 523), a *tribe* or *family*, literally those sprung from one mother, is rendered *people* in Num. 25:15 and Ps. 117:1, and *nations* in Gen. 25:16; Ezra 4:10; and throughout the Book of Daniel.

§3. *Nations and People in the N.T.*

The word ἔθνος (*1484*) first occurs in the N.T. in the phrase "Galilee of the *Gentiles*" (Matt. 4:15). Here the title is brought into close juxtaposition with λαός (*2992*), which is used in the words that immediately follow: "The *people* that sitteth in darkness hath seen a great light."

Other passages in which the words ἔθνος (*1484*) and λαός (*2992*) are contrasted follow. Luke 2:32, "A light for the purpose of revealing the truth to Gentiles, and [the] glory of thy people Israel." Acts 4:25, 27, "Why did the Gentiles rage, and the people imagine vain things? . . . For of a truth against thy holy servant[1] Jesus, whom thou hast anointed, both Herod, and Pontius Pilate, with the Gentiles, and the people [plural] of Israel, were gathered together." Acts 15:14, "God determined to take from among the Gentiles a people for his name." Acts 26:17, "Delivering thee from the people, and from the Gentiles, unto whom now I send thee." Acts 26:23, "That Christ should suffer, and that he should be the first that should rise from the dead, and should shew light unto the people and to the Gentiles." Rom. 15:10, "Rejoice, ye Gentiles, with his people." Rom. 15:11, "Praise the Lord, all ye Gentiles; and laud him, all ye people [plural]." I Pet. 2:9, "A holy nation and peculiar people."

The exact interpretation of the phrase "all nations" or "all the Gentiles" is sometimes attended with difficulty. We meet with it in the following passages. Matt. 24:9, "Ye shall be hated by all nations." Matt. 24:14, "This gospel of the kingdom shall be preached in all the world, as a witness to all nations" (compare Mark 13:10). Matt. 25:32, "All nations shall be gathered before him." Matt. 28:19, "Make disciples of all nations." Mark 11:17, "My house shall be called a house of prayer for all nations." Luke 21:24, "They [the Jews] shall be carried

---

1. See Chap. 1, §5.

captive to all nations." Luke 24:47, "That in his name should repentance and remission of sins be proclaimed to all nations." Acts 14:16, "In past times suffered all the Gentiles to walk in their ways." Acts 15:17, "That the residue of men might seek after the Lord, and all the Gentiles upon whom [now] my name is called." Rom. 1:5, "We have received grace and apostleship, for obedience to the faith among all nations." Rom. 15:11, "Praise the Lord, all ye nations." Rom. 16:26, "Made known to all the Gentiles." Gal. 3:8, "In thee shall all nations be blessed." Rev. 12:5, "To rule [or feed] all nations." Rev. 15:4, "All nations shall come and worship before thee." Rev. 18:3, "All nations have drunk of the wine of the wrath of her fornication." Rev. 18:23, "By thy sorceries were all nations deceived."

With these passages may be compared Ps. 67:2; 72:11, 17; 82:8; Isa. 2:2; 25:7; 61:11; and 66:18. These texts set forth the Divine promises to all nations of the earth. This expression, however, cannot always be understood in its full and literal sense, as will be seen by the examination of I Kings 4:31; I Chron. 14:17; Jer. 27:7; and Zech. 14:2.

§4. *Tribe or Family*

Two words are rendered *tribe*, namely, Matteh (מַטֶּה, 4294) and Shêbet (שֵׁבֶט, 7626—Assyrian *sibdhu*, rod), both of which originally signify a *rod*. The founder of a family was its root, while the ancestor of each subdivision (and so the subdivision itself) was a rod or stem. Hence the rod was the symbol of the tribe (Num. 17:2), and perhaps the heads of the tribes had rods, batons, or scepters of office. Shêbet (7626) first appears in Gen. 4:9, 10 (cf. vv. 16, 28). Matteh (4294) is first used of a tribe in Exod. 31:2. Both words are used freely in the same sense in the Pentateuch and Joshua. Shêbet (7626) is the more favored word in Judges, I and II Samuel, I and II Kings, and Psalms, and is found occasionally in Isaiah, Ezekiel, Hosea, and Zechariah. Matteh (4294) only occurs twice in I Kings, is frequent in I Chronicles, hardly ever in the prophetical books.

The *family* is a still further subdivision, and is called Mishpâchâh (מִשְׁפָּחָה, 4940). The only exceptions were as follows: in II Chron. 35:5, 12, the word Âb (אָב, 1), the *ancestry* or *house of fathers*, is used. In Judg. 6:15, 'Eleph (אֶלֶף, 505—Assyrian *alapu*), a *thousand*, is adopted (compare its use in the prophecy of Bethlehem, which was so small among the *thousands* of Israel, Mic. 5:2). In I Chron. 13:14 and Ps. 68:6 we find the word Bayith (בַּיִת, 1004), a *house*.

In Gen. 47:12 the Hebrew is Ṭaph (טַף, 2945), which is generally rendered *little ones;* this rendering, however, has lately been questioned.

Dr. Payne Smith, late Dean of Canterbury, suggested in his Bampton Lectures that Israel was divided into three great classes. First, there were the nobles, heads, or princes, whose genealogies were given in the Books of Numbers and I Chronicles. Secondly, there were the retainers, who formed the strength of these noble houses, not necessarily descended in a direct line from Jacob but forming households or clans under the various nobles. The Hebrew name for these households was Ṭaph (טַף, 2945), which the LXX renders οἰκία (3614) and συγγένεια (4772).[2] They were circumcised, were sharers of the covenant, and were part of the commonwealth of Israel. Dr. Payne Smith holds the English rendering *little ones* to be a mistake, because, while the Ṭaph (2945) included the children, it also included a great deal more, namely, the whole household or body of retainers. Thirdly, there was the *mixed multitude* or ʻÊreb (עֶרֶב, 6154) that had gradually united itself with the destinies of Israel and that included Egyptians, Arabs, and, in course of time, Canaanites. They appear to have had no landed property assigned to them, and were not sharers in the covenant.

Each tribe was divided into families (**Mishpâchâh**, 4940) that bore the names of the leading descendants of Jacob. Thus the men of the tribe of Reuben formed four families, and these were subdivided into *houses* (Num. 1:2). Similarly, in Josh. 7:17, 18, in the history of Achan, we find the tribe of Judah thus divided into families, houses, and individuals. The number in each *house* must have been large. The chiefs of the *houses* were important men, and were called "chief fathers" in Num. 31:26, and "heads of the fathers" in Josh. 14:1.

2. But only once in each case. The usual renderings are παιδίον (3813), τέκνον (5043), and σῶμα (4983).

23

Earth, World, Heaven

§1. *The Soil or Land*

Three Hebrew words are rendered *land*. **Sâdeh** (שָׂדֶה, 7704) signifies a field, a plot of land, or an estate. It is rendered *land* in I Sam. 14:14; II Sam. 9:7; 19:29; II Kings 8:3, 5; Neh. 5:3, etc. **'Erets** (אֶרֶץ, 776), which is very largely used, signifies a territory, or even the whole earth. It is systematically adopted by Moses and other writers in the expression, "A *land* flowing with milk and honey." **'Ădâmâh** (אֲדָמָה, 127) properly means the *soil*, regarded as a productive agent. It is used of the land or ground in the sense in which a farmer would speak of it. This word is used with remarkable consistency of the land of Canaan, of the Jew's own land, and of the fruits of the land. It occurs in Gen. 28:15, "I will bring thee again into this land," where it is in contrast with "all the families of the earth." In Gen. 47:20 we read, "Joseph bought all the land [i.e., *soil*, 'Ădâmâh, 127] of Egypt for Pharaoh . . . so the land [i.e., the whole territory, 'Erets, 776] became Pharaoh's." Other instances where the two words occur in juxtaposition are Lev. 20:24; Deut. 29:28; II Kings 25:21; Jer. 16:15; 23:7, 8; Ezek. 7:2; 12:19; 33:24. In these passages 'Ădâmâh (127) is used in a peculiar sense, to mark Israel's "own land," while 'Erets (776) is used more generally of the territory of the Canaanites or of some other people.

'Ădâmâh (127) is used in Deut. 21:1, 23, with regard to the defilement of the land caused by the presence of a slain body, or of a body that remained unburied. It was regarded as holy or sacred, and death was a defilement because it was the outward and visible sign of sin.

In the passages that relate to the restoration of Israel to their native soil 'Ădâmâh (127) is consistently used. See Isa. 14:1, 2; Jer. 16:15; Ezek. 11:17; 34:13, 27; 36:24; 37:12, 14, 21; Amos 9:15; Zech. 2:12.

'Ădâmâh (127) is rendered *earth* about fifty times, and always in the sense above designated, as *ground* or *soil*. Thus it is used of the beast of the earth (Gen. 1:25); of Cain being cursed from the earth, so that it should not yield its fruit to him (Gen. 4:11); of the face of the earth (Gen. 6:1, 7); of rain falling on the earth (Gen. 7:4); of the blessing to be given to all the families of the earth (Gen. 12:3; 28:14). Compare its usage in Exod. 10:6. In Exod. 20:24 it is used of the "altar of earth," a point interesting to be observed, as making the soil on which man lives and from which he takes his name a participator with the rite of sacrifice. Perhaps it was for an altar that Naaman asked for two mules' burden of soil (II Kings 5:17). 'Ădâmâh (127) is also used of the earth that was put on a man's head as a mark of sorrow (I Sam. 4:12). It occurs with touching significance in Ps. 146:4, "His breath goeth forth, he returneth to his earth; in that very day his thoughts perish."

In Isa. 24:21, where we read, "The LORD shall punish the host of the high ones that are on high, and the kings of the earth upon the earth," we should have expected to find 'Erets (776). But 'Ădâmâh (127) is used to enforce the contrast between those that dwell on this soil with the inhabitants of other regions. Compare Isa. 45:9, "Let the potsherd strive with the potsherds of the earth," and Amos 3:2, "You only have I known of all the families of the earth."

§2. *The Earth*

The great difficulty that has to be dealt with in translating the word 'Erets (776) is to determine where it is used with reference only to a special territory, such as Canaan, and where it signifies the whole world. When the earth is spoken of in connection with heaven (as in Gen. 1:1; Isa. 49:13; and 65:17), it must have the larger meaning. The same will usually be the case when we read of the ends of the earth (Isa. 52:10), or the whole earth (Mic. 4:13). But in a great number of passages there is nothing but the context or the general analogy of Scripture to guide the translator or interpreter.

The distinction between the narrower and wider meaning of the term is important in considering the account of the Deluge, also in the interpretation of many prophetical passages. Thus in Ps. 37:11

we read, "The meek shall inherit the earth"; but in verse 29, where 'Erets (776) is also used, the A.V. reads, "The righteous shall inherit the land." See also verses 22 and 34. In Isa. 11:9 we read, "The earth shall be full of the knowledge of the LORD"; yet the earlier part of the verse speaks only of God's "holy mountain." In Jer. 22:29 ("O earth, earth, earth") is the prophet appealing to the wide world, or to the land of Canaan? In Isa. 24:1 we read, "Behold, the LORD maketh the earth empty"; verse 3, "The land shall be utterly emptied"; verse 4, "The earth mourneth"; verse 13, "When thus it shall be in the midst of the land," etc. 'Erets (776) is used throughout the chapter, but to what does it refer? Ought it not to be rendered uniformly? Verse 21 seems to imply that it is used in the more extensive sense. In Amos 8:8 we read, "Shall not the land tremble for this?" and in verse 9, "I will darken the earth in the clear day." Zech. 14:9 says, "The LORD shall be king over all the earth," and verse 10 declares, "All the land shall be turned as a plain." Our translators seem almost to have indulged in variety in these passages for the sake of variety, but it is to the confusion of the English reader.

The Greek rendering for 'Ădâmâh (127) is always γῆ (1093). The same word is the most general rendering for 'Erets (776), but we also find χώρα (5561), *territory,* in about fifty passages, and οἰκουμένη (3625), the *inhabited earth,* in nine passages. There are other occasional renderings, but none that call for special notice.

The word for *earth,* in the sense of earthen vessels, potsherds, or potter's clay, is always **Cheres** (חֶרֶשׂ, 2789), except in II Sam. 17:28, where **Yâtsar** (יָצַר, 3335) is used, referring to the vessels being molded. In Dan. 2:10, "There is not a man upon the earth," the word **Yabbesheth** (יַבֶּשֶׁת, 3007) signifies *dry land;* while **Âphâr** (עָפָר, 6083), *dust,* is found in Gen. 26:15; Isa. 2:19; Dan. 12:2; Job 8:19; 28:2; 30:6; and 41:33. In most of these passages holes or cavities in the upper surface of the earth are referred to.

In the N.T., it is to be remembered, as in the O.T., that where the Greek representative of 'Erets (776) is found in contrast or juxtaposition with heaven, we know that it must signify *the earth* as a whole. This would apply to such passages as the following: "Till heaven and earth shall pass" (Matt. 5:18); "Thy will be done in earth, as it is in heaven" (Matt. 18:18).

In some passages the interpretation is in doubt, e.g., Matt. 5:5: "Blessed are the meek: for they shall inherit the earth." Here our Lord is making use of the LXX rendering of Ps. 37:11, in which passage it is natural to suppose that the land of Canaan would be *primarily* referred to. Here, however, the Hebrew word is 'Erets (776), as was noticed above, and thus the larger sense of the word is admissible. In Eph. 6:3, "[That] thou mayest live long on the earth," the Hebrew word quoted (from Exod. 20:12) is 'Ădâmâh (127), and the land of Canaan is primarily meant.

The context in these and other cases is the only means whereby the reader can decide whether by γῆ (*1093*) is signified the soil, the territory, or the world.

§3. *The World*

The general word translated *world* in the A.V. is Têbêl (תֵּבֵל, 8398—Assyrian *tabulu*, dry land). There are a few exceptions. Thus in Isa. 38:11 we read, "I shall behold man no more with the inhabitants of the world." Here the word Chedel (חֶדֶל, 2309) may perhaps signify the place of rest, cessation, forbearance.[1] In Ps. 17:14, "From men of the world," and 49:1, "Inhabitants of the world," we find the word Cheled (חֶלֶד, 2465), which may refer to the transitory state of things in this world that "passeth away." It is rendered *age* or *time* in Job 11:17; Ps. 39:5; and 89:47. 'Erets (776) is used in Ps. 22:27; Isa. 23:17; 62:11; and Jer. 25:26. 'Ôwlâm (עוֹלָם, 5769) is found in Ps. 73:12, "These are the ungodly, who prosper in the world"; Eccles. 3:11, "He hath set the world in their heart"; and in Isa. 45:17; 64:4.

By Têbêl (8398) is signified, first, the solid material on which man dwells, and that was formed, founded, established, and disposed by God; and secondly, the inhabitants thereof. It is usually rendered οἰκουμένη (*3625*) in the LXX, never κόσμος (*2889*), which was originally used only to denote *order* and *ornament* but had acquired a new meaning in our Lord's time.

The origin of the word is a little doubtful. A word spelled similarly, and used in Lev. 18:23 and other passages, signifies *pollution, confusion,* or *dispersion* (from בָּלַל, 1101). It is supposed, however, by Gesenius to be connected with the root Yâbal (יָבַל, 2986), *to flow,* and to indicate the stream of people with which the world is flooded.

In only one or two passages does the word Têbêl (8398) or

---

1. We find the root rendered *forbear* in Ezek. 3:27; *frail* in Ps. 39:4; and *rejected* in Isa. 53:3.

οἰκουμένη (3625) appear to refer to a limited portion of the earth. Perhaps Isa. 24:4 may be mentioned as an example.

The expression "round world" (which occurs in the P.B. version in Ps. 18:15; 89:12; 93:2; 96:10; and 98:8) simply stands for Têbêl (8398). It is to be found in Coverdale's Bible, and is traceable to the old Latin version, *Orbis terrarum* (*the circle of lands*, i.e., *the world*), the earth being regarded by the ancients as a disk, though not as a globe.

In the N.T. the word οἰκουμένη (3625) is certainly used of the Roman Empire in Luke 2:1, and perhaps in the quotation in Rom. 10:18, where the larger sense of the word implied in the Psalms could hardly be intended. In other passages we must understand the word as signifying all the earth, e.g., in Matt. 24:14; Acts 17:31; Heb. 1:6; 2:5. Prophetic students have a right to either interpretation in Rev. 3:10; 12:9; and 16:14. But the Roman use of the word is not so likely to be adopted by John as the Jewish.

§4. *Heaven*

The Hebrew word generally in use to represent the heavens and also the air is **Shâmayim** (שָׁמַיִם, 8064—Assyrian *samami*). Sometimes it signifies the atmosphere immediately surrounding the earth, in which the fowls of "the air" fly. Sometimes it is used of the space in which the clouds are floating. In other places it refers to the vast expanse through which the stars are moving in their courses. Shâmayim (8064) is also opposed to **Sheʾôwl** (שְׁאוֹל, 7585), the one being regarded as a place of exaltation, the other of degradation; the one being represented as the dwellingplace of the Most High and of the angels of God, the other as the abode of the dead.

In Ps. 77:18, where we read, "The voice of thy thunder was in the heaven," the word **Galgal** (גַּלְגַּל, 1534) probably signifies a *whirlwind*. The LXX has ἐν τῷ τροχῷ (1722, 3588, 5164—*in the wheel* or *whirlwind*). In Ps. 68:4, "Extol him that rideth upon the heavens," we find the word **Ărâbâh** (עֲרָבָה, 6160—Assyrian *erbu*), which generally means a *desert*; hence *clouds of sand*, and *clouds* generally. In Ps. 89:6 and 37, the word **Shachaq** (שַׁחַק, 7834), rendered *heavens*, originally signifies a cloud of fine particles; compare our expression "a cloud of dust." In Isa. 5:30, "The light is darkened in the heavens thereof," our margin has "in the destructions thereof"; the Hebrew word **Ărîyphîym** (עֲרִיפִים, 6183) used here probably signifies *darkness*.

In all but these few passages the word **Shâmayim** (8064) is used where *heaven* is found in the A.V. It is to be noticed that the form of the word is neither singular nor plural, but dual. This may be only an ancient form of the plural, but it is supposed by some commentators to imply the existence of a lower and an upper heaven, or of a physical and spiritual heaven—"the heaven and the heaven of heavens." The original idea represented by the root is generally considered to be height, and if this is a right conjecture, the word fairly answers to its Greek equivalent οὐρανός (3772), and to its English translation *heaven*. It includes all space that is not occupied by the terrestrial globe, and extends from the air we breathe and the winds we feel around us to the firmament or expanse that contains the innumerable stars. This it includes, and exceeds; for where our intellect ceases to operate, and fails to find a limit to the extension of space, here faith comes in. And while before the eye of the body there is spread out an infinity of space, the possession of a super-material nature brings us into communion with a Being whose nature and condition cannot adequately be described by terms of locality or extension. The heavens and the heaven of heavens cannot contain Him. The countless stars are not only known and numbered by Him, but are called into existence and fixed in their courses by His will and wisdom. Wherever He is, there the true heaven is; and the glories of the firmament faintly shadow forth the ineffable bliss that those must realize who are brought into relationship with Him.

While God is regarded as the God or King of heaven, we read in the prophecy of Jeremiah of the "queen of heaven" (7:18; 44:17, 18, 19, 25). In the margin this title is rendered "frame of heaven" (מְלָאכָה, 4399, for מַלְכָּה, 4436). If the former is the right interpretation, the heathen goddess Astarte or Venus is probably referred to; if otherwise, the prophet is reprobating the worship of the frame, structure, or workmanship of heaven, or, in other words, of the stars, as a substitute for the worship of Him who created all these things.

The usage of the word *heaven* in the N.T. generally answers to that which is to be traced through the Hebrew Bible, but more stress is laid on the spiritual heaven, on the Father who is there, and on the Son who came from heaven, and who has returned thither to remain hidden from the eye of man until the time of the restitution.

There are, indeed, the same distinct spheres designated by the word οὐρανός (3772) in the N.T. as by **Shâmayim** (8064) in the O.T.

There is the air, or dwellingplace of the fowls of the air (Matt. 6:26); there is also the vast space in which the stars are moving (Acts 2:19); but in by far the greater number of passages *heaven* signifies the dwellingplace of the Most High and the abode of the angelic hosts. The titles "kingdom of God" and "kingdom of heaven" are really identical in their signification, though presenting the truth in slightly varied aspects. God is the King of heaven, and His will is done by all its angelic inhabitants. When the kingdom of *God* is spoken of as coming upon earth, we are to understand a state of things in which the subjection of man's will to God is to be completed and the destruction of all that is contrary to God's will, whether in things physical or in things spiritual, is to be accomplished. When, on the other hand, it is the kingdom of *heaven* that is announced, we are to understand that the organization of the human race in whole or part, and also perhaps their dwellingplace, will be rendered harmonious with the other portions of the family of that heavenly Father in whose house are many mansions.

The popular phraseology about "going to heaven" represents the truth, but certainly not in the form in which it is generally presented in Scripture. We rarely read that the godly will go *to heaven*, either at death or after the resurrection. We are rather told of a kingdom being set up *on earth*, of a heavenly city descending from above and taking up its abode in the new or renewed earth.

§5. *The Host of Heaven*

In Deut. 4:19 the people of Israel were specially warned lest they should lift up their eyes unto heaven, and when they saw the sun, and the moon, and the stars, all *the host of heaven* (τὸν κόσμον τοῦ οὐρανοῦ—3588, 2889, 3588, 3772), should be driven to worship them and serve them. Death by stoning was to be the punishment of any such departure from the true God (Deut. 17:3, 5). To what an extent the people failed in this matter, and how grievously they suffered in consequence, will be seen by referring to II Kings 17:16; 21:3, 5; II Chron. 33:3, 5; Jer. 8:1–3; 19:12, 13. Not only was the host of heaven worshiped, but altars were set up in honor of the stars even in the precincts of the Temple. What a contrast with this impiety is presented by the opening words of the prayer of the Levites recorded in Neh. 9:6:

Thou, even thou, art LORD alone; thou hast made heaven, the heaven of heavens, with all their host, the earth, and all things that are therein, the seas, and all that is therein, and thou preservest them all; and the host of heaven worshippeth thee.

The folly of worshiping the host of heaven is forcibly illustrated by the fact that as the heavenly bodies owe their structure and continuance to God, so will they perish when He withdraws His hand. "All the host of heaven shall be dissolved, and the heavens shall be rolled together as a scroll: and all their host shall fall down, as the leaf falleth off from the vine, and as a falling fig from the fig tree" (Isa. 34:4). This passage is taken up and adopted by our Lord, who says, "After that tribulation, the sun shall be darkened, and the moon shall not give her light, and the stars of heaven shall fall, and the powers that are in heaven [i.e., the host of heaven] shall be shaken" (Mark 13:24, 25). Here the expression *powers* ($\delta\upsilon\nu\acute{\alpha}\mu\epsilon\iota\varsigma$, *1411*) is the usual rendering adopted by the LXX for host ($\acute{\eta}$ $\delta\acute{\upsilon}\nu\alpha\mu\iota\varsigma$ $\tauο\hat{\upsilon}$ $ο\grave{\upsilon}\rho\alpha\nuο\hat{\upsilon}$—*3588, 1411, 3588, 3772*).

In I Kings 22:19 Micaiah says, "I saw the LORD sitting on his throne, and all the host of heaven [$\acute{\eta}$ $\sigma\tau\rho\alpha\tau\iota\grave{\alpha}$ $\tauο\hat{\upsilon}$ $ο\grave{\upsilon}\rho\alpha\nuο\hat{\upsilon}$—*3588, 4756, 3588, 3772*] standing by him on his right hand and on his left." The context shows us that the prophet was speaking not of the physical but of the spiritual heaven, and that by the host of heaven he meant the intelligent beings who exist in that spiritual sphere in which God dwells and whose business it is to carry out His purposes of mercy and of wrath. With this passage may be compared the sublime vision contained in Rev. 19:11-14, when the heavens are opened and the seer beholds the Faithful and True One called the Word of God riding on a white horse: "and the armies which were in heaven [$\tau\grave{\alpha}$ $\sigma\tau\rho\alpha\tau\epsilon\acute{\upsilon}\mu\alpha\tau\alpha$ $\tau\grave{\alpha}$ $\grave{\epsilon}\nu$ $\tau\hat{\omega}$ $ο\grave{\upsilon}\rho\alpha\nu\hat{\omega}$—*3588, 4753, 3588, 1722, 3588, 3772*] followed him upon white horses, clothed in fine linen."

§6. *The Firmament*

The Hebrew word **Râqîy'a** (רָקִיעַ, *7549*) stands for *firmament*, i.e., the space in which the stars are set (Gen. 1:7, 8). Our interpretation of the word is derived from the Greek $\sigma\tau\epsilon\rho\acute{\epsilon}\omega\mu\alpha$ (*4733*), through the Latin *firmamentum*. It means that which is *fixed* and *steadfast*, rather than that which is solid. The word once occurs in the N.T., namely, in Col. 2:5, "the steadfastness [$\sigma\tau\epsilon\rho\acute{\epsilon}\omega\mu\alpha$, *4733*] of your faith in Christ"; and other forms of the root are used in the same way. The application of this word to the heavenly bodies is simple and beautiful: they are not fickle and uncertain in their movements, but are regulated by a law that they cannot pass over. "By the word of the LORD were the heavens made [ἐστερεώθησαν, 4732]; and all the host of them by the breath of his mouth" (Ps. 33:6). "I have made the earth, and created man upon it: I, even my hands, have stretched out [ἐστερέωσα, 4733] the heavens, and all their host have I commanded" (Isa. 45:12). "Mine hand also hath laid the foundation of the earth, and my right hand hath spanned [ἐστερέωσε, 4733] the heavens" (Isa. 48:13).

The Hebrew word is derived from **Râqa'** (רָקַע, 7554), *to spread out.* This verb is found in Job 37:18, "Hast thou with him spread out the sky, which is strong, and as a molten looking glass?"; Ps. 136:6, "To him that stretched out the earth above [or over] the waters"; Isa. 42:5, "He that spread forth the earth"; 44:24, "That spreadeth abroad the earth by myself."

The *firmament,* then, is that which is spread or stretched out— hence an *expanse.* This is the rendering received by many at the present time. Perhaps, guided partly by this usage of the Hebrew word and partly by the rendering of the LXX, we may attach two ideas to the term, namely, *extension* and *fixity,* or (to combine them in one) *fixed space.* The interplanetary spaces are measured out by God, and, though the stars are ever moving, they generally preserve fixed relative positions; their movements are not erratic, not in straight lines, but in orbits, and thus, though ever changing, they are always the same.

24

Destruction, Death, Hell

§1. *Various Words Signifying Destruction*

The destiny of man after death is the most serious of all questions. If Scripture invariably prophesied smooth things, we should readily accept its verdict. But there are passages in the N.T. that point in another direction. Hence the necessity of studying the O.T. terminology on the subject.

More than fifty Hebrew words have been rendered *destroy, destruction,* or *perish.* Some of them need only a brief mention, but others are of greater importance.

'Êyd (אֵיד, 343) is occasionally so rendered, as in Job 18:12 and Prov. 1:27. It is usually rendered *calamity,* and signifies that which oppresses and straitens, the "tribulation and anguish" of Rom. 2:9. 'Âçaph (אָסַף, 622), which occurs in I Sam. 15:6, means *to gather,* and we might render the passage, "lest I include you with them." Compare Ps. 26:9; also Zeph. 1:2, 3. 'Âsham (אָשַׁם, 816) is found in Ps. 5:10, "destroy thou them," i.e., condemn them or deal with them as guilty. In II Chron. 22:7, the *destruction* of Ahaziah is literally his *treading down;* and in Isa. 10:25, the destruction of the Assyrians means their being brought to nought or wasted away (so far as this world is concerned). In Prov. 21:7, "The robbery of the wicked shall destroy them," the verb Gârar (גָּרַר, 1641) means *to saw, sweep away,* or *drag down.* The destruction of the seed royal by Athaliah (II Chron. 22:10) is described by a word that signifies *the infliction of a pestilence* (דֶּבֶר, 1698); compare the use of the words *pestilent* and *pestilential* in our own language. Dakkâ' (דַּכָּא, 1793—Assyrian *dakû*), *to dash in pieces* or *crush*, is used in Job 6:9; 34:25; Ps. 90:3, "Thou turnest man to destruction."

Bâla' (בָּלַע, 1104—Assyrian *balû*), *to swallow up*, is used several times, e.g., in Job 2:3, "to destroy him without cause"; Ps. 55:9, "Destroy, O Lord, and divide their tongues"; Isa. 25:7, 8, "He will destroy in this mountain the face of the covering cast over all people, and the veil that is spread over all nations. He will swallow up death in victory." Here the same word is rendered *destroy* in one verse and *swallow up* in the other; the last clause might be rendered, "He will utterly destroy death." See R.V.

Dâmâh (דָּמָה, 1820), *to be silent*, or *to cease*, is rendered *destroy* in Ezek. 27:32, "What city is like Tyrus, like the destroyed in the midst of the sea?"; and in Hos. 4:5, 6, "I will destroy thy mother. My people are destroyed for lack of knowledge." We might perhaps give a more literal rendering here, and say, "My people are silenced for lack of knowledge."

In Deut. 7:23 and in I Sam. 5:9, 11, the word **Hûwm** (הוּם, 1949) is supposed to signify *commotion* or *confusion*; the similar word **Hâmam** (הָמַם, 2000), signifying *discomfiture*, is found in Exod. 23:27; Deut. 2:15; and Ps. 144:6. **Hârag** (הָרַג, 2026), *to kill*, is used in Ps. 78:47, "He destroyed their vines with hail." **Hâraç** (הָרַס, 2040), *to tear down*, occurs in I Chron. 20:1; of the destruction of Rabbah, in Ps. 11:3; of the destruction of foundations, in Isa. 14:17; of the destruction of cities, in Isa. 19:18, where we read of "the city of destruction," or, as the margin has it, *of Heres*, or *of the sun*." It also occurs in Ps. 28:5 and Isa. 49:17, 19.

Châbal (חָבַל, 2254), *to bind*, is used in Ezra 6:12; Prov. 13:13; Eccles. 5:6; Mic. 2:10; Isa. 10:27, "the yoke shall be destroyed because of the anointing"; 54:16, "I have created the waster to destroy"; Dan. 2:44, "In the days of these kings shall the God of heaven set up a kingdom, which shall never be destroyed"; 4:23, "Hew the tree down, and destroy it"; 6:26; 7:14.

In Prov. 31:8, the persons described as "appointed to destruction" are literally *sons of change* or *passing away* (חֲלוֹף, 2475—Assyrian *khalafu*). **Chârab** (חָרַב, 2717), *to dry up*, occurs in Judg. 16:24, "the destroyer of our country"; and in II Kings 19:17; Ezra 4:15; Ps. 9:6, "Destructions are come to a perpetual end." The exhaustion of a country, city, or individual is evidently referred to in these passages.

In seven passages in the Proverbs destruction is literally a "breaking up" (מְחִתָּה, 4288); in Ps. 74:8, "Let us destroy them altogether," the idea of violent dealing (יָנָה, 3238) is implied; in Exod. 15:9, the verb signifies *to take possession* (יָרַשׁ, 3423), and the passage is rendered in the margin, "My hand shall repossess them." In Job 21:20, *calamity* (פִּיד, 3589) is represented; while in Job 9:22; Lev. 26:44; and II Chron. 31:1, **Kâlâh** (כָּלָה, 3615), *to finish, to complete,* and so *to bring to an end,* is used. **Kârath** (כָּרַת, 3772), *to cut off,* is rendered *destroy* in Exod. 8:9; Lev. 26:22; Judg. 4:24; and I Kings 15:13. **Mûwl** (מוּל, 4135), which also signifies *to cut off,* is found in Ps. 118:10–12; **Kâthath** (כָּתַת, 3807), *to beat,* in Deut. 1:44; II Chron. 15:6; and Job 4:20; **Mûwth** (מוּת, 4191—Assyrian *matu*), *to die,* in II Sam. 20:19 and Job 33:22; and **Mâchâh** (מָחָה, 4229), *to blot out,* in Gen. 6:7; 7:4, 23, in the history of the Deluge; also in Judg. 21:17 and Prov. 31:3.

In Prov. 15:25, "The LORD will destroy the house of the proud," the word **Nâçach** (נָסַח, 5255—Assyrian *nasakhu*) signifies *to pluck up,* and hence *to root out.* In Job 19:26, "Though after my skin, even this body, is destroyed" (R.V.), the word **Nâqaph** (נָקַף, 5362) means *to cut down.* In Isa. 42:14, "I will destroy" is literally "I will make desolate" (נָשַׁם, 5395). In Ps. 9:6, "Thou hast destroyed cities," **Nâtha'** (נָתַע, 5421), *to tear,* is used; and in Exod. 34:13; Deut. 7:5; Job 19:10; Ps. 52:5; and Ezek. 26:12, **Nâthats** (נָתַץ, 5422), *to tear down* or *beat down,* is found. **Tsâdâh** (צָדָה, 6658), *to cut down,* is the word in Zeph. 3:6. **Çâphâh** (סָפָה, 5595), *to scrape,* is found in Gen. 18:23, 24, "Wilt thou also destroy the righteous with the wicked? . . . wilt thou also destroy and not spare the place for the fifty righteous?" It is also found in I Chron. 21:12 and Ps. 40:14.

Shâbar (שָׁבַר, 7665—Assyrian *sabaru*), *to shiver* or *break in pieces,* is rendered *destroy* about thirty times, e.g., in Prov. 16:18, "Pride goeth before destruction"; 29:1, "He, that being often reproved hardeneth his neck, shall suddenly be destroyed, and that without remedy"; Isa. 1:28, "The destruction of the transgressors and of the sinners shall be together"; 59:7, "Wasting and destruction are in their paths"; 60:18, "Violence shall no more be heard in thy land, wasting nor destruction within thy borders." **She'îyâh** (שְׁאִיָּה, 7591), *desolation,* occurs in Ps. 73:18 and Isa. 24:12; the word **Shôw'âh** (שׁוֹאָה, 7722) has the same meaning in Ps. 35:8, 17; and 63:9; **Shâmêm** (שָׁמֵם, 8074), *to lay waste,* or *to be astonished,* in Eccles. 7:16 and Hos. 2:12; **Shâçâh** (שָׁסָה, 8154), *to spoil,* in Jer. 50:11; **Shâkôl** (שָׁכֹל, 7921), *to bereave,* in Deut. 32:25. **Shâdad** (שָׁדַד, 7703), *to deal violently,* is rendered *destroy* ten times, e.g., in Ps. 137:8, "O daughter of Babylon, who art to be destroyed" (P. B. version, "wasted with misery"); Hos.

7:13, "Destruction unto them! because they have transgressed against me"; Joel 1:15, "The day of the Lord is at hand, and as a destruction from the Almighty shall it come."

The Chaldean word used of the destruction of the temple by Nebuchadnezzar in Ezra 5:12 is **Çâthar** (סְתַר, 5641), which in Hebrew means *to hide*. In Ps. 17:4, the word P^eriyts (פְּרִיץ, 6530) signifies a *violent man*; in Job 30:24 and 31:29, we find Pîyd (פִּיד, 6365), *calamity*; in Prov. 13:19, 21, Ra' (רַע, 7451), *evil*; in Ezek. 7:25, Q^ephâdâh (קְפָדָה, 7089), *cutting off*; in Jer. 46:20, the word for destruction is taken from the nipping (קֶרֶץ, 7169) of the gadfly. Qeteb (קֶטֶב, 6986) or **Qôteb** (6987) *contagion*, is found in Deut. 32:24; Ps. 91:6; and Hos. 13:14, "O death, I will be thy destruction." **Tsâmath** (צָמַת, 6789), *to cut off*, is the word used in II Sam. 22:41; Ps. 18:40; 69:4; 73:27; 101:8.

In Num. 24:17 we read, "A sceptre shall rise out of Israel, and shall smite the corners [or smite through the princes] of Moab, and destroy all the children of Sheth." The word Qûwr (קוּר, 6979), here rendered *destroy*, is somewhat doubtful. Some take it as meaning *dig*—hence *dig through* or *spoil*; others consider that it is used in a favorable sense of "building up the wall" of Sheth; but see Isa. 22:5, where it means *to break down* a wall.

§2. *The Root* Âbad

The words hitherto noticed, though very numerous, are used in only a few passages and do not play a conspicuous part in Scripture. They point to destruction as a calamity, as a work of breaking down or tearing up, as an act of violence, or as a deed of desolation. They apply to nations, cities, and individuals, and are used in just such senses as we should give them in ordinary history, without at all referring to the destiny of the individual in any state of existence beyond this world. Four words, however, remain to be considered, each of which is used in a great number of passages, and with some important variations of meaning.

Âbad (אָבַד, 6—Assyrian *abadu*), *to perish*, and in its causative form *to destroy*, is largely used throughout the O.T. This word is rendered *perish* in about a hundred passages. When used of persons it generally signifies *death*, when used of lands it implies *desolation*. The same is the general state of the case in its various forms with regard to its Greek equivalents ἀπόλλυμι (622), ἀπώλεια (684), and ὄλεθρος (3639). The name *Abaddon* (Rev. 9:11) is rendered *Apollyon,* the destroyer.

It is applied to the case of Korah's company, who "perished from among the congregation" (Num. 16:33); to the Amalekite nation, which should "perish for ever" (Num. 24:20, see also verse 24). It is held out as a threat to Israel that they should "utterly perish from off the land" if they became idolatrous (Deut. 4:26; contrast 30:18); it is used of the nation's ancestor, "a Syrian ready to perish" (Deut. 26:5). Esther uses it with regard to her apprehension of death as the alternative of success, "If I perish, I perish" (Esther 4:16). It is applied to the memory of the wicked, which dies out of the minds of their survivors (Job 18:17), and to the disappearance of the wicked man from the earth (20:7); it is used of men perishing for want of clothing (31:19). It is applied to the way or course taken by the wicked in contrast with the way of the righteous (Ps. 1:6). It is used of the heathen (as such) perishing out of the land (Ps. 10:16), of the wicked perishing before the presence of God as wax melts before the fire (68:2), of the heavens perishing while God endures (102:26), of man's thoughts perishing when he dies (146:4).

In Eccles. 7:15 'Âbad (6) is applied to a just man perishing in his righteousness. And in Isa. 57:1, 2, we read, "The righteous perisheth, and no man layeth it to heart: and merciful men are taken away, none considering that the righteous is taken away from the evil to come. He shall enter into peace." These passages are important, showing that the perishing of the outer man in death is perfectly consistent with entrance into peace.

The passages that have been cited are fair samples of the whole. They show that the word refers to the death of the righteous or the wicked; to the downfall and dissolution of nations; to the desolation of countries; to the withering away of herbage and crops; to the fading away of strength, hope, wisdom, knowledge, and wealth. The word is applied to man with reference to his whole position on earth, while his future destiny is left apparently untouched by it.

A brief examination of the usage of the active voice where it is rendered *destroy* or *destruction* will suffice. The word is applied to the destruction of temples, images, and pictures (Num. 33:52; Deut. 12:33); to defeat (Josh. 7:7); to national overthrow (Deut. 28:51); and to the taking away of life, whether by the hand of man or by the agency of God (II Kings 10:19; Exod. 10:7; Lev. 23:30; Deut. 7:10, 20; Job 28:22).

In Job 26:6 we read, "Hell [Sh*e*'ôwl, 7585] is naked before him, and destruction hath no covering"; and in Prov. 15:11, "Hell [She'ôwl, 7585] and destruction are before the LORD." These words apparently refer to the locality or condition of those who have died or have been destroyed. It is implied that although, so far as this world is concerned, they have perished, yet they are still in a state of existence and are within God's cognizance.

In Ps. 88:10–12 the question is heard, "Wilt thou shew wonders to the dead? shall the dead arise and praise thee? Shall thy loving-kindness be declared in the grave? or thy faithfulness in destruction? Shall thy wonders be known in the dark? and thy righteousness in the land of forgetfulness?" Here the dead, the grave or sepulcher, the state of destruction, the dark, and the land of forgetfulness, are synonymous; and the Psalmist, in his longing for present help, urges God not to put off His lovingkindness until that time when (so far as this life is concerned) it will be too late.

Âbad (6) is frequently rendered *lose*, e.g., in the following texts: Exod. 22:9; Lev. 6:3, 4; Deut. 22:3; and I Sam. 9:3, 20, with reference to a lost ox, sheep, or garment. In Ps. 119:176 it assumes a moral significance, "I have gone astray like a lost sheep; seek thy servant, for I do not forget thy commandments." In Jer. 50:6 we read, "My people hath been lost sheep: their shepherds have caused them to go astray." In Ezek. 34:4, 16, the LORD God says, "Neither have ye sought that which was lost. . . . I will seek that which was lost."

§3. *Destruction as Taught in the N.T.*

The word ὄλεθρος (3639) is found four times in the N.T. In I Cor. 5:5 "the destruction of the flesh" is spoken of. Here reference seems to be made to the special temporal chastisements that were inflicted in the apostolic age, and a contrast is drawn between the destruction of the flesh now and the salvation of the spirit in the day of Christ. In the other three passages reference is made to the punishment of the ungodly (see I Thess. 5:3; II Thess. 1:9; I Tim. 6:9).

Ἀπώλεια (684) in the N.T. specially represents the lot of those who go on the broad path (Matt. 7:13), who set themselves against the Gospel (Phil. 1:28), who live a carnal life (Phil. 3:19), who yield to lusts and covetousness (I Tim. 6:9), who draw back from Christ (Heb. 10:39), who deny the Lord that bought them (II Pet. 2:1, 3[1]), and wrest the Scriptures (II Pet. 3:16), and are, in a word, ungodly (II Pet. 3:7).

---

1. The A.V. has failed to preserve the connection between the *destructive* heresies and the *destruction* that ensues. See R.V.

The infliction of this ἀπώλεια (684) is synchronous with the Day of Judgment and the burning of the heaven and earth that now are (II Pet. 3:7). The whole event is prefigured by the destruction that came upon the earth at the Deluge, when the then world perished (ἀπώλετο, 622), and also by the destruction of Sodom and Gomorrah. The word also occurs in John 17:12, of Judas, the son of perdition; of another son of perdition in II Thess. 2:3; in Rev. 17:8, 11, of the beast; also in Acts 8:20; 25:16; and Rom. 9:22.

The verb ἀπόλλυμι (622) is applied to the waste of ointment (Matt. 26:8), to the destruction of physical objects, e.g., wineskins (Matt. 9:17), gold (I Pet. 1:7), food (John 6:27), and the hair of the head (Luke 21:18). In these cases it is not annihilation that is spoken of, but such injury as makes the object practically useless for its original purpose. It is applied to the destruction of the world in II Pet. 3:6 in exactly the same sense, for as the world was destroyed at the Deluge, so shall it be hereafter; it will be rendered useless as a habitation for man. Nevertheless, as after the first destruction it was restored, so it may be after the second. Again, the word is applied to perishing or being destroyed from off the face of the earth in death, when the physical frame that is the temple of life becomes untenanted; and a contrast is drawn between the power of those who can bring about the death of the body and of Him who can destroy both body and soul in Gehenna. Death is spoken of in this sense in Matt. 2:13; 8:25; 12:14; 21:41; 22:7; 26:52; 27:20 (and probably in Matt. 18:14; Rom. 2:12; 14:15; and I Cor. 8:11). The destruction of the body is compared to the disintegration of the seed that falls into the ground and dies. It is dismemberment and dissolution, and renders the body useless for the time being, so far as its original purpose is concerned, but it is not annihilation. The use of the word in the argument in I Cor. 15:18 is worthy of note. It here implies that, physically speaking, the Christian has perished, if Christ be not risen. There is not a word here about annihilation of the *person* (which would continue in Hades), but simply of the blotting out of *existence in the body.* See Isa. 51:1, 2, quoted above.

The word is also largely used in a moral sense, with respect to the inner man, as the opposite of salvation. It is applied to those "lost sheep" whom the Good Shepherd died to save (Matt. 18:11; Luke 15:32; cf. Isa. 53:6). All men are regarded as morally *destroyed,* i.e., they have failed to carry out the intention for which the race was called into being. To save them from this condition, God sent

His Son, and caused Him to be lifted up like the serpent in the wilderness (John 3:15, 16), not being willing that any should *perish*, but that all should come to repentance (II Pet. 3:9). Those who reject this salvation have contracted a new responsibility, and are, in a new sense, in the way of destruction ($\dot{\alpha}\pi o\lambda\lambda v\mu\acute{e}vo\iota\varsigma$, 622—I Cor. 1:18; II Cor. 2:15; 4:3; II Thess. 2:10). This final destruction affects evil spirits as well as men. We cannot comprehend what will be the nature of this destruction that affects the *spirit* or *person;* but the reading of such words as those uttered by the Lord in Matt. 10:28, 39 (as well as Matt. 16:25 and Luke 9:25), impresses the mind with the idea of the utter rejection and infinite degradation that shall be the lot of those who judge themselves unworthy of eternal life. Not only creation, but also redemption, has failed its purpose with them.

§4. *The Root* Shâchath

Shâchath (שָׁחַת, 7843—Assyrian *sakhatu*), a word that especially marks dissolution or corruption, is rendered *destroy* in about a hundred places. It first occurs in Gen. 6:13, 17, and 9:11, 15, with reference to both the moral corruption and also to the physical destruction of all that was living of the earth; and of the earth itself, which, as Peter said, "perished" (II Pet. 3:6). It is next used of the destruction of Sodom and Gomorrah (Gen. 13:10; 18:28; 19:13, 14, 29), a destruction that is regarded in both the O.T. and N.T. as a sample of the punishment of the ungodly. It is used in connection with the destruction of the firstborn in Egypt (Exod. 12:23), of trees (Deut. 20:19, 20), of the increase of the earth (Judg. 6:4, 5), of men in battle (Judg. 20:21, etc.), of cities (I Sam. 23:10), of nations (II Kings 8:19; 13:23).

In Ps. 55:23 we read, "Thou . . . shalt bring them down into the pit of destruction: bloody and deceitful men shall not live out half their days." This is a sample of a large class of passages in which wickedness is represented as bringing an untimely or violent death as its consequence. God, on the contrary, redeems the life of His people from destruction; that is to say, He prolongs their days (Ps. 103:4). This word is also used in Dan. 9:26, "The people of the prince that shall come shall destroy the city and the sanctuary"; and in Hos. 13:9, "O Israel, thou hast destroyed thyself, but in me is thy help." Lastly, the promise for the restored Jerusalem is, "They shall not hurt nor destroy in all my holy mountain" (Isa. 11:9; 65:25).

The chief LXX rendering of this word is διαφθείρω (1311); we also find in several passages φθείρω (5351), καταφθείρω (2704), ὁλοθρεύω (3645), ἐξολοθρεύω (1842), ἐξαλείφω (1813), and ἀπόλλυμι (622).

The verb διαφθείρω (1311) is used of physical corruption in Luke 12:33; II Cor. 4:16; Rev. 8:9. It is used of moral corruption in I Tim. 6:5, "men corrupted in mind," and Rev. 19:2. It is used in both senses in Rev. 11:18, "To *corrupt* those that are *corrupting* the earth."

The noun is used in only two passages, namely, in Acts 2:27, 31, and 13:34–37, in which Peter and Paul are applying Ps. 16:10 to the fact that our Lord's body was raised before corruption set in.

§5. *The Root* Shâmad

Shâmad (שָׁמַד, 8045), *to consume*, is rendered *destroy* in about eighty passages. It is usually rendered ἐξολοθρεύω[2] (1842), but sometimes ἀπόλλυμι (622). It is applied several times to the destruction of nations, cities, and families by war, especially in the Books of Deuteronomy, Joshua, and I and II Samuel. It is used of the destruction of the wicked in Ps. 37:38 and 92:7, "They shall be destroyed for ever"; 145:20, "All the wicked will he destroy"; Isa. 13:9, "He shall destroy the sinners . . . out of [the land]." The word occurs in Isa. 26:14, "They are dead, they shall not live; they are deceased, they shall not rise: therefore hast thou visited and destroyed them, and made all their memory to perish." This is an expression of the security in the mind of the speaker, who feels that there is no fear of the evil rulers rising again to play the tyrant or to mislead, but it is by no means to be taken as deciding the question whether these ungodly men may or may not have a future awaiting them.

Very often a qualifying expression is used, which shows that the destruction spoken of is relative, not absolute. Thus we find it in Ezek. 14:9, "[I] will destroy him from off the face of the earth"; Hag. 2:22, "I will destroy the strength of the kingdoms of the heathen." This points to the real meaning in other passages.

§6. *The Root* Châram

Châram (חָרַם, 2763) is a religious word of great importance, as will be seen from its usage. It represents the devotion of some object to

---

2. This word occurs only once in the N.T., namely, in Acts 3:23; it is a quotation from Deut. 18:19, but not from the LXX.

destruction or to a sacred use (answering to the double sense of the Latin *sacer*), not for the gratification of any selfish purpose, but as a religious act. It is rendered *devote* or *dedicate* in Lev. 27:21, with reference to a field; in verses 28 and 29 with reference to man, beast, and land; and the direction is given that the devoted object (if an animal) should not be redeemed but put to death. With regard to the land, its devotion rendered it the property of the priest (Num. 18:14; Ezek. 44:29). This word was applied to the destruction of nations, partly because they were regarded as under the Divine doom, and partly also because the substance of the nations destroyed was dedicated to the LORD. Thus we read in Mic. 4:13, "Thou shalt beat in pieces many people: and I will consecrate [or devote] their gain unto the LORD, and their substance unto the LORD of the whole earth." In Ezra 10:8 it is used of the forfeiture of the substance of those who did not come to the Passover, which was accompanied by putting them out of the congregation. Also in Dan. 11:44 it is used of the way in which the king should "make away" many.

The word is used of the *accursed* (i.e., devoted) city and substance of Jericho in Joshua 6 and 7, and in the reference to Achan's conduct in Josh. 22:20 and I Chron. 2:7.

The idols and their silver and gold are also described as *cursed* (i.e., devoted) in Deut. 7:26; 13:17. In Isa. 34:5 the Edomites are described as "the people of [God's] curse," i.e., devoted to destruction by God; and this accounts for the use of the word in II Chron. 20:23, "The children of Ammon and Moab stood up against the inhabitants of Mount Seir utterly to slay . . . them" (i.e., to devote them to destruction); without knowing it, they were carrying out the Divine purpose. In Isa. 43:28 God says, "[I] have given Jacob to the curse," i.e., I have devoted the people to destruction. This was a consequence of their idolatry and rebellion.

This same word, rendered *curse*, is the last word in the solemn conclusion of Malachi's prophecy (4:5, 6), "Behold, I will send you Elijah the prophet before the coming of the great and dreadful day of the LORD: and he shall turn the heart of the fathers to the children, and the heart of the children to their fathers, lest I come and smite the earth with a curse," i.e., lest I come and devote the land of Israel to destruction. Alas! the warning voice of Elijah was not attended to; Jerusalem did not recognize the day of its visitation, and it was smitten with a curse. The country was once more desolated, and the people scattered.

Châram (2763) is rendered *destroy* forty times. In almost all of these places reference is made to the destruction of the natives of Canaan and the surrounding country by Israel. The destruction of nations by Nebuchadnezzar is described by the same word in II Kings 19:11 and Isa. 37:11, perhaps because he was unwittingly carrying out the work of God in his destruction. In Isa. 11:15 the destruction of the land of Egypt by the LORD is referred to; and in Jer. 25:9, the destruction of Judah by the King of Babylon. The word is also used in Zech. 14:11, where the bright promise is given of a time when "there shall be no more utter destruction"—a hope that is carried forward in the N.T. in the words, "There shall be no more curse" (Rev. 22:3).

With regard to the extermination of the Canaanites, the following points may be noticed. *First*, it was not taken in hand to accomplish personal revenge, for Israel had no grudge against Canaan; the people had to be almost goaded into the land. *Second*, it was not done to gain plunder, for all plunder was regarded as Chêrem (2764), *devoted to God*, and in that sense accursed. *Third*, it was not done to gratify thirst for military glory. For the Hebrews were the smallest of nations, and were told beforehand that if they conquered it would not be in their own strength, but in God's. *Fourth*, it was not to be regarded as a reward for merit; they were a rebellious and stiffnecked people, and would have perished in the wilderness had not God remembered His holy covenant. *Fifth*, the extermination of the Canaanites was to be a security against idolatry and demoralization on the part of Israel. *Last*, these nations had filled up the measure of their iniquity, and the Israelites in destroying them were acting magisterially as God's agents.

The most prominent LXX renderings of this word are ἐξολοθρεύω (1842), ἀναθεματίζω (332), ἀνάθεμα (331), and ἀνάθημα (334). The word ἀνάθημα (334) occurs in Luke 21:5, where we read of the temple being adorned with *gifts*. Ἀναθεματίζω (332) is found four times in the N.T. In Mark 14:71 it is used of Peter's cursing, which may have been a calling down of imprecation on his own head. So in Acts 23:12 and 14:21, certain men "bound themselves with an oath," i.e., invited the curse of God in case they failed to carry out their purpose.

It is not easy to fix the exact sense of ἀνάθεμα (331) in the N.T. With the exception of Acts 23:14, it occurs in only five passages, which are in Paul's Epistles. In Gal. 1:8, 9, he says that if anyone should preach any other gospel than he himself has preached to them, that he should be *anathema*. Again, I Cor. 16:22, "If any man love not the Lord Jesus Christ, let him be *anathema*." Paul does not say, let him be put away from among you, but, let him be regarded with aversion as one on whom the Lord will pour down indignation.

Again, the Apostle says (I Cor. 12:3) that whatever spirit calls Jesus *anathema* is not of God. He is here giving a plain test by which the dullest comprehension could discern spirits. Whatever spirit prompts a man to speak of Jesus as an accursed object, that spirit cannot be of God.

The only other passage is Rom 9:3, where Paul seems to have almost prayed or wished that an *anathema* may have come on him from Christ, for the sake of his brethren. In Father Simon's translation of the N.T., the passage reads thus: "I could wish myself to be an anathema, for the sake of Jesus Christ, for my brethren," etc. He considered that the Greek ἀπὸ (575—from) might be rendered *because of*, or *for the sake of*, because the Hebrew preposition that answers to it in the O.T. is frequently used in this sense.

§7. *Meaning and Use of the Word* Sheʾôwl *or Hades*

The state that we call *death*, i.e., the condition consequent on the act of dying, is to be viewed in three aspects: first, there is the *tomb* or sepulcher, the local habitation of the physical frame called **Qeber** (קֶבֶר, 6913—Assyrian *qabru*), Gen. 50:5; secondly, there is the *corruption* whereby the body itself is dissolved, which is represented by the word **Shâchath** (שַׁחַת, 7843), discussed above; and thirdly, there is **Sheʾôwl** (שְׁאוֹל, 7585), which represents the locality or condition of the departed. The A.V. translates **Sheʾowl** (7585) by the words *hell, the grave, the pit*; the LXX usually renders it Ἅδης (86); the R.V. has unfortunately put **Sheʾôwl** (7585) in the O.T., and *Hades* (Ἅδης, 86) in the N.T. The original meaning of the Hebrew and Greek words is uncertain, but the following passages illustrate its usage: Gen. 37:35, "I will go down into the grave unto my son mourning" (compare 42:38; 44:29, 31). I Sam. 2:6, "The Lord killeth, and maketh alive: he bringeth down the grave, and bringeth up." Job 7:9, 10, "As the cloud is consumed and vanisheth away: so he that goeth down to the grave shall come up no more. He shall return no more to his house, neither shall his place know him any more." Job 14:13, "O that thou wouldest hide me in the grave, that thou wouldest keep me secret, until thy wrath be past, that thou wouldest appoint me a set time, and remember me!" Ps. 30:3, "Thou hast brought up my soul from the grave: thou hast kept me alive, that I should not go down to the pit." Ps. 49:14, 15, "Like sheep they are laid in the grave; death shall feed on them; and the upright shall have dominion over them in the morning; and their beauty shall consume in the grave from their dwelling. But God will redeem my soul from the power of the grave: for he shall receive me." Isa. 38:10, "I shall go to the gates of the grave." Hos. 13:14, "I will ransom them from the power [or hand] of the grave; I will redeem them from death: O death, I will be thy plagues; O grave, I will be thy destruction." Num. 16:30, 33, "They go down quick [i.e., alive] into the pit."

The word *hell* stands for She'ôwl (5785) in the following among other passages: Deut. 32:22, "A fire is kindled in mine anger, and shall burn unto the lowest hell." II Sam. 22:6 (see also Ps. 18:5; 116:3), "The sorrows of hell compassed me about; the snares of death prevented me." Job 11:8, "It is as high as heaven; what canst thou do? deeper than hell; what canst thou know?" Job 26:6, "Hell is naked before him, and destruction hath no covering." Ps. 9:17, "The wicked shall be turned into hell, and all the nations that forget God." Ps. 16:10, "Thou wilt not leave my soul in hell; neither wilt thou suffer thine Holy One to see corruption." Ps. 139:8, "If I ascend up into heaven, thou art there: if I make my bed in hell, behold, thou art there." Prov. 5:5, "Her feet go down to death; her steps take hold on hell." Prov. 15:1, "Hell and destruction are before the LORD; how much more then the hearts of the children of men?" Prov. 23:14, "Thou shalt beat him with the rod, and shalt deliver his soul from hell." Prov. 27:20, "Hell and destruction are never full; so the eyes of man are never satisfied." Isa. 14:15,"Yet thou shalt be brought down to hell, to the sides of the pit." Ezek. 31:16, 17 (see also v. 15 above), "I made the nations to shake at the sound of his fall, when I cast him down to hell with them that descend into the pit: and all the trees of Eden, the choice and best of Lebanon, all that drink water, shall be comforted in the nether parts of the earth. They also went down into hell with him unto them that be slain with the sword." Amos 9:2, "Though they dig into hell, thence shall mine hand take them; though they climb up to heaven, thence will I bring them down."

Jonah 2:2, "Out of the belly of hell cried I, and thou heardest my voice."

These are the most notable passages in which the word She'ôwl (7585) occurs. There is no reason to doubt that what the grave or pit is to the body, She'ôwl (7585) is to the soul. It is the *nether world*, and perhaps this would be the best rendering for the word. Not in one single passage is it used in the sense of the place of punishment after the resurrection, concerning which little, if anything, is definitely revealed in the O.T. It is contrasted, as regards its locality, with heaven, the one being regarded as *down* and the other *up*. It is spoken of as an abode for those who have departed from the way of life and have chosen the path of evil. Concerning those who live to the LORD, if they enter it, they are to be delivered from its hand by the power of God; death shall not have dominion over them. It is dark and silent, a place where none can praise God. Its very name possibly signifies a place about which men inquire—an impenetrable hiding place. It involves deprivation of the only kind of existence about which we have any definite knowledge, but some passages where it occurs imply a certain companionship. Though man knows so little about it, She'ôwl (7585) is naked and open before God. He can find men there; He can hide them there; He can redeem them thence.

It is surprising to notice how few references there are to this region or condition in the N.T., it being only mentioned twelve times altogether. In Matt. 11:23 and Luke 10:15, it is used figuratively of the casting down of Capernaum from her exaltation; and in the same way it is said of the Church of Christ, that the gates of Hades shall not prevail against it (Matt. 16:18).

In Luke 16:23 the rich man entered *Hades*, not *Gehenna*.

In Acts 2:27 Peter quotes the sixteenth Psalm, regarding the interpretation of which there is some difference of opinion. The ordinary rendering is, "Thou shalt not leave my soul in hell," but there are critics who consider that the passage, both in the O.T. and N.T., ought to be rendered, "Thou shalt not consign my soul to Hades"; while others are of the opinion that it should be translated, "Thou shalt not leave my dead body in the grave." That the word Nephesh (5315), *soul*, may sometimes be translated *dead body* is true (see Chap. 4); and that the word *Hades* is often translated *grave* we have also seen to be true. So far as the usage of the words, therefore, is concerned, there is no objection to this last rendering;

but the belief of the early Church as to the meaning of the text was in accordance with the more generally received translation.[3]

In I Cor. 15:55, the A.V. has adopted the rendering *grave* for Hades. But, according to many early authorities, the right reading is *death*, not *Hades*. In Rev. 1:18 (and, according to some MSS., in 3:7) the Lord is described as possessing the keys of Hades and death, i.e., it is He that can open the door of the nether world and call forth the dead into resurrection life. In Rev. 6:8 Death and Hades are described as the agents of slaughter; and in Rev. 20:13, 14, they are said to yield up the dead that had been swallowed up by them, and then to be cast into the lake of fire.

§8. *The Word* Gehenna

The word *Gehenna* (as it is transliterated into Greek) means the valley of Hinnom, in Hebrew Gêy-Hinnôm (גֵּי־הִנֹּם, 2011-1516), immediately outside Jerusalem (see Josh. 15:8). In several passages (II Kings 23:10; II Chron. 28:3; and 33:6) it is the scene of degraded idolatrous customs, and in Jer. 19 it is described as not only a center of iniquity, but also a place of retribution. In this sense it was used by the Jews in our Lord's time (see, e.g., Pirke Aboth), and the Lord Himself takes it as the place or condition of punishment. It is only used by Him (Matt. 5:22, 29, 30; 10:28; 18:9; 23:15, 33; Mark 9:43, 47; Luke 12:5) and in James 3:6.

§9. *Death*

The general word to represent dying is Mûwth (מוּת, 4191—Assyrian *mutu*); other words, however, are occasionally used. Thus **Nâphal** (נָפַל, 5307—Assyrian *napalu*), *to fall*, occurs in Gen. 25:18, "He died [or *fell*] in the presence of [or *before*] all his brethren." **Shâdad** (שָׁדַד, 7703—Assyrian *sadadu*), *to destroy*, is found in Judg. 5:27, "There he fell down *dead*" (i.e., destroyed). **Gâva'** (גָּוַע, 1478), *to breathe out* or *expire* (ἐκπνέω, 1606), is used in Gen. 6:17, "Everything that is in the earth shall die"; 7:21; Num. 20:3, "Would God that we had died when our brethren died before the LORD"; 20:29; Job 27:5; 29:18; 36:12; Ps. 88:15; 104:29; Zech. 13:8. This word (ἐκπνέω, 1606) is used only with reference to the death of our Lord in the N.T. (see Mark 15:37, 39; Luke 23:46).

3. See Pearson on the Creed.

Nᵉbêlâh (נְבֵלָה, 5038), a *carcass*, is used in Lev. 7:24, "The fat of the beast *that dieth* of itself," literally "the fat of a carcass." So also in Lev. 17:15; 22:8; Deut. 14:8, 21; Ps. 79:2; Isa. 26:19, "Thy dead men shall live, together with my dead body shall they arise"; Jer. 26:23; 34:20; 36:30; Ezek. 4:14; 44:31. Another word signifying *carcass* (פֶּגֶר, 6297—Assyrian *pagru*), is used in II Chron. 20:24, 25; Jer. 31:40; 33:5; 41:9.

Rᵉphâ'îym (רְפָאִים, 7497—Assyrian *rapu*, to be weak), which in other places is rendered *giants*, is used of the dead in Job 26:5, "Dead things are formed from under the waters, and the inhabitants thereof"; Ps. 88:10, "Wilt thou shew wonders to the dead? shall the dead arise and praise thee?" Prov. 2:18, "For her house inclineth unto death [Mûwth, 4191], and her paths unto the dead." See also Prov. 9:18; 21:16; Isa. 14:9; 26:19.

The Hebrew reduplicated form, "Dying thou shalt die" or "Thou shalt surely die" is found several times in the O.T., and is quoted in the N.T. in Matt. 15:4; Mark 7:10. It has sometimes been supposed that this expression, being so very emphatic, refers to something more than death, and implies the judgment that follows; but this cannot fairly be inferred from the form in question.

§10. *Use of the Word Death in the N.T.*

The word θάνατος (2288, death) answers in the LXX both to Mûwth (4191) and to Deber (דֶּבֶר, 1698), *pestilence*. It has a spiritual signification in the N.T., which calls for a short discussion.

Our Lord said to His disciples (Matt. 16:28), "There are some standing here who shall not taste of death until they see the Son of Man coming in his kingdom." The words are given in another form by Mark (9:1), "There are some . . . who shall not taste of death until they see the kingdom of God come with power." See also Luke 9:27.

The object of this passage was to prepare the minds of the disciples for the grand truth that death, which had been hitherto the terror of the world, was to lose its *taste* or *sting* in the case of those who united themselves to the Lord by faith. Christ Himself was to die, He was to suffer the pains of death, His soul was to be exceeding sorrowful even unto death, but by death He was to overcome him who had the power of death, and to deliver them who through fear of death had been all their lives subject to bondage. He thus introduced a new view of life and death, telling His disciples that he who would save his life by denying the Lord should lose it, while he who was willing to lose his life for the Lord's sake should save it. The Lord would be ashamed of the one on the Great Day, but would confess the other.

The entrance into a new life that takes place through faith in Christ involves death in another sense. It is a cutting off of human nature from its old modes and principles of existence—in other words, it is death to sin. Just as in physical dissolution the body ceases to feel, the heart to beat, the hands to work, and the feet to walk, so in this mystical death the body and all its members are to be no longer servants to sin. The same breach or gulf is to be made between the Christian and sin as there is between a dead man and the outer world in which he used to live and move and have his being. This death is related to the crucifixion of Christ, who "died to sin." The believer is baptized into Christ's death, he dies with Christ, is made conformable to His death, is crucified with Christ (Rom. 6:5; II Cor. 5:14; Gal. 2:19, 20; Col. 2:20; 3:3). In I Pet. 2:24, the word rendered *dead* in the A.V. and R.V., and which only occurs there, signifies severance (ἀπογίνομαι, 581).

The *second death* is mentioned only in the Book of Revelation (2:11; 20:6, 14; 21:8). This is a condition of things that follows after the resurrection. Those that overcome and are faithful unto death shall not suffer injury from it. Those that have part in the first resurrection shall not be subjected to its power. It is thus described in Rev. 20:14, 15, "Death and Hades [i.e., perhaps, those evil spirits that have the power of death and Hades] were cast into the lake of fire. This [i.e., being cast into the lake of fire] is the second death. And whosoever was not found written in the book of life was cast into the lake of fire." Again, we read (21:8) that while he who overcomes shall inherit all things, he who does not overcome, but gives way to instability, unbelief, idolatrous abominations, murder, fornication, witchcraft, idolatry, and lies, shall have his part in the lake that burns with fire and brimstone, which is the second death.

25

Satan, Tempter

Our knowledge of beings of a less material nature than ourselves, whether good or evil, is gained chiefly from Scripture, though an independent belief in the existence of spirits has been widespread for ages. The intrusion of wild, strange, bold, and blasphemous suggestions into the heart of the Christian in his holiest moments is a phenomenon not easily reconcilable with any other theory. Evil is often breathed into men's hearts, they know not how. Their intellects are sharpened while their consciences are deadened. They are impelled the wrong way by an evil force that is *in* them but not *of* them. Fountains of vileness and sin are opened and almost created in their hearts, and they are in danger of being plunged into every kind of violence. Whence are all these things? Are they to be accounted for by natural causes? Is man the sole originator of his wrongdoing? Has he only himself to blame? Scripture tells us that this is not the case. It unfolds to us the fact that the children of men are beset by tempters who try to make men as much as possible like themselves.

§1. *The Words Devil and Satan*

The word **Sâ'îyr** (שָׂעִיר, 8163) is translated *devil* in Lev. 17:7, "They shall no more offer their sacrifices unto devils"; and in II Chron. 11:15, "He ordained him priests for the high places, and for the devils, and for the calves which he had made." In each of these passages the LXX translates Sâ'îyr (8163) *vain things* (μάταια, 3152), by which no doubt they meant idols. The first passage evidently refers to a false worship that had become common in Israel during their stay in Egypt; and the second, pointing as it does to the introduction of idolatry by Jeroboam after his return from Egypt, would lead us in the same direction. The word Sâ'îyr (8163) originally signifies *a goat*, and is usually so rendered; and it is probable that goat worship is referred to in these passages.

Sâ'îyr (8163) is translated *satyr* in Isa. 13:21, "Satyrs shall dance there"; see also Isa. 34:14. In these passages the Sâ'îyr (8163) is introduced in company with the owl and the wild beast of the desert as freely taking up its abode among the ruins of ancient cities. There can be little doubt that goats are referred to in these passages, but the LXX adopts the word *demon* (δαιμόνιον, 1140) in the first of them. The idea that evil spirits haunt desolate places and ruins is a very old one.

The word Shêd (שֵׁד, 7700—Assyrian *sedu*, spirit) is rendered *devil* twice: in Deut. 32:17, "They sacrificed unto devils, not to God"; or, as it is in the margin, "to devils which were not God" (cf. I Cor. 10:20); and in Ps. 106:37, "Yea, they sacrificed their sons and their daughters unto devils."

In each of these cases, and in all places where *devil* occurs in the plural number in the A.V. of the N.T., the Greek word is *demon* (δαιμόνιον, 1140). The same rendering has been given in Ps. 96:5, and in Isa. 65:11, where some form of idolatry is specified in the words "that prepare a table for *that troop*,"[1] or, as it is in the margin, Gad (גַּד, 1408); and in Isa. 34:14, where we read, "The wild beasts of the desert" (צִיִּים, 6728). But little light is thrown by these passages on the real meaning of δαιμόνιον (1140), as understood by the Jewish readers of the LXX in our Lord's time. Its use in the Apocrypha answers to our idea of evil spirits.

Sâṭân (שָׂטָן, 7854) is, properly speaking, an *adversary* or *plotter*, or one who devises means for opposing another. The word is used either in its verbal or substantival form in the following passages: Num. 22:22, "The angel of the Lord stood in the way for an adversary against him." I Sam. 29:4, "Lest in the battle he be an adversary to us." II Sam. 19:22, "What have I to do with you . . . that ye should this

1. David Mill has an interesting dissertation on this point. He considers that *Gad* is the god of fortune, answering to *Meni* in the other part of the verse. He hints that there is a connection between the words *Gad*, ater-gatis, and *God*, and (possibly) ἀ-γαθός (18); he also thinks that there is a reference to Fortune in the use of the name God in Gen. 30:11. He likewise connects Achad (259), which we have naturally translated *one* in Isa. 66:17, with the name of *Hecate*.

day be adversaries unto me?" I Kings 5:4, "There is neither adversary nor evil occurrent." I Kings 11:14, "The Lord stirred up an adversary unto Solomon." Ps. 38:20, "They also that render evil for good are mine adversaries." Ps. 71:13, "Let them be confounded and consumed that are adversaries to my soul." Ps. 109:4, "For my love they are my adversaries." Verse 6, "Let Satan [without the article in the Hebrew and in the Greek] stand at his right hand." Verse 20, "Let this be the reward of mine adversaries from the Lord." Verse 29, "Let mine adversaries be clothed with shame."

In these passages the LXX renders by the verb διαβάλλω (1225), ἐπίβουλος (L-S 626A), or διάβολος (1228).

In I Chron. 21:1 we read that "**Sâtân** [7854] stood up against Israel, and provoked David to number Israel." There is no article here in the Hebrew or Greek (διάβολος, 1228); therefore the word might be rendered *an adversary*, as in other passages. Turning to the corresponding passage, II Sam. 24:1, we read, "And again the anger of the Lord was kindled against Israel, and he moved David against them to say, Go, number Israel and Judah." As in I Kings 11:14 we were told plainly that "The Lord stirred up *a Satan* against Solomon," so, putting these two parallel passages together, we may gather that "The Lord stirred up *a Satan* against Israel." The Bible reminds us more than once that provocations to evil are not only permitted but ordered by God, both to test those who are strong in faith and to show those who are depending on themselves how vain it is for them to trust in any one but the living God. The instruments that are used for this purpose are in some cases evil spirits.

Satan is referred to very definitely in Job 1:6–12 and 2:1–7. In these passages we have the definite article both in the Hebrew and in the Greek (ὁ διάβολος—3588, 1228), and we have a confirmation of the view that the previous passages suggested: that human opposition to what is good is secretly instigated by a being who lives in another sphere of existence, who is *the adversary*, or, to use the Greek translation in its modern English form, *the devil*; that he is permitted by God to put men's faith to the test by the infliction of various evils, but that he can do nothing without such permission.

In the vision recorded by Zechariah (3:1, 2) we read thus: "He shewed me Joshua the high priest standing before the angel of the Lord, and *Satan* [*the* adversary, not, as in the A.V. margin, "*an* adversary"] standing at his right hand *to resist* [lit., *to satan*—שָׂטָן, 7853] him. And the Lord said unto [the] *Satan*, The Lord rebuke thee, O

Satan." Here again there is an article in the Hebrew and Greek; and Satan is brought into conflict with the angels of God, as at the opening of the Book of Job, where the LXX renders "sons of God" as "angels of God." The same being is evidently referred to, and he is engaged in the same work, but is subjected to the rebuke of God.

The word Sâṭân (7854) is regarded as an equivalent title with *the devil* in the N.T., just as *evil spirit* is often substituted for *demon* in the parallel accounts of the same event in the Gospels. He is regarded as the enemy of souls, leading them into sin, and aiming at their destruction. He appears to have had influence over the bodies of men, and death is regarded as his masterpiece. But the Son of God by dying overcame "him that had the power of death, that is, the devil" (Heb. 2:14).

Where the word διάβολος (1228) occurs in the N.T. with the definite article, we may conclude that *the* adversary, Satan, is referred to. The following are instances of its usage: our Lord was tempted by the devil (Matt. 4); the enemy who sowed tares is the devil (Matt. 13:39); the fire is prepared for the devil and his angels (Matt. 25:41); the devil takes the good seed out of man's heart (Luke 8:12); the devil put it into the heart of Judas to betray the Lord Jesus (John 13:2). There is no definite article in Acts 13:10, where Paul addresses Elymas as the son of διάβολος (1228); probably, however, this passage may be classed with the others; compare the Apostle John's words "children of the devil" (I John 3:10). The devil is identified by name with Satan in Rev. 20:2.

The word occurs without the article, and in a more general sense, in I Tim. 3:11; II Tim. 3:3; Titus 2:3; and also in John 6:69, where our Lord says, "One of you is a devil," i.e., an adversary or false accuser.

The verb δαιμονίζομαι (1139) is only used in the Gospels, and expresses the case of those who are suffering from the agency of demons. These mysterious beings are constantly referred to in the N.T. as being cast out through the Lord's power. In John 10:20, the being possessed with a demon is regarded as equivalent to madness.

In Acts 17:18 the Athenian philosophers give the word its more classical usage, and accordingly it is rendered *gods,* that is to say, *demigods* or *genii.*[2] In this sense it seems to be understood in I Cor. 10:20, 21; I Tim. 4:1; James 2:19; Rev. 9:20; 16:14.

---

2. See, however, Chap. 2.

§2. *Temptation*

The word *tempt,* or *temptation,* occurs sixteen times in the O.T. In Mal. 3:15 the Hebrew word is **Bâchan** (בָּחַן, 974), to *prove* or *test,* as metals are tested in the crucible (see v. 10, where the same Hebrew word is rendered *prove*). In the remaining passages we find **Nâçâh** (נָסָה, 5254), literally *to test by the smell,* hence *to put to the proof.* In all these passages (with one exception, namely, Gen. 22:1, where we are told that God *tempted* or *tested* Abraham) the word is used with reference to the way in which man has put God's power or forbearance to the test. Thus in Exod. 17:2, 7, we are told that Israel *tempted* God in the wilderness, and the place was therefore called *Massah* (Maççâh—מַסָּה, 4532), a name derived from the word **Nâçâh** (5254). In Ps. 78:41 we read, "They turned back and tempted God, and limited the Holy One of Israel." This *limitation* was the setting of an imaginary boundary to God's power and goodness, and thus calling Him forth to step over that boundary. The temptations in the wilderness are referred to several times in both the Pentateuch and Psalms, and usually in the same sense. In three passages, however (Deut. 4:34; 7:19; and 29:3), reference is made not to the provocations that God endured when His forbearance was put to the test in the wilderness, but to the mode in which His purpose toward Israel and His power of working wonders were proved and demonstrated by His conduct towards Pharaoh and his people.

The usage of the two words will be more clearly seen if we compare other passages where they occur.

Bâchan (974) is found in the following passages: Gen. 42:15, 16, "Hereby ye shall be proved. . . . that your words may be proved, whether there be any truth in you." I Chron. 29:17, "Thou triest the heart." Job 23:10, "When he hath tried me, I shall come forth as gold." Ps. 7:9, "The righteous God trieth the hearts and reins"; so Jer. 11:20. Ps. 11:4, 5, "His eyelids try the children of men. The Lord trieth the righteous." Ps. 17:3, "Thou hast proved mine heart." Ps. 81:7, "I proved thee at the waters of Meribah." Ps. 139:23, "Try me, and know my thoughts." Prov. 17:3, "The fining pot is for silver, and the furnace for gold: but the LORD trieth the hearts." Isa. 28:16, "Behold, I lay in Zion for a foundation a stone, a tried stone"; the LXX, as quoted in the N.T., adopts the word *elect* (ἐκλεκτός, 1588) in this passage. Jer. 17:10, "I the LORD search the heart, I try the reins, even to give every man according to his ways"; see also Jer. 20:12. Ezek.

21:13, "It is a trial." Zech. 13:9, "I . . . will try them as gold is tried."
Mal. 3:10, "Prove me now herewith"—an idea taken up in the fif-
teenth verse, where the same word is used in the words, "They that
tempt God are even delivered."

Nâçâh (5254) occurs in Exod. 15:25, "There he proved them"; Exod.
16:4; 20:20; Deut. 8:2, 16; 13:3; Judg. 2:22; 3:1, 4; II Chron. 32:31. In
Deut. 4:34 it is rendered *assay* as well as *temptation;* and in Deut.
28:56, it is rendered *adventure* in the A.V. In Judg. 6:39 Gideon says,
"Let me prove, I pray thee, but this once with the fleece." I Sam.
17:39, David girded on Saul's armor and he assayed[3] to go (lit., he
was on the verge of starting), but he put the armor off again, since
he had not *proved* it.

In I Kings 10:1, the queen of Sheba came to Solomon "to prove
him with hard questions." Compare II Chron. 9:1.

It is also used in Job 4:2 (*assay*); Job 9:23 (*trial*); Eccles. 2:1 and 7:23;
also in Dan. 1:12 and 14, where it is rendered *prove.*

The two words occur together in Ps. 26:2, "Examine [Bâchan, 974]
me, O LORD, and prove [Nâçâh, 5254] me"; and in Ps. 95:9, "When
your fathers tempted [Nâçâh, 5254] me, proved [Bâchan, 974] me,
and saw my work."

A consideration of these passages leads to the conclusion that
the various evils and struggles and difficulties that are prompted
from within, or that befall man from without, are ordered by God as
part of the great system of probation or testing to which every child
of Adam is being subjected. The agency of the Evil One is permitted
for the purpose of bringing a man into that sort of contact with evil
that will serve to test his real principles.

The LXX translates Bâchan (974) by ἐτάζω (L-S 700A), ἐξετάζω (1833),
φαίνομαι (5316), φανερός γίνομαι (5318, 1096), μανθάνω (3129), κρίνω
(2919), διακρίνω (1252), δοκιμάζω (1381, the most usual word), δικαιόω
(1344—Ezek. 21:13), ἐπιστρέφω (1994), ἀνθίστημι (436), and ἐκλεκτὸς
(1588, Prov. 17:3 and Isa. 28:6).

Nâçâh (5254) is always translated by πειράζω (3985) or one of its
compounds.

§3. *Temptation in the N.T.*

The word ἐτάζω (L-S 700A) does not occur in the N.T., but ἐξετάζω
(1833) is used three times to represent accurate, scrutinizing search

---

3. It would have been better to put "he essayed."

(Matt. 2:8; 10:11; John 21:12); φαίνομαι (5316) is used to indicate the result of such scrutiny in II Cor. 13:7; and so φανερὸς γίνεσθαι (5318, 1096) is found in the sense of being brought to the test in Luke 8:17, "There is nothing secret, that shall not be made manifest"; I Cor. 3:13, "Every man's work shall be made manifest"; see also I Cor. 11:19; 14:25; I John 3:10.

There is some difficulty in giving a consistent rendering to διακρίνω (1252) in the N.T. It often answers, both in sense as well as etymology, to the word *discern,* as in Matt. 16:3, "Ye can discern the face of the sky"; I Cor. 11:31 (R.V.), "If we discerned ourselves [i.e., our own motives] we should not be judged [by the Lord]." In other passages the word is used in a causative sense, as when we read, "Who maketh thee to differ?" in I Cor. 4:7; so perhaps we should understand I Cor. 11:29, "Not making a distinction between ordinary food and that which represents the body of Christ."

In Jude 9 we read of Michael contending (διακρινόμενος, 1252) with Satan. But in verse 22, where the same part of the verb occurs, it has been rendered, "On some have compassion, making a difference"; might it not be rendered "contending with them," in accordance with the previous passage?[4] The verb has this sense also in Acts 11:2, where we read that "they that were of the circumcision contended with [Peter]."

In the passive voice the word has come to signify *doubting,* i.e., the subjection of the mind and will to fluctuations and contending impulses. Thus we read in Matt. 21:21, "If ye have faith, and doubt not"; so Mark 11:23; Acts 10:20; Rom. 4:20 (where the A.V. reads, "He staggered not at the promise"); Rom. 14:23; James 1:6; 2:4.

The word δοκιμάζω (1381) is also used of the process of scrutiny whereby a man is brought to the test. It is sometimes used as a substitute for διακρίνω (1252), as in Luke 12:56, which may be compared with Matt. 16:3 quoted above. So the man says of his yoke of oxen, "I go to prove them," Luke 14:19; Rom. 2:18, "Thou discernest what is excellent." Compare Rom. 12:2, "That you may make proof of what is that good, and acceptable, and perfect, will of God"; I Cor. 3:13, "The fire shall test every man's work"; I Cor. 11:28, "Let a man scrutinize himself"; compare verse 31, where διακρίνω (1252) is used. Compare also II Cor. 8:8, 22; 13:5; Gal. 6:4; Eph. 5:10; Phil. 1:10; I Tim. 3:10; I John 4:1.

4. But the text is uncertain. See R.V.

Sometimes the verb signifies that the scrutiny has been satisfactory; it is then rendered *to approve*. So we read in I Thess. 2:4, "We have been approved of God." Compare Rom. 1:28, "They did not approve of retaining God in their knowledge." In this verse the Apostle carries on the idea contained in the verb δοκιμάζω (*1381*) a little further, for he proceeds, "Wherefore God gave them up to a reprobate mind" (ἀδόκιμον νοῦν—*96, 3563*). They rejected Him, so He rejected them.

The word ἀδόκιμος (*96*) has usually been rendered *reprobate*, as in II Cor. 13:5, where we have the same connection of words as in the passage last quoted, "Prove [δοκιμάζετε, *1138*] your own selves . . . unless ye be reprobate" (ἀδόκιμοι, *96*). In one place, however, and that a very remarkable one, our translators have preferred to render ἀδόκιμος (*96*) by *castaway*, namely, in I Cor. 9:27, where Paul says, "I bring my body into subjection, lest, while I have preached to others, I myself should be unable to pass the scrutiny [of the last day]." James and Peter concur in using the expression "the trial of your faith." Here the word is δοκίμιον (*1383*—James 1:3; I Peter 1:7), and the idea suggested is that the faith that a Christian professes has to be submitted to the test of affliction and temptation, just as gold is put into a crucible and passed through the fire.

The word δόκιμος (*1384*) is used several times by Paul, and signifies the condition of him who has stood the test and is approved. See II Tim. 2:15, and compare James 1:12, "When he is tried," i.e., approved. In accordance with these passages, we can understand Rom. 5:4, where we read that "patience [worketh] experience" (δοκιμήν, *1382*). This doubtless means that as tribulation is the occasion whereby endurance or patience is developed, so this endurance becomes a test or proof that our faith is living and true.

When we turn from these various Greek words that stand for the Hebrew word Bâchan (*974*) to πειράζω (*3985*), which always represents the word Naçah (*5254*), we notice a marked difference of sense. The scrutiny or testing process that we have been considering is exercised by men, aided by the enlightenment of the Holy Spirit in this life, and will be brought to bear on the hearts and lives of all men by God hereafter. But πειρασμός (*3986*) is almost always represented in the N.T. as the work of the devil or of those who are following his guidance. Thus Christ during His earthly ministry "suffered, being tempted," and those temptations, which were of various kinds, were thrown in His path sometimes by Satan himself, and sometimes by the Pharisees and others, who sought to entangle Him in an offense against God or man. In the Acts we read of Ananias and Sapphira tempting the Spirit of God (Acts 5:9), and of Peter asking the brethren why they tempted God by imposing the law of Moses on the Gentile converts (15:10). In James 1:13, 14, we have the whole history of temptation, so far as the operations of the human heart are concerned. Satan's operations are implied, but not directly stated. A man is said to be led away when he is baited (δελεαζόμενος, 1185) by his own passions. But who is it that uses these things as a bait? Not God. Let no man say, *in this sense,* I am tempted of God. Not man; for he cannot bait the hook with which he himself is to be beguiled and destroyed. It must, then, be the Evil One, who makes use of the inclinations of the heart as a means of dragging him to ruin.

When we ask God not to lead us into temptation, we mean, Lead us not into that position, and put us not into those circumstances in which we should be in danger of falling an easy prey to the assaults of Satan. In connection with this prayer, we have the promise that with every temptation in which God permits us to be placed, He provides a way of escape that we may be able to go through without falling. He allows the way *in,* and He makes the way *out* (τὴν ἔκβασιν—3588, 1545), I Cor. 10:13.

Only one or two passages in which the verb occurs are to be interpreted differently. In II Cor. 13:5, "Examine yourselves" means to put yourself to the test, as we see from the context, which shows that the word is used as a parallel to the verb δοκιμάζω (1381). In this sense we must understand the use of the word in Heb. 11:17, where the writer refers to the temptation of Abraham in the matter of the offering of Isaac. God put Abraham's faith and obedience to the test, while Satan tempted him to disobey.

26

Witchcraft, Divination, Soothsaying

Superstition is the natural complement to materialism. The mind of man, having once become warped in religious matters, does not cling with unerring sagacity to the truth that there is a God, but goes aside into bypaths, sometimes resting in that which is material, and seeking to exclude the idea of spiritual existences altogether from the mind; at other times oscillating in the direction of what is now called *spiritualism*, a system known in earlier days by the ruder name of *witchcraft*. Few things are more fascinating than the thought that the secrets of the hidden world or of the unknown future may be unfolded through dealings with the departed, or that one person may, by going through certain mysterious processes, exercise a powerful influence over the will or destiny of another. Incantations, drugs, clouds of smoke, the conjunction of the stars, the voice or flight of birds, the passage of the clouds, mesmerism, animal magnetism, electrobiology—these and such like have been used in various ages and countries to take the place of religion, and by their means men have mimicked the supernatural dealings of God. But they are all abominable (Deut. 18:10–12), and are to give way before the simple voice of the inspired prophet. Accordingly, the Ephesian converts acted on a true instinct, and in plain harmony with the teaching of the O.T., when they discarded their "curious arts" and burned all their books at a great sacrifice (Acts 19:19). How dishonoring to God these practices are the prophet Isaiah plainly shows (Isa. 8:19). And how unprofitable to man they are our Lord teaches when He declares that if men believe not Moses and the prophets, neither will they be persuaded though one rose from the dead (Luke 16:31).

§1. *Witchcraft*

With one exception, which will be referred to under the head of *Divination*, the word for *witch* and *witchcraft* throughout the O.T. is Kâshaph (כָּשַׁף, 3784—Assyrian *kasipu*). The original meaning of this word is unknown, but if we may judge from the use of cognate forms in Arabic and Syriac, it may be taken to refer to the performance of religious rites, either in the way of prayer or of secret communications with another world.

Witchcraft was adopted in very early days as a method of trading on the religious instincts and superstitions of mankind. It was largely carried on by the female sex, though not confined to it. Thus Kâshaph (3784) is applied to the *sorcerers* of Egypt in Exod. 7:11, to Israelite sorcerers in Jer. 27:9 and Mal. 3:5, and to those of Chaldean origin in Dan. 2:2. It is also used of *sorcery* in Isa. 47:12. That the Canaanites were well acquainted with the art is evident from the fact that their city 'Akshâph (אַכְשָׁף, 407) must have been specially named from it (Josh. 11:1; 12:20; 19:25).

The word is rendered *witch* or *witchcraft* in the following passages: Exod. 22:18; Deut. 18:10; II Kings 9:22; II Chron. 33:6; Mic. 5:12; Nah. 3:4.

With regard to the exact nature of the art represented by this word, little is known; but the general rendering of the LXX, which is φαρμακεία (5331), leads to the supposition that the use of drugs, probably to produce clouds of smoke, was part of the process. The art, whatever it might be, was denounced as one of the works of the flesh in Gal. 5:20, and is referred to in Rev. 9:21; 21:8; 22:15. See also Acts 19:19.

§2. *Divination*

The one exception noticed above is I Sam. 15:23, where we read that "rebellion is as the sin of witchcraft"; but it would be better to say "the sin of divination." The word used is Qâçam (קָסַם, 7080—LXX μαντεύω, 3132). It stands for Joseph's divining cup. The original meaning of the word seems to be *to divide* or *partition out*. Its first appearance is where the elders of Moab go to Balaam with "the rewards of divination in their hand" (Num. 22:7), and where the seer announces, "Surely there is no enchantment against Jacob, neither is there any divination against Israel" (23:23). Balaam is directly called a *diviner* (A.V. *soothsayer*) in Josh. 13:22. We meet with it among the list of similar practices in Deut. 18:10 and 14, where we are given to understand that it was common among the Canaanites.

The Philistines had their diviners (I Sam. 6:2), and the witch of Endor was asked "to divine by the familiar spirit" (I Sam. 28:8). In Isa. 44:25, it is said of God that He "frustrateth the [significant] tokens of the liars [i.e., their false miracles], and maketh diviners mad"; and in Jer. 14:14, false prophets "prophesy unto you a false vision and divination, and a thing of nought, and the deceit of their heart." See also Jer. 27:9; 29:8; Ezek. 12:24; 13:6, 7, 9, 23; 21:29; 22:28; Mic. 3:6, 7; Zech. 10:2.

In Isa. 3:2 the word is rendered *prudent;* and in Prov. 16:10 we read that "a divine sentence," i.e., a word of divination, "is in the lips of the king." The diviners were doubtless shrewd men, well acquainted with the affairs of those whom they had to do with and able to deliver their prognostications in oracular and enigmatical language.

Three special modes of divination are alluded to in Ezek. 21:21: "The king of Babylon stood at the parting of the way, at the head of the two ways, to use divination: he made his arrows [or knives] bright, he consulted with images [or teraphim], he looked in the liver."

The ordinary word for a *diviner* in the LXX is μάντις (L-S 1080A), a *seer* or *soothsayer.* This art is referred to only once in the N.T., namely, in Acts 16:16, where we read of the Philippian damsel that she got for her masters much gains by divining (μαντευομένη, 3132).

§3. *The Familiar Spirit*

The familiar spirit is 'Ôwb (אוֹב, 178), literally, *a bottle* (see Job 32:19, where the word is used), and hence perhaps the hollow sound that might be produced by the wind or breath in an empty bottle or skin. The LXX renders the word ἐγγαστρίμυθος (L-S 467A), ventriloquist; so that the process called 'Ôwb (178) must probably have depended in some degree on the power of producing some peculiar sound that might represent the voice of the dead. This point is alluded to in Isa. 8:19, where we read of "them that have familiar spirits," together with "wizards that peep, and that mutter" (lit., that chirp or squeak, see 10:14; and that utter a low sound or speak indistinctly, see 59:3). Also in Isa. 29:4 we read, "Thou shalt be brought down, and shalt speak out of the ground, and thy speech shall be low out of the dust, and thy voice shall be, as of one that hath a familiar spirit, out of the ground, and thy speech shall whisper [or chirp] out of the dust." The idea that the dead, if they could speak at all, would be represented as speaking out of the ground, is very old and very natural; see Gen. 4:10, "The voice of thy brother's blood crieth unto me from the ground."

In one passage (II Kings 21:6) the LXX renders the word by θελητής (L-S 788B), by which was meant perhaps a person with a strong will who could act on the feelings of others. If this were not a solitary instance, one might be inclined to connect 'Ôwb (178) with the root 'Âbâh (אָבָה, 14), *to will*, and to class the dealings referred to with those that are now called animal magnetism, and possibly to introduce the ἐθελοθρησκεία (1479) or "will worship" of the N.T. (Col. 2:23) into the same category. The word 'Ôwb (178) also occurs in Lev. 19:31; 20:6, 27; Deut. 18:11; II Kings 21:6; 23:24; I Chron. 10:13; II Chron. 33:6; and Isa. 19:3.

The most interesting passage, however, is that in which "the witch of Endor" is described (I Sam. 28:3, 7–9). We are first told that "Saul had put away those who had familiar spirits . . . out of the land," then that he charged his servants to seek out a woman who dealt in this forbidden art. Accordingly, they find out for him a "mistress of 'Ôwb [178]," and he visits her in disguise and asks her to divine to him by 'Ôwb (178), and to bring up him whom he should speak of to her. The woman, under a promise of secrecy, is ready enough to gratify his wishes, and asks whom she shall raise up. Her business then was *necromancy*, a real or pretended dealing with the departed, the "inquiring of the dead," which is called necromancy in Deut. 18:11. There is no indication from other parts of Scripture where 'Ôwb (178) is referred to that there was usually any *appearance*. But generally a voice, which was supposed to be that of the departed person, was heard to proceed, as it were, from the ground, sometimes muttering indistinctly and sometimes "peeping," that is to say, piping or chirping like the thin shrill notes of a bird.

Saul says, "Bring me up Samuel" (I Sam. 28:11). No sooner are the words uttered than, to her astonishment, the woman perceives

Samuel. She screams with terror, and says to her visitor, "Why hast thou deceived me? for thou art Saul" (v. 12). There was no sham here. God had permitted the prophet to appear, perhaps clad in judicial robes of office, so that she said, "I saw gods [or judges[1]] ascending out of the earth" (v. 13).

Did the woman really bring up Samuel? She professed afterwards that she had done so (v. 21), but the narrative rather implies that it was not so. Certainly there is no encouragement here for Spiritualism or Theosophy, especially when we remember that "Saul died for his transgression . . . and *also for asking counsel of one* that had a familiar spirit . . . and enquired not of the Lord" (I Chron. 10:13, 14).

§4. *The Wizard and Magician*

The word for *wizard* is **Yidde'ônîy** (יִדְּעֹנִי, 3049), literally, *a knowing one.* They are always ranked with those who deal in **'Ôwb** (178), and are to be regarded with equal abhorrence. They are referred to in Lev. 19:31; 20:6, 27; Deut. 18:11; I Sam. 28:8, 9; II Kings 21:6; 23:24; II Chron. 33:6; Isa. 8:19; and 19:3. These *knowing* persons were no doubt wise in their generation, *prudent* like the diviners, and skilled in the art of preying on the follies and superstitions of those who came into contact with them. The LXX rendering is usually ἐπαοιδός (L-S 610A), an *enchanter,* or γνώστης (1109), a *knowing person.*

The magicians were **Charṭummîym** (חַרְטֻמִּים, 2748), a name that is supposed to be derived from **Chereṭ** (2747), a *graving tool* (compare the name Khartoum). The LXX sometimes calls them ἐξηγηταί (L-S 593A), *explainers.* Perhaps they were engravers of hieroglyphics and possessed that secret knowledge that those sculptures represented, which they communicated to the people with considerable reserve. Although at first sight it might be supposed from the facts narrated concerning them in the Book of Exodus that they were possessed of preternatural powers, yet it may well be doubted if they had access to any other secret influences than those that natural science is daily bringing to light, or than those by means of which the Indian juggler astounds his European spectators.

---

1. See Chap. 2.

§5. *The Soothsayer and Enchanter*

The Chaldean soothsayer whom we read of in the Book of Daniel
(2:27; 4:7; 5:7, 11) was no doubt an astrologer, who pretended to do
what astrologers in many countries and in various eras have professed to do, namely, to calculate the destinies of man by interpreting the movements and conjunctions of the heavenly bodies. Their
name is derived from G^ezar (גְּזַר, 1505), which is literally *to cut.*
Whether this name was applied to them from their marking out the
heavens into certain divisions for purposes of observation, or
whether they derived it from the fact that they cut off or decided
the fate of those who came to them for advice, is a matter that
perhaps cannot now be determined.

The astrologer of Dan. 1:20, etc., is 'Ashshâph (אַשָּׁף, 825, 826), for
which the Greek rendering is μάγος (*3097*). Compare Matt. 2:1, where
Wycliffe rightly puts *astronomers.*

Another mode of attempting to obtain information was by the
examination of the clouds. Hence the use of the word Ânan (עָנַן,
6049), κληδονίζω (L-S 958B), *to observe the clouds.* These observers
are ranked with all the other intruders into unlawful pursuits in
Deut. 18:10 and 14, under the title of *soothsayers.* They are mentioned in Isa. 2:6, where it is said of Israel that they "are soothsayers
like the Philistines." See also Mic. 5:12. They are spoken of in Isa. 57:3
as the sons of the *sorceress,* and are classed with the vile, the
impure, and the idolater. In Jer. 27:9, the A.V. calls them *enchanters;*
and in several passages (Lev. 19:26; II Kings 21:6; and II Chron. 33:6)
they are described as *the observers of times,* that is to say, persons
who by examining the clouds profess to be able to tell at what exact
crisis any event is to be expected to take place, and when a good
opportunity arrives for doing a certain work.

The word Cheber (חֶבֶר, 2267), *binding* or *fascination,* is rendered
enchantment in Isa. 47:9, 12, where reference is made to Babylon;
and is rendered *charmer* in Deut. 18:11, and in Ps. 58:5 where the
serpent charmer is referred to. In the early part of the same verse,
Lâchash (לָחַשׁ, 3907), *to whisper,* is used for the art of the serpent
charmer, and is also used in the same connection in Jer. 8:17, and in
Eccles. 10:11, where the A.V. has *enchantment.*

In Isa. 19:3, *charmers* are described as 'Iṭṭîym (אִטִּים, 328), those
who speak with a soft low voice. These are perhaps serpent

charmers. The word itself is used of Ahab going *softly* (I Kings 21:27), as a sign of his humility and repentance.

The *enchantments* of the Egyptians are Lahaṭîym (לַהֲטִים, 3858) in Exod. 7:11, and Lâṭ (לָט, 3909) in Exod. 7:22; 8:7, 18. Both of these words signify *secrecy*, and imply that these learned men practiced what in the Middle Ages would be called "the black art," or perhaps what we call "sleight of hand."

Only one other word has to be noticed, namely, Nâchash (נָחַשׁ, 5172), which is supposed to signify *to whisper* or *hiss*, and hence is applied to the serpent. It is rendered *enchantment* in Lev. 19:26; Deut. 18:10; Num. 23:23; 24:1 (with reference to Balaam); II Kings 17:17; 21:6; II Chron. 33:6. These passages imply that it was Canaanitish rather than Egyptian in its origin and connection. The word is used in a modified sense in I Kings 20:33, "The men did diligently observe whether any thing would come from him"; they prognosticated as to Ben-hadad's fate from Ahab's words. It is also the word used by Joseph's steward in Gen. 44:5, 15, where the A.V. has *divine* or *make trial*, and perhaps was specially used by Joseph's order as a word of Canaanitish origin that the sons of Jacob would understand. The LXX renders it by the word οἰωνισμός (L-S 1211A), *augury*, or the interpreting of events by the flight of birds; but divination by means of pictures, which were supposed to be formed by liquid in a cup, may be referred to. The verb is used in Gen. 30:27, where Laban says, "I have learned by experience that the LORD hath blessed me for thy sake." Two persons mentioned in the O.T. derive their name from this root, namely, Naasson (Nachshon), the son of Amminadab (Exod. 6:23), and Nehushta, the mother of Jehoiachin (II Kings 24:8).

27

Idol, Grove, High Place

Man is essentially an image-maker. His best works in art and mechanics are imitations of nature. His music is an attempt to present, not indeed to the eye, but to the ear, what may be called a picture of the varied feelings that occupy his heart. This tendency also shows itself in his religious worship, which he is inclined to make as symbolic as possible. Nay, he seeks to make a visible representation even of God Himself, and gradually to transfer to the work of his own hands that reverence and dependence that properly belongs to the one living and true God. There is a strange fascination in exaggerated religious symbolism. It engrosses and excites the mind, but is by no means of a healthy character. It tends little by little to supplant the simplicity of spiritual worship, and to turn man into an idolater. Idolatry in its first stage is a sort of symbolism. Some object is selected to represent the unseen Deity or to set forth one of His attributes. Little by little the material image takes the place of the spiritual reality for which it stands and idolatry ensues, bringing in its train that sensuality that is the sure attendant of every form of materialism. The highest functions of human nature are thus abnegated, and human life is debased. The first chapter of the Epistle to the Romans tells the story of idolatrous degradation with painful vividness. It fully accounts for the oft-repeated admonitions given by Moses on this special point, and for the severe penalties that God inflicted on the people in order to break through the evil fascination and to deliver them from the snare of materialism.

328

§1. *Idols*

Twelve different Hebrew words are represented by the English word *idol.* Some of them point to the fact that an idol is a thing of nought. Others signify the terror with which the worshiper of false gods is inspired, or the aversion with which the living and true God regards such objects. Others, again, refer to the shape of the idol, to the material of which it is made, or to the position in which it is placed.

In Isa. 66:3 the idol is ʾÂven (אָוֶן, 205—Assyrian *annu*), *iniquity,* or *a thing of nought.* Compare Bêyth ʾÂven (בֵּית אָוֶן, 1007), i.e., *house of idolatry,* which is referred to in Hos. 4:15; 5:8; and 10:5, 8. In Amos 5:5 we read that Bêyth-ʾÊl (בֵּית־אֵל, 1008) shall come to ʾÂven (205—A.V. *to nought*). Here there is evidently a play on the word. See Josh. 7:2.

The word ʾĔlîyl (אֱלִיל, 457), which is supposed to have the same meaning, is used in several places, e.g., Lev. 19:4; 26:1; I Chron. 16:26; Ps. 96:5; 97:7; Isa. 2:8, 18, 20; 10:10, 11; 19:1, 3; 31:7; Ezek. 30:13; Hab. 2:18; Zech. 11:17.

The nothingness of idolatry is brought out by the Apostle Paul, who reminds the Corinthians that "an idol is nothing in the world" (I Cor. 8:4), that the gods of the heathen are "vanities" (Acts 14:15), and "no gods" (Gal. 4:8).

In Jer. 50:38, where we read, "They are mad upon their idols," the word ʾÊymâh (אֵימָה, 367) is used, which implies that the idol was an object of terror. The same idea is probably represented by Miph-letseth (מִפְלֶצֶת, 4656), the designation of the idol that Maachah made[1] (I Kings 15:13; also in the corresponding passage, II Chron. 15:16). In II Chron. 15:8 idols are called *abominations,* Shiqqûwts (שִׁקּוּץ, 8251), a word that is often used to testify to God's hatred of the whole system of idolatry and that answers to the Greek βδέλυγμα (946).

The connection of *abomination* (βδέλυγμα, 946) with idolatry is brought out in Rom. 2:22, "Thou who abominatest idols, dost thou rob temples?" In Rev. 21:8, the *abominable,* that is, those who worship idols, are coupled with the fearful[2] and the unbelieving. In

---

1. David Mill considers that this was Pluto, the president of the infernal regions, whom he also identifies with Beelzebub the prince of flies, of nuisances, and of the power of the air. He thinks that Ashara or Astarte was Hecate or Luna, and that Chiun (Amos 5:26) was Saturn. But see Sayce, *Hibbert Lectures.*

2. The word δειλός (1169) here rendered *fearful* probably signifies *unstable,* in which sense it is used in the O.T.

Titus 1:16, Paul speaks of some who profess to know God, but by their works deny Him, and are abominable, i.e., practically on a level with idolaters. The *falsehood* of idolatry is brought out in Rev. 21:27, where to make an abomination and to make a lie are put side by side. Probably the cup containing abominations and whoredom, referred to in Rev. 17:4, represents the various forms of idolatry that "the woman" shall promote. Paul tells us that covetousness is idolatry, and in accordance with this truth our Lord tells the covetous Pharisees that what is lifted up among men is regarded as an abomination in the sight of God (Luke 16:14, 15).

Reference has now been made to all the passages in which the word βδέλυγμα (946) occurs in the N.T., with the exception of our Lord's reference to "the abomination of desolation, spoken of by Daniel the prophet" (Matt. 24:15; Mark 13:14; Dan. 9:27), which signifies that the desolation of Jerusalem was to be caused by an idolatrous power.

There is a word found several times in the O.T. that is rather ambiguous, namely, ʾÂtsâb (עָצָב, 6091). It is supposed to mean *that which causes labor,* either in the making of the idol or in the worshiping of it. The Greek rendering is sometimes λύπη (3077), *grief,* but usually εἴδωλον (1497). Scripture always conveys to us the idea that true worship is not wearisome to the child of God, whereas the worship of idols is hard labor without profit.

This word is used with reference to the false gods of the Philistines in I Sam. 31:9; I Chron. 10:9; II Sam. 5:21. In II Chron. 24:18 and Ps. 106:36, 38, it refers to the objects of Canaanite worship by which the Israelites were ensnared (see also Ps. 115:4 and 135:15). In Isa. 10:11, while 'Ĕlîyl (457) is used of Samaria's idols, ʾÂtsâb (6091) is used of Jerusalem's idols. In Isa. 46:1 it is applied to Bel and Nebo, which were "a burden to the weary beast." See also Jer. 50:2, where these same idols are described as broken in pieces. In Jer. 22:28, Coniah is described as "a despised broken *idol* ['Etseb, 6089]" (where some would translate the word *vase,* but unnecessarily). It is also used of the idols of Israel or Canaan in Isa. 48:5; Hos. 4:17; 8:4; 13:2; 14:8; Mic. 1:7; Zech. 13:2.

Another word for idol is derived from Galgal (גַּלְגַּל, 1534), *a wheel* or rolling thing, and signifies a trunk of a tree or a log of wood, or perhaps in some places a round stone. The word occurs only in Leviticus, Deuteronomy, I and II Kings, and Ezekiel. The LXX usually renders it εἴδωλον (1497), an *idol,* but sometimes ἐπιτήδευμα (L-S

666A), a *custom;* twice βδέλυγμα (946), an *abomination;* and in other passages ἐνθύμημα (L-S 567A), ἐπιθύμημα (L-S 634B), διάνοια (1271), and διανόημα (1270), words that would point to the tendency of the heart to idolatry rather than to the object of worship itself. It occurs in the following passages: Lev. 26:30 ("the carcases of your idols"); Deut. 29:17 (margin "dungy gods"); I Kings 15:12; 21:26; II Kings 17:12; 21:11, 21; 23:24; Ezek. 6:4, et al.

The word εἴδωλον (1497) is the only word used of idols in the N.T., whether these idols are outward and visible objects of worship or whether they are more subtle influences that attract the heart.

Idolatry is joined with *pharmacy* or witchcraft in Gal. 5:20. It is identified with covetousness in Eph. 5:5, and is classed with murder in Rev. 22:15.

§2. *The Image*

There are phrases that refer to the fact that an idol is fashioned into a certain shape or image. One such phrase—פֶּסֶל הַסֶּמֶל—is found in II Chron. 33:7 (see also v. 15). The word Çemel (סֶמֶל, 5566), meaning *image, figure,* or *likeness,* probably ought to be construed to be a standardized likeness of a false deity (in this case probably that of Asherah or Ashtoreth) in which it is imagined by its worshipers. The word Peçel (פֶּסֶל, 6459) signifies a *graven* or *carved image* or *statue,* in this case a specific representation of a false deity. So here it might be translated "a carved statue of the [standard] likeness." Çemel (5566) is also found in Ezek. 8:3, 5 ("the image of jealousy"), another reference to Asherah. In Isa. 45:16, the phrase חָרָשֵׁי צִירִים is translated "makers of idols." Chârâsh (חָרָשׁ, 2796) actually means *carver;* Tsîyr (צִיר, 6736) signifies *idol.* Temûwnâh (תְּמוּנָה, 8544), *likeness,* is used in Job 4:16. It does not, however, refer to an idol, but to some form or outline that presented itself in vision. The same word is used in Exod. 20:4, in the prohibition from making a *likeness* of anything; also in Deut. 4:23, 25; 5:8; and Ps. 17:15 ("I shall be satisfied, when I awake with thy likeness"). The LXX rendering is generally ὁμοίωμα (3667), *similitude.*

Tselem (צֶלֶם, 6754, 6755—Assyrian *tsalmu*), a *representation,* answering to the Greek εἰκών (1504), *image,* is the word used in Genesis (1:26, 27; 5:3; and 9:6) with reference to the fact that man was made in the image of God. In Num. 33:52 it is used of molten images, and it occurs in the following passages: I Sam. 6:5, 11 (the images of mice and hemorrhoids or tumors); II Kings 11:18 (the images of Baal); II Chron. 23:17; Ezek. 7:20; 16:17; 23:14 (images of men); Amos 5:26 (Moloch and Chiun); Dan. 2:31 passim and 3:1 passim, the image of which Nebuchadnezzar dreamed, and that which he set up on the plain of Dura. The word is also used in Ps. 73:20, "When thou awakest, thou shalt despise their image," that is to say, their form or appearance; and in Ps. 39:6, "Man walketh in a vain shadow" (lit., in an image).

In Lev. 26:1 the *graven image* is **Maskîyth** (מַשְׂכִּית, 4906), which is supposed to refer to hieroglyphics, or to little figures of Thoth and other Egyptian gods. This word also occurs in Ezek. 8:12, where reference is made to *chambers of imagery,* that is to say, chambers with figures painted and carved in relief such as still exist in Egypt and Assyria. In Num. 33:52 and Prov. 25:11, **Maskîyth** (4906) is rendered *pictures;* and in Ps. 73:7 and Prov. 18:11, there is reference to the mental process which we call *picturing up* or *imagination.*

§3. N.T. Teaching on Images

The word ὁμοίωμα (3667) means a *resemblance* or *figure,* whether bodily or moral. It is used with reference to idolatry in Rom. 1:23, whether bodily or moral. It is used with reference to idolatry in Rom. 1:23, where the Apostle Paul speaks of those who changed the glory of the incorruptible God into the resemblance of an image of a corruptible man. When our Lord is said to have been made in the likeness of men, the same word is used, but with what a difference! No lifeless stock or stone shaped by man's hand after the pattern of his fellowman! Rather He was a living Being partaking of all that is essential to human nature, yet absolutely free from stain of sin; and having a body destined to see no corruption, He was sent into human life, not from nothingness, but from the bosom of the Heavenly Father, and from that glory which He had before the foundation of the world.

The first passage in the N.T. in which the word εἰκών (1504) is used gives a good idea of its meaning. It is with reference to the *denarius* of which our Lord asks, "Whose is this image and superscription?" (Matt. 22:20). It is curious to observe that while idolaters are condemned for changing the glory of God into the similitude of the image of a corruptible man (Rom. 1:23), we are expressly told that man is "the image and glory of God" (I Cor. 11:7). Christ is said to be the image of God (II Cor. 4:4; Col. 1:15); the Christian is now in a moral and spiritual sense to be changed into the same image from glory to glory (Rom. 8:29; II Cor. 3:18; Col. 3:10); and hereafter, so far as his body is concerned, a similar resemblance shall be accomplished (I Cor. 15:49).

The word εἰκών (*1504*) is also adopted by the Apostle John when he describes the image of the beast in Rev. 13:14, 15.

A hot controversy was called forth shortly after the Reformation in England by the fact that in the English translations of the Scriptures the word εἴδωλον (*1497*) was translated *image.* Martin, in his controversy with Fulke, laid down that an idol signified a false god; Dr. Fulke, on the contrary, held that it meant an image, and that this was the best word, as it included a representation of the true God. Martin held, and rightly, that Peçel (פֶּסֶל, 6459), which is usually translated *a graven image,* only meant a *graven thing* (Latin *sculptile*—a carved or graven thing), and had no reference to an image; and he made a similar criticism on the word Maççêkâh (מַסֵּכָה, 4541), which is rendered *a molten image.* Fulke, however, answered that the object of the engraving in the one case, and of the melting in the other, was to make the material into an image that was intended to represent the invisible God, or to imitate one of His works, and so to be worshiped. This answer, coupled with the fact that εἴδωλος (1497) also answers to the Hebrew Temûwnâh (8544), as above noticed, may fairly justify our translators, and also their predecessors whose work was being criticized in translating εἴδωλον (*1497*) by the word *image.*

§4. *Other Objects of Worship*

We now pass to the consideration of words that represent certain specific objects that were closely connected with old forms of idolatry. Of these the first to be named is the *pillar, statue,* or *standing image,* the Hebrew name for which is Matstsêbâh (מַצֵּבָה, 4676), derived from the verb Nâtsab (נָצַב, 5324), *to stand,* and used of the object that symbolized Baal in the Canaanitish idolatry. The LXX usually adopts στήλη (L-S 1643B), *a pillar,* as its representative. It is first referred to in an idolatrous sense in Exod. 23:24, where the command is given to break down the *images* of the Canaanite gods; so in Exod. 34:13, where it is connected with *groves;* it is also found in Lev. 26:1; Deut. 7:5; 16:22; I Kings 14:23; II Kings 3:2 (image of Baal);

10:26, 27 (images of Baal); 17:10; 18:4; 23:14; II Chron. 14:3; 31:1; Jer. 43:13; Hos. 3:4; 10:1, 2; Mic. 5:13.

Another word used is **Chammânîym** (חַמָּנִים, 2553), *sun images,* perhaps *discs,* or perhaps *pyramidal stones* in the shape of a flame. This last is the idea that Gesenius inclines to, as in accordance with certain old Phoenician inscriptions that speak of Baal Hanan, the sun god. The word occurs in Lev. 26:30, "I will . . . cut down [cut off or smite] your images"; II Chron. 14:5; 34:4, 7; Isa. 17:8; 27:9; Ezek. 6:4, 6.

§5. *The Grove*

Closely connected with Baal statues and sun images stand the groves. But before discussing their nature, it is to be observed that the grove that Abraham is said to have planted, in Gen. 21:33, was doubtless a bona fide grove, or at least a tree. The word there used is **'Êshel** (אֶשֶׁל, 815), which is distinct from the heathen and idolatrous grove, and may be rendered *tamarisk.* With this exception, the general Hebrew word for a *grove* is **Ăshêrâh** (אֲשֵׁרָה, 842), usually rendered ἄλσος (L-S 73B—*grove*) by the LXX; but in two passages, Isa. 17:8 and 27:9, it is rendered δένδρον (1186—*tree*). The grove is first alluded to in connection with Canaanitish worship in Exod. 34:13, where it is coupled with the statue or pillar that has already been mentioned. We find it in the same connection in Deut. 7:5; 12:3; 16:21; I Kings 14:15, 23; II Kings 18:4; II Chron. 31:1; Isa. 27:9; and Mic. 5:14. It is introduced in connection with the worship of Baal in Judg. 3:7; 6:25, 26 (where we are plainly told that it was made of *wood,* and that it used to be set up by the altar of Baal); see also I Kings 16:33 and 18:19. In II Kings 17:16 the people are described as making a grove, and as worshiping not only Baal, but also "all the host of heaven"; so in II Kings 21:3 and 23:4, where we read of "the vessels that were made for Baal, and for the grove, and for all the host of heaven." See also II Chron. 33:3.

In I Kings 15:13 we read that Maachah made "an idol [or *horrible thing*] *in* a grove," or rather "*for* a grove." The same change in the rendering is needed in the parallel passage, II Chron. 15:16, the preposition in each case being **la** (לְ), *for,* not **ba** (בַּ), *in.*

The question now recurs, What was this **Ăshêrâh** (842), which we have rendered *grove?* It was certainly not what we call a grove of trees, nor was it a single tree planted in the earth;[3] but it was an object made of wood and set up by the side of an altar dedicated to Baal, and in some cases in company with a statue or pillar representing Baal. Gesenius, who is an authority on all matters connected with Phoenician and Canaanite worship, considers that 'Ăshêrâh (842) was a goddess, identical with Ashtoreth (Astarte, or Venus).[4]

It appears not unlikely that grove worship was a form of that tree worship which has been found almost all over the world, and which drew its origin from the trees in the garden of Eden. The 'Ăshêrâh (842) was probably, in the first instance, a representation of *the tree of life*, though the traditional idea soon passed away and was probably superseded by the idea of the reproductive powers of nature. We cannot now say in what form it was, but it may possibly have been in the form of a *cross*, which would have been the simplest artificial symbol for a tree, and which appears to have been adopted for this purpose in various countries and in ages long anterior to Christianity.[5] Assyrian sculptures afford elaborate representations of this tree of life. Compare II Kings 21:7, where we read of a "graven image of the grove," literally, "the likeness the grove," evidently a symbolic figure. In II Kings 23:7 we are told of certain women who "wove hangings for the grove," and who did the work in "the houses of the Sodomites." These *hangings* are literally *houses*, and were perhaps shrines or coverings for the symbolical figure.

§6. *The High Place*

Another object connected with idolatrous worship is the high place. The word used for it is Bâmâh (בָּמָה, 1116—Assyrian *bamahi*). The usual rendering in the LXX is ὑψηλός (5308), *high;* but we also find οἶκος (3624), a *house;* ἄλσος (L-S 73B), a *grove;* βουνός (1015), a *hill;* εἴδωλον (1497), an *idol;* ἁμαρτία (266), *sin* (Mic. 1:5); θυσιαστήριον (2379) and βωμός (1041), an *altar;* ἔρημος (2048), a *desert;* στήλη (L-S 1643B), a *pillar;* λίθοι (3037), *stones;* ἔδαφος (1475), a *foundation;* τράχηλος (5137), a *neck;* and ἰσχὺς (2479—Deut. 32:13), *strength.*

---

3. It is hardly ever said to be *planted;* usually it is described as *made.*

4. The Tel el-Amarna tablets show that he was right, except in identifying Asherah, the South Canaanite goddess of fertility, with Astarte or Asrate (*Sayce*).

5. See this subject discussed at length in Fergusson's work on Tree and Serpent Worship; see also the article on "Pre-Christian Crosses" in the *Edinburgh Review,* October 1869.

The word appears without reference to idolatry in Deut. 32:13, "He made him ride on the high places of the earth," where it is only used in a general sense. The same, perhaps, may be said of its usage in Deut. 33:29. In Job 9:8, the *waves* of the sea are literally *high places*. A high place is spoken of in I Sam. 10:13, where it seems to signify a hill, as also in II Sam. 1:19, 25; 22:34. See also Num. 21:28; 22:41; Ps. 18:33; 78:69; Isa. 15:2; 16:12; Jer. 48:35; Amos 4:13; 7:9; Mic. 1:3, 5; Hab. 3:19. With regard to some of these passages, it may be doubtful whether the word is used in its general or special sense.

In the days of Solomon (I Kings 3:2–4), we are told that "the people sacrificed in high places, because there was no house built unto the name of the LORD until those days"; and when Solomon went to Gibeon, "where was a great high place," he offered a thousand burnt offerings on the altar.[6] Here the LORD appeared to him, but did not rebuke him for what he had done. At that time the permanent temple was not built, and consequently full liberty was allowed. Shortly afterward, however, Solomon built high places for Chemosh and for Molech, the idols of Moab and Ammon, and then "the LORD was angry with him" (I Kings 11:7, 9). See Lev. 26:30; Num. 33:52. Jeroboam also made "houses of high places" (I Kings 12:31), with priests, altars, and golden calves. These priests of the high places burned incense on the altar at Bethel, and were denounced by the man of God who came out of Judah. The building and use of high places with statues and groves now became very common in both kingdoms. See I Kings 14:23; 22:43; II Kings 12:3; 16:4 (Ahaz "sacrificed and burnt incense in the high places, and on the hills, and under every green tree"); 17:9, 29, 32. Asa,[7] Jehoshaphat, and afterwards Hezekiah, removed them, as far as possible, but Jehoram and Manasseh rebuilt them (II Kings 21:3). Josiah again destroyed them, but the passion for these idolatrous rites was not easily to be rooted out. They appear to have been sometimes natural eminences, and sometimes constructed of earth or stones; occasionally they seem to have been used as altars; at other times they were surmounted by the 'Āshêrâh (842). In the discussion on *pre-Christian crosses* already referred to (see note 5, this chapter), it is stated that the old emblems of the tree of life were constantly placed on hills or

---

6. In the parallel passage (II Chron. 1:3) it is stated that the tabernacle of the congregation was at Gibeon, and that the high place was connected with it.

7. Asa removed the high places from *Judah* (II Chron. 14:5), but not from Israel (15:17).

mounds. This may throw some light on the origin of the high place.[8]

§7. *The Teraphim*

The T^erâphîym (תְּרָפִים, 8655—Assyrian *tarpu,* a *specter*) have now to be noticed. This word, which is only used in the plural number, is not understood by the lexicographer or the antiquarian. The LXX gives various renderings, namely, εἴδωλον (*1497*), *idol;* γλυπτόν (L-S 352B), *carved object;* δῆλα (*1212*), *manifestations;* ἀποφθεγγόμενοι (*669*), *revealers;* κενοταφία (L-S 938B), *empty tombs.* The T^erâphîym (8655) appear to be material objects regarded as a sort of *fetish* or talisman, and consulted in emergencies. They are first met with in Gen. 31:19, 34, 35. Laban calls them his *gods,* but the inspired writer only calls them T^erâphîym (8655). In Judg. 17:5, they are connected with the images, with a house of gods and an ephod, but they are evidently distinct objects (see Judg. 18:14, 17, 18, 20). In I Sam. 15:23, T^erâphîym (8655) are parallel with divination (compare Zech. 10:2). In I Sam. 19:13, 16, they are put in the bed to occupy the place of David. In Ezek. 21:21 they are mentioned as used by the king of Babylon in divining. This fact, coupled with the use of these objects in the house of Laban, would lead us to look for a Chaldean origin for them.

8. When riding through the country of the Ammonites in 1860, the writer was struck with the great number of rude cromlechs that are visible on the hillsides. If these were for religious purposes, as seems most probable, may they not have been of the nature of high places?

28

Eternal, Age to Come

§1. *Various Words Marking Duration*

The O.T. words representing *duration*, and their Greek equivalents, call for careful consideration in consequence of the fact that the revelation of man's future destiny must depend to some extent upon their accurate interpretation.

One of the most frequent words used to mark duration is 'Ad (עַד, 5703—Assyrian *adu*), which is represented in English by the words *eternity, ever, everlasting, evermore, of old, perpetually, world without end*. This word is once used where there is a reference to *past* duration of a limited extent, namely, in Job 20:4, "Knowest thou not this of old, since man was placed upon earth . . . ?" It is used of a state of being that is at once past, present, and future with regard to God who inhabits eternity (κατοικῶν τὸν αἰῶνα—2730, 3588, 165), Isa. 57:15. It is applied to the endless duration of God's reign in Exod. 15:18, and in Ps. 10:16, where the LXX is very strong (εἰς τὸν αἰῶνα καὶ ἐπ᾽ αἰῶνα καὶ ἔτι—1519, 3588, 165, 2532, 1909, 165, 2532, 2089); to the throne of God, Ps. 45:6; to the Messianic kingdom, Ps. 89:29; to the duration of God's righteousness, praise, and commandments, Ps. 111:3, 8, 10. It is also used of the duration of national or individual confidence in God, e.g., Ps. 48:14, "This God is our God for ever and ever [εἰς τὸν αἰῶνα καὶ εἰς τὸν αἰῶνα τοῦ αἰῶνος—1519, 3588, 165, 2532, 1519, 3588, 165, 3588, 165]: he will be our guide even unto death" (εἰς τοὺς αἰῶνας—1519, 3588, 165); Ps. 52:8, "I trust in the mercy of God for ever and ever"; Ps. 119:44, "So shall I keep thy law continually for ever and ever" (διαπαντός, εἰς τὸν αἰῶνα καὶ εἰς τὸν αἰῶνα τοῦ αἰῶνος—1275, 1519, 3588, 165, 2532, 1519, 3588, 165,

338

3588, 165). The same word occurs in the title of the Messiah, as "the everlasting Father," i.e., the source of everlasting life, Isa. 9:6; see also Ps. 148:6; 104:5.

Again, the term is applied to the continued existence of the people of God, and to the personal confidence that they may have in God, whether for the present or for the hereafter: Ps. 9:18, "The expectation of the poor shall not perish for ever" (εἰς τὸν αἰῶνα—1519, 3588, 165); Ps. 22:26, "Your heart shall live for ever" (εἰς αἰῶνα αἰῶνος—1519, 165, 165); Ps. 37:27-29, "Depart from evil, and do good; and dwell for evermore [εἰς αἰῶνα αἰῶνος—1519, 165, 165]. For the Lord loveth judgment [righteousness], and forsaketh not his saints; they are preserved for ever [εἰς τὸν αἰῶνα—1519, 3588, 165]: but the seed of the wicked shall be cut off. The righteous shall inherit the land, and dwell therein for ever" (εἰς αἰῶνα αἰῶνος—1519, 165, 165); Isa. 45:17, "Ye shall not be ashamed nor confounded world without end" (ἕως τοῦ αἰῶνος καὶ ἔτι—2193, 3588, 165, 2532, 2089).

Lastly, it is used with reference to the case of evildoers, whether nations or individuals. Of Assher and Eber it is said that they "shall perish for ever" (Num. 24:20, 24). Ps. 9:5, "Thou hast put out their name for ever and ever" (εἰς τὸν αἰῶνα κὰ εἰς αἰῶνα αἰῶνος—1519, 3588, 165, 2532, 1519, 165, 165); Ps. 83:17, "Let them be confounded and troubled for ever" (εἰς αἰῶνα αἰῶνος—1519, 165, 165); Ps. 92:7, "The wicked . . . shall be destroyed for ever" (ἐξολοθρεύθωσις εἰς τὸν αἰῶνα τοῦ αἰῶνος—1842, 1519, 3588, 165, 3588, 165).

Netsach (נצח, 5331), with a preposition (ל), is rendered *always, constantly, ever, perpetual,* and also in its original meanings of *strength* and *victory.* It is usually rendered by the LXX εἰς τέλος (1519, 5056), *unto completion,* but sometimes εἰς νῖκος (1519, 3534), *unto victory.* It signifies completeness, and might usually be translated *utterly.*

It is used of God not "keep[ing] his anger for ever" (Ps. 103:9); and of the pleasures that are at His right hand forevermore (Ps. 16:11). God is several times appealed to not to forget His people nor to be absent from them forever (Ps. 13:1; 44:23; 74:1, 10, 19; 79:5; 89:46).

Netsach (5331) occurs in Job several times, either with reference to the utter destruction brought upon man (that is, upon the outward man) by God, or to the final deliverance that is to be obtained by the godly. See Job 4:20; 14:20; 20:7; 23:7; 36:7.

No man, says the Psalmist, can cause his fellowmen to live forever, i.e., can ensure them against death (Ps. 49:9). The destructions of the wicked, that is, their evil machinations against the godly, are described as having "come to a perpetual end," or, in other words, as being utterly frustrated (Ps. 9:6). **Netsach** (5331) is also used of the desolation of Edom and Babylon (Amos 1:11; Jer. 50:39).

This word occurs in a slightly different form in the Hebrew heading of several Psalms. The LXX uniformly renders it εἰς τὸ τέλος (1519, 3588, 5056); the A.V. has "to the chief musician." Perhaps the real meaning is that the Psalm is one of victory, and to be sung with emphasis.

Three times in the N.T. we read that he who endures to the end (εἰς τέλος—1519, 5056) shall be saved. In I Thess. 2:16 we are reminded of Ps. 9:6, for we read that "wrath is come upon them to the uttermost."

The phrase εἰς νῖκος (1519, 3534) occurs only twice in the N.T., namely, in Matt. 12:20, where Isa. 42:3 is quoted, and in I Cor. 15:54, where the quotation is from Isa. 25:8. It is curious that in these two places the Hebrew le-Netsach (5331) is found, but not the phrase εἰς νῖκος (1519, 3534) in the LXX, the quotation being in each place a new translation from the Hebrew.

Tâmîyd (תָּמִיד, 8548) marks *continuity* or *perpetuity*. It is usually applied to the permanence of the Mosaic ritual through the history of the Hebrew nation. The LXX generally renders it διαπαντός (1275), but occasionally διὰ τέλους (1223, 5056). It is used of the showbread (Exod. 25:30); of the lamp (27:20); of the signet of holiness (28:38); of the pillar of cloud and fire (Num. 9:16); of the *daily* sacrifice (Dan. 12:11); of God's eye resting on the land of Israel (Deut. 11:12); of the sustenance afforded to Mephibosheth (II Sam. 9:10); of the constant realization of the presence of God ("I have set the LORD always before me," Ps. 16:8); "Mine eyes are ever toward the LORD," Ps. 25:15; of the constant remembrance of sin ("My sin is ever before me," Ps. 51:3); of devotional feelings and conduct (Ps. 34:1; 38:17; 71:6; 119:44).

God says of Jerusalem, "I have graven thee upon the palms of my hands; thy walls are continually before me" (Isa. 49:16). And to the godly man it is said, "The LORD shall guide thee continually" (Isa. 58:11). Lastly, of the heavenly Jerusalem it is predicted, "Thy gates shall be open continually; they shall not be shut day nor night" (Isa. 60:11).

The word διαπαντὸς (1275) occurs ten times in the N.T. Two of these passages are quotations from the O.T., namely, Acts 2:25 and Rom. 11:10, taken from Ps. 16:8 and 69:23, in which **Tâmîyd** (8548) is used. In other passages it is used of the continual service rendered to God (Luke 24:53; Acts 10:2; Heb. 9:6; 13:15). It is also used in Matt. 18:10, where we read of Christ's little ones, that their angels in heaven continually behold the face of God.

'Ôrek (אֹרֶךְ, 753—Assyrian *arahu*) denotes *length* without any reference to limit. It is translated *forever* in Ps. 23:6, "I will dwell in the house of the LORD for ever"; and Ps. 93:5, "Holiness becometh thine house, O LORD, for ever." In each case the LXX has εἰς μακρότητα ἡμέρων (*1519*, L-S 1075B, *2250*).

Dôwr (דּוֹר, 1755—Assyrian *duru*) signifies a *generation*. In Ps. 10:6, "I shall never be in adversity," the words are literally, "I shall not be in adversity from generation to generation"; and so in Ps. 77:8 ("Doth [the LORD's] promise fail for evermore?"). The word Dôwr (1755), like the Greek γενεά (*1074*) and the English *generation*, is often used in a large and indefinite sense, sometimes perhaps referring to an age or century, as when the LORD promised to Abraham that his seed should be rescued "in the fourth generation" (Gen. 15:16).

Dôwr (1755) is applied to the continuous covenant made between God and Noah (Gen. 9:12), εἰς γενεὰς αἰωνίους (*1519, 1074, 166*); to the remembrance of God's name or memorial (Exod. 3:15; Ps. 9:7; 102:12; 135:13); to the feeling that was to be kept alive against the Amalekites (Exod. 17:16); to the permanence of God's thoughts (Ps. 33:11), mercy and truth (40:11), wrath (85:5), existence (102:24), and dominion (145:13; Dan. 4:3); to the judgment of Edom (Isa. 34:10), and to the desolation of Babylon (Isa. 13:20).

A parallel expression is used in Luke 1:50 and Eph. 3:21 with regard to the continuance of God's mercy and of the glory that is to be ascribed to Him in Christ Jesus.

The word Tsᵉmîythûth (צְמִיתֻת, 6783) is rendered *forever* in Lev. 25:23, 30, where reference is made to the continuous possession of land. But in the LXX we find εἰς βεβαίωσιν (*1519, 951*), an expression that is preserved in the N.T. in Heb. 6:16, where we read that an oath is "for confirmation." Perhaps there is here a special reference to the continuity of the promise through the oath sworn to Abraham.

Qedem (קֶדֶם, 6924—Assyrian *qudmu*), which means *ancient* or *ancient time*, is used in Deut. 33:27 of the *eternal* God; in Prov. 8:22 of God's "works *of old*" (πρὸ τοῦ αἰῶνος—*4253, 3588, 165*); and in Hab. 1:12 of God's existence from everlasting (ἀπ' ἀρχῆς—*575, 746*). The Greek rendering adopted in the last passage is often found in the N.T.

This phrase is applied to periodical or recurrent rites, such as the lament for Jephthah's daughter (Judg. 11:40); the feast in Shiloh (Judg. 21:19); the worship in Shiloh (I Sam. 1:3, 21; 2:19; 20:6); and to the offering of sacrifices (Job 1:5; Amos 4:4).

It is used of the permanence of man's duty (Deut. 5:29); of God's promises (Deut. 6:24) and of His threats (Deut. 28:33); of the continuance of evil in the heart (Gen. 6:5) and of wicked devices (Ps. 52:1). It is also used of permanent relations between man and man, or between nation and nation, e.g., between Saul and David (I Sam. 18:29), Rehoboam and Jeroboam (II Chron. 12:15), David and Achish (I Sam. 28:2), Hiram and David (I Kings 5:1). See also Jer. 35:19; 31:36; 32:39.

The word 'Êth (עֵת, 6256—Assyrian *ittu*), which marks a *season* or *opportunity*, is used of duration in Job 27:10; Ps. 10:5; Prov. 6:14; 8:30; and Eccles. 9:8. The LXX renders it ἐν παντὶ καιρῷ (1722, 3956, 2540), "on every occasion." Compare Eph. 6:18.

§2. *The Word* 'Ôwlâm

No word is so largely used to express duration as 'Ôwlâm (עוֹלָם, 5769). It has twice been rendered *long*, namely, in Eccles. 12:5, where we read of a man going "to his long home" (εἰς οἶκον αἰῶνος αὐτοῦ— 1519, 3624, 165, 846); and Isa. 42:14, "Shall I *long* be silent?" (ἀεί, 104). Five times it is rendered *always*, namely, Gen. 6:3, "My spirit shall not always [εἰς τὸν αἰῶνα—1519, 3588, 165] strive with man"; I Chron. 16:15, "Be ye mindful always of his covenant"; Job 7:16, "I would not live alway" (i.e., in this world); Ps. 119:112, "I have inclined mine heart to perform thy statutes alway"; also in Jer. 20:17.

It is translated *perpetual* with reference to the covenant made with Noah (Gen. 9:12), to the priesthood of the house of Levi (Exod. 29:9), to the Sabbath as a sign of God's covenant (Exod. 31:16), and to various other religious rites. It is used with a negative in several passages, e.g., in II Sam. 12:10, of the sword never departing from David's house; in Ps. 15:5, of the godly man never falling. See also Ps. 55:22; Isa. 14:20; 25:2; Joel 2:26.

In Isa. 60:15 'Ôwlâm (5769) is rendered *eternal*: "I will make thee an eternal excellency." It is rendered *forever* in a large number of passages, e.g., Gen. 13:15, of the land being given to Abraham; Exod. 21:6, of the slave serving his master forever (εἰς τὸν αἰῶνα—1519,

3588, 165). See also Ps. 12:7; 29:10; 61:4; 73:26; 81:15; 112:6; 125:2; Eccles. 3:14; Isa. 40:8; 51:6; Dan. 7:18; 12:3.

Some passages where 'Ôwlâm (5769) is rendered αἰώνιος (166), and used with reference to God's judgments upon the wicked, may here be cited: Ps. 78:66, "He put them to a perpetual reproach"; Jer. 18:16, "He hath made their land desolate, and a perpetual hissing"; 23:40, "Perpetual shame"; 51:39 (cf. v. 57), "I will make them drunken, that they may rejoice, and sleep a perpetual sleep"; Ezek. 35:5, 9, "Because thou hast had a perpetual hatred. . . . I will make thee perpetual desolations"; compare Zeph. 2:9. In Dan. 12:2 the word is applied not only to everlasting life but also to everlasting contempt, which shall be the lot of many after the resurrection.

In the passages quoted, which are a considerable proportion and a fair specimen of the whole, the LXX rendering is usually αἰώνιος (166) or εἰς τὸν αἰῶνα (1519, 3588, 165). These Greek phrases, therefore, when they reappear in the N.T., must be interpreted in accordance with the usage of the word 'Ôwlâm (5769). They give a conception that, though negative, is sufficiently clear. Eternity is endlessness; and this idea is only qualified by the nature of the object to which it is applied, or by the direct word of God. When applied to things physical, it is used in accordance with the revealed truth that the heaven and earth shall pass away, and it is limited by this truth. When applied to God, it is used in harmony with the truth that He is essentially and absolutely existent, and that as He is the *causa causarum* (Cause of causes, i.e., the First Cause of all things) and without beginning, so in the very nature of things it must be held that no cause can ever put an end to His existence. When the word is applied to man's future destiny after the resurrection, we naturally give it the sense of *endlessness* without any limitation, except such as the postresurrection state shall involve; and this is not revealed.

§3. *Use of the Word Eternal in the N.T.*

The use of the words αἰών (165) and αἰώνιος (166) in the N.T. deserves careful attention. In a number of passages our Lord speaks of "this *age*" (αἰών, 165), of its cares (Matt. 13:22), of its end (13:39, 40, 49; 24:3; 28:20), of its children (Luke 20:34). Similarly, the Apostle Paul speaks of conformity to this age (Rom. 12:2), of the seeker of this age (I Cor. 1:20), of its vaunted wisdom (I Cor. 2:6; 3:18), of its rulers (I Cor.

2:6, 8), of its god (II Cor. 4:4), of its being a present evil age (Gal. 1:4), of the age of the world (Eph. 2:2), and of those who love it (II Tim. 4:10).

In John 9:32 it is said, "Since the world began," etc. Here we find ἐκ τοῦ αἰῶνος (1537, 3588, 165), which points backwards, as εἰς τὸν αἰῶνα (1519, 3588, 165) does forwards. We find ἀπ᾽ αἰῶνος (575, 165) in the same sense in Acts 3:21; 15:18; Eph. 3:9; and Col. 1:26; also πρὸ τῶν αἰώνων (4253, 3588, 165) in I Cor. 2:7.

There are a few passages that speak in a very special way of an αἰών (165) or *age to come*, e.g., Mark 10:30; Luke 18:30; 20:35; and of its powers, Heb. 6:5. Some interpreters connect these passages with the Millennium. In Eph. 2:7 the Apostle speaks in the plural number of the *ages* to come.

In other passages we have the expressions εἰς τὸν αἰῶνα (1519, 3588, 165), εἰς τοὺς αἰῶνας (1519, 3588, 165), εἰς τοὺς αἰῶνας τῶν αἰώνων (1519, 3588, 165, 3588, 165); see, e.g., Luke 1:33, 55; John 12:34; 13:8; Rom. 9:5; Gal. 1:5; I Tim. 1:17. Some translators have rendered these passages literally, and without respect to their usage in the LXX (e.g., "unto *the age*," "unto *the ages*," etc.). In I Tim. 1:17, God is called "the King of ages" (A.V. King eternal); while in Heb. 1:2 and 11:3 He is said to have made "the ages" (A.V. the worlds). The rendering of the A.V. is no doubt right in the first case, and probably in the second also. Ages and worlds bear the same relation to each other as time and space do, and the process of creating worlds was the means of bringing ages into being.[1]

In I Cor. 10:11 we read that even upon those who lived in apostolic days the ends of the ages had come (A.V. ends of the world); and in Heb. 9:26 we are told that Christ has come once in the completion of the ages (A.V. end of the world) to put away sin. The word *age* is here thought to answer rather to the sense in which the word *dispensation* is now used, and a more literal rendering would have been preferable.

In II Peter 3:18 we meet with the expression εἰς ἡμέραν αἰῶνος (1519, 2250, 165), to the Day of the Age (A.V. for ever), by which we understand the dawn of eternity.

The adjective αἰώνιος (166) is used more than forty times in the

---

1. ʿÔwlâm (5769) has been occasionally rendered *world* in the A.V., as in Eccles. 3:11, where, however, some would render the words, "He hath put [a conception of] *eternity* in their hearts." It is curious that several translators have rendered the last verse of Psalm 139, "Lead me in the *way of the world*." In later Hebrew ʿÔwlâm (5769) was constantly used in this sense.

N.T. with respect to *eternal life*, which is regarded partly as a present gift, partly as a promise for the future. It is also applied to God's endless existence in Rom. 16:26; to the endless efficacy of Christ's atonement in Heb. 9:12; 13:20; and to past ages in Rom. 16:25; II Tim. 1:9; Titus 1:2.

This word is used with reference to *eternal fire* (Matt. 18:8; 25:41; Jude 7); *eternal punishment* (Matt. 25:46); *eternal judgment* or *condemnation* (Mark 3:29; Heb. 6:2); *eternal destruction* (II Thess. 1:9). The word in these passages implies *finality*, and apparently signifies that when these judgments shall be inflicted, the time of probation, change, or the opportunity for retrieving one's fortune will have gone by absolutely and forever. We understand very little about the future, about the relation of human life to the rest of existence, and about the moral weight of unbelief, as viewed in the light of eternity. If, on the one hand, it is wrong to add to God's word, on the other we must not take away from it; and if we stagger under the doctrine of eternal punishment as it is set forth in Scripture, we must be content to wait, cleaving to the Gospel of God's love in Christ, while acknowledging that there is a dark background that we are unable to comprehend.

Index of Subjects

Index of Texts

Index of Hebrew
and Aramaic Words

Index of Greek Words

ἐλεημοσύνη (1654), 130, 182
ἐλεήμων (1655), 126
ἔλεος (1656), 129, 181
ἐλπίζω (1679), 121, 122, 123
ἐλπίς (1680), 121, 123, 124, 130
ἐμαυτῷ (1683), 87
ἐνθύμημα (L-S 634B), 331
ἐντέλλομαι (1781), 228, 234
ἐντολή (1785), 228, 229, 231, 234, 235
ἐξαγοράζω (1805), 141
ἐξαλείφω (1813), 303
ἐξαναλίσκω (L-S 584A), 112
ἐξετάζω (1833), 317
ἐξηγηταί (L-S 593A), 325
ἐξιλάσκομαι (L-S 594B), 93, 149, 150
ἐξιλασμός (L-S 594B), 93
ἐξολοθρεύω (1842), 303, 305, 339
ἐξομολογέω (1843), 243, 244
ἐπαινέω (1867), 242, 243
ἐπαοιδός (L-S 610A), 325
ἐπερωτάω (1905), 89n
ἐπερώτημα (1906), 89n
ἐπίβουλος (L-S 626A), 314
ἐπίθεμα (L-S 633B), 223
ἐπικάλεισθαι (1941), 245n
ἐπισκέπτομαι (1980), 229, 234
ἐπίσκεψις (L-S 656B), 229
ἐπισκοπεῖν (1983), 234
ἐπισκοπή (1984), 229, 230, 234
ἐπίσκοπος (1985), 230, 234
ἐπιστήμη (L-S 660A), 90
ἐπιστρέφω (1994), 103, 108, 317
ἐπιτήδευμα (L-S 666A), 330
ἔπω (2036), 226
ἔργον (2041), 101
ἔρημος (2048), 335
ἔρως (L-S 695B), 129
ἐτάζω (L-S 700A), 317
εὐαγγελίζομαι (2097), 244, 246, 246n
εὐδοκέω (2106), 159
εὐδοκία (2107), 84, 159
εὐθύς (2117), 117
εὐλογέω (2127), 243
εὐλογημένος (2127), 244
εὐλογητός (2128), 244
εὐλογία (2129), 243
εὐχαριστήσας (2168), 243
εὐχαριστία (2169), 243

Ζεύς (2203), 40
ζυγός (2218), 109

ἡμέρα (2250), 112, 280n, 341, 344

ἡγεμονικός (L-S 763A), 85

θάνατος (2288), 310
θεῖος (2304), 43
θέλημα (2307), 84, 85, 159
θελητής (L-S 788B), 324
θέλω (2309), 83, 86
θεός (2316), 26, 36, 39, 40, 45, 89n, 187, 206
θεραπεύω (2323), 43
θνητός (2349), 60
θυμιάω (2370), 223
θυσία (2378), 159, 207, 210, 211, 214, 220
θυσιάζω (L-S 812B), 211
θυσιαστήριον (2379), 213, 214, 335
θύω (2380), 211, 214, 217

ἱερατεία (2405), 267
ἱεράτευμα (2406), 267
ἱερατεύω (2407), 267
ἱερεύς (2409), 267
ἱερόν (2411), 257n
ἱερουργεῖν (2418), 267
ἱκανός (2425), 45
ἱλάσκομαι (2433), 153
ἱλασμός (2434), 93, 149, 150, 154
ἱλαστήριον (2435), 149
ἵλεως (2436), 153
ἰσχὺς (2479), 335

καθαρίζω (2511), 93, 163, 165, 191
καθαρισμός (2512), 149, 150, 165
καθαρός (2513), 168, 191
καθαρότης (2514), 161n
καθίστημι (2525), 229
καιρός (2540), 342
κακός (2556), 95
καλός (2570), 109
καρδία (2588), 80
κάρπωμα (L-S 880A), 222
καταγγελεύς (2604), 42n
καταγγέλλω (2605), 42n
κατακρίνω (2632), 277
καταλλαγή (2643), 152
καταλλάσσω (2644), 152
καταργέω (2673), 233n
κατασκηνόω (2680), 123
καταφθείρω (2704), 303
κατείδωλος (2712), 40
κατευθύνω (2720), 117, 118
κατοικέω (2730), 338
κατοικητήριον (2732), 257
κατορθόω (L-S 929B), 117